D1565799

Literary critics and cultural historians have for too long written the question of 'race' out of mainstream accounts of English literature. In *Constructions of 'the Jew' in English literature and society* Bryan Cheyette draws on a wide range of literary texts and social and political perspectives from the 1870s to the 1940s to show that the emerging cultural identity of modern England involved constructing Jews both as a force that could be transformed by a superior culture, and as 'a race' outside 'the English nation'. Dr Cheyette combines cultural theory, discourse analysis and new historicism with close readings of work by Arnold, Trollope and George Eliot, Buchan and Kipling, Shaw and Wells, Belloc and Chesterton, T. S. Eliot and Joyce to argue that 'the Jew' lies at the heart of modern English literature: not as a fixed myth or stereotype, but as the embodiment of confusion and indeterminacy.

CONSTRUCTIONS OF 'THE JEW' IN ENGLISH LITERATURE AND SOCIETY

CONSTRUCTIONS OF
'THE JEW' IN ENGLISH
LITERATURE AND SOCIETY

Racial representations, 1875–1945

BRYAN CHEYETTE

Queen Mary and Westfield College, University of London

CAMBRIDGE
UNIVERSITY PRESS

Published by the Press Syndicate of the University of Cambridge
The Pitt Building, Trumpington Street, Cambridge, CB2 IRP
40 West 20th Street, New York, NY 10011-4211, USA
10 Stamford Road, Oakleigh, Melbourne 3166, Australia

First published 1993

Printed in Great Britain at the University Press, Cambridge

A catalogue record for this book is available from the British Library

Library of Congress cataloguing in publication data

Cheyette, Bryan
Constructions of 'the Jew' in English literature and society:
racial representations, 1875–1945/Bryan Cheyette
p. cm.
Includes bibliographical references and index.
ISBN 0 521 44355 5
1. English literature–20th century–History and criticism. 2. English literature–19th
century–History and criticism. 3. Jews–Great Britain–History–20th century.
4. Jews–Great Britain–History–19th century. 5. Literature and society–Great Britain.
6. Great Britain–Ethnic relations. 7. Religion and literature. 8. Jews in literature.
9. Race in literature.
I. Title.
PR151.J5C47 1993
820.9'35203924–DC20 92-38292 CIP

ISBN 0 521 44355 5 hardback

PR
151
.J5
C47
1993

TAG

This book is dedicated to my wife Susan,
to my parents, Jack and Sonia,
and my sister, Nicola.

Contents

Preface

More than most authors, I suspect, it has often occurred to me during the composition of this book that, in an ideal world, it would not have had to be written. Biographers and historians of literature, in my ideal, would have long since noted the race-thinking in the work of virtually everyone published before the Second World War. Literary critics, following suit, would have played their part and subjected the racial discourse of a favoured author to the same degree of close reading as, over the years, has been applied to other aspects of a writer's work. But, of course, such musings are far from the truth. Instead, the question of 'race' has, for the most part, been written out of literary-historical studies of nineteenth- and twentieth-century writers. At best, biographies might include a few pages at the end to explain one or two 'unfortunate' passages which are usually deemed to be inconsequential aberrations. Or, a literary critic might be spurred to the defence of a cherished author against the pernicious charge of 'racism' or 'antisemitism'. Such are the involuntary strategies that are used to trivialize and marginalize those repressive aspects of liberal culture which, in effect, enables them to continue.

In an attempt to redress the balance, this book demonstrates the extent to which race-thinking about Jews was, in fact, a key ingredient in the emerging cultural identity of modern Britain. From Matthew Arnold's *Culture and Anarchy* onwards, I have located semitic racial representations at the centre of literary production and more widespread social and political discourses. Instead of a colonial or genocidal history of racism and antisemitism, this book is at pains to show the way in which racialized constructions of Jews and other 'races' were at the heart of domestic liberalism. Unlike other studies of pre-war 'literary antisemitism', which mistakenly foreground the Holocaust, my approach is to stress the enlightened expectation that a superior 'culture' can modernize and civilize even 'the Jew'. My aim is to understand the question of racial representations in terms of a dominant liberalism and not as an aberrant or exotic phenomenon that is, by definition, outside of mainstream society.

Along with the wider social context of this book, I try not to lose sight of specific literary texts nor the particular politics or histories of the writers under consideration. None of the authors discussed in detail have been chosen because they are especially pernicious but, on the contrary, because they are typical of broader modes of thinking. It is for this reason that some of the more notorious 'literary antisemites', such as Ezra Pound and Wyndham Lewis, are referred to only in passing in this study. This is not least because both writers are considered to be peculiarly fascistic and therefore reinforce the supposed exceptional or pathological nature of racial discourse in liberal democracies. Indeed, the writers examined in this book, taken as a whole, exemplify the broadest possible social and philosophical outlook to demonstrate the extent to which semitic racial representations saturated all aspects of British culture.

By using a common critical vocabulary, I have tried to reconstruct semitic racial representations in terms that can be easily applied to other historical and national cultures. I refer throughout to semitic discourse – as opposed to a discrete historiography of antisemitism – precisely because I wish to use a language that is generally enabling and not morally loaded. Instead of the uneasy silence that currently surrounds the subject of this book, I have tried to develop ways of reading that allow other literary critics and cultural theorists to discuss the question of racial representations in different social and political contexts. After all, much of the material in this book will be familiar to many readers of nineteenth- and twentieth-century English literature. The crisis of representation, which I have foregrounded throughout this study, is also a well-known problematic for teachers and students of late Victorian, Edwardian and modernist English literature. At the same time, the familiar canon of critical concerns has, inevitably, been qualified in this work. By highlighting a racial discourse that cuts across the ordering of texts purely in relation to aesthetic criteria, I have attempted to point to other possible ways of reading literature than those that have been more usually privileged in English literary studies. This has resulted in the juxtaposition of authors such as Matthew Arnold and James Joyce, or George Eliot and John Buchan, or G. K. Chesterton and T. S. Eliot, who, as a rule, are placed in distinct categories. It is my hope that by confronting the critical commonplaces concerning the literature under discussion, I will enable other literary critics and cultural historians to think about the question of racial discourse in nineteenth- and twentieth-century literature as a routine area of inquiry. Only in this way can the humanizing pretensions of European and American literary studies be both challenged and upheld. While the issue of 'racism' and 'antisemitism' remains merely a specialist discipline – of interest only to its victims and a few concerned individuals – then it will, in effect, continue to be ignored.

Acknowledgements

A number of libraries have enabled me to carry out the research for this book. I would like to thank, in particular, the library staff of the University of Sheffield, the University of Leeds, the British Library, Sussex University, the Hebrew University, Jerusalem, and the Houghton Library, Harvard University. All have helped me in my task with friendly efficiency. I would also like to thank Mrs Valerie Eliot, who has kindly given me permission to quote from T. S. Eliot's unpublished lecture, 'The Bible as Scripture and Literature' (1932). Copyright of this unpublished lecture remains with Mrs Eliot. I am also grateful to the National Trust, which has given me permission to quote from Rudyard Kipling's unpublished correspondence. I would like to thank *The Wellsian, Joyce Studies* and *Shaw: The Annual of Bernard Shaw Studies* for permission to reprint material published in different form in these journals.

Over the years, I have become indebted to a large number of friends and colleagues for many small and not so small kindnesses with regard to this book. As a postgraduate at the University of Sheffield, I benefited from the preliminary guidance of Colin Holmes and the erudition and continued enthusiasm of Kenneth Graham. Neil Roberts also made some helpful initial comments on my doctoral thesis and I was most fortunate to have had Tony Kushner as a fellow postgraduate at this time. Along with Bill Williams and David Feldman, I owe a good deal to David Cesarani who stimulated me, at an early stage, to think about my subject-matter in new and exciting ways. In my year as a research fellow in Jerusalem, I was encouraged greatly by Harold Fisch who has taken a consistently encouraging and practical interest in my work. At the University of Leeds, Richard Brown, Vivien Jones, Lynette Hunter, Sally Shuttleworth, Alistair Stead and John Whale have all usefully commented on chapters or sections of this book. I am also deeply indebted, in this regard, to Homi Bhabha and Benita Parry and, at Queen Mary and Westfield College, to Lisa Jardine and Jacqueline Rose. I would, finally, like to acknowledge the help and advice of Todd Endelman, Jonathan Frankel, Hyam Maccoby, Maxim Silverman, John Schwarzmantel, David Sorkin, Nadia Valman and Steve Zipperstein as well as the anonymous readers of this book, whose recommendations on the initial typescript were most pertinent. In recent years I have benefited, more than I can say, from the wisdom and encouragement of Janina Bauman, Zygmunt Bauman and Gabriel Josipovici.

The forbearance of many friends has enabled me, over more than a decade, to come to terms with an often painful and always complex subject. My family, to whom this book is dedicated, have provided me with the kind of emotional and practical support which has made writing this work easier than it might have been. For many years my wife, Susan Cooklin, has had to live with this book in ways in which she would not have chosen for herself. She has been a source of strength and undiminished love which has remained remarkably unaffected by the inordinate amount of time spent by her husband in front of a word-processor.

CHAPTER I

Introduction: semitism and the cultural realm

Jews have no beautiful philosophy of life, but they are
sympathique.
Oscar Wilde, cited in *Oscar Wilde* (London, 1989) by
Richard Ellmann, p. 547

Jew-mania was the one evil which no one foretold at the close of
the last war ... [N]o prophet, so far as I know, had foreseen this
anti-Jew horror, whereas today no one can see the end of it.
There had been warnings, of course, but they seemed no more
ominous than a poem by Hilaire Belloc.
E. M. Forster, 'Jew-Consciousness' (1939), collected in
Two Cheers for Democracy (London, 1951), p. 25

Any study of the representation of Jews in English literature and
society is peculiarly fraught with difficulties. The recent prolonged
and often heated debates on whether or not the life and work of the
literary critic Paul de Man and the philosopher Martin Heidegger
were complicit with Nazism shows the extent that, even in the
academic community, a largely repressed European past still has the
capacity to return and haunt the present. Zygmunt Bauman, with
reference to the discipline of Sociology, has shown that the Holocaust
has been systematically marginalized and belittled in relation to
social theories of modern civilization. With no less culpability, the
humanities have also failed to engage with the implications of a post-
Holocaust understanding of European civilization.[1] George Orwell,

---

[1] The journal *Critical Inquiry* (Volumes 14–15, 1988–9) contains the most varied account of the
implications of the Heidegger and Paul de Man 'affairs' for the academic community.
Zygmunt Bauman, *Modernity and the Holocaust* (Oxford, 1989), p. xi, rightly notes that the
large number of specialist works and institutions devoted to the Holocaust means that, in
effect, a 'substantive analysis' of the Holocaust is 'eliminated from the core canon of the
discipline'. There is a parallel danger that the growing number of specialist works devoted
to 'Holocaust literature' will, similarly, make it easier for the 'core canon' of English and

in an article published in February 1945, predicted with startling
prescience why discussions of the 'antisemitic strain in English
literature' would fail to enter public discourse but would instead,
after the War, either be ignored or generate a 'storm of abuse':

There has been a perceptible antisemitic strain in English literature from
Chaucer onwards, and without even getting up from this table to consult a
book I can think of passages which *if written now* would be stigmatized as
antisemitism, in the works of Shakespeare, Smollett, Thackeray, Bernard
Shaw, H. G. Wells, T. S. Eliot, Aldous Huxley and various others...
Anyone who wrote in that strain *now* would bring down a storm of abuse
upon himself, or more probably would find it impossible to get his writings
published.[2]

The over-simple association of fictional constructions with mass
murder has enabled literary critics and biographers, with a few
notable exceptions, to disregard the Jewish representations in the
literature of their chosen subject.[3] Specialist studies have, in
particular, colluded with this post-War 'stigmatization' and have
slipped too easily from English literary texts into the horrors of
European history. A recent study of 'the Jew in the Victorian novel',
for instance, was written with 'the memory of Nazi Germany still
fresh' and, as a consequence, includes an opening précis of Leon
Poliakov's multi-volume history of antisemitism. In America, academic debate has centred around the issue of whether or not to teach
'literary antisemitism' given what is presumed to be the potentially
'lethal' charge of a literary text. With such crude teleological
assumptions at the heart of discussions of the 'antisemitic strain in
English literature', mainstream English literary criticism has been
able to conceive of this supposedly genocidal 'strain' as a phenom-

Comparative Literature to leave any 'substantive analysis' of the Holocaust and its
implications to 'the specialists'.
[2] George Orwell, 'Antisemitism in Britain', *Contemporary Jewish Record* (April, 1945) in Sonia
Orwell and Ian Angus (eds.), *The Collected Essays, Journalism and Letters of George Orwell*:
1943–1945, 4 vols. (London, 1970), III, p. 385 (Orwell's emphasis).
[3] In recent years, notable exceptions to this rule include Stephen Greenblatt 'Marlowe,
Marx, and Anti-Semitism', *Critical Inquiry* (Winter, 1978), 291–307, M. J. C. Echeruo, *The
Conditioned Imagination From Shakespeare to Conrad: Studies in the Exo-Cultural Stereotype* (London,
1978), Robert Casillo, *The Genealogy of Demons: Anti-Semitism, Fascism, and the Myths of Ezra
Pound* (Evanston, 1988), Christopher Ricks, *T. S. Eliot and Prejudice* (London, 1988), Ira B.
Nadel, *Joyce and the Jews* (London, 1989), Derek Cohen and Deborah Heller (eds.), *Jewish
Presences in English Literature* (Montreal, 1990), and Andrea Freud Loewenstein, *Loathsome
Jews and Engulfing Women: Metaphors of Projection in the Works of Wyndham Lewis, Charles
Williams and Graham Greene* (New York, 1993).

enon that is ultimately 'external' to English literary production and dismiss it as an 'inexplicable' or trivial 'commonplace'.[4]

Not unlike Michel Foucault's history of sexuality, 'literary antisemitism' has been conceived of as an open 'secret' or unacknowledged commonplace that, during intermittent 'storms of abuse', is also spoken about '*ad infinitum*'. This unhappy state of affairs has, furthermore, been unwittingly reinforced by influential studies of the 'Jew in English literature' which have defined Jewish literary representations as fixed 'stereotypes', 'myths' or 'images' that have remained essentially the same across the centuries and are thus, in the words of Hannah Arendt, 'natural consequences of an eternal problem'. The privileged cultural realm of literature remains essentially unthreatened by the naturalized construction of an eternal mythic 'Jew'. The mythic 'Jew', that is, exists quite comfortably in the realm of 'culture' which is, supposedly, above and beyond the messy contingencies of history and the crude expediencies of politics. As Homi Bhabha has rightly maintained, the 'Great Tradition' is 'thrown into disarray' *only* when it is reconstructed from the margins and shown to contain at its core 'questions of cultural difference and racial discrimination'.[5]

[4] Anne Aresty Naman, *The Jew in the Victorian Novel: Some Relationships Between Prejudice and Art* (New York, 1980), p. 49 and chapter 2 and Charlotte Klein, 'The Jew in English and German Fiction and Drama 1830–1933', unpublished Ph.D thesis, University of London (1967), are both unduly influenced by 'the memory of Nazi Germany'. Mark Howard Gelber, 'What is Literary Anti-Semitism?', *Jewish Social Studies* 47 (Winter 1985), 1–20 and 'Pedagogical Guidelines for Literary Antisemitism', *Patterns of Prejudice* 20 (January 1986), 35–44 has usefully catalogued the debate in America on whether to banish 'antisemitic' texts from the literary canon. For the dismissal of John Buchan's literary 'antisemitism' as a trivial commonplace that was 'too passive to be scandalous' see Gertrude Himmelfarb, 'John Buchan: An Untimely Appreciation', *Encounter* (September, 1960), 50 and 46–53 which is reprinted as chapter 9 of her *Victorian Minds* (London, 1968). Cassillo, *The Genealogy of Demons*, chapter 1, cites those literary critics who construct Pound's 'antisemitism' as an unimportant 'external' phenomenon. As a result of such marginalization from mainstream literary criticism, Ricks, *T. S. Eliot and Prejudice*, p. 29, believes that there is no possibility of a 'solution' to our lack of understanding of T. S. Eliot's 'antisemitism'.
[5] Hannah Arendt, *The Origins of Totalitarianism* (Cleveland, 1958), p. 7 and Michel Foucault, *The History of Sexuality*, 3 vols. (London, 1976), I, p. 35. Edgar Rosenberg, *From Shylock to Svengali: Jewish Stereotypes in English Fiction* (Stanford, 1960) and Harold Fisch, *The Dual Image: A Study of the Jew in English Literature* (London, 1959) are both influential 'mythic' accounts of the eternal 'Jewish stereotype'. See also, in this context, Lionel Trilling, 'The Changing Myth of the Jew' (1931) republished in *Commentary* (August, 1978), 24–34 and Hyam Maccoby, *The Sacred Executioner: Human Sacrifice and the Legacy of Guilt* (London, 1982). Rosenberg's acknowledged ahistoricity can be explained by his vigorous response to M. F. Modder, *The Jew in the Literature of England* (Philadelphia, 1939) and David Philipson, *The Jew in English Fiction* (Cincinatti, 1911) both of which are written from a naively whiggish perspective. Homi Bhabha, 'Representation and the Colonial Text: A Critical Exploration of Some Forms of Mimeticism' in Frank Gloversmith (ed.), *The Theory of Reading* (Brighton,

This study of semitic 'cultural difference' is an attempt to rewrite the discipline of late nineteenth- and early twentieth-century English Literature by placing a dominant racialized discourse at the heart of what constitutes the received definitions of literary 'culture'. At the same time, this work wishes to problematize the reductive construction of a homogenous 'Western Judeo-Christian' culture in current theories of 'colonial discourse' which does not recognize the ambivalent position of 'the Jew' within a supposed 'common culture'.[6] The potentially damaging split within various theories of racial difference is, nonetheless, insignificant when compared to the resilience of a superficially universalizing, aesthetic construction of English literature, even in the face of the most blatant historical contingencies. As late as 1949, the Fellows of the Library of Congress were to unashamedly award Ezra Pound the first Bollingen Prize for poetry with the following justification:

... To permit other considerations than that of poetic achievement to sway the decision [to award Pound the Bollingen Prize] would destroy the significance of the award and would in principle deny the validity of that objective perception of value on which civilized society must rest.[7]

The binary opposition between a 'civilized' aesthetic realm and its 'other', in this case Pound's fascist politics, is a distinction which is derived, in particular, from Matthew Arnold's *Culture and Anarchy: An Essay in Political and Social Criticism* (1869). Arnold's influential definition of 'culture' – as an erasure of the differences between 'Hebraism' and 'Hellenism' – is the admittedly arbitrary starting point for my work. The arbitrariness of this beginning, moreover, should not be underestimated. It would, perhaps, have made equal sense to begin with Benjamin Disraeli's Young England trilogy of the 1830s and 1840s which, in its own way, prefigured Britain's Imperial pretensions in the nineteenth century. But it is precisely Arnold's

1984), p. 102 and his 'The Other Question: Stereotype and Colonial Discourse', *Screen* 24 (November – December, 1983), 18–36 are influential reworkings of the received vocabulary to which I am indebted.
[6] Marshall Grossman, 'The Violence of the Hyphen in Judeo-Christian', *Social Text* 22 (Spring, 1989), 115–22 addresses directly the reductive use of 'Judeo-Christian culture' in Henry Louis Gates's (ed.) otherwise admirable volume, *'Race', Writing and Difference* (Chicago, 1986), p. 4 and p. 6. It is a sign of the plurality of *'Race', Writing and Difference*, however, that Tzvetan Todorov, in his response to this work, 'Race, Writing, and Culture', published in this volume, p. 376 criticizes Gates for the 'absence' of any discussion of antisemitism in his text.
[7] Library of Congress Press Release Nó. 542, Febuary 20, 1949, cited in Cassillo, *The Genealogy of Demons*, p. 9.

acknowledged position at the centre of liberal culture that makes his work a compelling point of origination. Whereas Disraeli remained firmly outside of Victorian liberal verities, Arnold, in many ways, continues to symbolize them. Unlike Disraeli's use of a racial discourse, which always remained at the heart of his thinking, Arnold positioned fixed racial differences between 'Aryans' and 'Semites' as something that should be transcended by his ideal of 'culture'. All of the texts under discussion, as in Arnold's *Culture and Anarchy*, try and contain a racialized 'other' within a transcendent order. The acculturated 'Jew', in terms of this ambivalent Arnoldian liberalism, is an extreme example of those that may draw closer to 'grace' and 'beauty' by surpassing an unaesthetic, worldly Hebraism. This ideal of 'culture' signifies a transforming site of humanizing perfection even though, as George Steiner has argued, such 'civilizing' processes are no longer at the centre of our contemporary 'post-culture'.[8]

The confident Victorian expectation that 'culture' can modernize and order an 'anarchic' reality underpins this study, and the literary works under consideration, even when we are painfully aware that the Holocaust has made Arnold's sense of a transforming 'culture' seem bitterly ironic. Unlike the many previous studies that read backwards from the 'anarchy' of the Holocaust, we shall deliberately foreground this Arnoldian ideal of 'culture' where Jews, newly assimilated into the nation-state, exemplify the Enlightenment virtues of tolerance, justice and equality. This liberal inclusiveness, however, is always ambivalent because it is buttressed by a spurious universalism which assumes that 'the Jew' will be transfigured in a higher realm.[9] Within an increasingly exclusivist nation-state, that is, Jews are constructed in equivocal terms as both the embodiment

[8] George Steiner, *Extraterritorial* (London, 1976), pp. 163–79 and Jacques Derrida, 'Violence and Metaphysics: An Essay on the Thought of Emmanuel Levinas' in *Writing and Difference* (London, 1978) for a 'post-cultural' reading of Arnold's *Culture and Anarchy*.

[9] Richard Cumberland's play *The Jew* (1794), based on Gotthold Lessing's influential *Nathan der Weise* (1779), anticipated the nineteenth-century representation of Jews in terms of Enlightenment 'civilizing' discourses. There is a strong link, in these terms, between the eighteenth-century 'Noble Savage' and their nineteenth-century semitic counterparts, such as Maria Edgeworth's *Harrington* (London, 1817) and Charles Dickens's *Our Mutual Friend* (1864–5). Frantz Fanon, *Black Skins, White Masks* (Paris, 1952), chapters 5 and 6, discusses the implications of this historical parallel and, following on from Fanon, Hayden White in his *Tropics of Discourse: Essays in Cultural Criticism* (Baltimore, 1978), chapter 9, rightly describes the 'Noble Savage theme' as a 'fetish' which he defines as 'any natural object believed to possess magical or spiritual power' (p. 184) and as 'simultaneously ... monstrous forms of humanity and as quintessential objects of desire' (p. 194). Such fetishization will recur in the semitic representations which make up this study.

of a transformable cultural Hebraism and, at the same time, as an
unchanging racial 'other'. The stark doubleness of a semitic discourse
will, in general terms, thus be seen to constitute 'the Jew' as
encompassing the possibility of a new redemptive order as well as the
degeneration of an untransfigured past.

The fear that a supposedly homogenous national culture was being
overwhelmed by an unassimilable 'other' was reflected in Henry
James's 'sense of dispossession' in New York where, after a twenty-
year absence, he longed for 'the luxury of some such close and sweet
and *whole* national consciousness as that of the Switzer and the Scot'.
New York, James writes in *The American Scene* (1907), had been
vanquished by the 'ubiquitous alien' and James's reparative desire
for a '*whole* national consciousness' is not dissimilar to his belief in the
organic wholeness of the novel. James also talks specifically in *The
American Scene* about the 'Hebrew conquest of New York' and the
'unsurpassed strength of the [Jewish] race' which could 'redeem' the
city but was also as 'alien' and uncertain as the unknowable 'future':
'Who can ever tell ... what the genius of Israel may, or may not,
really be "up to"?' As well as this exclusivist construction of the
Jewish 'race', James's own national displacement and fascination
with the 'international theme' can also be said to point to a repressed
sense of identification with the 'genius of Israel'.[10] This ambivalence
was given its starkest form in George Du Maurier's *Trilby* (1894), a
best-selling novel which 'acquired existence first as a note in James's
scribbler'. Du Maurier's Svengali is both an outstanding musical
genius and a sexually rapacious, racialized 'other'. He is, in other
words, the extreme embodiment of both 'culture' and 'race'. George
Meredith, in the opening chapter of *One of Our Conquerors* (1891), was
not the only English writer at the turn of the century to imagine a
future London, not unlike James's New York, as a Hebraized
dystopian city. But if the disruptive new order is unremittingly
'semitic', then this racialized sense of alienation also included the
power of 'culture' to transform 'the Jew'.

[10] Henry James, *The American Scene*, ed. Leon Edel, (London, 1968) pp. 86–7 and 132–3. I am
grateful to Homi Bhabha for this point and to Jonathan Freedman who has kindly let me
have sight of his unpublished 'Henry James and the Discourses of Anti-Semitism'. This is
the most nuanced and comprehensive account of Jamesian 'antisemitism' to date and
builds, sensibly, on Leo B. Levy, 'Henry James and the Jews: A Critical Study', *Commentary*
25 (September 1958), 243–9 and Ross Posnock, 'Henry James, Veblen, and Adorno: The
Crisis of the Modern Self', *Journal of American Studies* 21 (1987), 31–54. A great many of the
writers in this book will be seen to have a repressed identification with 'the Jew', as will be
discussed in the Conclusion.

The inter-connection between 'culture' and 'race' was initially raised in James's early 'conversation' on George Eliot's *Daniel Deronda* (1876). At the heart of James's criticism of Eliot's novel is 'Constantius's' complaint that George Eliot misrepresents Jews 'as a person outside of Judaism – aesthetically', which is later juxtaposed with the centrality of Jewish racial difference ('the big horrid Jewish nose'). This all-important opposition – between aestheticism and racial difference – is specifically illustrated with reference to Deronda's artistic mother:

PULCHERIA: I don't *see* the princess, in spite of her flame-coloured robe. Why should an actress and prima-donna care so much about religious matters?

THEODORA: It was not only that; it was the Jewish race she hated, Jewish manners and looks. You, my dear, ought to understand that.

PULCHERIA: I do, but I am not a Jewish actress of genius; I am not what Rachel was. If I were, I should have other things to think about.[11]

James returns to this theme in his *The Tragic Muse* (1890) where the potential artistic transcendence of the 'Jewish race' is emphasized by the actress, Miriam Rooth, who rebuffs Peter Sherringham after he notes that her 'Jewish ancestry' makes her 'very sufficiently of Rachel's tribe'. Echoing the snobbish 'Pulcheria', Miriam tells Sherringham that: '"I don't care, if I'm of her tribe artistically. I'm of the family of artists; *je me fiche* of any other! I'm in the same style as that woman [Rachel]; I know it"'.[12] Not unlike her medieval and Elizabethan counterparts, Rachel, along with Sarah Bernhardt and a myriad of 'belles juives', was commonly constructed as succumbing to the transforming power and universality of Christianity which, by the nineteenth century, was synonymous with 'culture'. James could, therefore, fetishize the Jewish actresses of the Théâtre Français and, at the same time, litter his novels with Jewish art dealers who

[11] Henry James, '*Daniel Deronda*: A Conversation', *The Atlantic Monthly* 38 (December 1876), 684–94. It is not insignificant that this 'conversation' is now widely read as an appendix to F. R. Leavis's *The Great Tradition* (London, 1972). I am referring to this appendix above, pp. 291, 299 and 284–304. Leon Edel, *Henry James: The Treacherous Years*, 1895–1900 (London, 1969), pp. 162–4 notes that James urged his friend Du Maurier to write *Trilby* over a six-year period.

[12] Henry James, *The Tragic Muse* (Penguin edition: London, 1978), p. 141. In Henry James, *The Art of the Novel*, ed. R. P. Blackmur (New York, 1934), p. 91 James says of *The Tragic Muse* that 'I never "go behind" Miriam ... she is thoroughly symbolic' and, as the consummate art object at the end of the novel, Nick Dormer, when painting her, ambivalently relocates the 'element of race' and the 'Hebrew strain' (p. 444) within Miriam. Freedman, 'Henry James and the Discourses of Anti-Semitism', usefully discusses the interchangeability of 'the artist' and 'the Jew' in this novel.

remained racially untransformed or 'materialistic'. It is this Jamesian or Arnoldian ambivalence, and not a crude 'antisemitism', that will characterize the Jewish representations within the liberal cultural realm of this study.[13]

I prefer 'semitic discourse' as a way of defining this Arnoldian ambivalence – as opposed to 'antisemitism' or 'philosemitism' – because this term has the added advantage of eschewing the inherent moralizing attached to these latter terms, especially when they are narrowly applied to illustrate a particular individual's 'hostility' or 'affinity' towards 'the Jews'. I could also have usefully applied 'allo-semitism' to the texts under discussion, as suggested by the Polish critic and novelist Artur Sandauer, which explicitly foregrounds difference.[14] Although 'semitic discourse' suggests that there are unassailable limitations on the imaginative reconstruction of 'the Jew', it is, I believe, a flexible enough term to be applied to a literary text. Instead of employing a predetermined 'system' that 'explains' a given set of representations, the one ironically consistent feature of the literary representations under consideration is the protean instability of 'the Jew' as a signifier. The radical emptiness and lack of a fixed meaning in the constructions of 'semitic' difference in this study results in 'the Jew' being made to occupy an incommensurable number of subject positions which traverse a range of contradictory discourses. This indeterminate, fluid reading of 'the Jew', exploited to the full in literary texts, results in semitic representations being utilized in a bewildering variety of contexts. It is precisely the slipperiness of these constructions that shall be seen to undermine

---

[13] Edel, in his 'Introduction' to *The American Scene*, p. xviii, argues that 'to be anti-semitic' James 'would have had to be a bigot; and a bigot would not have seen the immigrant Jew as having an "intensity of aspect" and "the unsurpassed strength of his race"'. This study tries to avoid such narrow apologetic definitions of 'antisemitism'. For James's 'materialistic' art dealers see Levy, 'Henry James and the Jews', and for the sexual fetishizing of Jewish women, Jean Paul Sartre, *Anti-Semite and Jew* (New York, 1948) pp. 50–1, Hyam Maccoby, 'The Delectable Daughter', *Midstream* 16 (November, 1970), 50–60 and Stephen Wilson, *Ideology and Experience: Antisemitism in France at the Time of Dreyfus* (Oxford, 1983), chapter 15.

[14] Artur Sandauer, *Collected Works: Volume 3* (Warsaw, 1985), pp. 449–52 utilizes 'allo-semitism' in a seminal critique of the recieved vocabulary. For examples of a conventional approach to these issues based mainly on extremist individuals and organisations see Colin Holmes, *Anti-Semitism in British Society 1876–1939* (London, 1979). My use of 'semitic discourse' is not, however, to discount the historical formation of the term 'antisemitism' which was widely popularized by Wilhelm Marr's pamphlet, *The Victory of Judaism over Germanism* (1879). It is precisely the dehumanizing political discourse that lies behind Marr's post-liberal construction of 'antisemitism', as opposed to individualized acts of 'hostility' or 'affinity' towards 'the Jews', that informs this study.

fatally the supposed certainty that an author, especially of a literary realist text, might have in their ability to represent 'reality'. With the advent of explicitly modernist texts, the very incoherence of 'the Jew' was to be a potent expression of the impossibility of fully 'knowing' anything.

That writers inside an imperial culture were able to define 'the self' in relation to a semitic 'other' points ultimately, as Edward Said has noted, to the power of such narratives to segregate and exclude in the name of a higher 'culture'.[15] But it is not just the difference in power relations between a dominant and subordinate culture that results in a radically unstable construction of 'the Jew'. The indeterminacy of the semitic representations under consideration meant that 'the Jew' can be constructed to represent both sides of a political or social or ideological divide. To name just a few of the ambivalent oppositions within each of the following chapters: Jews are represented as *both* the embodiment of liberal progress *and* as the vestiges of an outdated medievalism; as a bastion of empire *and* one of the main threats to empire; as prefiguring a socialist world state *and* as a key force preventing its development; as the ideal economic man *and* the degenerate plutocrat *par excellence*; as the modern alienated artist *and* the incarnation of a corrupt worldliness. To some extent, this doubleness points to a received Christological discourse which has constructed Jews as *both* 'a deicide nation [*and*] also a nation... on whose redemption the fate of mankind hangs'.[16] The historical positioning of Jews within the reformist bourgeois democracies of the nineteenth century was, therefore, to have quasi-messianic overtones as Enlightenment rationalism and the forces of modernity were said to have 'emancipated' even 'the Jews'. At the same time, the accommodation of pre-modern Jews from the 'East' within the borders of the nation-states of the 'West' was, as the century progressed, represented as threatening the very foundations of, in our case, the 'English nation'. Paul Gilroy has usefully shown, with reference to contemporary anti-Black racism, that in Britain 'race' is

---

[15] Edward Said, *Orientalism* (London, 1978) pp. 5–6 and *passim*. However, both Homi Bhabha, 'The Other Question', and Dennis Porter, '*Orientalism* and Its Problems' in Francis Barker, Peter Hume, Margaret Iversen and Diane Iversen (eds.), *The Politics of Theory* (Colchester, 1983), pp. 179–211, are important qualifications of Said's overly rigid construction of orientalism as a monolithic power structure which has been in place 'since antiquity' (p. 58).

[16] Fisch, *The Dual Image*, p. 15 and Andrew Benjamin, 'Kitaj and the Question of Jewish Identity', *Art and Design* (Winter, 1988), 61–4 for an interesting reworking of this theme.

a 'cultural-biological' category that exists in 'plural form' and 'can change, assuming different shapes and articulating different political relations'. A semitic discourse is similarly 'plural' and historically situated within broader 'systems' which helped construct an increasingly exclusivist 'English nation' that, by the time of the Aliens Act of 1905, was beginning to severely qualify a reformist State liberalism.[17]

That a semitic discourse was, by the 1870s, to be utilized ambivalently by both a 'cultural' inclusivism, however flawed, as well as a 'racial' exclusivism points to the reason for the particular chronology of this work. By the turn of the century, an increasingly beleaguered liberalism was being strenuously qualified from the radical right by diehard Imperialists and from the political left by socialists who wished to universalize 'the nation'. These post-liberal discourses, I believe, culminated imaginatively in the politically disparate 'modernist' *avant garde* but were also prefigured in the breakdown of literary 'realism' in the late Victorian novels of George Eliot and Anthony Trollope and the Edwardian 'romances' and plays of John Buchan, Rudyard Kipling, H. G. Wells and George Bernard Shaw. An Arnoldian definition of 'culture' attempted to elide the chronic class and ethnic divisions in the English nation-state which, by the time *Culture and Anarchy* was published, were rightly deemed to have had an 'anarchic' potential. The authoritarian Chester–Belloc grouping, in the Edwardian period, was the most extreme expression of a racialized sense of 'anarchy' that could no longer be contained by an all-embracing Arnoldian 'culture'. I have chosen this time of 'crisis' and continual redefinition of the limits of liberalism in England because, to a large extent, the ambivalent reconstruction of 'the Jew' is at its apogee during this period. From the 1870s to the 1940s, each of the post-liberal discourses that will be examined – roughly grouped together as Imperialism, socialism, distributism, modernism, and fascism – rewrote the liberal construction of 'the Jew' in their own terms. Writers are selected for detailed discussion precisely because their literary production is intimately related with such socio-political discourses and with the

---

[17] Paul Gilroy, *There Ain't No Black in the Union Jack* (London, 1987), p. 43. My only quibble with Gilroy is that this 'plurality' and the 'emptiness of racial signifiers' (p. 40) is not merely characteristic of a 'new racism' as he argues. For the historical legacy of this not so 'new racism' see David Feldman, 'The importance of being English: Jewish Immigration and the decay of liberal England' in David Feldman and Gareth Steadman Jones (eds.), *Metropolis London: Histories and Representations Since 1800* (London, 1989).

wider historical issues which surround them. The selection of writers discussed, therefore, is by no means comprehensive, not even for the limited chronology of this study.[18]

While the historicizing of the semitic discourse under consideration avoids the essentialism that may be associated with the eternally 'mythic' construction of 'the Jew', it should be stressed that it is as subjects of a 'discourse' and not as historical subjects that 'Jews' are situated in the literary texts under consideration. Even those writers who were personally intimate with individual Jews or with 'Jewish culture' – including British-Jewish writers – still operated within a 'discourse' that was already in place and that was already 'known' to them.[19] 'The Jew' within discourse becomes, as Robert Casillo has argued in relation to Ezra Pound, the 'unrecognised double of the confusion and uncertainty' which is at the 'core' of a writer's textual production. It is Pound's assignment of difference and 'confused otherness' to 'the Jews' that enables him, according to Casillo, to 'provisionally and questionably' carry out his 'major project of calling things by their right names'. When Pound's literary texts exceed their own categories and assumptions 'the Jew', in this reading, becomes the carrier of this uncertainty and the archetypal transgressor of boundaries.[20]

I want to extend this important reading of Pound's writings into all of the literary texts under consideration and note that it is the very slipperiness and indeterminacy of 'the Jew' – as constructed within a semitic discourse – that enables an uncertain literary text to explore the limits of its own foundations, whether they be the ideal of literary 'realism'; or of liberal 'culture'; or the Empire; or socialist

[18] Obvious omissions from a detailed analysis are Joseph Conrad, D. H. Lawrence, Virginia Woolf and Dorothy Richardson. Other writers, such as Ezra Pound, Graham Greene, Wyndham Lewis and Charles Williams have been the subject of recently published full-length studies.

[19] My 'The Other Self: Anglo-Jewish Fiction and the Representation of Jews in England, 1875–1905' in David Cesarani (ed.), *The Making of Modern Anglo-Jewry* (Oxford, 1990), pp. 97–111, is an account of internalization of a semitic discourse by British Jewry. Dorothy Richardson's mammoth *Pilgrimage* sequence of thirteen novels contains a series of racialized 'Jewish' representations based on her intimate acquaintance with a number of British-Jews and, even after many years of marriage to Leonard Woolf, Virginia could still represent a 'Jewish neighbour' in *The Years* (1937), pp. 365–68, as leaving 'a ring of Jewish grease on the bath'.

[20] Casillo, *The Genealogy of Demons*, p. 18. Bauman, *Modernity and the Holocaust*, p. 39, has emphasized that the 'conceptual Jew' was an imagined force which 'visualized the horrifying consequences of boundary-transgression... he was the prototype and arch-pattern of all nonconformity, heterodoxy, anomaly and abberation'. See also the Conclusion to this study for a further discussion of these wider theoretical issues.

universalism; or nationalist particularism; or 'modernist' post-liberalism. 'The Jew', like all 'doubles', is inherently ambivalent and can represent both the 'best' and the 'worst' of selves. Unlike marginalized 'colonial subjects' who were, for the most part, confined racially to the 'colonies' in the late nineteenth century, Jews were, simultaneously, at the centre of European metropolitan society and, at the same time, banished from its privileged sphere by a semitic discourse.[21] It is the proximity of Jews within the European imperial orbit that made them *both* a powerful 'self' and a powerless 'other', a key touchstone for the racial boundaries of European 'culture' and the 'Englishness' of modern English literature. Semitism lies at the indeterminate 'centre' of many of the texts which make up the received literary canon but, just as the 'canon' itself is made up of texts wrenched from their political and social context, 'the Jew' remains unacknowledged as a silent 'double'; a racial 'comm-onplace' that is crudely differentiated from the discourse of English literary criticism. The main aim of this book is to break this institutional silence and to reveal the radical potentiality of literary texts to internalize and expose the inherent contradictions within a dominant semitic discourse.[22]

[21] Karl Miller, *Doubles* (Oxford, 1987) is an important general discussion of the literary 'double' and Bhabha, 'The Other Question', locates a Lacanian 'ambivalence' within theories of 'colonial discourse'. See also Bhabha, 'DissemiNation: Time, Narrative and the Margins of the Modern Nation' in his *Nation and Narration* (London, 1990) pp. 291–322 which positions his earlier theories of ambivalence within the context of 'the modern nation'. The non-Lacanian emphasis of this study also locates a discursive ambivalence within individual texts as well as specific historical, political and social contexts.

[22] For an excellent account of the 'Englishness' of Leavisite literary criticism see Francis Mulhern, 'English Reading', in Bhabha (ed.), *Nation and Narration*, pp. 250–64. I should emphasize that the term 'literary text' includes so-called 'popular' texts which I will endeavour to insert back into the 'literary' canon throughout this study.

CHAPTER 2

The promised land of liberalism: Matthew Arnold, Anthony Trollope and George Eliot

Hebraism and Hellenism – between these two points of influence moves our world. At one time it feels more powerfully the attraction of one of them, at another time of the other; and it ought to be, though it never is, evenly and happily balanced between them.

> Matthew Arnold, *Culture and Anarchy: An Essay in Political and Social Criticism* (1869), edited by R. H. Super (Michigan, 1965), pp. 163–4

And we, then, what are we? what is England ... why, my very name expresses that peculiar Semitico-Saxon mixture which makes the typical Englishman ...

> Matthew Arnold, 'On the Study of Celtic Literature' in *Essays in Criticism* (1865), edited by R. H. Super (Michigan, 1962), pp. 334–5

INTRODUCTION

This chapter examines the fiction and social criticism of Matthew Arnold, Anthony Trollope and George Eliot, all of whom can be described variously as nineteenth-century 'liberal' authors. Beginning with Arnold's influential use of the binary opposition 'Hebraism and Hellenism' in his *Culture and Anarchy*, we will note the extent that a racial vocabulary underpins these culturally differentiating terms. Within the contradictory discourses of 'race' and 'culture', 'the Jew' will be seen to be constructed as both an object that can be spectacularly civilized (embodying Arnold's ideal of 'culture') and, at the same time, as an unchanging semitic 'other'. This ambivalence will be seen to be a product of the competing needs of the liberal nation-state which situates 'the Jew' in both a particularist 'English' community and an assimilating, universalist framework.

13

Anthony Trollope's fiction will be discussed as an example of the contradictory impulses inherent in the liberal 'realist' novelist. Trollope, that is, includes a 'balanced' representation of reality where the intentions of the racialized outsider must first be 'known' before he or she is accepted into his privileged national community. His fiction, therefore, constructs the racial origins of 'the Jew' as a problem that, only after thorough investigation, can be situated in a narrowly defined 'English' nation. Within these constraints, Trollope's 'Jews' either regulate their own racialized behaviour or are excluded from an idealized, homogeneous England. By the 1870s, however, an increasingly pessimistic Trollope began to lose faith in the capacity of 'the Jews' to regulate their worst excesses and in his mode of realism to adequately 'know' the dark intentions of the semitic 'other'.

The breakdown of a 'realist' narrative in Trollope's fiction, and the fear that his Old England had succumbed to a Hebraic commercialism, will be seen to anticipate George Eliot's post-realist *Daniel Deronda* (1876). We will examine why her 'experimental' novel situated 'the Jews' in a future spiritual realm that can not be 'known' and the implications that this has for the 'realist' form of the novel. Eliot explicitly displaces the 'promised land' of a progressive liberalism in this novel onto a Judaized 'promised land' of the future. But, in so doing, she articulates the confusion inherent in *Culture and Anarchy* and constitutes both racially and culturally determined 'Jews' with radically differing futures. The verities of liberal 'progress' – and the anxieties surrrounding assimilated Jews as signs of this 'progress' – will be shown to be a central feature of the cultural production of the 1870s which culminated in the fierce polemics surrounding Benjamin Disraeli's Eastern Question (1876–8).

MATTHEW ARNOLD: CULTURE AND AMBIVALENCE

In a letter to his mother, just after the publication in book form of *Culture and Anarchy* (1869), Matthew Arnold predicted with some confidence that his chapters on 'Hebraism and Hellenism' in this seminal work are 'so true that they will form a kind of centre for English thought and speculation on the matters treated in them'. A year later he concluded that 'more and more will turn' on the 'distinction' between Hebraism and Hellenism and 'on dealing wisely [with this distinction] everything depends'. Two decades after Arnold's death G. W. E. Russell, Arnold's contemporary biographer, confirms the centrality of this 'famous conjunction' which, by 1904, was most 'closely associated with [Arnold's] memory' even to the extent that the Arnold family was itself thought to be of 'Jewish extraction'. Arnold's 'remote ancestors', Russell tells us, had 'emigrated from Germany to Lowestoft' and might well have belonged to 'the ancient Race'.[1] The vague Judaization of Arnold's family was, indeed, an unanticipated consequence of his 'famous conjunction' and indicates the extent to which English 'culture' was racialized by the turn of the century.

Most historians agree that the immediate catalyst for the widespread public acceptance and use of a racial construction of 'the Jew' was Disraeli's Eastern Question of 1876–8. One of the most prominent contemporary commentators on this foreign policy crisis was Goldwin Smith, a Professor of Modern History and a long-standing political enemy of Disraeli, who wrote that: 'had England been drawn into this conflict, it would have been in some measure a Jewish war, waged with British blood to uphold the objects of Jewish sympathy or to avenge Jewish wrongs'.[2] Goldwin Smith's attack on Disraeli's 'Jewish' Eastern policy quickly became a more general critique of Jewish emancipation and the mid-Victorian liberal consensus which allowed Anglo-Jews to be assimilated into the British State as 'Englishmen of the Mosaic Persuasion'. This critique of a universalist liberalism is demonstrated by Smith's insistence on a 'Jewish race':

The secret of Lord Beaconsfield's life lies in his Jewish blood ... Certainly a century and a quarter of residence in England on the part of his ancestors and himself has left little trace on the mind and character of Lord Beaconsfield. He is in almost every essential ... a Jew.[3]

---

[1] G. W. E. Russell (ed.), *Letters of Matthew Arnold 1848–1888*, 2 vols. (London, 1895), II, p. 11 and p. 33 and G. W. E. Russell, *Matthew Arnold* (London, 1904) pp. 162–3. George Meredith, in a letter to Lucien Wolf dated January 20, 1906, argued that 'we get Spinoza, and some noble English – the Arnolds [and] Browning' from 'the Arab Jew'. For this see C. L. Cline (ed.), *The Collected Letters of George Meredith*, 3 vols. (Oxford, 1970), III, p. 1339. Hilaire Belloc also Judaized the 'Arnold Families' in his *The Jews* (London, 1922), p. 47. These associations were undoubtedly popularized by the portrait of Dr Arnold as an Old Testament patriarch in Lytton Strachey's *Eminent Victorians* (London, 1918).

[2] Colin Holmes, *Anti-Semitism in British Society 1876–1939* (London, 1979), pp. 11–12, cites Goldwin Smith and Disraeli's Eastern policy as the catalyst for the origins of a widespread racial antisemitism in the mid-1870s. The popular second edition of Arnold's *Culture and Anarchy* was also published at this time.

[3] 'The Political Adventures of Lord Beaconsfield' *Fortnightly Review*, 23 (April – June, 1878), 480 and 447–93. F. W. Hirst, *Early Life and Letters of John Morely*, 2 vols. (London, 1927), II,

This widespread privileging of 'race' over 'culture' goes back, ironically, to the early Victorian Dr Thomas Arnold, Matthew Arnold's father, who considered Jews to be fundamentally incompatible with the 'teutonic' element in 'our English race'. Dr Arnold was one of the leading campaigners against Jewish emancipation (the admission of Jews into Parliament in the 1830s and 1840s) on the grounds that 'the Jews are strangers in England, and have no more claim to legislate for it than a lodger has to share with the landlord in the management of his house ... For England is the land of Englishmen, not of Jews'.[4] None was more vociferous in defending the belief in England as a narrowly constituted 'Christian nation' than Dr Arnold who proposed, as Lionel Trilling has shown, an 'almost mystic homogeneity' between Church and State which was intended to exclude Jews and non-Christians from Parliament as well as other 'Christian' institutions such as Christ's Hospital and the University of London. In petitioning against the 'Jew Bill' of the 1830s and 1840s, Dr Arnold wished to 'expose that low Jacobinical notion of citizenship, that a man acquires a right to it by the accident of his being, littered inter quatuor maria, or because he pays taxes'. Instead of confusing the 'right of taxation' with the 'right of general legislation', Dr Arnold believed that Jews should 'tax themselves in a Jewish House of Assembly, like a colony or like the clergy of old'.[5]

In terms of Dr Arnold's racial construction of the 'English' nation, the 'citizenship' of British Jews represented the irrevocable decline of a particularist Englishness, and a form of radical liberalism based on the universalism of the future. William Hazlitt made out the radical case for the 'emancipation of the Jews' by arguing that Jewish emancipation was 'but a natural step in the progress of civilization' which would oppose the 'prejudice' and 'intolerance' of an illiberal England rooted in the past. By privileging 'culture' over 'race', Hazlitt's ideal of the civilizing 'toleration' of 'the Jews' exactly

---

p. 50 attributes this article to Goldwin Smith. For a recent discussion of Smith in this context see David Feldman, *Englishmen and Jews: English Political Culture and Jewish Society, 1840–1914* (New Haven, 1993).

[4] A. P. Stanley, *The Life and Correspondence of Thomas Arnold*, 2 vols. (London, 1958), II, p. 27 and pp. 28–9 and Russell, *Matthew Arnold*, p. 163. Frederic E. Faverty, *Matthew Arnold: The Ethnologist* (Illinois, 1951), chapter 4 is useful for Dr Arnold's identification of 'the English' with the 'Teutonic race'. Thomas Arnold, *The Inaugural Lecture* (London, 1843), p. 26 is an example of his construction of a distinct 'English race'. For this in general see A. MacDougall, *Racial Myth in English History* (London, 1982).

[5] Stanley, *Thomas Arnold*, p. 330 and pp. 464–5 and R. J. Cambell, *Thomas Arnold* (London, 1927), pp. 115–40. See also Lionel Trilling, *Matthew Arnold* (London, 1949), p. 60.

reverses Dr Arnold's belief in the necessity of their internal coloni-
zation.[6] The acceptance in 1858 of religiously identifying Jews into
the House of Commons clearly signalled a future that opposed the
narrow boundary-ridden 'Christian nation' envisaged by Dr Arnold.
Above all, it signified the ascendancy of a liberal bourgeois culture
(institutionalized by the second Reform Bill of 1867) which, unlike
feudal England, did not need the past to validate it. This lack of
historical validation made Jews – and other racial minorities –
vulnerable to particularist definitions of Englishness predicated on
the fixity of the past. The anxious juxtaposition of Victorian economic growth with the stability and spirituality of the past reflected,
as Martin Weiner has demonstrated, a profound unease with a
modernization process which threatened to deny the 'imprint of the
old aristocracy'. By the 1870s, Jews were no longer 'lodgers' in a
Christian nation but were able to participate in a civil society as
'Englishmen of the Mosaic Persuasion' with their religion merely a
matter of personal 'conscience'. The feared erasure of the past could
thus be projected onto the uncontained and boundaryless 'economic'
ascendancy of 'the Jews'.[7]

Hazlitt's association of the 'progress of civilization' with the
'emancipation of the Jews' was reinforced by the fact that Jews were
the most significant group after the 1850s to take up the liberal offer
of a modernizing universalism. In stark contrast to his father,
Matthew Arnold situated a universalist 'culture' at the heart of this
civilizing process and enthusiastically welcomed the final entry of
British Jews into the Houses of Parliament. The displeasure expressed
by Dr Arnold at the election of Jewish members of Parliament was
matched, if not surpassed, by his son's unmitigated joy at the
ennoblement in 1885 of Sir Nathaniel Rothschild, the first Jewish
peer:

---

[6] Edgar Rosenberg, *From Shylock to Svengali: Jewish Stereotypes in English Fiction* (Stanford,
1960), Appendix VIII, cites William Hazlitt, *The Tatler*, 28 March, 1831. Our discussion of
G. K. Chesterton and Hilaire Belloc in chapter 5 will elaborate on Edwardian theories of the
'internal colonisation' of 'the Jews'.

[7] Martin Weiner, *English Culture and the Decline of the Industrial Spirit 1850–1980* (Cambridge,
1981), p. 10 and chapter 1 discusses the feared erasure of aristocratic values in these terms.
Robert Colls and Philip Dodd (eds.), *Englishness: Politics and Culture 1880–1920* (London,
1986), p. 22 and chapter 1 outlines the construction during the 1880s of a coercive
Englishness fixed in the past. It is worth remembering that even those who supported Jewish
'emancipation' predicated their support on the supposed rational utilization of Jewish
'wealth'. For an example of this reasoning see Thomas Macaulay on the 'Civil Disabilities
of the Jews', *Edinburgh Review* 104 (January, 1831), 363–74.

I feel really proud ... and happy for the British public to have, by this peerage, signally marked the abandonment of its old policy of exclusion ... What have we not learned and gained from the people who we have been excluding all these years! And how every one of us will see and say this in the future![8]

As a liberal of 'the future', the accommodation of Jews within the British state had a profound significance for Arnold. By the 1880s, he had long since constructed universalist Jews such as the actress Rachel, Heinrich Heine, Spinoza and Constance de Rothschild as individuals with a special place in the pantheon of 'culture'. Arnold, significantly, used Heine's distinction to combine the 'Hebraic' virtues – hard work, thrift and moral duty – with a 'Hellenic' tradition which stands for the disinterested pursuit of knowledge, beauty and truth. In this way, he attempted to replace his father's racial exclusion of 'the Jew' with a much broader national 'culture' which could include even the racial 'other'. Arnold's avowed 'central target' in *Culture and Anarchy* was the 'bad civilization of the English middle class', the purveyors of a distorted modernization, that were deemed by him to be overly 'hebraized'. But the supposed centrality of this 'target' points to an inherent instability at the heart of his construction of Hebraism. As well as embodying the virtues of 'conscience' – the subjugation of oneself to the Law – Hebraism also represented for Arnold the 'anarchy' of bourgeois individualism (or 'doing what one wants') which, he believed, was increasingly divorced in late Victorian England from the 'sweetness and light' of the Hellenic tradition. Hebraism, according to this formulation, was thus both one of the 'points of influence [which] moves our world' and a force that, at least at this point in history, needed to be transcended by Hellenism.[9] The ambivalence of this construction of Hebraism – a term which could be applied equally to individuals as well as historical epochs – is especially apparent when the racial discourse underlying the contending forces of 'Hebraism and Hellenism' is made explicit:

[8] Cited in Russell, *Matthew Arnold*, pp. 163–4.
[9] Matthew Arnold, *Culture and Anarchy*, ed. R. H. Super (Michigan, 1965), pp. 163–4 and p. 255. All future reference's to Arnold's *Culture and Anarchy* will be cited in the body of the text from this edition. See also Matthew Arnold, *Lectures and Essays in Criticism*, ed. R. H. Super (Michigan, 1962) for Arnold's essays on Spinoza and Heine and Ruth apRoberts, *Arnold and God* (Berkeley, 1983), pp. 157–75 for a recent discussion of Arnold's relationship with Jews as 'cultured' beings. Stefan Collini, *Arnold* (Oxford, 1988), pp. 77–8 usefully discusses *Culture and Anarchy* in relation to 'the bad civilization of the English middle class'.

Science has now made visible to everybody the great and pregnant elements which lie in race, and in how signal a manner they make the genius and history of an Indo-European people vary from those of a Semitic people. Hellenism is of Indo-European growth, Hebraism is of Semitic growth; and we English, a nation of Indo-European stock, seem to belong naturally to the movement of Hellenism. But nothing more strongly marks the essential unity of man, than the affinities that can be perceived, in this point or that, between members of one family of peoples and members of another. And no affinity of this kind is more strongly marked than that likeness in the strength and prominence of the moral fibre, which notwithstanding immense elements of difference, knits in some special sort the genius and history of us English ... to the genius and history of the Hebrew people. (173–4)[10]

By emphasizing both the 'essential unity of man' and, at the same time, the 'scientific' or ethnographic basis of 'semitic' racial difference – in opposition to 'we English, a nation of Indo-European stock' – Arnold unwittingly exposes the central ambivalences at the heart of the liberal accommodation with its Jewish 'other'. It is precisely by foregrounding racial particularity that liberalism can then lay claims to 'civilize' or 'universalize' the racial 'others' that it 'emancipates'. But once racial difference is constructed in this fashion, then the uncontained 'semitic growth' of Hebraism can always be represented as a potentially disruptive or 'anarchic' force. While Arnold intended to privilege 'culture' over 'race', he is no less scathing about an untransfigured or unhellinized Jewish particularity than Dr Arnold was about non-Christianized Jews. In *Literature and Dogma* (1873), for instance, Arnold makes an 'extraordinary distinction' with regard to the 'Hebrew people':

In spite of all which in them and in their character is unattractive, nay, repellent, – in spite of their shortcomings even in righteousness itself and their insignificance in everything else, – this petty, unsuccessful, unamiable people, without politics, without science, without art, without charm, deserve their great place in the world's regard, and are likely to have it more, as the world goes on, rather than less.[11]

This 'distinction' is echoed in the Preface to *Culture and Anarchy* where, with no less ambivalence, Arnold argues that 'as our idea of

[10] Faverty, *Arnold: The Ethnologist*, pp. 162–85 has an important discussion of Arnold's influence by European ethnography and, in particular, Ernest Renan. Renan is discussed usefully in this context in Edward Said, *Orientalism* (London, 1978) and in Shmuel Almog (ed.), *Antisemitism Through the Ages* (Oxford, 1988), chapter 18.
[11] Matthew Arnold, *Dissent and Dogma*, ed. R. H. Super (Michigan, 1968), p. 199. See Faverty, *Arnold: The Ethnologist*, p. 169 for an elaboration of this quotation which can be found originally in the work of Ernest Renan.

perfection widens beyond the narrow limits which the over-rigour of Hebraizing has tended to confine it, we shall yet come to Hebraism for that devout energy in embracing our ideal, which alone can give to man the happiness of doing what he knows' (255). Hebraism, in this way, is divided between a 'narrow' philistine legalism and the 'devout energy' of its historical form which, although emptied of any meaningful content, is still a necessary vehicle for the institutionalizing of Hellenic truth and beauty.

In chapter 5 of *Culture and Anarchy*, Arnold compares the Hebraic philistinism of the contemporary English middle-classes with the Hebraism of the 'first days of Christianity' (187). The transition from Judaism to Christianity required the Hellenic 'free play of the mind' to break down the Hebraic 'fixed rule' of law which had become 'mechanical and had thus lost its vital motive power' (187–8). This 'importation of Hellenism, as we have defined it, into Hebraism' (188) both denotes for Arnold the transfiguration of Judaism into the higher form of Christianity as well as the transformation of the 'anarchic' middle-classes into the higher world of 'culture'. In a letter written a decade after *Culture and Anarchy*, Arnold could thus argue that St Paul's 'sentiment about the Jews answers to mine about our middle class'. This slippage is what makes Hebraism both an alien 'semitic growth' and, at the same time, a metonym for the English Puritan tradition.[12]

Arnoldian 'culture' aimed to unite inclusively people of all classes and assimilate the racial 'other' into the British state. But whereas a universalist 'culture' relies on the 'best selves' within each class to transcend their Hebraic individualism, the racialized 'Jew' is emptied of all content ('without politics, without science, without art, without charm') and is merely a mode of action for bringing about 'perfection' or, what he calls, 'the happiness of doing what [one] knows'. Although Arnold's ideal of 'culture' is far from synonymous with Victorian liberalism, *Culture and Anarchy*, nonetheless, re-enacts the ambivalent process of liberal accommodation with its racial 'other'. The 'other', in these terms, must divest itself of its racial particularism before being assimilated into a supposedly 'universalist' culture.[13] As we have seen, this is the secular rep-

---

[12] Russell, *Letters of Matthew Arnold*, II, p. 155. 'St Paul and Protestantism' and 'Literature and Dogma' in Arnold, *Dissent and Dogma*, pp. 20–6 and p. 225 both trace a 'Hebraized' English Puritanism.

[13] Geoff Dench, *Minorities in the Open Society: Prisoners of Ambivalence* (London, 1985) for an elaboration of this argument.

resentation of the transformation of Judaism into Christianity, the master-text which anticipates the 'importation of Hellenism ... into Hebraism' in late Victorian England. When Arnold wrote to his mother on Christmas Day 1867 arguing that both he and his father wanted to 'get rid of all that was purely Semitic in Christianity', he was reflecting this ambivalent 'cultural' transformation of 'the Jew'. In other contexts, Arnold was to stress the 'native diversity between our European bent and the Semitic bent' and this racial exclusivism clearly undermined his 'cultural' inclusivism: 'we are none the better for trying to make ourselves Semitic, when Nature has made us Indo-European'. Such racial differentiation was essential to Arnold's biblical criticism – as it was to his father's before him – and it is this racialized semitic discourse that underpins his social criticism of the 'bad civilization of the English middle-class' as being 'unnaturally' Hebraic.[14]

In *Literature and Dogma*, Arnold came to believe that Hebraic 'conduct' was 'three-fourths of life' precisely because it could institutionalize his Hellenic, Indo-European ideals. 'Hebraic' action was, in this way, both the necessary correlative to Hellenic beauty and an uncontainable force that signified the future. Universalist, Hellenized Jews such as Rachel, Heinrich Heine, Spinoza and Constance de Rothschild could become, by transcending their Jewish past, the representatives for Arnold of the 'perfection' brought about by the containment of Hebraism within Hellenism (which is not dissimilar from the traditional Christian belief that the 'conversion of the Jews' would bring about the messianic era).[15] Spinoza's life, in Heine's words, quoted with relish by Arnold, became 'a copy of the life of his divine kinsman, Jesus Christ'. These sentiments are also echoed in Arnold's Preface to *Culture and Anarchy* where, we are told, 'the conception which cultivated and philosophical Jews now entertain of Christianity and its Founder, is probably destined to become the conception which Christians themselves will entertain' (251). This is almost certainly a reference to Arnold's friendship with Constance de Rothschild who embodied not only the 'best self' of

[14] Russell, *Letters of Matthew Arnold*, I, p. 381 and Arnold, *Essays in Criticism*, 'On the Study of Celtic Literature', p. 301 and p. 369. The influence of Ernest Renan can also be found in the belief that the English were overly 'Hebraic'. For this see Faverty, *Arnold: The Ethnologist*, p. 173.
[15] Arnold, *Dissent and Dogma*, p. 175. For the prevalence of the belief in the messianic potential of early Victorian Jewry see W. H. Oliver, *Prophets and Millennialists: The Users of Biblical Prophecy in England from the 1790s to the 1840s* (Oxford, 1978).

Arnold but, more popularly, the transforming hopes of liberal England. Wealthy, assimilated Jews thus became a *tabula rasa* on which could be inscribed the 'best' of English culture. Arnold's purveyors of culture, following this reasoning, were thereby constructed as 'aliens': 'persons who are mainly led, not by their class spirit, but by a general *humane* spirit, by the love of human perfection' (146). The Jew as 'alien' – a semitic race 'other' to the Indo-European English – was to signify both the ideas of cultural perfection as well as an unchanging racial difference.[16]

Within *Culture and Anarchy*, a semitic discourse positioned 'the Jew' as the spiritual and cultural embodiment of the 'essential unity of man' precisely because their transformation was proof positive of the civilizing power of a necessarily superior 'culture'. If Arnold's generalizations were 'scrupulously empty', so that critics of the future could interpret them in the most apposite way possible, then this did not prevent his vocabulary from being steeped in the ambivalent semitic discourse at the heart of Victorian liberalism. This racial differentiation, to a large extent, represented the limits of his romantic self-identification as a 'man of culture' with the Jewish 'chosen people'. In 'The Function of Criticism at the Present Time', for instance, the critic is identified with the Patriarch Moses who espies 'the promised land' of culture which criticism can only 'salute from afar'. By writing as a 'man of culture', Arnold was an outsider *par excellence*, hence his self-identification with acculturated Jews. But Arnold also wrote as a 'man of the future'. In this latter sense, his construction of 'the Jew' was split between their necessary but impossible racial transcendence and the as yet unwritten spiritual 'promised land'.[17]

George Eliot's *Daniel Deronda* was to be an 'epic' treatment of the theme of a Judaic 'promised land' and, in a poem entitled 'Rachel' (1867), Arnold was to acknowledge as 'ours' the 'contending powers' within his subject: 'Germany, France, Christ, Moses, Athens, Rome. / The strife, the mixture in her soul, are ours; / Her genius and her

---

[16] Arnold, *Essays in Criticism*, 'Spinoza and the Bible', p. 182 and, for references to Arnold's friendship with Constance de Rothschild, see apRoberts, *Arnold and God*, pp. 167–75. The favourable impact of the Rothschilds in Victorian Britain is charted in Anne and Roger Cowen (eds.), *Victorian Jews Through British Eyes* (Oxford, 1986), pp. 32–55. For the split identity resulting from an Arnoldian discourse of 'culture' see Sander Gilman, *Jewish Self-Hatred: Anti-Semitism and the Hidden Language of the Jews* (Baltimore, 1986), p. 2 and *passim*.

[17] Jonathan Arac, *Criticial Genealogies: Historical Situations for Post-Modernist Literary Studies* (New York, 1987), pp. 119–20 and p. 127.

glory are her own'. The question of 'race' was, in this way, always intertwined with such acts of Judaic self-identification. Writing with the needs of a particularist nation in mind, Arnold utilized a semitic discourse that was in turn used to exclude 'others' from the national community. His ideal of the modernizing universalist State in *Culture and Anarchy*, on the other hand, was only able to institutionalize an 'alien' cultural transcendence in an unrealizable future. But such is the continued importance of *Culture and Anarchy* that it exposes the competing needs of a universalist State, built on the foundations of an exclusivist national community, which was expanding its sphere of influence throughout the late Victorian period.[18] The ambivalent discourse that results from these competing needs shall now be explored in more detail in the fiction of Anthony Trollope.

ANTHONY TROLLOPE AND THE REALISM OF 'RACE'

Matthew Arnold's ideal of an even and happy 'balance' between 'Hebraism and Hellenism' can, in a rather less grandiose way, be applied to the fiction of Anthony Trollope. Trollope, after all, considered himself to be the most 'balanced' of novelists whose autonomous 'characters' transcended mere 'causes' and, like Arnold's definition of 'culture', synthesized all oppositions into a higher realm of 'truth'. The very liberality of Trollope's fictional 'realism', in the words of one of his most sophisticated critics, excludes 'literary stereotypes' as 'unreal': 'Outright villainy is as foreign to Trollope's realistic world as is [outright] heroism... Trollope's most villainous men are those who act like stage villains; their behaviour is that of a literary stereotype, jarring with the realistic behaviour of those who share their fictional world'. Most recent accounts of Trollope emphasize the multifarious 'mixture of good and bad' in his 'attitude towards groups and individuals' and reinforce his sense of an incontestable verisimilitude located in his model 'characters'.[19]

---

[18] For Arnold's idealization of the modernizing, universalizing State see Raymond Williams, *Culture and Society, 1780–1950* (London, 1958), pp. 131–6 and, for this argument in general, see Dench, *Minorities in the Open Society*, pp. 8–9.

[19] William Kendrick, *The Novel Machine: The Theory and Fiction of Anthony Trollope* (Baltimore, 1980), pp. 69–70 and *passim* is the most sophisticated discussion of Trollope's fictional 'realism'. For recent apologetic readings of Trollope in terms of the liberality of his conception of 'character' see Stephen Wall, *Trollope and Character* (London, 1988), and Richard Mullen, *Anthony Trollope: A Victorian in his World* (London, 1990), p. 469 who,

Trollope's *An Autobiography* (1883), in particular, defines his realist fiction in opposition to a Dickensian satirical unscrupulousness. This, he believed, was inherently 'dishonest' because, as he says, 'the vices implied [in satire] are coloured so as to make effect rather than represent truth' (335). Realism is more 'truthful', less stereotypical, because it does not 'take up one side and cling to that' but scrupulously sees both sides of 'a cause' (94–5). Trollope's political creed, as an 'advanced … conservative Liberal' (291), achieves a higher truth by being 'balanced' between liberalism and conservatism and his fiction, reflecting his politics, is represented as virtuous precisely because his 'characters' do not have a particular axe to grind. Trollope's autobiography thereby castigates unnecessary 'political doctrine' as well as 'satire' and the 'sensation novel' for axe-grinding instead of upholding the innate equanimity of the world:

A man who entertains in his mind any political doctrine, except as a means of improving the condition of his fellows, I regard as a political intriguer, a charlatan, and a conjurer, – as one who thinks that, by a certain amount of wary wire-pulling, he may raise himself in the estimation of the world. (294)

Trollope's whiggish emphasis on 'improving the condition of his fellows' – a vague and non-doctrinal belief in a general 'tendency towards equality' (294) – also contains the notion that 'inequality is the work of God' (292) and that those who 'raise [themselves] in the estimation of the world' therefore disturb a God-given equilibrium between 'equality' and 'inequality'. An unqualified equality, not unlike Arnold's sense of 'anarchy', is 'offensive and presents to the imaginations of men ideas of communism, of ruin, and insane democracy' (294). Elsewhere, Trollope writes, 'I dislike universal suffrage; I dislike vote by ballot; I dislike above all things the tyranny of democracy'. Such contradictions were an essential part of Trollope's fictional practice which attempted to contain these various 'offensive' tendencies in his idealized sense of 'character'. Balanced with Trollope's all-inclusive 'liberal' realism is, therefore, a 'conservative' exclusivity which sees 'inequality' as the 'work of God' and privileges 'the aristocrat' as 'of all men the best able to rule'.

---

especially at this point, describes Trollope's 'Jewish characters' as a 'mixture of good and evil'. For a less apologetic reading of Trollope on this issue and in general see R. H. Super, *The Chronicler of Barsetshire: A Life of Anthony Trollope* (Ann Arbor, 1988). All references to Trollope's *An Autobiography* are to the World's Classics edition (Oxford, 1950) and will be cited in the body of the text.

Political power, for Trollope, is not achieved by political doctrines but is naturally situated in the old Whig families who, in the words of John Halperin, are 'the Conservative progenitors of Victorian Liberalism'.[20]

Trollope's liberal inclusiveness is thereby bounded by his construction of an aristocratic Englishness, rooted in a particularist past, which was to be the site of political progress in his fiction. Just as Arnold's supposedly all-embracing notion of 'culture' was fixed racially – 'we English [are] a nation of Indo-European stock' – Trollope constructs an aristocratic Englishness as a vehicle to uphold seemingly universal values. Both Arnold and Trollope, in this way, might be said to be trying to 'balance' opposed forces in Victorian liberalism which wanted to both extend a reformist, universalizing State and, at the same time, maintain a particularist nation whose values were rooted in the past. That Trollope feared the destructive power of an unchecked 'commercialism' is aptly summed up in the well-known opening aside at the beginning of *Dr Thorne* (1858):

> England is not yet a commercial country in the sense in which that epithet is used for her; and let us hope that she will not soon become so. She might surely as well be called feudal England, or chivalrous England. If in western civilized Europe there does exist a nation among whom there are high signors, and with whom the owners of the land are the true aristocracy, the aristocracy that is trusted as being best and fitted to rule, that nation is the English. ... Buying and selling is good and necessary; ... but it cannot be the noblest work of man; and let us hope that it may not in our time be esteemed the noblest work of an Englishman.[21]

His wish to locate bourgeois 'commercialism' within a 'feudal England' meant, as Raymond Williams has argued, that Trollope's fiction was especially concerned with the relation between 'the inheriting landed families and the connected and rising cadet and professional people'. This latter class, of course, included Trollope himself. It is for this reason that many of Trollope's central characters are outsiders who are fearful of rejection by their aristocratic

---

[20] Trollope, *North America* (London, 1862), p. 188 cited in John Halperin, *Trollope and Politics: A Study of the Pallisers and Others* (London, 1977), p. 20 and pp. 14–15. For other important accounts of Trollope's politics and its relationship to his fictional 'realism' see Patrick Brantlinger, *Spirit of Reform: British Literature and Politics, 1832–1867* (Cambridge, Mass., 1977), p. 244 and chapter 9 and Kendrick, *The Novel Machine*, p. 96 and *passim*, to whom I am indebted for this discussion.

[21] Trollope, *Dr Thorne* (London, 1908), p. 10 and Weiner, *English Culture*, p. 31 for a discussion of this passage.

superiors and are thus, in the words of Jonathan Raban, 'haunted by the continuous possibility of disgrace, humiliation, suicide or madness'.[22] Trollope's 'characters', in other words, were positioned for the most part within a changing but narrowly defined 'English nation'. As Victorian England began to expand to incorporate exactly those 'commercial' forces that he feared might destroy it, his fiction was to be increasingly the site on which his 'advanced conservative Liberalism' was to work through its own contradictions and ambivalences.

Defined against the age-old wisdom, values and traditions of the 'true aristocracy', British Jews, who were recently allowed to sit in Parliament, were vulnerable to the charge of being 'conjurers' who were intriguing to 'raise [themselves] in the estimation of the world'. It was precisely this capacity for political 'intrigue' that made Victorian Tories the '*nouveaux riches* of the political arena' in Trollope's eyes. This view was clearly expressed in *The Bertrams* (1859) where Trollope, in a long authorial aside, describes the political background of the 1840s and 1850s for the benefit of a newly elected Member of Parliament:

At this time men had not learnt thoroughly by experience, as now they have, that no reform, no innovation ... stinks so foully in the nostrils of an English Tory politician as to be absolutely irreconcilable to him. When taken in the refreshing waters of office any such pill can be swallowed. This is now a fact recognized in politics. Let the people want what they will, Jew senators, cheap corn, vote by ballot, no property qualification, or anything else, the Tories will carry it for them if the Whigs cannot. A poor Whig premier has none but the Liberals to back him; but a reforming Tory will be backed by all the world – except those few whom his own dishonesty will personally have disgusted.[23]

Anticipating the semitic discourse surrounding the Eastern Question in the 1870s, the 'Jew senator' Benjamin Disraeli was to be increasingly Trollope's *bête noire*, who represented the worst kind of 'reforming Tory' and dishonest parvenu, an arch 'conjurer' and 'political intriguer' *par excellence*. As early as *Barchester Towers* (1857), Trollope pointedly evokes the figure of 'Sidonia' in Disraelian terms as 'a most remarkable man' who quickly reverts to being 'a dirty little' moneylender. Disraeli's construction of Sidonia in *Coningsby*

---

[22] Raymond Williams, *The Country and the City* (London, 1973), p. 214 and Jonathan Raban, *For Love and Money* (London, 1987), p. 76.

[23] Halperin, *Trollope and Politics*, p. 16 and Trollope, *The Bertrams* (London, 1859), p. 165.

(1844), as a Jewish racial aristocrat, is crudely undermined by Trollope in *Barchester Towers*.[24] By the time of Trollope's posthumous autobiography, Disraeli's novels are said to have 'the glory of pasteboard', 'the wealth of tinsel' and the 'wit of hairdressers':

> An audacious conjurer has generally been his hero, – some youth who, by wonderful cleverness, can obtain success by every intrigue that comes to his hand. Through it all there is a feeling of stage properties, a smell of hair-oil, an aspect of buhl, a remembrance of tailors, and that pricking of the conscience which must be the general accompaniment of paste diamonds. (259–60)

Those, like Disraeli, who use 'clever' words to 'conjure' up a false reality stand in contradistinction to the 'realist' novelist whose words, more humbly, merely mirror the world. Beneath the glittering surface of Disraeli's Byronic heroes is, for Trollope, the hidden truth of their real 'origins' – the 'remembrance of tailors' – echoing his earlier reconstruction of the romantic figure of Sidonia as a 'dirty little' moneylender.[25] Far from evoking the 'progress of civilization', the election of 'Jew senators' to the House of Commons and the embourgeoisement of British Jewry represented a disruption of the fragile equilibrium between the historical forces of 'inequality' and 'equality'.

Just as the 'orthodox liberalism' of Dr Arnold had defined England racially in the 1840s to exclude 'the Jew' from the compass of 'the nation', the morality of Trollope's 'Jews' also needed to be established unequivocally by him. In his more 'advanced' way, Trollope did not wish simply to exclude 'the Jews' but he, instead, intended them to know their place within a necessarily superior 'feudal England'. It is not simply that, as Halperin would have it, 'the Jews' in Trollope's novels are fixed and unchanging 'obnoxious and greedy... moneylenders'. Within Trollope's fiction, it was precisely the uncertainty caused by unknown, possibly 'semitic', *arrivistes* that meant that the hidden 'reality' of his 'Jews' could not just be assumed stereotypically. Mr Solomon Aram in *Orley Farm*

---

[24] Trollope, *Barchester Towers*, 2 vols. (Oxford, 1953), I, p. 79 and Mullen, *Anthony Trollope*, p. 190 for Trollope's dislike of Disraeli in this context. For an early satire of Disraeli's *Coningsby* (London, 1844) see Thackeray's *Codlingsby* written under the pseudonym of D. M. Shrewsbury and collected in *Contributions to 'Punch'* (New York, 1903).

[25] Kendrick, *The Novel Machine*, pp. 71–2 and *passim* notes that, for Trollope, 'poetry and romance designate territories outside the boundaries of the realistic novel'. See also Donald Stone, 'Trollope, Byron and the Conventionalities' in J. H. Buckley (ed.), *The World of Victorian Fiction* (Harvard, 1975) for a discussion of this.

(1862), for instance, is a relatively considerate solicitor 'of the Hebrew persuasion' who was 'not a dirty old Jew with a hooked nose'.[26] He might almost pass for a 'Christian attorney' but for the fact that 'his eyes were closer than is common with most of us, and his nose seemed to be somewhat swollen about the bridge'. Repeated throughout Trollope's corpus, this racial typology can, obviously, be said to limit Trollope's 'Jews' so that 'when one knew that [Aram] was a Jew one saw that he was a Jew' (II, 129). But the fact that Trollope's readers needed to be given a paradoxical 'knowledge' of Aram's supposedly 'Jewish' physiognomy before he could be 'seen' as a Jew reflects the ambivalence behind his use of a semitic discourse. Trollope's Jews, above all, are not what they seemed and Aram, later on in the novel, is pointedly characterized by his 'air of pretence' rather than his 'steady and assured well-being' (II, 219). It was such 'pretence' that enabled 'the Jew' in the first place to cross the racial boundaries into a privileged Englishness.

That Jews might successfully 'pass' as 'English gentlemen' challenges and qualifies the power of Trollope's 'realist' narrative to 'know' its subjects. Unlike 'negroes', who were firmly circumscribed within Trollope's racial typology, 'the Jews' were able to challenge the ascendancy of a particularist Old England.[27] As Trollope's 'English nation' is perceived to be threatened by a universalizing 'commercialism', then his all-inclusive 'realism' – showing the world as it 'really' is – is an attempt to contain those forces that are 'other' to an authentic Englishness rooted in the past. Trollope's fiction, that is, includes the racialized 'other' only to exclude or contain it within his construction of 'the real'. His Jewish representations are, in this

---

[26] Halperin, *Trollope and Politics*, p. 160 and Trollope, *Orley Farm*, World's Classics edition, 2 vols. (Oxford, 1956), II, p. 129. Further references to this edition will be in the body of the text. Rosenberg, *From Shylock to Svengali*, chapter 6, Anne Aresty Naman, *The Jew in the Victorian Novel: Some Relationships Between Prejudice and Art* (New York, 1980), chapter 4 and Derek Cohen and Deborah Heller (eds.), *Jewish Presences in English Literature* (Montreal, 1990), chapter 4 all discuss Trollope's fixed Jewish stereotypes in these reductive terms. Apart from Halperin, there is the usual gulf between Trollope's place in specialist studies of 'Jewish stereotyping' and mainstream criticism of Trollope. Super, *The Chronicler of Barsetshire*, p. 202 and *passim*, speaks generally about Trollope's 'sturdy, matter-of-fact Victorian anti-Semitism' and is an honourable exception to this rule.

[27] Halperin, *Trollope and Politics*, p. 21 cites Trollope's *North America*, p. 190 and pp. 181–2 where Trollope argues that it was inconceivable to him 'that the Negro can be made equal to the white man' as 'the negro is the white man's inferior through laws of nature ... He is not mentally fit to cope with white men'. For this see also Iva G. Johnson, 'Trollope, Carlyle, and Mill on the Negro: An Episode in the History of Ideas', *Journal of Negro History* 52 (July, 1967), 185–99.

way, 'balanced' precariously between inclusion in the world of 'realism' and exclusion from the authentic world of a racially fixed 'feudal' England.

Trollope's first and only full-length representation of Jewish life, the novella *Nina Balatka* (1867), is also one of his most marginal works. It was published anonymously in Blackwood's magazine in 1866, and written in a deliberately uncharacteristic 'romantic' style to suit its subject-matter. As with *The Bertrams*, where Jews were located in Palestine as a rather exotic group who indulge in strange unEnglish practices (such as throwing stones on the Grave of Absalom) Trollope, in *Nina Balatka*, locates a Jewish milieu in a timeless other-worldly 'ghetto' in contemporary Prague.[28] The fact that, as Trollope argues in his autobiography, there is no 'English life' in *Nina Balatka* meant that there could, in this work, be 'more of romance proper than had been usual with me' (206). Jews in *Nina Balatka* are, therefore, not a danger to the 'reality' of Englishness – as they were to become in subsequent novels by Trollope – but, instead, they threaten a more nebulous foreign Catholicism. The unreal 'romantic' nature of *Nina Balatka* meant that the categories of 'Jew' and 'Christian' are used in this novella to signify religious and racial differences which are not rooted in a concrete social or political 'reality' but are merely a part of the 'symbolic scenery' of the story. As Joan Cohen has shown, Trollope's Prague 'is a mysterious place. It seems dark and empty of people. Though Nina travels continually between the Jewish quarter and her Christian home she seldom meets or even sees anyone'. *Nina Balatka*, in these terms, is rather like a 'fairy tale', where the 'threatening landscape' of Trollope's other-world is divided into 'Jewish' and 'Christian' quarters – symbolically linked together by the bridge over the Moldau – which denotes the impossible gap which separates these religious and racial enemies.[29]

The overall tone of *Nina Balatka* is set by its opening lines which inform the reader that 'Nina Balatka was a maiden of Prague, born of Christian parents, and herself a Christian – but she loved a Jew; and this is her story' (1). The disruptive clause – 'but she loved a Jew' – indicates the disturbing role of 'the Jews' in this story as they

---

[28] Trollope's *The Bertrams*, p. 26 and *An Autobiography* pp. 204–6. Further references to *Nina Balatka* will be to the World's Classics edition (Oxford, 1946) and will be in the body of the text.

[29] Joan Mandel Cohen, *Form and Realism in Six Novels of Anthony Trollope* (The Hague, 1976), p. 84.

move out of their 'ghetto' into the arms of the children of 'Christian parents'. If *Nina Balatka* is *sui generis* in its style and subject-matter in relation to the rest of Trollope's fiction, it is largely because of the unqualified 'hatred' which the Prague 'Christians' felt for 'the Jews'. Such vehement Jew-hatred – which 'in those earlier days ... could satisfy itself in persecution' (1) – was long since considered 'medieval' and unEnglish in Victorian Britain and Trollope's severely mediated liberalism was still shaped according to these assumptions.[30] Much of Trollope's fiction, written soon after *Nina Balatka*, nonetheless echoes this 'romantic tale' by concerning itself with the 'problem' of Jews assimilating into the 'English nation' and the 'prejudice' or 'hatred' which this causes amongst Trollope's supposedly indigenous community. The address for one of the most problematic of these upwardly mobile Jewish assimilators, the Rev. Joseph Emilius, is Bohemian Prague and the initially troublesome Madame Marie Max Goesler in *Phineas Redux* (1874) also displays an intimate knowledge of the Prague 'ghetto'.

A clue to the connection between Trollope's 'romantic' Eastern other-world and the 'realistic' world of his subsequent fiction can be found in Anton Trendellsohn's contradictory 'dreams' of equality which anticipate the difficulties, as Trollope perceived them, of accomodating emigrant Jews once they had reached the shores of England. After settling in London, Trendellsohn 'believed that he would be rich, and was sure that he knew the ways of trade'. His entrepreneurial ambitions, before succumbing to the benign influence of Nina Balatka, were nevertheless still bounded worryingly by his Jewishness:

To be a Jew, always a Jew, in all things a Jew, had been ever a part of his great dream. It was as impossible to him as it would be to his father to forswear the religion of his people. To go forth and be great in commerce by deserting his creed would have been nothing to him. His ambition did not desire wealth so much as the possession of wealth in Jewish hands, without those restrictions upon its enjoyment to which Jews under his own eye had ever been subjected. (70)

Only after Nina Balatka had 'come across his path', did the Judeo-centric Anton 'shape his dreams anew' and accommodate himself to the 'freedom' of 'far cities'. Here, presumably, his desire for the

---

[30] For a discussion of these assumptions see Bryan Cheyette, 'The Other Self: Anglo-Jewish Fiction and the Representation of Jews in England, 1875–1905' pp. 97–111, in David Cesarani (ed.), *The Making of Modern Anglo-Jewry* (Oxford, 1990).

'possession of wealth in Jewish hands' was to be tempered by his 'union' with Nina:

[H]e would show the world around him, both Jews and Christians, how well a Christian and a Jew might live together. To crush the prejudice which had dealt so harshly with his people – to make a Jew equal in all things to a Christian – this was his desire; and how could this better be fulfilled than by his union with a Christian? (71)

The duality in Trendellsohn's notions of 'equality' – one bounded by his Jewishness the other by his 'union with a Christian' – indicates the doubleness in Trollope's representation of Trendellsohn. On the one hand Trendellsohn is reduced to a racial category with 'jet-black hair', a 'dark' skin ('no white man could be more dark and swarthy than Anton Trendellsohn') and 'eyes [which] were too close together in his face'. In short, Trendellsohn was 'a very Jew among Jews ... the movement of the man's body was the movement of a Jew' (11). This exclusivist representation is tempered by Trollope's inclusivist moralizing which 'balances' Trendellsohn's racial attributes with his 'Christian forbearance to his Christian debtor, Josef Balatka' and his loyalty and 'Christian chivalry' (119) towards Nina. The tension between Trendellsohn's racial Jewishness and 'Christian' patterns of behaviour is, however, exposed when the 'inborn suspicion of his nature' (181) jeopardizes his marriage to Nina and almost causes her to commit suicide.

Trollope ends his story with 'a Jew and his wife [taking] their leave of Prague, and start[ing] for one of the great cities of the west' (191), which once again emphasizes Anton and Nina's 'union' as well as their continuing racial difference. It is this tension which is explored in the Palliser novels and *The Way We Live Now* (1875). In these novels, the wilfully transgressive 'Jew' confronts the boundaries of the 'English nation' by combining the dangers of a universalizing 'commercialism' with a preternatural 'romantic' racial particularism which had only just been rampant in the dark 'ghettos' of the East. Anton, nonetheless, restrains his racialized behaviour – acting as a 'Christian' in a 'dark' Jewish skin – and thereby anticipates Trollope's later models of 'forbearance' in the face of superior 'English' values. For this reason it may well be significant, as Richard Mullen has argued, that Trollope has Anton sign a letter 'A. T.', thereby signifying the anonymous author of the story. That Anton's initials are the same as Trollope's points also to the

stereotypical 'Jew' as an unconscious Trollopian self who, like his
rigidly 'commercial' author, is an alien outsider needing to be
accepted by a hostile society.[31]

The figure who acts as an idealized model for the ambivalent
assimilation of the Jewish racial 'other' into Trollope's fictional
aristocracy, and who also carries over the 'fairy tale' element from
Nina Balatka, is undoubtedly Madame Max Goesler. She is introduced in the second volume of *Phineas Finn* (1869) – a novel which
was written in the winter of 1866–7 soon after *Nina Balatka* – and she
is an important character in the Palliser series until her final
appearance in *The Duke's Children* (1880). Madame Goesler was
initially characterized as the familiar Oriental Jewess, a construction
that was utilized previously by Trollope in his representation of the
eroticized Rebecca Loth in *Nina Balatka* and the exotic 'Jewesses' in
The Bertrams.[32] At one point in *Phineas Finn*, Madame Goesler is
described as being seated on her sofa with her feet tucked beneath her
'as though she were seated somewhere in the East' (180). Trollope's
initial representation of Goesler emphasizes this exoticism by
focussing on her wealth ('she is very rich and has a small house in
Park Lane' (26)); her mysterious antecedents ('no one, I take it,
knows much of her' (29)); her Jewishness ('her enemies say that her
father was a German Jew' (26)) and, above all, her rampant
sexuality:

She was a woman probably something over thirty years of age. She had
thick black hair, which she wore in curls – unlike anybody else in the world.
... Her eyes were large, of a dark blue colour, and very bright, and she used
them in a manner which is as yet hardly common with English women. She

---

[31] Mullen, *Anthony Trollope*, p. 470 for this astute point. Trollope's *An Autobiography*, pp. 1–19
is an account of his youthful social ostracism and sense of himself as an outsider. This work
passim also gives ample evidence of Trollope's necessary 'commercialism' as an author.

[32] All references to *Phineas Finn* (London, 1869) will be taken from the Everyman edition
(London, 1929) and included in the body of the text. Rebbeca Loth in Trollope's *Nina
Balatka*, is described as 'dark, with large dark-blue eyes and jet-black tresses ... who knew
herself to be all a queen' (pp. 82–3) and the unnamed 'Jewesses' in *The Bertrams*, p. 94 who,
'though already mothers', were 'glorious specimens of feminine creation' who 'were
somewhat too bold, perhaps; there was too much daring in their eyes, as, with their naked
shoulders and bosoms nearly bare, they met the eyes of the men who were looking at them'.
This Orientalist tradition of 'Eastern' exoticism was commonly applied to representations
of Jewish women in our period. It is staggering, therefore, that Jane Nardin, *He Knew He was
Right: Women in the Novels of Anthony Trollope* (Illinois, 1988) pp. 193–201 and *passim* ignores
completely the racial dimension in Trollope's representations of women. For a brief account
of this important topic see Olivier Cohen-Steiner, 'Jews and Jewesses in Victorian Fiction:
From Religious Stereotype to Ethnic Hazard', *Patterns of Prejudice* 21 (Summer 1987),
25–34.

seemed to intend that you should know that she employed them to conquer you ... But perhaps her greatest beauty was in the brilliant clearness of her dark complexion ... (21)

Such is the erotic power of Madame Goesler that Trollope's pen, at one point, 'may not dare to describe the traceries of yellow and ruby silk' which ran across the Goesler 'bosom' (22). As well as her Oriental sexuality, Goesler's uncertain 'dark' racial origins also make it difficult for Trollope's 'realist' fiction to accommodate her. The Duke, for instance, associates her with a houri he had once seen in Greece, 'there was something of the vagueness of mystery in the very blackness and gloss and abundance of her hair, – as though her beauty was the beauty of some world which he had not yet known' (180). Her generic and racial otherness marks Goesler out as a figure whom the reader can only 'know' problematically and, as Stephen Wall has argued, Trollope spends most of the second volume of *Phineas Finn* 'wondering what, exactly, Madame Max was like, and finding this out experimentally'.[33]

The main way that Trollope 'finds Goesler out' is by having the aged Duke of Omnium succumb to her sexual power, which results in a proposal of marriage. Goesler is initially tempted by this offer as it is both the pinnacle of her special 'ambitions' – 'she played her game with great skill and great caution' (151) – and, above all, it is a means of exacting 'revenge' on those that had 'ill-used and scornfully treated her' (181). Just as Anton Trendellsohn wished to avenge Christian 'prejudices' by marrying Nina Balatka, Madame Goesler similarly threatens to become the Duchess of Omnium as a means of 'revenge' for past wrongs.[34] Instead of a vengeful marriage with the Duke of Omnium, Goesler's acknowledged sense of inferiority in relation to the aristocracy turns out to be the main reason why she rejects his offer. Goesler refuses the Duke because she calculated that she was 'not fitted by birth and position to be the wife of the Duke of Omnium' (194). Her interestingly ambiguous social calculation meant, therefore, that she would not be able to live at 'ease' among

[33] Wall, *Trollope and Character*, p. 145. See also Naman, *The Jew in the Victorian Novel*, pp. 105–7 for a discussion of Madame Max Goesler in these terms.
[34] Wall, *Trollope and Character*, p. 148 for this interpretation. For a negative reading of Madame Goesler along these lines see Rebecca West's *The Court and the Castle* (London, 1958), chapter 3. Anton, interestingly, also has 'jet-black hair ... clustered round his ears': 'Had it been allowed to grow, it would almost have hung in ringlets; but it was worn very short as though its owner were jealous even of the curl' (p. 11). He is, as Rachel Feldberg has argued in an unpublished essay, jealous and possessive even of a ringlet and, like Madame Goesler, needs to control his more primitive racial characteristics.

her 'superiors' as the Duchess of Omnium. In this, she demonstrates
the self-imposed racial limitations that constitute Trollope's ideal
model of 'Jewish' assimilation into the heart of Old England.

Trollope is clear about the racial chaos that would ensue if
Madame Goesler were to marry the Duke. Lady Glencora, who
wished 'her fair-haired, curly-pated, bold-faced little boy' (156) to
be the Earl of Silverbridge, is horror-stricken at the thought of 'some
little sizen-cheeked half-monkey baby, with black, brown, and yellow
skin' (156–7) as the heir to the Duke of Omnium. Throughout this
period of indecision with regard to the 'extent of her ambition'
towards the Duke, Madame Goesler veers from being represented in
this grotesque mode as both the 'wicked witch' and the 'good fairy'.
But such violently opposed reactions to the semitic 'other' are
represented in *Phineas Finn* as being perfectly understandable when
one is ignorant of a character's racial origins. In this way, Trollope's
fiction panders to the 'natural' prejudices which his readers might
have had towards a figure who was not bounded by the limitations of
her 'race':

Had the Duke forgotten himself and his position for the sake of some fair girl
with a pink complexion and grey eyes... Lady Glencora thought that she
would have forgiven it better. (193)

In a parallel conflict between the 'blonde' Lady Laura Standish and
Madame Goesler, over Phineas Finn in *Phineas Redux* (1874), Lady
Laura could similarly have 'borne' Phineas Finn's marriage to
Madame Goesler if Goesler had not been a 'swarthy' 'German
Jewess' (II, 225).[35] This unpleasant castigation of Madame Goesler
was, in this case, a product of Lady Laura's own character flaws as
Goesler, by the time of *Phineas Redux*, had demonstrated time and
again her uncompromising integrity in relation to a superior
Englishness (even refusing the Duke's bequest to her).

By understanding her place in the social order of things Goesler,
paradoxically, came to embody Trollope's 'advanced conservative
Liberalism' and is rightly described as 'the most perfect gentleman in
Trollope's novels'. Once Goesler is seen to have tempered her
initially unbounded ambitiousness – and realized the limitations of
her race and sexuality – she ceases to be a threatening figure and, in
subsequent Palliser novels, is eventually indistinguishable from the

---

[35] This is a familiar erotic and racial opposition. See, for example, Sir Walter Scott's *Ivanhoe*
(1819) and a later reworking of this theme in George Du Maurier's *The Martian* (1897).

Palliser circle as a deracialized and desexualized 'close friend' of Lady Glencora's. Goesler's marriage to Phineas Finn is particularly appropriate as both are 'stranger[s] in the world of the Pallisers' who offer the detached rationale of the outsider for the continuation of an increasingly threatened social order. Nonetheless, after successfully containing Madame Goesler in *Phineas Finn*, her initially disturbing otherness is displaced onto two further mysterious travellers from the East, Joseph Emilius in *The Eustace Diamonds* (1873) and *Phineas Redux* and Ferdinand Lopez in *The Prime Minister* (1876).[36]

When proposing to the disreputable Lady Eustace in *The Eustace Diamonds*, the Reverend Joseph Emilius would have 'asked a Duchess to marry him, with ten times Lizzie's income' without 'a blush or a quiver in his voice' (707). The comparison here with Madame Goesler is telling. Unlike Goesler, the fashionable romantic clergyman from Mayfair, who quotes from Byron and the Bible to Lizzie Eustace, is unable to regulate his inner rapaciousness. In contrast to the indeterminacy which defines Madame Goesler, Joseph Emilius is marked from the beginning as a 'Jew [born] in Hungary' who was known in Bohemia as 'Mealyus' (335). By the time of *Phineas Redux*, Trollope reverts to calling Emilius 'Yosef Mealyus' and, in this way, linguistically reverses the mid-Victorian process of Jewish assimilation into British society. Whereas Madame Goesler's sexual and racial difference is eventually sublimated, Emilius, by the end of *Phineas Redux*, is universally regarded as a 'foreigner and a Jew, by name Yosef Mealyus' (*PR* II, 287). That Lizzie eventually succumbs to this Jewish 'imposter' indicates both the dangers of her foolish romanticism – to her 'poetry was life and life was poetry' (*ED*, 526) – and the ability of Emilius to 'conjure' a false reality precisely by confusing 'poetry' with 'life'.[37]

Like Disraeli, Emilius constructs himself as a racial aristocrat – 'the blood that runs in my veins is as illustrious as your own, having descended to me from the great and ancient nobles of my native country' – but he is quickly re-written by Trollope as a 'nasty,

---

[36] Shirley Robin Letwin, *The Gentleman in Trollope: Individuality and Moral Conduct* (London, 1982), p. 74 on Madame Max as Trollope's 'perfect gentleman' and Robert Tracy, *Trollope's Later Novels* (Berkeley, 1978), p. 26 for the importance of the 'detached rationale' of the 'outsider'. I will be citing *The Eustace Diamonds*, Penguin edition (London, 1986); *Phineas Redux*, World's Classics editon (Oxford, 1983); and *The Prime Minister*, Panther edition (St Albans, 1973) in the body of the text.

[37] For this argument see Stone, 'Trollope, Byron and the Conventionalities', p. 199 and Kendrick, *The Novel Machine*, p. 66.

greasy, lying, squinting Jew preacher' (*ED*, 710). It is Madame
Goesler's intimate knowledge of the Prague 'ghetto' in *Phineas Redux*
that finally vindicates Phineas Finn and exposes Emilius as a
murderer and a bigamist. That the 'key' (in all senses) to Finn's
innocence in this novel is to be found in the dark streets of the Jewish
'ghetto' indicates both the unfortunate necessity of accommodating
the racial 'other' and the dangers of their unknowable powers of
deception. If Emilius is the Disraelian analogue for self-deception in
the private sphere in *The Eustace Diamonds* then, more worryingly still
for Trollope, the Conservative leader Mr Daubeny in *Phineas Redux* is
the analogue for this form of self-deception in the public sphere.[38] By
the time of *Phineas Redux*, Disraeli had already completed his first
ministry of eleven months (from February to December 1868), which
provided the political context for this novel, and, during the last
decade of Trollope's life, Disraeli was to enter his first full Conservative ministry (1874–80). In *The Way We Live Now* (1875) and
The Prime Minister (1876), the mysterious 'conjuring' that characterizes Prime Minister Daubeny in *Phineas Redux* had finally entered
the public sphere. It is in this corrupt world that the deceptive racial
'other' was able to flourish. By the mid-1870s, the forces of deceit and
unreality were perceived by Trollope, among many others, to be in
the ascendancy and increasingly difficult to contain.

The racial origins of Ferdinand Lopez in *The Prime Minister*, like
those of Madame Goesler, are clouded in uncertainty. Most
disturbing for Trollope, however, is that although his origins are
unclear, Lopez, as soon as he appeared in London, was immediately
'admitted on all sides' to the 'precious rank' of 'gentleman' (22).
Unlike Goesler who, over a long period of time, had to prove her
'superiority of inward being' – Trollope's definition of a gentleman
in his *Life of Cicero* (1880) – Lopez, in the words of Shirley Letwin,
'skillfully use[d] the outward marks of a gentleman to violate what
they promised'.[39] Rather like Trollope's condemnation in his
autobiography of the 'sensation novel' as being overly concerned
with the 'development of plot' (*A*, 227) as against the 'truth of
character' (*A*, 229), Lopez in *The Prime Minister* is all 'plot' – or
devious machinations – who is defined exclusively in terms of his
inner lack of 'character'. Because it is possible in the 1870s to become a 'gentleman' without 'ancestry' (22), Lopez uses his false

[38] Halperin, *Trollope and Politics*, p. 174 and chapter 7 for this argument.
[39] Letwin, *The Gentleman in Trollope*, pp. 248–9 and p. 252.

'rank' to marry into one of 'the oldest families in England' (46). In a repetition of the plot of *Nina Balatka*, Lopez is bitterly opposed in his marriage to Emily Wharton by her father, Abel Wharton, QC, 'a man of old fashions' (37) who challenges Lopez because he 'is not the son of an English gentleman' (43). In an important distinction, demonstrating the limits of liberalism in Trollope's fiction, Wharton argues:

I have always been for absolute toleration in matters of religion, – have always advocated admission of Roman Catholics and Jews into Parliament, and even to the Bench. In ordinary life I never question a man's religion. It is nothing to me whether he believes in Mahomet, or has no belief at all. But when a man comes to me for my daughter – . (45)

Here Wharton distinguishes between the accommodation of religious or racial minorities into the universalist state and the private assimilation of these minorities into the particularist 'family' of England. If the 'world as it was now didn't care whether its sons-in-law were Christian or Jewish, whether they had the fair skin and bold eyes and uncertain words of an English gentleman, or the swarthy colour and false grimace and glib tongue of some inferior Latin race', Wharton did 'care for these things' (134). Rather like the 'prejudices' against Joseph Emilius in *Phineas Redux*, Wharton's diatribes against the 'swarthy son of Judah' (46) or the 'greasy Jew adventurer out of the gutter' (137) – which are dismissed by Emily as 'the prejudices of an old man' (21) – are proven right by the end of the novel.

Critics have argued that Wharton's 'prejudices' against his prospective son-in-law are qualified by Trollope's supposedly 'sympathetic' view of Lopez who eventually commits suicide.[40] His sense of 'himself as a victim' (392), however, drives Lopez to even greater peaks of revenge against Wharton and Plantagenet Palliser, Trollope's fictional Prime Minister. Far from being defined by the 'balanced' autonomy of his 'character', Lopez's irrational vengeance is a racially defined emotion that Anton Trendellsohn first articulated in the Prague 'ghetto' and Madame Goesler threatened to unleash in *Phineas Finn*. That his vengeance drives Lopez to challenge the moral authority of Plantagenet Palliser – Trollope's 'perfect gentleman' (*A*, 361) in the Palliser series – indicates the serious social and political ramifications of admitting those without 'the faintest notions

---

[40] Wall, *Trollope and Character*, pp. 177–88 and Super, *The Chronicler of Barsetshire*, pp. 332–5 for this argument.

of the feelings of a gentleman' (500) into the bastions of Englishness.
By the time of Trollope's later novels, the private frailties of overly
'emotional' women have considerable public implications. 'Corsair-
figures', such as Lopez and Emilius, were thus able to advance, in all
senses, due to the unreal 'romantic' propensities of those such as
Lizzie Eustace, Emily Wharton and Glencora Palliser. It is, after all,
Lady Glencora's susceptibility to Lopez's Byronic charm, echoing
Emily Wharton's initial attraction to Lopez, that threatens to end
Plantagenet Palliser's political career. By the 1870s, Trollope's
'realism' can no longer contain the slippery 'romanticism' of the
Jewish 'other' which has moved from the margins of Trollope's mid-
Victorian texts to the very centre of his later work.[41]

As an explicitly axe-grinding 'satire', *The Way We Live Now* tries to
avoid the uncertainty of being a 'realist' work which cannot fully
'know' its 'Jewish' subjects. The non-realistic form of Trollope's
novel succumbs to its subject-matter as it charts, comprehensively,
the collapse of 'feudal English' values and, in turn, the lack of any
firm national foundations on which to situate a sense of 'reality'. In
an inversion of the Palliser series, *The Way We Live Now* has at its
heart not the ideal self of Plantagenet Palliser but the racial and
generic anti-self, Augustus Melmotte. Melmotte, significantly, is an
intertextual figure, deriving from both Charles Maturin's *Melmoth the
Wanderer* (1828) and Charles Dickens's Mr Merdle in *Little Dorrit*.[42]
As an unreal figure that is self-consciously textualized rather than
realized, Melmotte is the apotheosis of the romantic obfuscator who
confuses 'poetry' with 'life' as he 'could make money as dear or
cheap as he pleased' (I, 31). His empty rhetoric, in this way,
generates an economic unreality that signifies the destructive
'commercial profligacy of the age' (*A*, 353).

[41] Charlotte Klein, 'The Jew in Modern English Literature', *Patterns of Prejudice* 5 (March–April, 1971), 23–31 usefully discusses Trollope in these terms and Patrick Brantlinger, *Rule of Darkness: British Literature and Imperialism, 1830–1914* (Ithaca, 1988), pp. 5–10 argues that Trollope 'offers a paradigm of the evolution from early to late Victorian Liberal attitudes toward the Empire' and charts his increasingly pro-imperialist belief in 'English' racial superiority in the 1870s. There is an obvious parallel here with Trollope's growing pessimism towards 'the Jew' in his later fiction and, also, the growing threat of his fictional women's 'romantic propensities'. For this latter fear see Stone, 'Trollope, Byron and the Conventionalities', pp. 179–203.
[42] Trollope's *An Autobiography*, pp. 353–6 has an anxious self-justification of his use of Dickensian 'satire'. For a recent stimulating account of this novel in this context see Christopher Herbert, *Trollope and Comic Pleasure* (Chicago, 1987), p. 180 and chapter 7. Further references to the World's Classics edition of *The Way We Live Now* (Oxford, 1975) will be in the body of the text.

In contrast to the rooted Englishness and stolid 'reality' of Plantagenet Palliser, the romantic 'wanderings' and uncertain cosmopolitan background of Melmotte make him, in the words of John Terry, the arbitrary 'motive force' of the novel and the false 'engine to which the unbiquitous drive for power, money and respectability is harnessed'. Given his empty unreality, it is significant that Melmotte's mysterious antecedents are not merely synonymous with his supposed Jewishness, as many critics of *The Way We Live Now* have assumed. Melmotte's indeterminacy, as opposed to his fixed racial Jewishness, defines him even when his textual presence includes previous invocations of the destructively 'vengeful' Jew which probably have their origin in Trollope's reading of Elizabethan drama:

People said of him that he had framed and carried out long premeditated and deeply laid schemes for the ruin of those who had trusted him, that he had swallowed up the property of all who had come in contact with him, that he was fed with the blood of widows and children... (I, 75).[43]

As with Melmoth the Wanderer and Mr Merdle, this Shylockian allusion is just another set of arbitrary textual references that fail to locate Melmotte in a 'known' reality. Instead of merely fixing Melmotte as a stereotype, Trollope associates his symbolic power with an indeterminate 'greasiness' which may or may not originate in his 'Jewishness'. Whereas 'the Jew' in the Palliser series is, eventually, either assimilated or excluded from his narrow realm of Englishness, Melmotte is a romantic writer *manqué* whose slippery unreality is defined, precisely, by not being fixed in a given time or place.[44]

In a further reversal of the Palliser series, Trollope abandons the 'truth of character' in *The Way We Live Now* for a world of 'dishonesty magnificent in its proportions' (*A*, 354) which reduces his supposedly autonomous 'characters' to the exigencies of 'plot'. When nothing is 'real' or bounded by national values, the mysterious

---

[43] Tracy, *Trollope's Later Novels*, pp. 32–69 for Trollope's reading of Elizabethan and Jacobean dramatists and John Terry, *Anthony Trollope* (London, 1977), p. 239. Naman, *The Jew in the Victorian Novel*, chapter 4 and Rosenberg, *From Shylock to Svengali*, chapter 6, both wrongly assume Melmotte to be 'Jewish' as do Cohen and Heller, *Jewish Presences*, chapter 4. Harold Fisch, *The Dual Image* (London, 1973), chapter 3, usefully identifies the figure of the 'Wandering Jew' with nineteenth-century romanticism but also describes Melmotte as a 'fantastically wicked Jew' (p. 65).

[44] T. S. Eliot, in his poetry, was to similarly emphasize the excremental sliminess of the indeterminate 'Jew' which is discussed in chapter 6.

forces of the East run rampant and are barely contained by the increasingly illusive 'inward being' of the English character. With the aristocracy made up not of 'land but of capital' after the Agrarian Depression of the 1870s, there is a fateful linkage made, in this novel, between financial speculators such as Melmotte and the impoverished aristocracy such as Lord Longestaffe, the Squire of Caversham.[45] Instead of being expelled or contained by public opinion, wolf-like Jews such as Samuel Cohenlupe, Member of Parliament for Staines, are close to the centres of power. Cohenlupe, in particular, controls Melmotte's City affairs and, eventually, absconds with his company's funds. Melmotte's befuddling of the language enables Jews like Cohenlupe to straddle dangerously both the pre-modern life of the 'ghetto' – 'crowds of dark, swarthy, greasy men' (I, 107) – as well as a modern, uncontrollable 'commercialism' which threatens to devour an Old England. In a world without self-regulation, there are simply no moral standards to test the 'inward being' of an Emilius or a Lopez. Only Ezekiel Breghart, Melmotte's banker, demonstrates a good deal of Goesler-like integrity in refusing the hand in marriage of Georginia Longestaffe when it is clear that she wishes to marry him purely for his money. The 'good natured' (II, 90) Breghart, like Trendellsohn before him, is constructed in racial terms:

He was a fat greasy man, good-looking in a certain degree, about fifty, with hair dyed black, and beard and moustache dyed a purple colour. The charm of his face consisted in a pair of very bright black eyes, which were, however, set too near together in his face for the general delight of Christians. (II, 91)

That Breghart is defined racially by his 'greasiness' and his failure to change his 'semitic' appearance (via the 'dyer's art'), indicates also his inability to fully assimilate into 'feudal England'. By the time of *Is He a Poppenjay?* (1878), the Dean of Brotherton is adamant that no 'good is ever done by converting a Jew', a pointed reference to Disraeli. However ill-disguised, by refusing to marry the daughter of an aristocrat, Breghart, like Madame Goesler, unambiguously embodies Trollope's sense of social order. By comparison, Georginia and her father, Lord Longestaffe, transgress the borders of Englishness by moving from rural England to the urban world of cosmopolitan finance. Even though Breghart insists on 'society' being open to him (II, 271), he is still able to exercise his own 'good

---

[45] Williams, *The Country and the City*, p. 298 for this linkage.

nature' and retain a private sense of integrity. Georginia, on the other hand, is willing to transgress all boundaries – national and racial – for the sake of a large dowry. Her 'greed and craftiness', as Tracy has noted, is more stereotypically 'Jewish' than the behaviour of Breghart.[46] Her justification of these transgressions points to the Hebraized 'commercialism' of England as a whole and, most seriously of all, the racial degeneration (through inter-marriage) of the aristocracy:

> [Breghart] was absolutely a Jew; not a Jew that had been, as to whom there might possibly be a doubt whether he or his father or his grandfather had been the last Jew of the family; but a Jew that was. So was Goldsheiner a Jew, who Lady Julia Stuart had married, or at any rate had been one a very short time before he ran away with the lady. [Georginia] counted up ever so many instances on her fingers of 'decent people' who had married Jews or Jewesses. Lord Frederic Framlinghame had married a girl of the Berrenhoffers; and Mr Hart had married a Miss Chute... (II, 92)

As with Goesler, Trollope needs Breghart to articulate his inferior place in relation to a racially exclusive Englishness and this results paradoxically in an ambivalent self-identification with 'the Jew'. On the one hand, Trollope concurs with the 'prejudiced' Lord Longe-staffe whose only 'real opinion' is that in 'admitting the Jews into Parliament... the glory of England was sunk forever' (II, 23). This 'opinion' is reinforced by the election to the House of Commons of Melmotte and Cohenlupe in *The Way We Live Now* and the attempted election of Lopez in *The Prime Minister*. Beauchamp Beauclerk pointedly notes, in an obvious reference to Disraeli, that 'Melmotte was not the first vulgar man whom the Conservatives had taken by the hand, and patted on the back, and told that he was god' (II, 37). To underline this Disraelian association, Trollope comments that 'anyone reading the Conservative papers at the time... would have thought that England's welfare depended on Melmotte's return... he knew nothing of the working of parliament, nothing of nationality' (II, 33–4). And yet, it is other 'outsider' figures such as Madame Goesler and Phineas Finn who, throughout the Palliser series, validate Trollope's 'advanced conservative Liberalism'. A central irony of Trollope's life was that his construction of an exclusivist Englishness is nearest, perhaps, in its philosophy to the Young

---

[46] Trollope, *Is He Popenjay?*, World's Classics edition, 2 vols. (Oxford, 1946), II, p. 165 and Tracy, *Trollope's Later Novels*, p. 174.

England doctrine of his *béte noire*, Benjamin Disraeli. But the closer
Trollope was to come to emulating Disraeli's imperial philosophy,
the greater was to be the vilification of his arch-enemy as in his
representation of Melmotte, in part, as a Disraelian double. Trollope,
significantly, even took an active part in the political campaign
against Disraeli, making an important speech at a 'national
conference' on the Eastern Question.[47]

By refusing to recognize the limitations of their racial origins
Disraeli, and assimilating Jews in general – such as Joseph Emilius
and Ferdinand Lopez – represented a blurring of the boundaries
between an aristocractic Englishness and an uncontainable 'commercialism'. If Madame Max, as a Jewish woman, could be safely
desexualized and deracialized by Trollope, then this form of
domestication (with the exception of the elderly Breghart) was not
possible for the rampantly sexual, young, upwardly mobile Jewish
male. They, after all, were in a position to take advantage of the
'romantic' susceptibilities of Trollope's flawed women. An indeterminate Jewishness also crossed the boundaries of his chosen
medium – the realist novel – which was to prove to be an increasingly
inadequate means of containing the ambivalent 'other'. Trollope's
use of such hated forms as the 'sensation novel', 'romance' and
'satire', in his most comprehensive semitic representations, points to
the ultimate failure of the 'realist' novel to incorporate 'the Jew'
within its 'balanced' aesthetic realm. I will now discuss George
Eliot's *Daniel Deronda* (1876), as a fruitful example of the realist
novelist going beyond the doctrines of liberal realism in order to
represent the ultimately unknowable semitic 'other'.[48]

---

[47] Halperin, *Trollope and Politics*, p. 118 and p. 295 cites references to this speech and Trollope's
political involvement with the Eastern Question and Trollope's *An Autobiography*, pp. 258–60
contains Trollope's most sustained attack on Disraeli. Tracy, *Trollope's Later Novels*, chapters
2 and 3, makes out a strong case for the similarity of the 'social doctrines' of Disraeli and
Trollope in contrast to the 'doctrine' of Walter Bagehot which is more usually associated
with Trollope. Brantlinger, *Rule of Darkness*, pp. 6–8 also relates Disraeli and Trollope in
relation to late Victorian attitudes to the Empire.

[48] Said, *Orientalism*, p. 72 and Homi Bhabha, 'Difference, Discrimination and the Discourse of
Colonialism' in Francis Barker, Peter Hume, Margaret Iversen and Diane Iversen (eds.),
The Politics of Theory (Colchester, 1983), p. 199, both suggest that an orientalist racial
discourse is, in Said's words, a 'form of radical realism' or, in Bhabha's, a 'regime of truth'
which is 'structurally similar to Realism'. I would wish to turn this argument on its head
and note that rather than a structural similarity, the 'realist text' is fragmented ultimately
by a semitic racial discourse.

GEORGE ELIOT: TOWARDS THE PROMISED LAND

In a continuation of Arnold's *Culture and Anarchy*, Eliot's slightly precious narrative persona in 'The Modern Hep! Hep! Hep!' (1879) places 'the Jew' at the centre of her understanding of liberal progress and makes explicit her intention of representing the 'specific affinities of disposition between our own race and the Jewish' (177).[49] Like Arnold, Eliot's persona has an ambivalent 'affinity' with 'the Jews' arguing in 'The Modern Hep! Hep! Hep!' that 'the superlative peculiarity of the Jews admitted, our affinity with them is only the more apparent when the elements of their peculiarity are discerned' (174). Just as Arnold's sense of 'culture' attempted to transcend racially differentiated Jews, Eliot's persona emphasizes both a higher 'affinity' with 'the Jews' and, at the same time, their 'superlative peculiarity'.

In contrast, however, with Arnold's championing of the supranational 'alien', Eliot's persona rejects the 'adverse moral influences of alienism' or 'cosmopolitan indifference' as a false 'universalism'. Instead, she privileges Jewish particularism as the 'ideal force' of nationalism (182–5) and stresses the historic affinities between 'the way we English got our island and the way the Israelites got Canaan' (176). In general, the Jewish 'sense of their supreme moral values' (177) and their ability to construct a national identity which inspires 'sacrifices of individual comfort ... for the sake of the ideal whole' (183–4) makes 'the Jews' a model for Eliot of what has been called an 'orderly, conservative and morally admirable people'.[50] The organicist ideal of 'separateness with communication', articulated by Daniel's grandfather in *Daniel Deronda*, is thereby embodied in the Jewish nation which, if restored to statehood, would be 'a special channel for special energies [which] may contribute some added form of national genius and an added voice to the councils of the world' (191). Arnold's construction of universalist Hellenized Jews as

---

[49] All further references to George Eliot's *Daniel Deronda* (1876) will be to the Penguin edition and will be cited in the body of the text. Eliot's 'The Modern Hep! Hep! Hep!' (1879) is contained in her collection of essays, *The Impressions of Theophrastus Such* (Edinburgh and London, Blackwood edition, n.d.) and will also be cited in the body of the text.

[50] Deirdre David, *Fictions of Resolution in Three Victorian Novels* (New York, 1981) p. 153 and chapters 7–9 for an excellent discussion of *Daniel Deronda* in these terms. Other useful accounts of this novel include Catherine Gallagher's 'George Eliot and *Daniel Deronda*: The Prostitute and the Jewish Question' in Ruth Yeazell (ed.), *Sex, Science and Society* (Baltimore, 1986), pp. 56–7 and William Baker's *George Eliot and Judaism* (Salzburg, 1975).

a *tabula rasa* for the inscription of the ideal of 'culture' is self-consciously reversed in *Daniel Deronda*. Not unlike her essay, Eliot's novel projects her ideal of nationalism onto particularist Jews who supposedly contain 'that sense of special belonging which is the root of human virtues, both public and private' (183). As with Arnold's description of an overly Hebraic Englishness, Eliot was to represent an increasingly 'cosmopolitan' (173) or 'denationalised' (182) contemporary England which was deemed to be devoid of a sense of 'national' history or a 'higher' purpose. In this, Eliot was also echoing Trollope's racially degenerate England of *The Way We Live Now* and *The Prime Minister*.

Just as a fixed racial differentiation lies behind Arnold's sense of a transcendent 'culture', Eliot's ideal of nationalism was also underpinned by a rigid particularism which highlights the 'superlative peculiarity' of Jews and Englishmen as well as their historical 'affinity'. In a Trollopian representation of an exclusivist Englishness, Eliot's persona in 'The Modern Hep! Hep! Hep!' emphasizes what she calls the 'national life in our veins. Because there is something English which we feel to be supremely worth striving for, worth dying for, rather than living to renounce it' (188). It is in these exclusivist terms that the sense of 'affinity' with 'the Jews' breaks down:

Let it be admitted that it is a calamity to the English, as to any other great historic people, to undergo a premature fusion with immigrants of alien blood; that its distinctive national characteristics should be in danger of obliteration by the predominating quality of foreign settlers. ... [W]hat must follow from the predominance of wealth acquiring immigrants, whose appreciation of our political and social life must often be as approximate or fatally erroneous as their delivery of our language? (186–7)

It is the ambivalence of 'the Jews' in 'The Modern Hep! Hep! Hep!', who are positioned uneasily between their racial 'peculiarity' and a cultural 'affinity', that shall be located in *Daniel Deronda*. Eliot's novel both incorporates the binary oppositions made in her essay – between 'national' and 'denational' Jews and Englishmen – and, at the same time, undermines these distinctions. As with the 'fatally erroneous' language of the 'foreign settler', Eliot's indeterminate narrative is unsure of what discourse to 'deliver' in her novel. As Gillian Beer has shown, *Daniel Deronda* is a work which is both preoccupied with racial origins and yet is 'distrustful of fixed beginnings'.[51] Henleigh Mallinger Grandcourt, for instance, is described initially in relation to a fixed national stereotype, 'the correct Englishman, drawing himself up from his bow into rigidity ... seeming to be in a state of internal drill' (145). But Eliot quickly undercuts this representation in a well-known authorial aside: 'Attempts at description are stupid: who can all at once describe a human being? ... We recognise the alphabet; we are not sure of the language' (145–6). Her sense of the difficulty of achieving a homogeneous narrative – from the individual letters of 'the alphabet' to 'the language' itself – pervades *Daniel Deronda*. Because the universal 'language' of liberal progress no longer adequately represents the future, Eliot increasingly utilizes the particularist vocabulary of 'race' and 'nation' in her novel. This also, however, turns out to be an uncertain 'language' that cannot, quite, be fully understood.

Eliot's novel is, on the one hand, structured in terms of an all-encompassing racial spectrum which stretches from the cosmopolitan, 'denationalised' Leubronn (which opens *Daniel Deronda in medias res*) to the final vision of a future 'national' Jewish Palestine. But, countering this narrative movement towards the 'ideal force' of nationalism, Eliot also emphasizes the textual impossiblity of fully 'knowing' either the origins or history of her characters. The epigraph for the chapter which introduces Daniel Deronda begins pointedly with the seminal belief: 'Men, like planets, have both a visible and an invisible history' (202). Deronda's 'invisible' history means that he is a *tabula rasa* who is 'nothing other' than his as yet unknown racialized 'vocation'. It is difficult to 'see' Deronda in this incomplete state, hence the need for certain defining traits, such as the routine 'grasping of his coat-collar', as if the reader is continually meeting him for the first time. The 'invisibility' of Deronda's vocation renders his character passive and featureless as, that is, someone who is defined by *not* having the 'appropriate nose' (205) of the Malinger family. This absence of 'character' is, however, the necessary precondition for Eliot's displacement of her nationalist ideals onto her eponymous hero.[52]

[51] Gillian Beer, *Darwin's Plots: Evolutionary Narrative in Darwin, George Eliot and Nineteenth-Century Fiction* (London, 1985 edition), p. 223 and chapters 6–7, along with Sally Shuttleworth, *George Eliot and Nineteenth-Century Science: The Make-Believe of a Beginning* (Cambridge, 1984), chapter 8, convincingly make out a case for the ambiguity of 'origins' in *Daniel Deronda*.

[52] Shuttleworth, *George Eliot and Nineteenth-Century Science*, p. 176, along with Beer, *Darwin's Plots*, for this reading and Alan Mintz, *George Eliot and the Novel of Vocation* (Cambridge,

Daniel eventually achieves his epic vocation by transforming himself into one of Disraeli's 'youthful heroes going to seek the hidden
tokens of their birth and ... inheritance' (573). But such Disraelian
romanticism, associated throughout Eliot's novel with Deronda,
serves further to emphasize the imponderable ideal of Jewish
nationalism as an other-realm, or unknown 'promised land', that is
defined against a rational, modernizing liberalism. Thus, when
Mordecai in the Philosopher's Club confronts Gideon, an assimilated
'rational Jew', it is with a vocabulary that reflects Eliot's own shift
from liberal realism to the other-worldly epic:

> I too claim to be a rational Jew. But what is it to be rational – what is it to
> feel the light of the divine reason growing stronger within and without? It
> is to see more and more of the hidden bonds that bind and consecrate change
> as a dependent growth – yea, consecrate it with kinship: the past becomes
> my parent, and the future stretches towards me the appealing arms of
> children. (587–8)

Mordecai's prophetic ability to discern 'the hidden bonds that bind
and consecrate change', coupled with his construction of the 'future'
in exclusivist familial terms, parallels Eliot's own epic narrative. Like
Eliot, Mordecai wishes to go beyond the 'rote-learned language of a
system' (560) and he, therefore, emphasizes the kabbalistic tradition
of preordained 'pathways' which ultimately prefigure the met-
empsychosist passage of souls into 'perfection' (599–600). Such is the
indeterminacy of the Judaic spiritual realm in this novel which
challenges the received 'language' of liberal progress.

In a telling ambivalence, Mordecai's transcendent kabbalism, and
the Jewish prayer which anticipates the 'unity of mankind' (802), is
written in the silent other-language of Hebrew which Daniel, halfway through the novel, had 'somehow, in deference to Mordecai, ...
begun to study' (466). That the universalist message of 'separateness
with communication' is expressed by both Mordecai and Daniel's
grandfather in the Hebrew language signifies what Colin MacCabe
has appropriately called an 'undifferentiated plenitude' in *Daniel
Deronda*. At the climactic point of her self-dissolution, as she realizes
herself to be a 'mere speck' in comparison with the 'wide-stretching'
East (875–6), Gwendolen remembers Daniel studying Hebrew. To

Mass., 1978), chapter 7 is useful for the importance of 'vocation' in Eliot's novel. For a
Jamesian reading of Deronda as 'passive and featureless' see Ruth Raider, '"The Flash of
Fervour"': *Daniel Deronda*', in Ian Gregor (ed.) *Reading the Victorian Novel: Detail into Form*
(London, 1980), p. 266 and chapter 13 to whom I am indebted for this discussion.

be sure, Daniel does assimilate into a 'symbolic language community', in Sally Shuttleworth's apposite phrase, but it is a textual community, like the future Jewish Palestine, whose content cannot be 'known' by Eliot's readers.[53]

In rejecting the false universalism of a materialist rationalism – the 'promised land' of liberal progress – Eliot constructs a spiritual Judeo-centric universalism which is 'beyond the liberal imagination'. By associating a mystical transcendence with Jewish particularity, Eliot introduces a double narrative into her novel which both attempts to reach 'beyond the modes of self-transcendence available in England at the time' and is, at the same time, confined by a racialized discourse.[54] This split between cultural transcendence and racial fixity is at the heart of *Daniel Deronda*. Mordecai's nationalism contains a 'higher' Arnoldian synthesis defined in physiological terms as a nation of 'one growth' of 'whom it may be truly said that ... religion and law and moral life mingled as the stream of the blood in the heart' (590). But the specificity of the 'Hebrew blood' (594) of 'Israel' fixes 'the Jew' as a racial category: 'the heritage of Israel is beating in the pulses of millions' (596). While Mordecai's Jewish nationalism expresses a timeless 'reconciliation' of 'East and West' (597), it also emphasizes the particularist need for the transfiguration of materialist Jews in the here and now. There are, Mrs Meyrick comments, 'Ezras and Ezras in the world; and really it is a comfort to think that all Jews are not like those shopkeepers who *will not* let you get out of their shops' (628). Throughout the novel Daniel (as well as Mrs Meyrick, Hans, the Arrowpoints and Gwendolen) continually note the 'ugly', 'vulgar', 'narrow', 'unpoetic' or 'unrefined' nature of Jews and Judaism. The Cohen family, in particular, who are studied 'zoologically' by Daniel, contrast starkly with Daniel, Mordecai and Mirah.[55] Such ambivalence is highlighted in 'The Modern Hep! Hep! Hep!' when Eliot's persona states that:

[53] Colin MacCabe, *James Joyce and the Revolution of the Word* (London, 1978), p. 24 (although he mistakenly fixes Eliot as a 'Classic Realist' novelist in this book) and Shuttleworth, *George Eliot and Nineteenth-Century Science*, p. 187. Edward Said in his *The Question of Palestine* (New York, 1979), pp. 60–9 makes the point that the 'promised land' of 'Palestine' is itself an absence in Eliot's novel.

[54] Mintz, *George Eliot and the Novel of Vocation*, p. 158 and Robert Pryer, 'Beyond the Liberal Imagination: Vision and Unreality in *Daniel Deronda*', *Victorian Studies* 4 (September 1960), 33–54. See also U. C. Knoepflmacher, *Religious Humanism and the Victorian Novel* (Princeton, 1965), chapter 2 for a still useful discussion of these issues.

[55] David, *Fictions of Resolution*, p. 141. See also Naman, *The Jew in the Victorian Novel*, pp. 203–7 and May Daniels, 'The Cohen Family in *Daniel Deronda*', *The Jewish Quarterly* 26 (Numbers 3–4, 1978–9) for this argument.

If we wish to free ourselves from the inconveniences that we have to complain of, whether in proletaries or in Jews, our best course is to encourage all means of improving these neighbours who elbow us in a thickening crowd, and of sending their incommodious energies into beneficent channels. (191)

The slippage in this passage from the 'incommodious energies' of 'proletaries' onto 'the Jews', as Deirdre David has argued suggestively, points to a wider subsumption in *Daniel Deronda* of material or class interests into a 'beneficent' nationalism. And yet, if the ideal of Jewish nationalism is a universally applicable mode for the representation and salvation of contemporary Britain, it is also an unknowable racial other-realm. This displacement of Eliot's ideals onto 'the Jews' is continually uncertain as 'the Jews' can signify both a quasi-biblical, spiritual community rooted in the past as well as a degenerate contemporary 'race' that is in need of immediate 'improvement'. In one partial reading, the repeatedly affirmed absorption into European Christian culture of Daniel and his grandfather makes Judaism 'the enabling milieu for Christianity' and Jews exemplary 'secularized religious beings'. Daniel's redemptive mission, in relation to degenerate or 'denationalised' Jews, is therefore displaced uneasily onto a late Victorian Britain perceived by Eliot to be in need of spiritual renewal.[56] Whether Eliot's 'epic' narrative is concerned with the fixed semitic particularity of 'the Jews' or an all-inclusive universalism, signified by the proclaimed 'unity of mankind', is an unresolved tension in *Daniel Deronda*. By positioning 'the Jew' at the centre of her hopes for the future renewal of England, Eliot was to construct competing 'national–racial' and 'aesthetic–cultural' versions of her object of desire.

At the beginning of *Daniel Deronda*, Eliot refers ironically to Gwendolen as a 'princess in exile' (71) at Offendene and, pointedly, notes that 'Gwendolen might still have played the queen in exile, if only she had kept her inborn energy of egoistic desire...' (71). Gwendolen's faith in her ability as a gambler at Leubronn, a continuous point of reference throughout the novel, represents not

[56] E. S. Shaffer, '*Kubla Khan' and the Fall of Jerusalem: The Mythological School of Biblical Criticism and Secular Literature, 1770–1880* (London, 1975), pp. 235 and 244 and chapter 6 for the influence of Feuerbach, in particular, on Eliot's Christianization of Daniel Deronda. Eliot was also particularly influenced in this regard by Emanuel Deutsch's writings on 'The Talmud', *Quarterly Review* 123 (October, 1867), 417–64 as can be seen in Baker, *George Eliot and Judaism*, chapter 6. David, *Fictions of Resolution*, p. 160 and chapter 8 has a continually useful account of the subsumption of class into racial interests in *Daniel Deronda*. Beer, *Darwin's Plots*, p. 202 is also worth reading on this subject.

the 'inborn energy of egoistic desire' but, as Neil Roberts puts it, 'the superstitions spun from the undisciplined ignorant ego'.[57] By containing such 'distant varieties of European type: Livonian and Spanish, Graeco-Italian and miscellaneous German, English aristocrat and English plebian' (36), Leubronn proves to be 'a striking admission of human equality' (36), the embodiment of 'denationality' and the false universalism of 'cosmopolitan' materialism. In her degenerate homelessness, Gwendolen – especially after the Stock Exchange failure of Grapnell and Co. – is analogous to the Jewish diaspora embodied in Lapidoth, the Cohen family and the 'Jew dealers' at Leubronn (whom she notes are 'so unscrupulous in taking advantage of Christians unfortunate at play!' (48)). That Daniel redeems Gwendolen's necklace from a Jewish pawnbroker and thereby increases her indebtedness to himself is, as Catherine Gallagher has noted, a succinct summary of the novel as a whole: 'a young man who thinks he has a mission to save wayward women turns out to have a mission to save a nation of usurers.' In his position as a 'redeemer' of both a materialist Jewry and an increasingly 'denationalised' England, Daniel bestrides both 'halves' of *Daniel Deronda* and relates 'everything in the book to everything else there'.[58]

Eliot, significantly, distinguishes in her essay between the English as 'a colonising people ... who have punished others' (172) and 'the Jews' as a powerless people in exile. But these 'races' are also brought together in Eliot's reading by a 'denationalised' assertion of will – whether it be the brutality of Empire or the amorality of international finance – which eschews the guiding light of a sense of national destiny. In an early conversation with Gwendolen, the sadistic Grandcourt inadvertently parodies Deronda's search for salvation in the East by recalling his own Eastern 'season or two' of 'tiger-hunting or pig-sticking': 'Everything here is poor stuff after that' (147). After his sojourn abroad, in a pale reflection of Eastern pig-sticking, Grandcourt can only 'master ... a woman who would have liked to master him' (365) and thereby exercises a 'poor' form of 'imperiousness' (481) in his marriage. Here the 'denationalised' assertion of will is represented in its extreme form by Grandcourt's 'empire of fear' (479) over Gwendolen. Just as Daniel's redemptive

[57] Neil Roberts, *George Eliot: Her Belief and Her Art* (London, 1975), p. 197.
[58] Gallagher, 'George Eliot and *Daniel Deronda*', p. 50 and G. S. Haight (ed.), *The George Eliot Letters*, 7 vols. (New Haven, 1978), VI, p. 290.

relation with Gwendolen has its authentic context in 'the East', Grandcourt's domestic form of 'colonial management' has a wider imperial context.[59] Such parallels are reinforced by the fact that both Grancourt and Deronda are supposed 'nephews' of Sir Hugo Mallinger. In a further Judaization of Imperial Britain, Daniel quickly learns to reject his Uncle's belief in 'the Whigs as the chosen race among politicians' (217). By replacing a Whiggish progressivism with the prophetic politics of the authentic 'chosen race', Daniel once again emphasizes the originating Hebraic beginnings of a politics which is no longer 'an inspired vocation'. Lacking Mordecai's 'prophetic' dimension, contemporary British politicians merely take care of the 'business of the country' (434).

As well as these constructions of 'the Jew' centred around the issues of race and the nation, the early chapters of *Daniel Deronda* also contain a conflicting set of aesthetic–cultural Judaic parallels. Gwendolen's comparison with herself and the actress Rachel juxtaposes Gwendolen's potential artistic vocation with that of the popular French–Jewish actress. Gwendolen's 'destiny', we are told, 'sometimes turned on the question whether she should become an actress like Rachel since she was more beautiful than that thin Jewess' (84).[60] It is Klesmer, significantly, the 'felicitous combination of the German, the Sclave, and the Semite' (77) who, first points out Gwendolen's lack of 'deep, mysterious passion' or 'sense of the universal' in her singing and opens up a 'sudden width of horizon ... round her small musical performance' (79). When introducing Klesmer Eliot asks if, in his music criticism, there was 'ever so unexpected an assertion of superiority? at least before the late Teutonic conquests?' (78). Even in this ironic mode, Eliot is evidently sympathetic to Bismarck's European expansionism in the 1860s and 1870s. This nationalist 'Teutonic' unification of Germany, in bringing together questions of race and the nation, is not unrelated to Mordecai's belief in the semitic unification of Israel. Klesmer's Germanic identification with the recent 'Teutonic conquests', and his critique of Gwendolen's artistic pretensions, offers a powerful alternative narrative to Deronda's redemptive relationship with Gwendolen. The 'inward sob of mortification' (80) and 'new sort of

[59] David, *Fictions of Resolution*, p. 180 for an interesting reading of Gwendolen's marriage in terms of 'colonial management'.

[60] George Henry Lewes, in his *Actors and the Art of Acting* (London, 1875), chapter 3, has a sympathetic account of the actress Rachel to match that of Matthew Arnold's discussed earlier.

pain' (82) that Klesmer's critical remarks cause Gwendolen, as well as references to the 'universal' and 'sudden width of horizon', obviously prefigure and undermine Daniel's salutary impact on Eliot's heroine.[61]

That art, like Deronda's Judaism, is a 'higher vocation' (302) is a parallel that is reinforced by Eliot's epigraph to the chapter where Gwendolen finally learns from Klesmer of her inability to enter the cultural pantheon: 'Among the heirs of Art, as at the division of the promised land, each has to win his portion by hard fighting: the bestowal is after the manner of prophecy, and is a title without possession' (293). The displacement of the biblical 'promised land' and sense of 'prophecy' onto 'Art' once again both pre-empts the Judaic 'higher vocation' and offers an alternative cultural mode of self-transcendence to Daniel's nascent Zionism. Klesmer's attack on the 'lack of idealism in English politics' (283) again upstages Daniel. Especially after his marriage to Catherine Arrowpoint, Klesmer becomes an assimilated 'Wandering Jew' (284) who is pointedly not fixed by his Jewishness but 'felicitously' wanders between 'the German, the Sclave and the Semite' and, clearly, cannot be contained by Mordecai's racially determined construction of 'the nation'.[62] In his aesthetic, supra-nationalist identification with assimilated Jews, such as Rachel and Spinoza, Klesmer embodies the Arnoldian ideal of 'culture' which disrupts fatally Eliot's nationalist construction of 'Jewish' idealism.

Klesmer's artistic cosmopolitanism prefigures an equally powerful narrative which also challenges the centrality of Mordecai's racial determinism in *Daniel Deronda*. Daniel's reunion with his mother, Princess Halm-Eberstein, acts as a dramatic and, yet, indeterminate centre for Eliot's novel by simultaneously 'releas[ing] a completely new set of possibilities' for Daniel as 'a Jew' and, at the same time, radically questioning a fixed, unchanging Jewishness.[63] By rejecting what her father wanted her to be, Daniel's mother challenges the rigid Judaic 'pattern' imposed on her: 'the Jewish woman; this is

---

[61] Roberts, *George Eliot*, chapter 9 makes out a convincing case for this reading of *Daniel Deronda* and Barbara Hardy, Penguin edition of *Daniel Deronda*, p. 887, notes Eliot's political sympathies for Bismarck.

[62] Klesmer, significantly, means 'musician' in Yiddish, the language of the Jewish diaspora (as opposed to the Hebrew of the nascent Jewish State).

[63] Beer, *Darwin's Plots*, p. 224 and Cohen and Heller, *Jewish Presences*, chapter 5, for this argument. To this extent, 'Pulcheria' is wrong to argue in James's 'Conversation' pp. 298–9 that she cannot '*see*' Deronda's mother and that, in Constantius's words, 'all the Jewish part is at bottom cold'.

what you must be; this is what you are wanted for ... her happiness is
to be made as cakes are, by a fixed receipt' (694). Like Klesmer, she
opposes a reductive racial identity by 'living a myriad lives in one'
(689) as a woman, an actress, a famous opera singer and, latterly, a
wife, mother and Jewess. The plurality of Halm-Eberstein's 'lives'
directly opposes Daniel's unproblematic assimilation into his Jewishness and Mirah's straightforward identification as a 'Jewish woman'.
To be sure, Halm-Eberstein's courageous act of will – in 'trading'
Daniel for her singing career – is itself severely qualified by Eliot's use
of a 'shopkeeping' metaphor and by Daniel's physical and philosophical metamorphosis as her father. Not only are Mordecai's beliefs
identical to Halm-Eberstein's father but Daniel is his 'young copy'
(692). But, as well as fulfilling his racial destiny, Daniel, in being
raised as an 'English gentleman' (690), can also be read as an
Arnoldian 'alien' or 'cultured cosmopolitan'.[64] Like the novel as a
whole, Daniel veers between a racially determined nationalism and
a displacement of this idealized nationalism onto textuality or 'art'.
The confusion inherent in Daniel's radically differing futures can be
said to have reached its apotheosis in George Du Maurier's *Trilby*
(1894). Svengali, in this best-selling novel, is both an outstanding
musical genius and a sexually rapacious, racialized 'other' *par
excellence*. In a less extravagant manner, Daniel's epic 'unmapped
country', signified by the contradictory discourses of 'race' and
'culture', indicates both an idealized realm beyond a spiritually
bankrupt England which is, at the same time, reduced to the question
of 'race'.

Because she is deemed to be outside of the dominant 'languages' of
'race' and 'culture' Gwendolen, to complete her story, needs neither
art nor nationalism as modes of transcendence. In her speck-like
aspect at the end of the novel, Gwendolen's escape from patriarchy,
like the nascent Jewish state, has clearly yet to begin. Although she is
finally a strong, independent woman, like Daniel's mother, Gwendolen is nonetheless left without a narrative line to continue her story.
Mordecai's Jewish nationalism is, on the one hand, positioned in the
novel in opposition to a masculine imperialist world based on an
economic and philosophical materialism. It is worth recalling in this
context that the future stretches towards Mordecai like 'the
appealing arms of children' (588). For this reason, Gwendolen's

[64] Beer, *Darwin's Plots*, pp. 224–5 and Gallagher, 'George Eliot and *Daniel Deronda*, p. 57, for
this argument.

specific story as a victim of patriarchy is displaced onto a feminized nationalism. This interchangeability of questions of nationality, race, class and gender in *Daniel Deronda* indicates, above all, that Eliot is uncertain in her novel as to what, exactly, signifies a 'Jewish' idealism.[65] The transcendence of a universalized 'promised land' of liberalism by a Judaized 'promised land' throws into disarray Arnold's assimilationist 'cultural' imperatives as it fatally particularizes them in terms of the 'Jewish race'. Eliot's 'experimental' postrealist novel, therefore, does not pursue the issue of gender in relation to historical change but, instead, foregrounds an ambivalent semitic discourse which was intended to provide an alternative vocabulary of 'the nation', to that of a materialist liberalism, which would help renew a society whose future direction was ever-more fraught with uncertainty.

CONCLUSION

It is not insignificant that the popular second edition of Matthew Arnold's *Culture and Anarchy*, Trollope's *The Way We Live Now* and *The Prime Minister* and George Eliot's *Daniel Deronda* were all published in the mid-1870s which was the period when, most historians would argue, a revitalized 'Jewish Question' entered the British political arena. Much of the semitic discourse at this time had, as we have seen, been in place for nearly half a century. Nonetheless, the urgency and frequency with which Jews after the 1870s were positioned as 'other' to the 'English nation' reflects the extent to which they came to symbolize the fruits of a universalizing State as opposed to the needs of a supposedly indigenous national community. The extreme ambivalence inherent in visions of the future in late Victorian Britain was projected onto Jews who were constructed as both the embodiment of racial particularism as well as that of a modernizing 'culture'. 'The Jew', in other words, came to represent simultaneously both the return to an exclusivist Englishness as well as a future all-inclusive nation-state.

Although Arnold wished to privilege 'culture' over 'race', his use of a racially differentiating vocabulary was to throw his cultural imperatives into disarray. This was apparent not only in Arnold's

---

[65] For the interchangeability of key discourses in *Daniel Deronda* see Gallagher, 'George Eliot and *Daniel Deronda*' and David, *Fictions of Resolution, passim*. F. R. Leavis in his 'George Eliot's Zionist Novel', *Commentary* 30 (1960), 317–25, an important revision of chapter 2 of *The Great Tradition*, usefully sketches Deronda as a 'feminine' figure by developing 'Pulcheria's' remarks that Deronda is 'not a man' (p. 319).

own writing but in the fiction of Trollope and George Eliot who, like Arnold, both constructed a materialistic 'English nation' in need of urgent spiritual renewal. But if acculturating Jews represented a potent transcendence of an empty materialism, their supposed racial difference could also undermine such hopes for the spiritual transformation of English society. Trollope's desire for a return to the 'feudal' values of Old England, where 'alien' outsiders clearly knew their place, delineated precisely the limits of his hierarchical Englishness. These limits, however, were to be threatened severely by his construction of 'the Jew' who was bounded by a superior Englishness but could also be driven by an unstoppable racial particularism. George Eliot, on the other hand, chose to foreground a not dissimilar 'Jewish' racial particularism as an 'ideal force' which could, potentially, revive an increasingly degenerate England. In a telling inversion of Arnold's *Culture and Anarchy*, Eliot's emblematic language of 'race' and 'nation' was drained of much of its impact in her novel by a rival narrative centred around the language of 'art' and 'culture'. Once again, 'the Jew' was impossible to pin down within the realist novel and could embody equally two competing vocabularies. In the next chapter, this contradictory revaluation of an overly universalized 'English nation' is expanded to include the Imperial arena. Here the slipperiness of 'the Jew' could represent both the racial hierarchies necessary to uphold the Empire and, at the same time, an all-encompassing liberalism that was weakening Britain's Imperial commitment to such an extent that it threatened to unleash anarchy upon the world.

CHAPTER 3

Empire and anarchy: John Buchan and Rudyard Kipling

'... God works by races, and one was appointed in due season and after many developments to reveal and expound in this land the spiritual nature of man. The Aryan and the Semite are of the same blood and origin, but when they quitted their central land they were ordained to follow opposite courses. Each division of the great race has developed one portion of the double nature of humanity, till after all their wanderings they met again, and, represented by their two choicest families, the Hellenes and the Hebrews, brought together the treasures of their accumulated wisdom and secured the civilisation of man.'

Benjamin Disraeli, Lothair (London, 1870) volume xi of the
1927 Bradenham edition, p. 397

INTRODUCTION

In contrast to those writers who attempted uneasily to contain a racialized 'Jew' within Arnoldian liberal notions of 'culture', the Imperialist writers in this chapter are quite explicit about privileging 'race' over 'culture' in their constructions of 'the Jew'. Benjamin Disraeli, in particular, rewrote in Imperial terms the binary oppositions utilized by Matthew Arnold in *Culture and Anarchy*. According to Disraeli, 'the Jew' represented 'religion, property and natural aristocracy', the very foundations of Empire. This influential reworking of Arnold was taken up by the later writer-colonialists, John Buchan and Rudyard Kipling. These authors adopted Disraelian racialized notions of 'the Jew' to counter socialist and radical liberal constructions of degenerate 'Jewish financiers' who were said to have caused the Boer War (1899–1902) for their own 'alien' capitalist interests.

The split in Disraeli's semitic discourse between Jews as the embodiment of 'race' and as falsely universalized 'communist'

conspirators was reflected especially in the fiction and politics of
Buchan and Kipling. Both writers were to divide 'the Jew' radically
in their fiction into loyal imperialists, who were conforming to their
racial 'bias', and dangerous subversives who represented an alternative universalism to that of the Empire. Anxieties concerning the
continuing power of the Empire, especially after the Boer War, were
projected onto 'the Jews' and the uncertain position of 'semitic'
racial difference within the colonial sphere. Buchan, in his popular
Imperial 'romances', and Kipling, in some of his most complex (and
most crude) short stories and poems, were both to incorporate a
radically divided semitic discourse into their imaginative literature.
'The Jews', in this sense, will be seen to have a distinct place within
the Empire as they were constructed, like Disraeli, as ideal colonial
'selves' and, at the same time, as feared 'others' who needed to be
differentiated and contained. These extraordinarily manichaean
constructions – which resulted in both the promotion of antisemitic
Jewish conspiracy theories as well as Zionist national aspirations –
will be given a specific political context in Imperial circles in the
inter-war years.

JOHN BUCHAN: 'RULING THE WORLD JUST NOW'

By the 1890s, the racial opposition between a 'civilised' and a
'semitic' foreign policy – that was at the centre of Disraeli's Eastern
Question – was playing itself out in relation to the Boer War and
Britain's unhappy Imperial presence in Southern Africa. The earlier
displacement of the 'immoral' aspects of British Imperialism onto a
racialized construction of Jewishness was, by the turn of the century,
a widely circulated strand of contemporary Liberal and Socialist pro-
Boer opinion. After the abortive Jameson Raid against Kruger's Boer
Republic in 1895, many pro-Boers regarded the inevitable full-scale
conflict as 'a war fostered by Jews for Jewish gain.'[1] Prominent
'Jewish financiers' based in Southern Africa were represented as a
'conspiracy' which, according to H. M. Hyndman's *Justice*, the
journal of the Social Democratic Federation, were planning to create
'an Anglo-Hebraic empire stretching from Egypt to Cape Colony

---

[1] Colin Holmes, *Anti-Semitism in British Society*, 1876–1939 (London, 1979), p. 70 and chapter 5.

and from Beira to Sierra Leone'. In a characteristic series of articles in April 1896 on 'Imperialist Judaism in Africa' Hyndman argued that:

It is high time that those who do not think that Beit, Barnato, Oppenheim, Rothschild and Co. ought to control the destinies of Englishmen at home, and of their Empire abroad, should come together and speak their mind.[2]

As the crisis between the British Empire and the Boer Republic came to a head in the late 1890s any subsequent warfare could, therefore, be blamed by Hyndman on a 'Jew-jingo gang' and a 'Jew press' which had brain-washed the public into supporting a 'piratical imperialism in the Transvaal and elsewhere.' Such sentiments, in common usage in this period, were echoed by the novelist Jerome K. Jerome who, in a letter to the MP Herbert Samuel, asserted that: ' ... those who prefer the cause of England, her fair name and her prosperity, to the success of the gold mines on the Rand, are denounced by the German Jew Press as unpatriotic!' J. A. Hobson, in his influential book on the South African War published in 1900, was to summarize this aspect of pro-Boer antisemitism by referring to the Boer War as a 'Jew–Imperialist design' because 'Jews are par excellence the international financiers'. As with the debate surrounding Disraeli's Eastern Question two decades before, a racialized view of 'the Jew' was utilized by pro-Boer campaigners to represent those (uncivilized) particularist forces that were perceived to be opposed to a progressive, universalist liberalism or socialism.[3]

John Buchan was a key member of Milner's 'kindergarten' in Southern Africa from 1901 to 1903, who helped to 'resettle' the land after the Boer War. Not surprisingly, he regarded such 'Jewish financiers' as Alfred Beit – who was closely associated with Cecil Rhodes and De Beers mining company – in radically differing terms from his liberal and socialist political opponents. As early as his contemporary account of his experiences in South Africa, *The Africa*

---

[2] Holmes, *Anti-Semitism in British Society*, p. 69 cites Hyndman. For further examples of this kind of conspiratorial politics see Claire Hirchfield, 'The British Left and the "Jewish Conspiracy": A Case Study of Modern Antisemitism', *Jewish Social Studies* (Spring, 1981), 95–112.

[3] Holmes, *Anti-Semitism in British Society*, p. 67, quotes Hobson and Hirchfield, 'The British Left and the "Jewish Conspiracy"', p. 99 cites Hyndman's *Justice*. For J. K. Jerome's letter to Herbert Samuel see S. Koss (ed.), *The Pro-Boers* (London, 1973) p. 149. The next chapter will discuss in more detail 'socialist' constructions of 'the Jew'.

Colony: Studies in the Reconstruction (1903), Buchan was to question whether the city of Johannesburg, known in England as 'Judasburg' or 'the New Jerusalem', was full of 'Semitic adventurers'. He concluded unequivocally that ' the first piece of cant to clear the mind of' is that 'Johannesburg is made up wholly of adventurers and Whitechapel Jews'. According to his biographer, Buchan argued elsewhere that 'Jewish financiers' in South Africa are: 'young men with several millions each, and their acumen and good sense is remarkable. Very different from the bloated Jew financier of the pro-Boer and Bellocian imagination.' As Rhodes and Beit helped to finance the abortive Jameson Raid at a cost of £400,000, the centrality of these financiers in colonizing Africa would have been clear to Buchan and was certainly articulated by many others at the time. J. B. Robinson, for instance, an English gold magnate who worked with Beit in South Africa, believed that individuals such as himself were 'laying the political foundations of the continent which will be the keystone of the arch of Empire ... '[4]

His biographers have claimed that Buchan can be distinguished from the pro-Boer 'antisemitism' of his political opponents by his relative 'sympathy' for the South African 'Jewish financiers'. But it would be a mistake to ignore the equally influential semitic discourse utilized in Buchan's colonial politics and fiction just because it did not conform to liberal or socialist constructions of 'the Jew'. Hugh Cunningham's reductive characterization of late Victorian 'conservative' discourses of patriotism as crudely 'antisemitic' is similarly unable to deal with such distinctions. Disraeli, in particular, was one of Buchan's 'political heroes' about whom he had once considered writing a biography. He even considered that he was doing the 'work of Disraeli' in relation to the Empire.[5] It is not surprising, therefore,

---

[4] 'The South Africa Settlement', *Nineteenth Century* (September, 1882) cited in Jamie Camplin, *The Rise of the Plutocrats* (London, 1978) p. 43 and chapter 3 and Janet Smith, *John Buchan: A Biography* (London, 1965) p. 125. See also John Buchan, *The Africa Colony: Studies in the Reconstruction* (London, 1903) pp. 313–14 and Buchan's autobiography, *Memory-Hold-The-Door* (London, 1940) p. 28. References to Buchan's fiction will be to first editions with the exception of *The Thirty-Nine Steps* (London, 1980 edition) and *Greenmantle*, *The Three Hostages*, *Prester John*, and *Mr Standfast*, which are all Penguin editions (London, 1981) and will be quoted in the body of the text.

[5] Smith, *John Buchan: A Biography*, pp. 156–7 and p. 187. See also Hugh Cunningham, 'The Language of Patriotism, 1750–1914' in Raphael Samuel (ed.), *Patriotism: The Making and Unmaking of British National Identity*, 3 vols. (London, 1989), I, pp. 77–8 and chapter 7. Recent accounts of Buchan have reacted strongly against the 'charge' that he is 'antisemitic'. David Daniell, in particular, in his *The Interpreter's House: A Critical Assessment of John Buchan*

that Buchan was to adopt a Disraelian vocabulary and represent
Jews in terms that were consistent with his vision of an expanding
Imperial world order. Disraeli left an influential legacy of Jewish
representations which were also an integral part of his racialized
Imperial philosophy. These representations were identified by
Disraeli as his 'Semitic principle' which was articulated especially in
an extraordinary *non sequitur* in his *Lord George Bentinck: A Political
Biography* (1851). Here Disraeli, *in medias res*, devoted a chapter of his
biography to a justification of his belief in Judaism as the originator
of aristocratic principles:

Let us observe what should be the influence of the Jews, and then ascertain
how it is exercised. ... The Jews represent the Semitic principle; all that is
spiritual in our nature. They are the trustees of tradition, and the
conservators of the religious element. They are a living and the most striking
evidence of the falsity of that pernicious doctrine of modern times, the
natural equality of man.[6]

Whereas Arnold attempted to privilege 'culture' over 'race' and
pinned his hopes on a progressive universalist State, Disraeli, not
unlike George Eliot, racialized 'the Jew' to demonstrate the 'falsity'
of liberalism and the consequent power of a superior spiritual Judeo-
Christian 'tradition'. This Disraelian legacy was utilized explicitly
by Buchan in his *A Lodge in the Wilderness* (1906), a semi-fictional
'symposium' on South Africa. Alfred Beit is fictionalized in this book
as 'Mr Loewenstein' who is described in the following terms by the
American Mrs Yorke:

(London, 1975) attempts to 'get Buchan right again' and to 'steer the necessary debate
about him off the territory of *canards* about Jew-hater and so on'. In an unfortunate image,
he describes as 'absurd' those who go 'sniffing around for the two mild references to Jews,
or non-existent racist sentiments' and argues erroneously that there is 'no general reference
to "a Jew"' in the 'whole Buchan *corpus*', p. xiii, p. 150 and pp. 205–7. Buoyed up by
Daniell's study, Buchan's son, Alistair Buchan, in his *John Buchan: A Memoir* (London, 1982)
speaks of Buchan's 'savage accusers' with regard to his 'antisemitism' (p. 251). For less
special pleading see Janet Smith's *John Buchan and His World* (London, 1979) pp. 80–1 and
Gertrude Himmelfarb, *Victorian Minds* (London, 1968), chapter 9.

6 *Lord George Bentinck: A Political Biography* (London, 1851) p. 323 and chapter 24 *passim*.
Further references to the 1927 Bradenham edition will be included in the body of the text.
Important recent accounts of Disraeli's semitic racial discourse include Daniel Bivona,
Desire and Contradiction: Imperial Visions and Domestic Debates in Victorian Literature (Manchester,
1990), chapter 1 and Patrick Brantlinger, *Rule of Darkness: British Literature and Imperialism
1830–1914* (Ithaca, 1988) pp. 146–71. See also the historical accounts by Todd Endelman,
'Disraeli's Jewishness Reconsidered', *Modern Judaism* 5 (1985), 109–21 and, from a radical
right perspective, John Vincent, *Disraeli* (Oxford, 1990) chapters 3 and 4.

'I like his face,' said Mrs Yorke thoughtfully; 'there is a fire somewhere behind his eyes. But then I differ from most of my countrymen in liking Jews. You can do something with them – stir them up to follow some mad ideal, and they are never vulgar at heart. If we must have magnates, I would rather Jews had the money. It doesn't degrade them and they have the infallible good taste of the East at the back of their heads. No Northerner should be rich, unless he happens to be also a genius.' (21)

Such is the Disraelian vision of mysterious Jewish orientals 'stirred up' to 'follow some mad ideal' which was especially influential in colonial circles at the turn of the century. These 'Easterners' would, at one and the same time, benefit the Empire while remaining unmistakably opposed to the 'Northern' Aryan races. As well as adopting the liberal construction of Judaism as a private matter of conscience, a number of British Jews were to internalize the 'conservative' discourse that Disraeli had promoted. In relation to the Empire, as Robert Huttenback has shown, it was not uncommon for British Jews to internalize 'Anglo-Saxon notions of racial singularity' and thus to 'think of themselves as a distinct race and to identify 'choseness' in the messianic sense with racial superiority'. From a eugenic point of view, Jews could also constuct themselves as a model racial group: 'a closely knit community, which had identified religion with a sense of racial destiny'.[7]

Ford Madox Ford, in a variety of his literary and journalistic works, was to foreground this double-edged representation of semitic 'racial superiority' from a more general conservative and Imperial perspective. In his *The Spirit of the People: An Analysis of the English Mind* (1907), for instance, he recounted the time when he stood on the London Docks and observed the 'many Jews from Odessa' arriving amongst other immigrants. Ford's conclusion that 'it is not impossible that one of the children of one of these adventurers may be, like Disraeli, the man who will help England to muddle through', was similarly predicated on Disraeli's 'Semitic principle'. He maintains, in the same book, that Disraeli was 'the most appealing of all England's real rulers during the nineteenth century' and, yet,

---

[7] G. R. Searle, *Eugenics and Politics in Britain 1900–1914* (Leiden, 1976) pp. 40–2 and Robert Huttenback, 'The Patrician Jew and the British Ethos in the Nineteenth and Early Twentieth Centuries', *Jewish Social Studies* 40 (Winter 1978), 61 and 49–62. See also my 'The Other Self: Anglo-Jewish Fiction and the Representation of Jews in England, 1875–1905' in David Cesarani (ed.), *The Making of Modern Anglo-Jewry* (Oxford, 1990) pp. 97–111.

Ford was also to single out Jewish 'Rand millionaires' as changing the 'whole tone of English society' after the Boer War:

It was undoubtedly the Rand millionaire who began to set the pace of social life so immensely fast. And the South African war meant the final installation of Mayfair which is the centre of English ... social life. The Rand millionaire was almost invariably a Jew; and whatever may be said for or against the Jew as a gainer of money, there is no doubt that having got it he spends it with an extraordinary lavishness, so that the whole tone of English society really changed about this time.[8]

This sense of evolutionary pessimism with regard to 'the Jew' was articulated in Ford's novel *Mr Fleight* (1913) where the dark side of the 'Semitic principle' is made apparent. In this novel, the aristocratic Mr Blood justifies, in the following terms, his cynical political and financial manipulation of the Scottish-Jewish Mr Fleight:

The appearance of the Jew in our society means that the Jew is an unrivalled soldier of fortune. He isn't part of our country; he hasn't got our morality, but he's extraordinarily able as a ruler. So our side [the Tories] takes him up and uses him. It doesn't matter to him which side he's on, because he can't begin to understand our problems or our ethics or our morality or our way of looking at things.[9]

This ambivalence – between the Jew as an 'extraordinarily able ruler' who is nonetheless not a part of 'our country' – is especially present in a colonial setting. For those that took Disraeli at his word and racialized history, 'other' races are both 'known' and fixed in terms of their place in an Imperial world order and, at the same time, are constructed as forces that are ultimately uncontrollable and beyond comprehension. Such is the radically divided Imperial construction of 'the Jew'. A colonial discourse could thus both locate a minority of Jews within the Imperial ruling 'racial aristocracy', as Buchan put it, as well as representing them as fundamentally 'other' to the Anglo-Saxon 'race'. In this fissured discursive context, John

---

[8] Ford Madox Ford, *Ancient Lights and Certain New Reflections* (London, 1911) pp. 235–6 and *The Spirit of the People: An Analysis of the English Mind* (London, 1907) pp. 32, 45 and 84. See also H. R. Huntley, *The Alien Protagonist of Ford Madox Ford* (Michigan, 1970) p. 28 for a useful discussion of these texts.

[9] Ford Madox Ford, *Mr Fleight* (London, 1913) p. 213 and Huntley, *The Alien Protagonist*, chapter 5.

Buchan in 1910 wrote his seminal story, 'The Grove of Ashtaroth',
collected in *The Moon Endureth* (1912).[10]

Lawson, the central figure in 'The Grove of Ashtaroth', is
described as a 'born colonial at heart' who plays polo and hunts a
little in season but does not 'propose to become the conventional
English gentleman' (100). Buchan tells the tale of Lawson's
possession by the goddess Ashtaroth when he builds a house in a
desolate grove in Southern Africa. According to the story's bluff
narrator, Lawson is strangely attracted to the 'Grove of Ashtaroth'
largely because of his unusual racial 'pedigree': 'his eyes … marked
him out from the ordinary blonde type of our countrymen. They
were large and brown and mysterious, and the light of another race
was in their odd depths' (100). It turns out that Lawson had a
'grandfather who sold antiques in a back street at Brighton' who
'still frequented the synagogue' and a mother who was 'a blonde
Saxon from the Midlands' (100–1). As Lawson continues to be
inexplicably captivated by the 'grove', it becomes clear to Buchan's
story-teller that Lawson's mixed 'pedigree' had resulted in an inner
racial conflict: 'the two races were very clear in him – the one
desiring gorgeousness, the other athirst for the soothing spaces of the
North … the Saxon mother from the Midlands had done little to
dilute the strange wine of the East' (102–3).

With a mysterious 'spell in the air' and 'an odd dead silence',
Lawson becomes increasingly enraptured with the land on which he
wants to make his new 'home' and insists that the Imperial company
which owns the site must sell it to him. After living for three years in
his new house, however, Lawson is utterly transformed. Instead of
the polo-playing 'fine make of a man' (100), who is introduced at the
beginning of the story, Lawson is a 'heavy, flaccid being who shuffled
in his gait' and, worse still, his 'pallid face' made him look 'curiously
semitic' (108). In this 'semitic' condition, Lawson was 'extraordinary successful in his [financial] speculations' (108), confirming
his status as a 'new millionaire' (100). The shocked narrator
concludes, however, that there is clearly something in the grove
which had 'turned a gentleman into a brute' (109):

Ashtaroth was the old goddess of the East. Was it not possible that in all
Semitic blood there remained, transmitted through the dim generations,

---

[10] *A Lodge in the Wilderness* (London, 1906) p. 29 defines imperialism ambivalently as the
'administration of vast tracks inhabited by lower races' by a 'racial aristocracy' in 'relation
to other subject peoples' and a 'democracy in relation to each other'.

some craving for her spell? I thought of the grandfather in the back street at Brighton and of those burning eyes upstairs. (116)

In this regressive racial state, Lawson indulges in grotesque pagan rites akin to 'black magic': 'the dance grew swifter and fierce. I saw the blood dripping from Lawson's body, and his face ghastly white above his scarred breast' (119). This is clearly a reference to the figure of Laputa in *Prester John* (1910), written in the same year as 'The Grove of Ashtaroth', who similarly prays to the 'God of Israel' with his heart 'black with the lusts of paganism' in a bid to incite the local population to destroy the Empire. Laputa, nonetheless, is eventually dismissed as a 'great savage with a knife' in this novel and is perceived to be fatally limited as a 'kaffir'. Lawson, on the other hand, is a 'born colonial at heart' who, because of his drop of 'semitic blood', has access to an indigenous Africa which threatened the very heart of Empire. Roy Turnbaugh has rightly argued that in Buchan's *fin de siècle* fiction, standards that proved reliable for high Victorian Imperial writers such as G. A. Henty are shown to be 'illusory': 'indeed many of Buchan's villains are [so] outstandingly English in appearance ... that the hero can detect no flaw in their facade'.[11] This frightening lack of differentiation is signalled at the end of this story when the Anglo-Saxon narrator who eventually 'saves [Lawson's] soul' (126) also, 'for one brief second', peers into the 'new world' which Lawson had succumbed too:

A strange passion surged up in my heart. I seemed to see the earth peopled with forms not human, scarcely divine, but more desirable than man or god. ... I do not know how the Semites found Ashtaroth's ritual; to them it may well have been more rapt and passionate than it seemed to me. For I saw in it only the sweet simplicity of Nature ... (119)

The ambiguous attraction of these forces – 'far older than creeds or Christendom' – to the 'prosaic, modern Christian gentleman, a half believer in casual faiths' (116) who narrates Lawson's story, points to an uncertainty at the centre of Buchan's fiction. Buchan's persona, Edward Leithen, for instance, begins *The Dancing Floor* (1926) by describing himself as someone who 'goes about expecting things,

---

11 This reading of *Prester John* (London, 1910) can be found in Roy Turnbaugh, 'Images of Empire: George Alfred Henty and John Buchan', *Journal of Popular Culture* 9 (Winter 1975), 737–8 and 734–41. For a recent disappointing account of Buchan's Hannay novels as 'texts about Buchan' see Christopher Shaw, 'The Pleasures of Genre: John Buchan and Richard Hannay' in Christopher Shaw and Malcolm Chase (eds.), *The Imagined Past: History and Nostalgia* (Manchester, 1989) p. 103 and chapter 7.

waiting like an old pagan for the descent of the goddess'. Only once did he catch the 'authentic shimmer of her wings' which turns out to be the story of *The Dancing Floor*. The 'authentic shimmer' of the pagan goddess is able to transport Leithen into another world echoing the experience of Lawson in 'The Grove of Ashtaroth'.

Leithen, like Buchan, is a self-confessed 'romantic' and it is Buchan's non-naturalistic 'romantic' construction of literature – as outlined in his 'The Novel and the Fairy Tale' (1931) – that echoes Disraeli's *Lothair* (1870) by containing an ultimate 'unity' beyond the differentiating 'reality' of race and Empire. In 'The Novel and the Fairy Tale', Buchan points to the mythic 'folk tale' as being at the heart of the novel because, in his view, it is part of the 'common stock of humanity' which may 'go back to the ancestry of our race' but belongs to 'no one country or age'. The attractiveness of this mythic unity – in the guise of the goddess Ashtaroth – similarly undercuts Buchan's differentiating racial discourse in 'The Grove of Ashtaroth'.[12] It is the inability of Buchan to 'know' what ultimately lies behind the racial facade of even the most loyal subject of the colonies that points to a considerable unease with the 'civilizing' mission of the Empire. The uncontainable power of the semitic race – going back at least to pagan times in 'The Grove of Ashtaroth' – is an especially acute example of a divided discourse which both complements the Imperial order and, at the same time, points to an ultimate anarchy beyond 'country or age' which can devastatingly undermine it.

By the time of *The Powerhouse* (1916), Buchan's villains were able to claim convincingly that the 'tenure' of the 'civilisation [which] we boast about' is essentially 'precarious': 'you think that a wall as solid as the earth separates civilisation from barbarism. I tell you that the division is a thread, a pane of glass. A touch here, a push there, and you bring back the reign of Saturn' (211). It has been generally assumed that it was Buchan's Calvinism that made him particularly aware of the 'unquiet depths that lay beneath the human surface' and that this religious awareness culminated in many of his novels in

---

[12] John Buchan, 'The Novel and the Fairy Tale', *English Association Pamphlet*, No. 79 (1931), 16. For a description of Leithen as Buchan's persona see Richard Usbourne, *Clubland Heroes* (London, 1953) p. 139, a reading which Daniell, *The Interpreter's House*, p. 197, agrees with. See also Bivona, *Desire and Contradiction*, pp. 20–2, for similar 'moments' of pre-historic 'unity' in Disraeli's fiction. The quote from *Lothair* that opens this chapter, for instance, emphasizes that 'the Aryan and the Semite are of the same blood and origin' before God banished them from their Edenic 'central land'.

a 'gothic, almost apocalyptic vision of the dark, destructive forces contained in human beings and society'. But, in fact, these supposedly 'Calvinistic' themes were commonplaces in popular fiction after the 1880s which Brantlinger has usefully dubbed 'Imperial Gothic'. A principal characteristic of 'Imperial Gothic' is the theme of an individual's decline brought about when the colonizer 'goes native' or is possessed by a racial 'other'. This kind of regression applies to the Imperial nation as a whole in the form of popular invasion scare stories or degeneration theories, where the precariousness of 'civilization' is foregrounded or where English society is imagined to be overwhelmed by 'barbaric' forces. The uncertainty about the extent and longevity of Imperial power – which was reinforced by the Boer War but which was long since a cause for apprehension – meant that theories of racial superiority and perceived alternative 'Imperial' powers were frequently invoked in this period whether they be 'Yellow Peril' scare stories or fears of invasion by alien races or, even, Dracula's empire of the 'undead'. 'The Grove of Ashtaroth' is, in these terms, a piece of 'Imperial Gothic'.[13]

The unease caused by the construction of Empire in relation to a dark double was at the heart of Buchan's popular Imperial novels. In the manichaean world of 'Imperial Gothic', a semitic discourse was to construct Jews ambivalently in relation to both a triumphalist and a degenerate view of Empire. While Jews were an important example of a successfully 'civilized' racial group, they were constructed like their colonial counterparts as 'mimic-men', whom Homi Bhabha has called: 'a flawed colonial mimesis, in which to be Anglicized, is *emphatically* not to be English'. If the Empire was increasingly understood as being unable to contain or 'civilize' its racial 'others', then one of the signs of this 'crisis of empire' was the radical ambivalence of Jewish racial representations who were an early domestic 'colony' that were meant to have been long since 'Anglicized'.[14] In the notorious first chapter of his best-selling *The*

---

[13] For the significance of Buchan's Calvinism see especially Himmelfarb, *Victorian Minds* pp. 268–72 and for the general impact of these 'Calvinistic' themes in Edwardian Britain see Brantlinger, *Rule of Darkness*, p. 249 and chapter 8 for his useful account of 'Imperial Gothic'.

[14] Homi Bhabha, 'Of Mimicry and Man: The Ambivalence of Colonial Discourse', *October* 28 (1984), 128 and 125–33. The phrase 'crisis of empire' is taken from Alan Sandisan, *The Wheel of Empire: A Study of the Imperial Idea in Some Late Nineteenth and Early Twentieth-Century Fiction* but, unlike Sandisan, I do not reduce this term to a writer's apolitical 'personal crisis' (p. 149 and p. 200). For a criticism of Sandisan's approach along these lines see Benita Parry, *Conrad and Imperialism* (London, 1983) p. 134.

Thirty-Nine Steps (1915), for instance, Buchan was to introduce a dark all-embracing conspiracy as an inversion of the Church of Empire. Retold to Richard Hannay by a very frightened American spy called Scudder, the reader soon learns that this particular 'conspiracy' is to 'get Russia and Germany at loggerheads':

> Away behind all the Governments and the armies there was a big subterranean movement going on, engineered by very dangerous people... sort of educated anarchists that make revolutions, but besides them there were financiers who were playing for money... The capitalists would rake in the shekels, and make fortunes by buying up wreckage. Capital... had no conscience and no fatherland. Besides, the Jew was behind it and the Jew hated Russia worse than hell... For three hundred years they have been persecuted and this is the return match for the pogroms. The Jew is everywhere, but you have to go far down the backstairs to find him. Take any big Teutonic business concern... if you're on the biggest kind of job and are bound to get to the real boss, ten to one you are brought up against a little white-faced Jew in a bathchair with an eye like a rattlesnake. Yes sir, he is the man who is ruling the world just now... (11–12)

It is, most importantly, the universalism of 'Capital' which has 'no conscience and no fatherland' which produces the dark side of Buchan's semitic representations. When Jews, with the 'infallible good taste of the East at the back of their heads', can 'do something' for the Empire then they are clearly fulfilling their 'ideal' colonial role by, in Buchan's words, forgetting 'their bank accounts'.[15] By entrusting Jews with the universalism of 'Capital' – 'if we must have magnates, I would rather Jews had the money' – then it is always possible that they will act in their own racial interests because of 'three hundred years of persecution'. When Hannay notes with some scepticism that Scudder's 'Jew-anarchists seemed to have got left behind a little', Scudder replies that these 'Jew-anarchists' have now 'struck a bigger thing than money, a thing that couldn't be bought, the old elemental fighting instincts of man' (12). This pre-modern racial 'instinct' underpins the degenerate modernity of the Jewish-conspiracy. Lawson, it is worth recalling, was also 'white-faced' and had 'burning eyes' as well as being an extraordinarily successful financier when he, too, threatened the 'arch of Empire'. While it is undoubtedly correct to point out that Scudder's Jewish-conspiracy theory is largely disproved as the rest of *The Thirty-Nine Steps* unfolds, nonetheless, as Gina Mitchell has argued, 'its impact remains – if

---

[15] Buchan, *Memory-Hold-The-Door*, p. 113.

only because it sustains the reader until it is replaced by another and much less dramatic explanation halfway through the book.' The 'impact' of Scudder's conspiracy, moreover, should be seen in the context of a wide range of popular fiction from the 1890s onwards which were similarly constructed around *fin de globe* visions of an animalistic world controlled by anarchic or materialist Jew-devils.[16]

The Jewish-conspiracy theories, which were incorporated into many apocalyptic Edwardian pot-boilers, were a key feature historically of an Imperial semitic discourse. Shortly after introducing the 'Semitic principle' in his Bentinck biography, Disraeli referred to the 1848 revolutionary uprisings in Continental Europe as the 'destruction of the Semitic principle' and an 'insurrection... against tradition and aristocracy, against religion and property':

[The] extirpation of the Jewish religion, whether in the mosaic or the christian form, the natural equality of man and the abrogation of property, are proclaimed by the secret societies who form provisional governments, and men of Jewish race are found at the head of every one of them. The people of God co-operate with atheists; the most skilful accumulators of property ally themselves with communists; the peculiar and chosen race touch the hand of all the scum and low castes of Europe! And all this because they wish to destroy that ungrateful Christendom which owes to them even its name, and whose tyranny they can no longer endure. (324)

By maintaining their racial difference, 'the Jews' could represent an Imperial world built on the foundations of 'religion, property, and natural aristocracy'. But those Jews who universalized themselves as 'communists' and denied the 'Semitic principle' also represented the conspiratorial forces of 'anarchy'. Whereas Arnold believed that Jews could contribute to a universal culture by transcending their racial particularity, Disraeli, on the contrary, popularized a vocabulary that showed that it was precisely a racialized semitism that signified the fundamentals of 'civilization' and Empire. As with Disraeli's inversion of Arnold, Buchan used a racial discourse which was thrown into disarray when 'the Jew' was represented, confusingly, as both an illustration of the fixity of 'race' as well as of an 'anarchic' universality.

---

[16] Gina Mitchell, 'John Buchan's Popular Fiction: A Hierarchy of Race', *Patterns of Prejudice* 7 (Number 6, 1973) 26 and 24–30. Representations of the 'Jew-devil' appeared in a wide range of popular fiction at this time. Some of the more significant exponents of this theme include William le Queux, T. Kingston Clarke, Marie Corelli, Guy Thorne and Frank Harris.

There is, in this discursive context, ample evidence in Buchan's fiction which reinforces Scudder's apocalyptic conspiratorial outlook. As early as *The Half-Hearted* (1900) we learn, without qualification, that Britain had been 'corrupted' by a 'gang of Jew speculators and vulgarians' (231). Shortly after this revelation, the narrator refers to the backstreets of Bardur where the 'foot of the Kashmir policeman rarely penetrates' and where there are housed 'certain Jewish gentlemen, members of the great family who have conquered the world' who are 'engaged in the pursuit of their unlawful calling' (233). This conspiratorial vocabulary is, once again, prefigured by Disraeli who, as late as *Endymion* (1880), notes that 'Semites exercise a vast influence over affairs by their smallest though most peculiar family, the Jews. There is no race gifted with so much tenacity, and such skill in organisation'.[17]

These double-edged constructions are repeated throughout Buchan's fiction. A figure such as Mr Julius Victor in *The Three Hostages* (1924) is, significantly, 'one of the richest men in the world ... who had done a lot of Britain's financial business in the War' (17) and whose word was 'weightier than that of many Prime Ministers' (18). Victor, who is described by the antisemitic Blenkiron as 'the whitest Jew since the Apostle Paul', is undoubtedly a victim of an anarchist conspiracy in *The Three Hostages* because of his search for 'peace in the world' (18). But, as the conspiracy against the ambiguously named Julius Victor includes a 'hideous untameable breed' of 'young Bolshevik Jews' (23) and a suspiciously recurring 'North London Jew with a dyed beard' (12), there is clearly represented in Buchan's text a corrupt racial potential even within the apostolic but all-powerful Victor. The 'dyed beard', we remember from Trollope's Breghart, is a poor disguise of one's innate 'Jewishness'. In *Greenmantle* (1916), written during the First World War, Hannay articulates the specific threat posed by Buchan's radically divided 'Jews':

That is the weakness of the German. He has no gift for laying himself alongside different types of men. He is such a hard-shell being that he cannot put out feelers to his kind. ... In Germany only the Jew can get outside himself, and that is why, if you look into the matter, you will find the Jew is at the back of most German enterprises. (72)

[17] Disraeli, *Endymion* (1880), 1927 Bradenham edition, p. 246. Vincent, *Disraeli*, rightly emphasizes in general the conspiratorial nature of Disraeli's semitic discourse which prefigured Buchan.

It is precisely the Jewish racial ability to 'get outside himself' that enabled individual Jews to work 'alongside different types of men' for the good of the 'universal Empire'. This confused discourse, however, meant that it was also possible for 'the Jew' to remain a particularist force 'at the back of most German enterprises'. Thus, in *Huntingtower* (1922), 'the Jews' are said by Saskia, the novel's heroine, to be 'behind' the 'respectable bourgeois' (102) who unleashes the dark conspiracy against her. In chapters 6 and 7 of *Mr Standfast* (1919), the 'Portuguese Jew' in the novel is also a dangerous German spy who speaks perfect German as well as Gaelic. The 'Bolshevik Jew', the 'Portuguese Jew' and the German-Jewish spy are all prominent figures in Edwardian popular fiction which were especially popularized during the First World War. In Buchan's oeuvre these representations of degeneracy are often juxtaposed, as in *The Three Hostages*, with more 'sympathetic' colonial representations of 'the Jew' which Buchan, as a 'Zionist', continued to promote throughout the 1920s and 1930s.

To be sure, Buchan's avowed Zionism resulted in him becoming the Chairman of the Parliamentary Palestine Committee in 1932 and a friend of Chaim Weizmann, the President of the World Zionist Organisation. It is, Buchan believed, because of 'the Jews' that 'Palestine is today by far the cheapest of our Imperial commitments'. This familiar represention of 'Jewish' materialism, harnessed to the 'ideals' of Empire, was to be the subject of his explicitly 'Zionist' novel, *A Prince of the Captivity* (1933).[18] Adam Melford, the central figure in this novel, is recruited into the British Secret Service by a Mr Macandrew who 'was clearly a Jew, a small man with a nervous mouth and eyes that preferred to look downward' (48). The symmetry between Macandrew's 'ardent Zionism' and Melford's avowed defence of the Empire is foregrounded in Buchan's narrative with both individuals deemed to be 'working for the peace and felicity of Jerusalem' (59). Macandrew's 'Zionism' is a major force for the restoration of a British Imperial order after the anarchy of the First World War and, in providing the novel with a dramatic

---

[18] John Buchan, 'Ourselves and the Jews', *Graphic* (5 April, 1930) 12. I will be referring to the contemporary edition of *A Prince of the Captivity* (London: Thomas Nelson and Sons, 1933) in the body of the text. Smith, *John Buchan: A Biography*, pp. 316–17, Daniell, *The Interpreter's House*, p. xii and p. 207 and Alistair Buchan, *John Buchan*, p. 251 all argue erroneously that Buchan's 'friendship' with individual Zionists meant that he could not be an 'antisemite'. For examples of Buchan's derogatory references to Jews in his 'letters and talk' see Smith, *John Buchan: A Biography*, pp. 155–6.

opening, it is the obverse of Scudder's 'Jewish world conspiracy' in
The Thirty-Nine Steps:

Adam often wondered what was in [Macandrew's] eyes. It appeared that
his real name was Meyer, and that he was a Belgian Jew, who had long
foreseen the war and had made many preparations. Adam discovered one
day the motive for his devotion to the British cause. The man was an ardent
Zionist, and the mainspring of his life was his dream of a reconstituted Israel.
He believed that this could not come about except as a consequence of a
great war, which should break down the traditional frontiers of Europe, and
that Britain was the agent destined by God to lead his people out of the
wilderness ... It was the only [subject] which made him raise his eyes and
look Adam in the face, and then Adam read in them the purpose which
makes saints and martyrs. (59)

Rather like the commonplace portrayal of British colonialists as
latter-day biblical prophets, Macandrew believed that Britain was
'destined by God to lead his [Jewish] people out of the wilderness'.
But this perception of 'Zionism' as a transcendent sacred order –
which was an integral part of 'the British cause' – is fatally disrupted
by Macandrew's assistant, Theophilus Scrope. Scrope 'had spent
much of his life in the East' and his sage-like advice to Adam is
'directed to one point': 'the everlasting temperamental differences
between East and West' (55–6). Buchan's text therefore both brings
together 'East and West' in terms of a sanctified 'Zionism' which is
then undermined by Scrope's emphasis on the irrevocable 'temperamental differences' between Europeans and their 'others'.

   The awkward Jewish money-lenders who are introduced at the
beginning of the novel – 'soft-spoken people with Scots names and
curved noses [who] would take no denial' (23) – are, after Scrope's
intervention, never quite displaced by the venerated Macandrew-
Meyer. Placing Macandrew's unifying 'Zionism' alongside Scrope's
fundamental differentiations between 'East and West' is reminiscent
of George Eliot's *Daniel Deronda* (1876) which Buchan admired.
Eliot's novel also juxtaposed an other-worldly Jewish nationalism
with, in Mrs Meyrick's words, 'Jews who *will not* let you out of their
shops'. Such crude manichaeanism resulted in Adam Melford being
'called by the Almighty' (103) to defeat a 'cosmopolitan' and
'devilish' conspiracy – known as the 'Iron Hand Movement' –
which was led by 'violent German nationalists' (331–2) and intended
to undermine the British Empire. The world of *A Prince of the Captivity*
is thus poised on a knife-edge as Europe's financiers, especially

Warren Creevey, waver between the British Empire and the Iron Hand Movement.

Creevey's fateful choice between empire and anarchy is signified, in part, by David Marrish, 'a small dark man' who was 'born in the Transvaal with a touch of Jew in him' (199–200). Like Lawson in 'The Grove of Ashtaroth', Marrish had a 'dead-white face and hot eyes' (202) and was possessed by a 'small crazy devil' (210) which needed to be exorcized by Adam. Once 'saved' from 'disaster' by Adam – who uses an old 'trick' from an African 'witch-doctor' (209) – Marrish is full of 'doglike worshipping affection' (221) for his Anglo-Saxon master. Unsurprisingly, Marrish turns out to be a willing servant of the Empire even though he had once tried to undermine it as a revolutionary socialist. In this increasingly manichaean world of Empire, the 'semite' is always fatally divided and his intentions, of necessity, must be anxiously made explicit. After *Daniel Deronda*, there were a series of popular novels which crudely represented 'Jewish financiers' as being harnessed to a Hebraic Palestine in a bid to create a timeless racial order where Jewish power can be utilized for the good of the Empire.[19] In this context, the Rothschilds are evoked in Disraelian fashion in Buchan's novel as an historical precedent who, in an important contrast with the wavering Creevey, 'made their great fortunes by helping a bankrupt Europe through the Napoleonic wars' (373).

Such was the uncertainty at the heart of Buchan's fissured world-view, that his Imperial verities were invariably expressed alongside a set of values that threatened to destroy the Empire. His expressed view of Empire, which saw the colonies as a means by which Britain was to 'enrich' the world through the universal application of its 'culture and traditions', was thereby contradicted in Buchan's *fin de siècle* fiction. In stark contrast to their declared 'civilizing' mission, Buchan's fiction positioned the isolated Englishman single-handedly against the unseen forces of evil.[20] This anxiety was especially reflected in a semitic discourse which constructed 'the Jew' as an

[19] Popular post-*Daniel Deronda* 'Zionist' novels include Sydney Grier, *The Kings of the East* (1900) and *The Prince of Captivity* (1902), Winifred Graham, *The Zionists* (1902) and Lucas Cleeve's *The Children of Endurance* (1904). Grier's *The Prince of Captivity* clearly anticipates Buchan's novel and also refers to Disraeli's *Alroy* (1833), where his problematical messiah, David Alroy, becomes the Jewish 'Prince of Captivity' by fulfilling his holy purpose of rebuilding the temple and restoring the Jews to Jerusalem.
[20] For this reading of Buchan see Turnbaugh, 'Images of Empire', 734–40. Buchan's retrospective view of Empire can be found in his *Memory-Hold-The-Door*, p. 130.

idealized colonial subject who was also a threatening alternative force, a shadowy double of the 'universal Empire'. After 1906, when the new Liberal government in London gave 'responsible government' to the Afrikaaners in the Transvaal, it seemed to those that fervently wanted to colonize Africa that the 'Jewish' universalist creed of liberalism had finally defeated them in the heartland of the Empire. From within a richly fragmented Imperial perspective, Rudyard Kipling was to give such semitic constructions a specifically literary context.

KIPLING: THE 'WHITE MAN'S BURDEN'

It was T. S. Eliot who first noted in his Introduction to *A Choice of Kipling's Verse* (1941) that Kipling's poetic 'reflections on the Boer war' are 'more admonitory than laudatory'. Most critics of Kipling's verse during this period would now agree with Eliot that the jingoism of 'The Lesson' (1901) – 'It was our fault, and our very great fault – and now we must turn it to use / ... We've had an Imperial lesson. It may make us an Empire yet!' – only represents one aspect of Kipling's Boer War verse. This poem needs, especially, to be contrasted with the condemnatory tone of 'The Islanders' (1902) which contains Kipling's well-known reference to the 'flannelled fools at the wicket or the muddied oafs at the goals'.[21] Along with Buchan, Kipling certainly believed that Southern Africa was ripe for Imperial development in the immediate aftermath of the Boer War. But Kipling had, it should be remembered, been exposed to more injury, disease and death during the Boer War than throughout all of his days in India. Martin Van Wyk Smith has rightly shown that this horrific exposure was to severly undermine Kipling's 'grandiose concept of empire'. Anticipating qualities which have come to be regarded as peculiarly those of First World War verse, Kipling's Imperialism was 'too brittle to outlast a real imperial war'.[22] As well

---

[21] T. S. Eliot (ed.), *A Choice of Kipling's Verse* (London, 1963 edition) p. 29. See also Bonamy Dobree, *Rudyard Kipling: Realist and Fabulist* (London, 1967) chapter 4. References to Kipling's fiction will be to first editions with the exception of 'The House Surgeon' (1909) and 'The Church that was Antioch' (1929) which are collected in Andrew Rutherford (ed.), *Rudyard Kipling: Short Stories*, Penguin edition, 2 vols. (London, 1971) and '"Bread Upon the Waters"' in *The Day's Work* (London, 1964).

[22] Martin Van Wyk Smith, *Drummer Hodge: The Poetry of the Anglo-Boer War* (1899–1902) (Oxford, 1978), p. 98.

as intensifying the fervour of patriotism at the turn of the century, Kipling, with such poems as 'The Dykes' (1902), also undoubtedly added to the apocalyptic mood in Britain at this time:

> Now we can only wait till the day, wait and apportion our
>   shame.
> These are the dykes our fathers left, but we would not look to
>   the same.
> Time and again we were warned of the dykes, time and again we
>   delayed;
> Now, it may fall, we have slain our sons, as our fathers we
>   have betrayed.

This nostalgic despair for a world of 'our fathers' and for 'the dykes' of an unassailable high Victorian Imperialism is, as in the case of Buchan, plainly at odds with the proclaimed mission of creating a 'great white nation' in Africa. Nonetheless, it would be folly to underestimate the widespead impact of Kipling's patriotic verse. 'The Absent-Minded Beggar' (1899), for instance, raised a quarter of a million pounds for soldiers' families and appeared in a variety of forms on tobacco jars, ash trays, packets of cigarettes, pillow cases and plates.[23] Many parodies of this verse appeared throughout the Boer War and those by T. W. H. Crosland in the *Outlook*, in particular, utilized a semitic discourse in its crudest form to oppose the war.

Crosland was the assistant editor of the *Outlook* from 1899 to 1902 and published two volumes of Kiplingesque pastiches, *The Absent-Minded Mule* (1899) and *The Five Notions* (1903). In both of these volumes, the layout and typography of Kipling's anthologies were carefully copied. Two decades later Crosland was to publish the appallingly Judeophobic *The Fine Old Hebrew Gentleman* (1922) which was foreshadowed in these pastiches. Here, for example, is 'The Five Notions', the title poem of Crosland's second volume:

> 'E 'ath a notion that the War
> Was a Imperial beano, gave
> By a 'eroic people for
> A people twenty times as brave.
>
> An' if you take his little book
> An' read wherever you may choose,
> Tho' you may look, an' look, an' look

---

[23] George Shepperson, 'Kipling and the Boer War' in John Gross (ed.), *Rudyard Kipling the Man, His Work and His World* (London, 1972) p. 84.

> You won't see nothin' of no Jews.
>
> As if old England, once agen,
> Raged in the field for honour's sake!
> An' certain 'Ebrew gentlemen
> 'Ad got no interests at stake!
>
> Ar – you might think from Rudyard's lines
> That Cecil went about in white;
> 'E never owned no dimon mines,
> 'E drank no fizz with Verner Beit![24]

In his typically unpleasant way, Crosland juxtaposes a racial discourse of 'Jewish' corruption with the language of patriotism – 'heroism', 'bravery' and 'honour'. This is not simply the 'parts of the picture of empire that Kipling left out', as Van Wyk Smith suggests, but this parody also demonstrates the radically different semitic constructions utilized by the Imperialist and the pro-Boer. Kipling, unlike Buchan, felt himself to be 'goaded' in his fiction into challenging the anti-war opposition at home. Pro-Boer public opinion was confronted especially in *Traffics and Discoveries* (1904) and, in this context, his fiction was to explicitly rewrite the liberal or socialist construction of 'the Jew'.[25]

Traffics and Discoveries was written, for the most part, in the immediate aftermath of the Boer War by an uncomplicatedly moralistic Kipling. In 'The Comprehension of Private Copper', written in 1902 and collected in this volume, Kipling associates pro-Boer politics with traitorousness and the decline of the Imperial Race. Private Alfred Copper's 'comprehension' is attained after he captures a 'renegid' Englishman who has been fighting for the Boers because the 'renegid's' father had been betrayed as a 'Uitlander' (literally a 'foreigner') by a vacillating British government. As the grievances of the Uitlanders were the pretext for British intervention in South Africa, C. A. Bodelson has rightly observed that Kipling's Cape Town journalism echoes directly the 'renegid's' complaints against the lack of British commitment towards its African Colonies. But Kipling was also to represent the 'renegid' Englishman as racially inferior and akin to his previous depictions of 'mixed races' in India. As Private Copper observes of his prisoner: 'you ain't 'alf-caste, but you talk *chee-chee* – pukka Bazar chee-chee' (168). Not unlike Buchan's 'Imperial Gothic', the deterioration of the British

---

[24] Van Wyk Smith, *Drummer Hodge*, p. 105 and Holmes, *Anti-Semitism in British Society*, p. 217.
[25] Van Wyk Smith, *Drummer Hodge*, p. 105 and Dobree, *Rudyard Kipling*, p. 87.

colonialist is deemed, by Kipling, to be a consequence of an equivocating policy towards the Uitlanders which has deprived them of the benefits of the Empire for the past eight years.[26] Private Copper thus begins to 'comprehend' the importance of Empire and of the Boer War in maintaining a racial Englishness abroad. In this context, Copper distances himself from the legitimate complaints of the 'renegid' by making fun of a copy of a liberal pro-Boer newspaper called 'Jerrolds Weekly' which was found on the 'traitor':

'You're the aristocrat, Alf. Old Jerrold's givin' it you 'ot. You're the uneducated 'ireling of a callous aristocracy which 'as sold itself to the 'Ebrew financier. Meantime, Ducky' – he ran his finger down a column of assorted paragraphs – 'you're slakin' your brutal instincts in furious excesses. Shriekin' women an' desolated 'omesteads is what you enjoy. Alf... Halloa! What's a smokin' 'ektacomb?'[27]

Once the necessity of defending the integrity of the Imperial Race in Africa has been properly 'comprehended', Kipling is at pains to show the irrelevance of the ''Ebrew financier' to the soldiers who have fought in the Boer War. In 'The Army and the Dream' (1904), which was also collected in *Traffics and Discoveries*, he was to go on and reconstruct a semitic discourse in specifically Imperial terms. Published originally in four extracts in the right-wing newspaper the *Morning Post*, 'The Army and the Dream' was an explicitly propagandistic account of an 'ideal England which has accepted military service as an integral part of national life'. In this model imperial world of an 'England trained and prepared for war by freely offered service', private day schools were to take part in a nation-wide military exercise. This exercise was to include Jewish Voluntary Schools who, in this story, beat the other day schools at their own 'game'. Based on this reading of the story, Kipling's biographers have made extravagant claims for his 'philosemitism'. But, while Kipling might allow British-Jewry into an exemplary colonial world on the grounds of political expediency, the Jewish Voluntary Schools by the end of the story are crudely opposed to a prevailing Englishness:

[26] C. A. Bodelson, *Aspects of Kipling's Art* (Manchester, 1964), chapter 8 and p. 157 has a useful reading of 'The Comprehension of Private Copper' and refers specifically to Kipling's Cape Town journalism in this context.
[27] 'Jerrold's Weekly' was probably based on the notorious *Reynold's Newspaper*, a popular Sunday weekly, which by 1899 was regularly promoting a 'Jewish world-conspiracy'. Hirchfield, 'The British Left and the "Jewish Conspiracy"', pp. 100–1 and 111.

'*To your Tents, O Israel! The Hebrew Schools stop the Mounted Troops.*' Pig, were
you scuppered by Jew-boys? ... By Jove, there'll have to be an inquiry into
this regrettable incident![28]

According to his autobiographical 'Baa Baa, Black Sheep', collected
in *Wee Willie Winkie* (1890), the nadir of humiliation for Kipling as a
schoolboy in the 'House of Desolation' was his 'thrashing ... before
the Jews' (293). As 'The Army of the Dream' was designed to show
the contemporary lack of preparedness of Britain's Imperial Armed
Forces, being 'scuppered by Jew-boys' was clearly an ideal way of
signifying the potential humiliation for the future defenders of the
Empire. Nevertheless, with characteristic economy, Kipling was also
to demonstrate in this story the importance of compulsory national
service for strengthening the racial back-bone of even Britain's 'Jew-
boys'.

The fear of a lack of 'national efficiency' after the Boer War meant
that Kipling did not write the 'great South African novel' that was
expected of him after he finally returned from Southern Africa in
1907. Instead, in *Puck of Pook's Hill* (1906) and *Rewards and Fairies*
(1910), a more inward-looking Kipling constructed what has been
described as an alternative 'moral history of England'. As well as
stressing the unchanging virtues of a particularist Englishness, a less
optimistic Kipling was provoked by the Boer War to doubt whether
England was 'the nursery of those virtues which the Empire and the
world needed'.[29] In *Puck of Pook's Hill*, which originally began as
nursery tales told to his children, Kipling uses his Sussex home as a
microcosm of these necessary English values so that the 'essence of
Englishness' is recreated in terms of what Alun Howkins has called
the 'rural and the Southern'. The last story of the volume, 'The
Treasure and the Law', includes in this setting a Disraelian
construction of 'the Jew' written, above all, in these pre-modern

---

[28] Angus Wilson, *The Strange Ride of Rudyard Kipling* (London, 1977) pp. 241–2 argues that
'The Army and the Dream' is an expression of Kipling's 'respect for the Jewish contribution
to Western civilisation'. See also Charles Carrington, *Rudyard Kipling his Life and Work*
(London, 1955) p. 315. While Kipling's post-war critics tend to ignore Kipling's racial
construction of 'the Jew', Christopher Ricks in his *T. S. Eliot and Prejudice* (London, 1988)
pp. 26–8 has recently reminded us that Kipling's 'antisemitism' was the cause of an
important exchange of letters between T. S. Eliot and Lionel Trilling in *The Nation* (16
October 1943 and 15 January 1944).

[29] J. H. Grainger *Patriotisms: Britain* 1900–1939 (London 1986) p. 76 and Alun Howkins,
'Kipling, Englishness and History' in Angus Ross (ed.) *Kipling* 86 (Brighton, 1987) pp.
25–6. See also Shepperson, 'Kipling and the Boer War', p. 87.

terms. In T. S. Eliot's pertinent phrase, it is the 'contemporaneity of the past' in *Puck of Pook's Hill* that relates Kipling's stories of England in the eleventh and twelfth centuries directly to his hopes concerning South Africa after the Boer War.[30] In a veiled reference to the pro-Boer antisemitism of the time, the 'Song of the Fifth River', which prefaces 'The Treasure and the Law', postulates a divine 'Jewish' relationship to the 'Secret River of Gold' or the world's money supply:

> When first by Eden Tree
> The Four Great Rivers ran,
> To each was appointed a Man
> Her Prince and Ruler to be.
>
> But after this was ordained,
> (The ancient legends tell),
> There came dark Israel,
> For whom no River remained.
>
> Then He That is Wholly Just
> Said to him: 'Fling on the ground
> A handful of yellow dust,
> And a Fifth Great River shall run,
> Mightier than these Four,
> In secret the Earth around;
> And Her secret evermore
> Shall be shown to thee and thy Race.'

This God-given chosen relationship to the 'Secret River of Gold' has resulted in 'dark Israel' having the legendary capacity to anticipate both 'droughts' and 'floods' and 'turn' them to their 'gain'. As a consequence, Jews are represented in the last stanza of the poem as having a mystical ability to follow the 'gold' throughout the ages:

> A Prince without a Sword,
> A Ruler without a Throne;
> Israel follows his quest.
> In every land a guest,
> Of many lands a lord,
> In no land King is he.
> But the Fifth Great River keeps
> The secret of Her deeps
> For Israel alone,
> As it was ordered to be.

[30] Alun Howkins, 'Kipling, Englishness and History', p. 28 and Eliot, *A Choice of Kipling's Verse*, p. 32. See also J. M. S. Tompkins, *The Art of Rudyard Kipling* (London, 1959) p. 77.

The story that accompanies this poem concerns the genesis of the Magna Carta when, as in the fiction of Buchan and Disraeli, there is postulated a moment of uncanny unity between those of different 'blood and origin'. In 'The Treasure and the Law', Kipling's all-important concept of 'the Law' is related to the signing of the Magna Carta at Runnymede which subsumes 'Jew and Christian' under a higher quasi-religious power (285). We learn that the Magna Carta was signed because King John needed to borrow money from 'the Jews' who, in return, 'sought Power-Power-Power! That is *our* God in our captivity. Power to use!' (293). Kipling, significantly, relates the legendary 'Song of the Fifth River' to his 'history' of the signing of the Magna Carta:

There can be no war without gold, and we Jews know how the earth's gold moves with the seasons, and the crops, and the winds; circling and looping and rising and sinking away like a river – a wonderful underground river. How should the foolish Kings know *that* while they fight and steal and kill? ... [M]y Prince saw peace or war decided not once, but many times, by the fall of a coin spun between a Jew from Bury and a Jewess from Alexandria ... Such power had we Jews among the Gentiles. (290–1)

In Kipling's conception of an exemplary past, there is a 'natural' union between what he calls 'the Sword', 'the Treasure' and 'the Law' (303). To a large extent, the idealized partnership between 'Jewish' financial power and the colonial 'Law' – backed up by the Imperial 'Sword' – is a calculated riposte to those pro-Boer conspiracy theorists who maintained that it was a degenerate 'Jewish plutocracy' that had caused the Boer War. But, in opposing this contention, it is obvious that Kipling was still using a semitic discourse which similarly constructed 'the Jews' as all-powerful financiers that might, eventually, act in their 'own' racial interest.

Kadmiel, who retells the story of the Magna Carta, is explicitly identified by Kipling with the romantic tradition of the omniscient, eternally Wandering Jew which Disraeli utilized in his portrayal of Sidonia.[31] As with Disraeli and Buchan, Kipling's construction of the

---

[31] Daniel Schwarz, *Disraeli's Fiction* (London, 1979) and Bivona, *Desire and Contradiction*, chapter 1 are good accounts of Disraeli's fiction in this context. See also Kipling's 'The Wandering Jew' in *Life's Handicap* (London, 1891) which is, however, not connected to the mythical figure of Ahasuerus. Another non-mythic 'Wandering Jew', Ahasuerus Jenkins, can be found in Kipling's 'Army Head-Quarters' (1886). Noel Annan, 'Kipling's Place in the History of Ideas', in A. Rutherford (ed.), *Kipling's Mind and Art* (London, 1964), pp. 113–14 discusses 'The Treasure and the Law' in the context of Kipling's anti-rationalism.

timeless particularist Jew conflicts with the Arnoldian assimilated
Jew who had been 'civilised' by a historically progressive liberalism.
To reinforce this point, the sympathetic Kadmiel is contrasted with
the vulgar modern figure of Mr Meyer, in this story, who is the
caricature Jewish parvenu who wears 'yellow gaiters' (302) and
pretends to be a country gentleman by cruelly shooting rabbits. Here
the parameters of Kiplings 'Law' are apparent, as it only allows
other 'races' into its privileged sphere if they conform to their
timeless but limited racial purpose. By denying their racial destiny, as
in the case of Mr Meyer – or the English 'renegid' in 'The
Comprehension of Private Copper' – such figures put themselves
beyond 'the Law'. The biblical resonances in the well-known fourth
stanza of Kipling's poem 'Recessional' (1897) are, in these terms, not
insignificant:

> If, drunk with sight of power, we loose
>   Wild tongues that have not Thee in awe,
> Such boastings as the Gentiles use,
>   Or lesser breeds without the Law –
> Lord God of Hosts, be with us yet,
> Lest we forget – lest we forget!

While Kipling is, undoubtedly, influenced here by the vernacular of
the Authorized Version, it is interesting to note that the Imperial
power in this stanza is identified with the biblically chosen Jews, as
opposed to the boastful 'Gentiles'. By becoming 'drunk with [the]
sight of power', and ignoring the responsibilities that go with their
superior racial destiny, the English nation threatens itself to
degenerate into 'lesser breeds without the Law'. Kipling's 'Law', in
these terms, is the 'natural' racial order that has existed for all time
and that must not be denied by either animals (pace *The Jungle Book*
(1894)) or equally differentiated human-beings.[32] In the case of
Kipling's semitic constructions, it is clear that those that do not
conform to the timeless ideal of Kadmiel but who, instead, become
'drunk with [the] sight of power' will pose a peculiar threat to 'the
Law' underpinning the Empire.

There is plenty of evidence in Kipling's Indian Stories, written
before his experience of Imperialist 'Jewish financiers' in South

---

[32] For Kipling's self-identification with 'the system of brutal justice that Kipling found and
admired in the Old Testament' see Sandra Kemp, *Kipling's Hidden Narratives* (Oxford, 1988)
p. 89 and for Kipling and 'the Law' see Eliot L. Gilbert, *The Good Kipling: Studies in the Short
Story* (Manchester, 1972) p. 45.

Africa, that Jews were perceived to be among the 'lesser breeds' who
might, potentially, undermine the foundation of Empire. When not
contained within the Imperial 'Law' the 'Jewish race', in these
stories, was no less threatening than Kipling's other 'native races'. In
a typical early Kiplingesque combination of vulgarity and complexity collected in *Life's Handicap* (1891), 'Jews in Shushan'
introduces the seminal figure of 'Ephraim the Jew' as he is known to
the natives of Shushan. He is introduced initially as a rather 'meek'
debt-collector who wishes to build a synagogue in Shushan by
forming a prayer quorum of ten Jews. After his initial 'meek'
appearance – 'never was Jew more unlike his dread breed' (338) –
Ephraim is, however, quickly transformed into a 'dread' example of
the dangers of semitic racial particularism. When the door which
shuts Ephraim 'off from the world of the Gentile' (341) is opened, he
is seen holding a 'half-maddened sheep' as the 'butcher to our
[Jewish] people':

He was attired in strange raiment... and a knife was in his mouth. As he
struggled with the animal between the walls, the breath came from him in
thick sobs, and the nature of the man seemed changed. When the ordained
slaughter was ended, he saw that the door was open and shut it hastily, his
hand leaving a red mark on the timber... A glimpse of Ephraim busied in
one of his religious capacities was no thing to be desired twice. (339–40)

Soon after this episode, Kipling comments didactically that Ephraim
'set at naught the sanitary regulations of a large, flourishing, and
remarkably well-governed Empire' (341). As Ephraim's racial quest
to build a Jewish community in Shushan is thwarted by the death of
his children and the other congregants, the consequences of Ephraim
obeying his own primitive Judaic laws – as opposed to 'the Law' of
Empire – is severly punished by Kipling in this story. His wife's
madness, brought on by the death of their children, obviously
denotes that Miriam had also been 'untrue to her race' (342).
Martin Seymour-Smith has recently noted that a Jewish 'Miriam'
was to reappear in a range of Kipling's texts throughout the next
three decades establishing, perhaps, an alternative set of representations to the dark forces which Ephraim unleashed on a 'well-ordered
Empire'.[33] In contrast to Miriam's later ennoblement, however,

[33] Martin Seymour-Smith, *Rudyard Kipling* (London 1989) pp. 114–15, 214–15 and 278–9,
traces the 'Miriam' motif in Kipling's work from his poem 'The Prayer of Miriam Cohen'
(1893) to 'They' (1904). In 'The Eye of Allah' (1926), for instance, John of Burgos's Jewish

'Jews in Shushan' ends on the disparaging racial note of a subaltern whistling 'Ten Little Nigger Boys'. Described as the 'dirge of the Jews of Shushan' (342), this is an obvious allusion to Ephraim's quest to form a prayer quorum of ten Jews in Shushan. It also, interestingly, brings together 'the Jew' and 'the nigger' as racial primitives which need to be 'governed' by a superior Imperial power. This is, clearly, a far cry from the later colonial role of British-Jews in South Africa and beyond.

It is in this tone of coarse belittlement that Kipling was to write 'His Chance in Life' which is collected in *Plain Tales from the Hills* (1888) and is related interestingly to the 'Jews in Shushan'. Set on the racial 'borderline' where 'the last drop of White blood ends and the full Black tide sets in' (71), the story concerns the 'very black' Michele D'Cruze who has only 'seven-eighths native blood in his veins'. The 'other' blood in him is part 'Portuguese', part 'Yorkshire platelayer' and part 'black Jew of Cochin' (73). In the typically divided racial context of Kipling's Indian stories, D'Cruze finds himself confronted with a native riot and a local Police Inspector who regards him as a 'Sahib' because of the 'old race-instinct which recognises a drop of White blood as far as it can be diluted' (75). Kipling notes caustically that 'the man with the Cochin Jew and the menial uncle in his pedigree' was 'the only representative of English authority in the place' (75). By bowing to this 'authority' and sending for the British Army to stem the riot, D'Cruze's heart becomes 'big and white in his breast' (76) and he learns to love a woman who is his social superior. But when faced with the authentic sign of 'Our Authority' (74), a young English officer, D'Cruze 'felt himself slipping back more and more into the native' as the 'white drop' of blood in 'his veins' began to 'die out' (77).

Only with the publication of *Kim* (1901), did Kipling treat the theme of a divided racial identity with maturity. What is clear from 'His Chance in Life', however, is that whether a 'Jew' was 'white' or 'black' depended ultimately on a wider relationship to an exclusively British Imperial 'authority'. This 'Law' applied especially to 'dark Israel' because of its dangerous indeterminacy which meant that it could be both 'white' and 'black' at the same time. That D'Cruze

mistress, like Miriam in 'Jews in Shushan', dies in childbed. Not that all of Kipling's Jewish women are paragons of suffering. A passenger in *The Light that Failed* (1891) p. 131 is described by Kipling's artist hero, Dick Heldar, as 'a sort of Negroid-Jewess-Cuban, with morals to match'.

was to end up earning an Imperial salary of sixty-six rupees to pay for his fiancée's dowry, contrasts markedly with Ephraim's loss of his family and friends for daring to remain a particularist Jew in the face of 'the Law' of Empire. Such were the stark options open to Kipling's Indian Jews situated awkwardly on the 'borderline' between 'white' and 'black'.[34]

Two widely divergent stories by Kipling, 'Bread Upon the Waters' (1896) and 'The House Surgeon' (1909), demonstrate especially the disturbing ambivalence in Kipling's semitic discourse where Jews can simultaneously represent the modernizing universalism of Capital – the 'dangerous solvent of society' – as well as the pre-modern Imperial 'race instinct'. In 'Bread Upon the Waters', a familiar tale of revenge collected in *The Day's Work* (1898), Kipling recounts the adventure of McRimmon, a ship owner, who 'cuts the liver out o' Holdock, Steiner, Chase, and Company, Limited' (246), an unscrupulous rival firm of shippers. In particular, Holdock, Steiner and Chase dismiss McPhee as a chief engineer after twenty years of exemplary service which includes 'two or three Royal Humane Society medals for saving lives at sea' (222). This dismissal is caused by McPhee's refusal to run his ship, the *Breslau*, to a recently introduced hazardous time schedule. Throughout the tale, McPhee's traditional sea-faring values are juxtaposed with a ruthless modernity which is specifically associated with 'Young Steiner', the son of the firm's founder. As McPhee narrates:

The old Board would ne'er ha' done it. They trusted me. But the new Board was all for reorganisation. Young Steiner – Steiner's son – the Jew, was at the bottom of it, an' they did not think it worth their while to send me word. (227)

Or,

Young Steiner, the Jew, was at the bottom of it. They sacked men right an' left that would not eat the dirt the Board gave 'em. They cut down repairs; they fed crews wi' leavin's and scrapin's... ' (231–2)

While Steiner's father presumably worked within the constraints of traditional practices, it is his son – one of the generation of Jews which should have become more 'civilized' in terms of conventional

---

[34] Sander Gilman, *Difference and Pathology: Stereotypes of Sexuality, Race and Madness* (Ithaca, 1985) is the best account of the cross-over in 'black' and 'Jewish' representations. See also Kemp, *Kipling's Hidden Narratives*, chapter 1 and Kipling, *Kim*, ed. Edward Said (London, 1987), pp. 7–46.

liberal thought – who symbolizes a rapacious financial efficiency and calculating disregard for the lives and customs of Britain's sailors. 'Young Steiner's' lack of sympathy causes McPhee to remark that 'there's more discernment in a dog than a Jew' (229). By turning a respectable firm of shippers into 'deevidend-huntin' ship-chandlers, deaf as the adders o' Scripture' (228), Steiner gives McRimmon an opportunity to bankrupt the 'Jew-firm' (248), something which he has waited fourteen years to do. McPhee even considers this prospect to be one of 'those singular providences' that proves that 'we're in the hands of Higher Powers' (248). Unlike 'The Treasure and the Law', where a materialist Judaism works hand in hand with the 'Higher Powers', 'Bread Upon the Waters' crudely reflects upon the dire consequences of a destructive Jewish modernity – released from its sacred Imperial obligations – which has become 'drunk with [the] sight of power'. The primitivism of the 'black Jews', which disturbs the 'order' of Empire in Kipling's India, is here linked to the corrupt modernity of the 'white Jews' who attack the very heart of the 'English nation'.

These contradictory aspects of the 'Jewish race' are brought together in one of Kipling's most influential and accomplished short stories, 'The House Surgeon', which is collected in *Actions and Reactions* (1909). In this complex story, as Sandra Kemp has shown, 'dream and fantasy are as essential a part of life as the conscious and the rational'.[35] This duality both structures the story and defines the 'Jewishness' of its main character, Maxwell M'Leod. In particular, M'Leod's naive materialism is juxtaposed throughout with the 'blasting gust of depression' (201) which pervades Holmescroft, the country house which the M'Leod family have recently purchased. The deft comic opening of 'The House Surgeon' invokes the multiple perspectives of Easter, Passover and the supernatural and gives the reader an intriguing glimpse of an unwritten ghost story 'about the Curse on the family's first-born' which 'turned out to be drains' (194) as opposed to a modern Egyptian plague. This superficially technical solution to the problem of combating evil is reflected in M'Leod's shallow methods of dealing with the 'Horror of great darkness which is spoken of in the Bible' (197). As M'Leod confides:

'...if I've spent a pound first and last, I must have spent five thousand. Electric light, new servants' wing, garden – all that sort of thing. A man and

---

[35] Kemp, *Kipling's Hidden Narratives*, p. 60.

his family ought to be happy after so much expense, ain't it?' He looked at me through the bottom of his glass'. (194)

This endeavour by M'Leod's 'moneyed innocence' to exclude the 'great darkness' indicates, as John Coates has noted, the reason why Kipling constructed M'Leod as an assimilated Jew who has changed his name and married a Greek in a bid to deny his 'dark' racial heritage.[36] M'Leod, in this reading of the story, replaces biblical knowledge and morality with a facile plutocratic modernity which dominates the story. His refusal to confront the timeless verities is signified by the 'fortifying blaze of electric light' (201) which envelops Holmescroft as well as the extra £1000 which M'Leod has paid his lawyer to ensure that no death has occured in the house since it was first built. This over-simple banishment of past suffering, however, points to the inadequacy of a modern Arnoldian synthesis between Hebrew and Hellene – as represented by M'Leod's marriage to a Greek woman – which is meant to lead to the painless progress of civilization.

The 'Perseus' figure, who narrates the story, soon discovers that a devout Calvinist had accidentally killed herself by falling out of a window at Holmescroft, her previous abode. By blaming her for committing suicide, Mary Moultrie had caused the guilt-ridden spirit of her sister to haunt Holmescroft. As Hyam Maccoby has argued, the skilful contrast between M'Leod's godlessness and Mary Moultrie's reprehensible presumption of God's purpose (rather like Ephraim in 'Jews in Shushan') indicates the richly ambiguous perspective of the 'pagan Saviour' of Holmescroft.[37] The narrator's 'most terrible of all dreams' reflects M'Leod's attempted banishment of 'all past evil' where, in trying to 'wipe [evil] out of our lives', we 'wake to the day we have earned' (201). But, as the narrator manages easily to expose M'Leod's dangerous folly, his worst nightmare turns out, ironically, to be merely the story of 'The House Surgeon'.

There is, interestingly, a curious symmetry between 'The House Surgeon' and Lionel Trilling's reading of Kipling which views his

---

[36] John Coates, 'Religious Cross Currents in "The House Surgeon"', *The Kipling Journal* 45 (September 1978), 3 and 2–7 and see also Hyam Maccoby, '"The Family Reunion" and Kipling's "The House Surgeon"', *Notes and Queries* (February 1968), 48–57.

[37] Maccoby, '"The Family Reunion" and Kipling's "The House Surgeon"', 50 and Coates, 'Religious Cross Currents in "The House Surgeon"', 5.

Imperialism as a manichaean ideology erected 'against the mind's threat to itself'. Recent literary criticism has, similarly, emphasized the 'peculiar divisions of voice and vocabulary that haunt Kipling's writings'.[38] To some extent, 'the Jew' – who in his 'modern' guise represses the 'primitive' within him – embodies this split within Kipling. The 'pagan' narrator in Kipling's story especially articulates a richly divided voice which unusually eschews both the language of the Old Testament – and thereby subtly distances the narrative from Mary Moultrie's Puritanism – as well as his potential role as a redemptive Christ-figure (which distinguishes him from Buchan's narrator in 'The Grove of Ashtaroth'). These contradictory perspectives are also reinforced in the two poems that end 'The House Surgeon'. On the one hand, Miss M'Leod sings 'With Mirth, Thou Pretty Bird' which joyously asserts the acceptance of one's natural shortcomings. But this implicit defence of the M'Leod's way of life is immediately undercut by 'The Rabbi's Song', an important coda to 'The House Surgeon', which stresses the need for a 'spiritual' transcendence of one's present condition:

> Our lives, our tears, as water,
>   Are poured upon the ground;
> God giveth no man quarter,
>   Yet God a means hath found;
> Though faith and hope have vanished,
>   And even love grows dim,
> A means whereby His banished
>   Be not expelled from Him![39]

Echoing 'The Treasure and the Law', Kipling's 'Rabbi' in this poem reiterates the sacred obligations of God's 'banished' people not to succumb to what is called 'the desolation / and darkness of thy mind' which has been caused by the Jewish rejection of Christ. The possibility that the 'whispering ghosts' of 'the past' will dominate 'the Jews' who have left their 'habitation' is an ironic commentary on M'Leod's life-long avoidance of those dark forces which have

---

[38] Kemp, *Kipling's Hidden Narratives*, p. 6 and Lionel Trilling, 'Kipling' in Rutherford, *Kipling's Mind and Art*, pp. 91 and 83–94. See also Abdul JanMohamed, *Manichean Aesthetics: The Politics of Literature in Colonial Africa* (Amherst, 1983).

[39] Unfortunately 'The Rabbi's Song' is not contained in the Penguin reprint of *The House Surgeon*. See Maccoby, '"The Family Reunion" and Kipling's "The House Surgeon"', 50 for the Old Testament vocabulary of this story.

surfaced with a vengeance at Holmescroft. 'The Rabbi's Song', however, is at pains to emphasize that such 'darkness' must be replaced by God's 'spirit'. If Jews continue to be 'expelled from Him', then their thoughts of their past 'habitation' will degenerate into 'madness' and 'terror' or, in the modern context of 'The House Surgeon', M'Leod's anarchic materialism. Unlike Robert Browning's related poetic persona, 'Rabbi Ben Ezra', where Jews are represented in terms of Browning's life-affirming liberalism – 'the best is yet to be' – Kipling's timeless 'Rabbi' speaks exclusively in the vocabulary of unchanging verities, which are rooted in an ideal past, and which apply to modern-day as well as to biblical Jews.[40]

Kipling's ambivalent Jewish representations were to reach a level of narrative complexity in 'The House Surgeon' which, it is worth noting, was to be echoed later in the poetry of T. S. Eliot. It would, nonetheless, be a mistake to distinguish, as Sandra Kemp has done, between Kipling as a 'public figure' who 'co-operated with the radical right-wing' and Kipling as a 'writer'. The problem with this distinction becomes especially apparent when we read a poem such as 'Gehazi' (1915). According to Eliot, this poem was both a piece of 'passionate invective rising to real eloquence' which was also 'inspired by the Marconi scandals'. The imaginative literature surrounding the 'Marconi Scandal' – a popular example of 'Jewish financial' corruption in the Edwardian period – will be examined in a later chapter. But it is obviously difficult to separate a 'public' and 'private' Kipling when he responds primarily as a 'writer' to a 'public' affair which was high on the 'radical right' agenda of political activities.[41]

By contrasting the biblical 'Judge of Israel' with the 'baseness' of the 'market place', 'Gehazi' contains many of the assumptions of Kipling's literature as a whole. Rufus Isaacs, the newly appointed Lord Chief Justice and one of the main protagonists of the 'Marconi Scandal' is, not unlike M'Leod in 'The House Surgeon', the degenerate double of his biblical counterpart. The stark duality

---

[40] Coates, 'Religious Cross Currents in "The House Surgeon"', 6 usefully compares Kipling and Browning in this context. It is not insignificant that M'Leod's assumed name (which sounds like 'my lord') has an absent 'c' which has been unilaterally restored by some of Kipling's critics and perhaps signifies M'Leod's fearful lack of C(hristianity). It might not be entirely coincidental that M'Leod, like Kipling's sometime literary agent J. B. Pinker, was a Scottish-Jew.

[41] Kemp, *Kipling's Hidden Narratives*, p. 2 and Eliot, *A Choice of Kipling's Verse*, pp. 15–16. Chapter 5 of this book discusses the semitic discourse surrounding the 'Marconi Scandal'.

between Isaacs' political status and his moral depravity is conveyed fervently by Kipling in his use of the metaphors of sickness and health in the final stanza of the poem:

> Thou mirror of uprightness,
>   What ails thee at thy vows?
> What means the risen whiteness
>   Of the skin between thy brows?
> The boils that shine and burrow,
>   The sores that slough and bleed –
> The leprosy of Naaman
>   On thee and all thy seed?
>   Stand up, Stand up, Gehazi,
>   Draw close thy robe and go.
>   Gehazi, Judge in Israel,
>   A leper white as snow!

Such are the dire consequences for Kipling of empowering those Jews that are not only nationless but are, more importantly, acting in their own debased 'racial' interests. What is significant about 'Gehazi', however, is that Kipling's political enemies at the time of the Boer War – such as the vehemently pro-Boer Hilaire Belloc and G. K. Chesterton – were, in the context of the 'Marconi Scandal', his political friends. The degeneracy of 'the Jews' meant that their potential for anarchy was, in the end, not to be contained by the order of Empire. Two years before leaving South Africa for good in March 1906, when Kipling was 'sick and wearied of the state of things here [in the Rand]', he wrote to his friend H. A. Gwynne to agree with him that 'a certain type of Jew-financier – I have Albu in my eye – is most dangerous and should be hampered but the danger then is (since they all hang together) of weakening the others and so bringing on a bigger smash'.[42] When not imbued with 'the Law' of Empire, Kipling's racialized Jews were to prove to be peculiarly untrustworthy. Such was one of 'the lessons' of his South African years which resulted in Kipling's eventual coincidence of interests with the previously traitorous pro-Boers.

By the time of the First World War, the subtle ambivalence of 'The House Surgeon' was to be replaced by the strident anger of 'Gehazi' as more and more godless Jews were perceived to be running amok and threatening the very heart of Englishness. Instead of recognizing

[42] Unpublished Letter to H. A. Gwynne, 27 March 1906 (letter number 34 in the Kipling Archive).

the 'sin' which had caused the loss of Empire in South Africa and the destruction of the First World War, Kipling argued instead that Jews like M'Leod were intoxicated with the golden calf of a universalizing materialism. This perception can be found in Kipling's autobiography *Something of Myself* (1937), where he was to contrast 'the Semitic strain' of America with 'the English tradition' because, for Kipling, America was increasingly like a 'too-much-at-ease Zion'.[43] Unlike Buchan, who was to retain his faith in the Jewish nationalist potential of 'the Semitic strain', Kipling after the First World War was to lose hope in 'the Jews' ever completely knuckling under to the harsh Anglo-Saxon responsibilities of 'the white man's burden'.

Whereas Buchan's Imperial constructions of 'the Jew' could lead him to a passionate 'Zionism', the same constructions could lead Kipling to a belief in a 'Jewish World Conspiracy'. H. A. Gwynne, Kipling's life-long friend, was by the early 1920s promoting the *Protocols of the Elders of Zion*, a widely circulated pamphlet that argued that 'Jewish communists' and 'Jewish financiers' were conspiring to control the world. After the Bolshevik Revolution, Kipling came to believe that this was 'absolutely in line with the work which the "international Jew" at his worst has accomplished and is accomplishing at the present moment'. But, unlike Gwynne, he stressed that such views were not 'fit for publication' and, although Gwynne quoted him as a supporter of the *Protocols*, Kipling was to confine his support to his private letters and diaries. Kipling, moreover, did not completely abandon the Imperial construction of 'the Jew' after the War and even corresponded with the Imperialist writer Henry Rider Haggard about a proposed novel concerning 'the Jew upon whom Doom has not begun to work'. The sketch of this novel located the 'Wandering Jew' in an idealized Middle Ages where Kipling, presumably, would have situated his 'race' in a pre-lapsarian spiritual order.[44]

---

[43] Rudyard Kipling, *Something of Myself* (London, 1937) p. 132. As early as his poem 'The Long Trail' (1892), Kipling could describe leaving 'English luxury' for 'a roving life' as being 'done with the Tents of Shem' which, according to Philip Mason, *Kipling, the Glass, the Shadow and the Fire* (London 1975) p. 97, signifies Heinemann, a 'Jewish' firm of publishers.

[44] Morton Cohen (ed.), *Rudyard Kipling to Rider Haggard. The Record of a Friendship* (London, 1965) pp. 110–11. This proposal most probably resulted in Kipling's 'The Church that was at Antioch' (1929). In an unpublished letter to Ian Colvin (2 August 1917), in my possession, Kipling argues that the 'domestic Jew rejoices' in the chaos of the First World War. Colvin, along with Kipling's friend, H. A. Gwynne, editor of the *Morning Post*, helped to promote the *Protocols of the Elders of Zion*. Kipling's letter to Gwynne (25 October 1919)

In the conspiracy-ridden 'radical right' circles, which he inhabited after the First World War, Kipling became convinced that he was the victim of a 'semitic hoax' when a forged poem, purporting to be from his hand, was published in *The Times* on 27 May 1918. The hoaxer tried to crudely implicate the Jewish writer Israel Zangwill in this deception by sending an obviously forged note from Zangwill to Kipling. Even after Sir Basil Thomson, Director of Intelligence at Scotland Yard, stated that Zangwill was not the culprit, Kipling continued to 'suspect more than a little' that a 'non-Aryan' hand was behind the hoax. In his autobiography Kipling went further and elaborated on ' ... the Oriental detachedness and insensitiveness of playing that sort of game in the heart of a life-and-death struggle'. But Kipling, in retrospect, had put the hoax forward a year to 1917, at the height of the bloodshed during the First World War.[45] By the time of his story, 'The Church that was at Antioch' (1929), Kipling's hard-bitten narrator could refer pointedly to a 'hellicat Judea' (237) or a 'Nation of Jews within the Empire' as being 'very particular and troublesome' (249) for the Roman Empire. This had obvious contemporary resonances during the troubled British Mandate period in Palestine in the 1920s and 1930s. While Buchan was to retain his faith in the 'Nation of Jews within the Empire', the same belief in a racialized Jewish power could be constructed not as an aid but as a threat to the Empire.

Given the doubleness of Imperial representations of 'the Jew', it is worth noting that in the 1917 English translation of the *Protocols*, Sergius Nilus had his blue-print for world domination supposedly presented to the 'Council of Elders by "the Prince of Exile", Theodor Herzl, at the First Congress of Zionists'. It is rather reductive for Edward Said to argue in this context that 'by a concatenation of events the Semitic myth bifurcated in the Zionist movement; one Semite went the way of Orientalism, the other, the Arab, was forced

was widely quoted by Gwynne. For this correspondence see Keith Wilson, 'The *Protocols of Zion* and the *Morning Post*, 1919–1920', *Patterns of Prejudice* 19 (Number 3, 1985) 6 and 5–14 and also Holmes, *Anti-Semitism in British Society*, pp. 139–41 and chapter 9. For a misreading of Kipling's intended novel on the theme of the Wandering Jew see Alun Howkins, 'Rider Haggard and Rural England: An Essay on Literature and History', in Shaw and Chase, *The Imagined Past*, p. 92 and chapter 6.

45 Kipling, *Something of Myself*, pp. 225–6. For an account of this hoax see Gordon Phillips, 'The Literary Hoax that Fooled the Thunderer and did Kipling Down', *The Times*, 1 August 1977. Kipling and Israel Zangwill had, in fact, a friendly if irregular correspondence since the 1890s which is located in the Kipling Archive, University of Sussex and the Central Zionist Archive, Jerusalem.

to go the way of the Oriental'.[46] This over-simple opposition between a colonial 'Zionism' and a racialized 'Arab' does not, however, take account of the fact that the 'Zionist movement' could itself be the object, and not just the perpetuator, of a dominant semitic discourse. In 1901, H. R. Haggard was to sum up these ambivalences when he asked, in a reference to the 'wailing of the Jews in the Temple Wall in Jerusalem', 'why do they wail, when a few of their financiers could buy up the country [of Palestine]?' Haggard had previously elaborated on this viewpoint in his account of his travels through Palestine after he had himself visited the 'Wailing Wall':

But surely they might add [to prayers] other more practical attempts to recover the heritage of their race. For instance, they might persuade their wealthier brethren to buy out the Turk. There are a dozen gentlemen on the London Stock Exchange who could do this without much individual inconvenience... Surely it is only a question of price? Are they held back by indifference and apathy – or, perchance, by the mysterious chain of some Divine decree? Or they might drill, buy arms, and make an insurrection. I am informed, however, that they prefer to await the advent of their Messiah, a man of blood and power, a Jewish Napoleon, who when he appears will bring about the glory and temporal advancement of the race'.[47]

Two decades later, this construction of the infinite financial power of a 'dozen gentlemen on the London Stock Exchange', which might be utilized to rehabilitate the Empire, was to be the basis of Haggard's belief that Bolshevism in England was a 'great Jewish plot' and that 'behind even the ordinary vapouring Communist' in Russia stands the 'sinister figure of the Jew'. The obverse of Haggard's colonialist 'Zionism' was, therefore, not only the 'Oriental Arab' but also the construction of 'the Jew' as a dark double of Empire. Other writers, such as Olive Schreiner, similarly veered between an idealized

[46] Edward Said, *Orientalism* (London, 1978) p. 307 and Norman Cohn, *Warrant for Genocide: The Myth of the Jewish World-Conspiracy and 'The Protocols of the Elders of Zion'* (London 1967) pp. 69–70 and p. 103 which argues that 'countless editions of the *Protocols* have connected that document with the [First Zionist] congress'.

[47] Henry Rider Haggard, *A Winter Pilgrimage, Being an Account of Travels Through Palestine, Italy, and the Island of Cyprus, Accomplished in the Year* 1900 (London, 1901) pp. 341–2 and 'The Commercial Future of Palestine: Debate at the Article Club', *Jewish Chronicle*, 22 November 1901, 14. Wendy Katz, *Rider Haggard and the Fiction of Empire: A Critical Study of British Imperial Fiction* (Cambridge, 1987) is an excellent account of the range of 'Jewish' constructions in Haggard's fiction and unpublished diaries which have been previously omitted from D. S. Higgins (ed.), *The Private Diaries of Sir Henry Rider Haggard 1914–1925* (London, 1980). Howkins, 'Rider Haggard and Rural England: An Essay on Literature and History', p. 92 and *passim* is over-reliant on Higgins. His conclusion, 'unlike Kipling, [Haggard] did not see Jews as an overwhelming threat' is not borne out by the evidence collected in Katz, a volume which Howkins does not refer to.

'Zionism' and a blanket condemnation of 'Jewish finance' in her journalism and fiction. Joseph Conrad, in particular, was to give this ambivalence a memorable literary dimension in *Nostromo* (1904).[48] Conrad, in this novel, represents the figure of Hirsch as a cowardly 'hooked-nose' or 'hooked beak' Jew with a 'practical mercantile soul' (190–1) who, after spitting in Sotillo's face, arguably achieves the one act of defiance against oppression in the novel. Hirsch's resulting murder by Sotillo, after he is brutally tortured, is left to baffle both Nostromo and Monygham. They discover Hirsch's crucified body 'erect and shadowy against the stars' where it seems to be transformed into a Christ-like symbol of transcendence:

The light of the two candles burning before the perpendicular and breathless immobility of the late Señor Hirsch threw a gleam afar over land and water, like a signal in the night. (378)

Nostromo's call to 'avenge' Hirsch is fatally undermined as he marches unaware to his own death: 'You man of fear!' he cried. 'You will be avenged by me – Nostromo' (385). Monygham's previous description of Hirsch as 'part of the general atrocity of things' (368) also prefigures the doomed Nostromo. But that was the point of the ambivalent figure of Hirsch who, like all of the transformations of 'the Jew' in this chapter, is constructed to represent the colonial desire for the 'semitic race' to become part of a transcendent order. Constructions of 'the Jew' in an Imperial context are, in this way, dangerously confused and divided as they simultaneously reinforce the eternal foundation of 'race' and, at the same time, introduce the threat of a more vigorous 'universal' power made up of those 'Jews' that succumb to their own racial particularism. As Kipling was to eventually conclude in his autobiography, 'Israel is a race to leave alone. It abets disorder'.[49]

[48] Katz, *Rider Haggard and the Fiction of Empire*, pp. 149–52 cites Haggard's diaries and his fiction on p. 46 and pp. 118–19. Olive Schreiner's support for 'the beautiful dream of the Zionist' can be found in her *A Letter on the Jew* (Cape Town, 1906) p. 5 and her crude representation of the 'Jew financier' in her posthumous *From Man to Man* (London, 1926) which was begun in the 1880s. Further references to the Penguin edition of *Nostromo* (London, 1983) will be in the body of the text.

[49] Kipling, *Something of Myself*, p. 224. Parry, *Conrad and Imperialism*, chapter 6 and especially p. 111 and p. 115 analyses the redemptive and racial discourses in Conrad's *Nostromo*. Conrad, significantly, in his only other semitic construction, in the short story 'Prince Roman', *Tales of Hearsay and Last Essays* (London 1928, uniform edition) p. 39 and p. 44 associates 'the Jew Yankel' with the aristocratic old order and describes him as a 'Polish patriot'. Frederick Karl, *Joseph Conrad: The Three Lives* (London, 1979) *passim*, however, also makes plain Conrad's life-long construction of Jews in relation to a degenerate modernity.

CONCLUSION

Whereas Victorian liberal writers constructed a transcendent future
for their object of desire, Imperialists such as Disraeli, Buchan and
Kipling were at pains to contain 'the Jew' within a racial order
which was located in an idealized past. The Bible, in these terms, was
not merely an Arnoldian master-text through which Jews might
assimilate into English 'culture'. On the contrary, it was to provide
the writers in this chapter with an ancient mythology which had long
since organized the world in terms of unchanging 'aristotcratic'
verities. When Jews complied with their allotted colonial role, they
were deemed to be living out a universal racial destiny which
confirmed the unquestionable superiority of the newly 'chosen'
Imperial Race. Jews thus had a spectacularly over-determined
function within Imperial thinking. Those who conformed to the God-
given civilizing mission of Empire were in turn constructed as the
ideal embodiment of how racially differentiated colonial subjects
should behave. A racialized 'Jewish materialism' was represented, in
this way, as both serving the interests of Empire and, above all, as
containable within its borders.

Both Buchan and Kipling were to locate a supposed Jewish
financial power within the realm of Empire in terms which were to
oppose liberal and socialist constructions of mythologized 'Jewish
financiers' in Southern Africa. Buchan, especially, consistently
positioned Jews at the centre of his Imperial order and his Zionism,
in particular, translated the age-old racial destiny of 'the Jews' into
modern terms. A supposedly 'Jewish' liberalism was, therefore,
contained within the higher order of Empire. But when the colonies
were perceived to be weakening, as in the case of Southern Africa,
those modernized Jews that were thought to be 'outside' of the
interests of Empire were constructed as a peculiar threat. A Jewish
racial particularism that was not managed within an Imperial order
was constructed in the writings of Buchan and Kipling as a dark
double of Empire or as a degenerate 'chosen race' compared to the
'civilizing' Imperial Race. The same representations that were
deemed to uphold the Empire could, thus, be also used to construct
Jewish Conspiracy theories which threatened to unleash an anarchic
materialism throughout the world.

The ambivalence or unknowability of the Jewish 'race' meant
that, as in the case of Trollope, it could not be completely confined

within the borders of a racialized Englishness. But unlike liberal writers, who attempted to 'balance' past virtues with present realities, Kipling and Buchan located all value in an indeterminate past. In the next chapter, the 'socialist' writers, George Bernard Shaw and H. G. Wells, exactly reverse the Imperialist position. Following on from Matthew Arnold and George Eliot, Shaw and Wells construct a rationalist view of the future where all forms of particularist individualism will die out. In this extreme re-working of the liberal position, Jewish racial difference is both transcended in a socialist world-state while, at the same time, the Jewish diaspora prefigures the internationalism of the future. Once again, 'the Jew' stands on the cusp of a transfiguring ideology and, as with Imperial writers, exposes the structural ambivalences within an apparently all-explaining view of the world.

CHAPTER 4

The 'socialism of fools': George Bernard Shaw and H. G. Wells

But is the Jew of the usury gold becoming our despot-king of Commerce?

George Meredith, *One of Our Conquerors* (London, 1891), p. 8

... I have always refused to be enlightened and sympathetic about the Jewish Question. From my cosmopolitan standpoint it is a question that ought not to exist.

H. G. Wells, *Experiment in Autobiography* (London, 1934), p. 353

INTRODUCTION

Whereas John Buchan and Rudyard Kipling privileged 'race' within the sphere of Empire, the fiction, drama and social criticism of George Bernard Shaw and H. G. Wells offered a vision of the world which understood semitic racial difference in terms of an ordered 'scientific' socialism. As part of a radical anti-capitalist tradition, late Victorian constructions of 'the Jew' were a potent symbol of capitalist disorder. Instead of the Arnoldian 'cultural' transfiguration of individual Jews, a socialist rationalism was predicated on, among much else, the disappearance of all forms of Jewish particularity. By imagining the transcendence of Jewish racial difference, the 'socialism of fools' (as it became known) also associated the universalized 'Jew' with the emerging utopian world order. Jews, in this way, were at the heart of socialist expectations concerning the radical transformation of society which, in contradictory fashion, also encompassed definitions of Judaism as being irredeemably capitalist.

This structual ambivalence was articulated in a wide variety of texts by the 'socialist' authors, George Bernard Shaw and H. G. Wells, who both utilized extensively a semitic discourse in their

94

literature and journalism. Shaw, in particular, was to represent Jews equivocally as both the embodiment of a Hebraic liberal capitalism as well as the most revolutionary of 'races'. His paradoxical construction of a Nietzschean 'superman' – who needed to evolve biologically beyond 'this world' to bring about fundamental social changes – was positioned in opposition to 'the Jew' as the embodiment of worldly man. Semitic representations were pointedly transient in Shaw's fiction and drama because they were deemed to be outside of the evolutionary Life Force. And yet, Shaw's 'Jews' often had a considerable dramatic impact as a necessary counter to the supra-worldly 'superman'. H. G. Wells, in contrast to Shaw's ambivalent self-identification with 'the Jew', was to 'scientifically' apply the logic of Shaw's belief in the eugenic evolution of mankind. In a rationally ordered society, Jewish racial difference was a phenomenon that must be eliminated along with other 'inferior races'. By assimilating into 'mankind' Jews were nonetheless capable, in Wells's utopian social criticism, of prefiguring a socialist world state. But, in contrast to his utopian writing, Wells's fiction invariably constructed semitic racial difference as the embodiment of a disorderly capitalist plutocracy. During the inter-war years Shaw and Wells were both, for the most part, to associate 'the Jew' not with the progressive evolution of society but with the regressive forces that were preventing its rational development.

GEORGE BERNARD SHAW: SUPERMAN AND JEW

In his foreword to *An Unsocial Socialist* (1884), written in 1930, Shaw describes his novel's 'original design' as being 'only the first chapter of a vast work depicting capitalist society in dissolution'. The seriousness of this 'design' can be gauged from the fact that, at the same time as completing this work, Shaw was reading a French translation of Marx's *Das Kapital* in the British Library reading room. A recent convert to the 'religion' of socialism, Shaw joined the Fabians in 1884, the year in which his novel was published, after being courted by H. M. Hyndman's Social Democratic Federation which he had also seriously considered joining. Shaw's 1930 foreword also claimed that the 'opinions' of the novel's eponymous hero, Sidney Trefusis, 'anticipated those of the real Lenin' and it is not surprising in this context that it has been described as 'the first

notable British Socialist novel', although R. F. Dietrich, in particular, has argued against this 'Leninistic' interpretation.[1]

An Unsocial Socialist, the last and best of Shaw's five 'novels of his
nonage', was originally entitled *The Heartless Man* largely because of
Trefusis's 'heartless' treatment of Henrietta Jansenius, his first wife,
whom he had impetuously eloped with. By the second chapter,
however, Trefusis ends his marriage of five weeks so that he can
'return to my old lonely ascetic hermit life' (11). He justifies this
decision later on in the novel by telling Henrietta that the 'first
condition of work for me is your absence' (77). Henrietta is the
daughter of John Jansenius, a Jewish banker, and is represented in
familiar Orientalist terms by Shaw to reinforce her role as a 'luxurious
creature' (10) whose exotic beauty is so distracting for Trefusis that
it makes it impossible for him to carry out the higher task of 'Socialist
propagandism' (11):

> [Henrietta] was of the olive complexion, with a sharp profile: dark eyes with
> long lashes; narrow mouth with delicately sensuous lips; small head, feet,
> and hands, with long taper fingers; lithe and very slender figure moving
> with serpent-like grace. Oriental taste was displayed in the colors of her
> costume, which [was] ... decorated with a profusion of gold bangles. (9)

In stark contrast to Madame Max Goesler, whose racial otherness
prevented her from marrying into a conventional English family,
Henrietta's 'serpent-like' exoticism does not preclude her, in a
pleasing Shavian paradox, from representing the height of con-
ventionality.[2] This is made clear in an extraordinary chapter in *An
Unsocial Socialist* where Trefusis accounts for his father's capitalist
wealth and power by explaining to Henrietta Marx's theory of
'surplus value' (259) which justifies Trefusis's overriding need to
'liberate those Manchester labourers who were my father's slaves'
(76). In response to Trefusis's 'Socialist propagandism', Henrietta
offers him a 'long idyll' where she would 'dress as a dairymaid, and
have a little pail to carry milk in ... [and] housekeep for you' (77). It
is precisely this sentimental obfuscation of life's harsh economic

---

[1] David Smith, *Socialist Propaganda in the Twentieth-Century British Novel* (London, 1978) p. 3
and, for an opposing viewpoint, R. F. Dietrich, *Portrait of the Artist as a Young Superman: A
Study of Shaw's Novels* (Gainesville, 1969) p. 168 and pp. 150–74. See also Michael Holroyd,
Bernard Shaw: The Search for Love (London, 1988) p. 131 for this period of Shaw's life. I will
be referring to the Virago Modern Classics edition of *An Unsocial Socialist* (London, 1980)
introduced by Holroyd which includes Shaw's 1930 Foreword to the novel.

[2] See chapter 2 for a discussion of Madame Max Goesler in these terms and Rana Kabbani,
Europe's Myths of Orient (London, 1986) for nineteenth-century Oriental exoticism.

realities that makes Henrietta such a threat to Trefusis's socialism. Shaw's description of Henrietta's father especially reinforces the dangers of complacently conforming to society's Hebraic norms:

Mr. Jansenius was a man of imposing presence, not yet in his fiftieth year ... His handsome aquiline nose and keen dark eyes betrayed his Jewish origins, of which he was ashamed. Those who did not know this naturally believed that he was proud of it, and were at a loss to account for his permitting his children to be educated as Christians. Well instructed in business and subject to no emotion outside the love of family, respectability, comfort and money, he had maintained the capital inherited from his father, and made it breed new capital in the usual way ... [H]e had the satisfaction of being at once a wealthy citizen and a public benefactor, rich in comforts and easy in conscience. (13)

Jansenius's 'love of the family, respectability, comfort and money' clearly corresponds to the ideal liberal representation of the acculturated Jew, even to the extent that Jansenius educates his children 'as Christians'. That Jansenius has 'no emotion' outside of this worldly bourgeois sphere and is 'easy in conscience' about 'breeding new capital' indicates the extent to which the socialist Trefusis must overcome the anarchic capitalist system as represented by Jansenius and his daughter. By embodying a 'dissolute' capitalist system Jansenius points, most importantly, to a widespread socialist conflation of an 'anti-capitalism' with an 'anti-semitism' which was dubbed, in the 1890s, the 'socialism of fools'. Karl Marx's influential pamphlet, 'On the Jewish Question' (1843), had long since argued that 'emancipation from haggling and from money, that is practical real Judaism, would be the same as the self-emancipation of our age'. If Judaism is synonymous with capitalism, then the disappearance of Judaism is considered to be the equivalent of mankind's 'self-emancipation'.[3] Here is one of the earliest and most revealing accounts of the reactionary potential that was supposed by many socialists to be contained within Judaism.

Shaw would have been familiar with a specifically late Victorian version of the 'socialism of fools' which was a commonplace in

[3] August Bebel, a leader of the German Social Democratic Party, first identified the 'socialism of fools' in a long speech to his party in 1893. For an exhaustive treatment of this history see Robert Wistrich, *Socialism and the Jews* (Oxford, 1982) and Jacob Katz, *From Prejudice to Destruction: Anti-Semitism, 1700–1933*, chapters 9 and 13. Karl Marx's 'On the Jewish Question' is cited in Wistrich, pp. 27–8 and is discussed in detail in Julius Carlebach, *Karl Marx and the Radical Critique of Judaism* (Oxford, 1980) and Stephen Greenblatt's stimulating 'Marlowe, Marx, and Anti-Semitism', *Critical Inquiry* (Winter, 1978), 291–307.

socialist and radical circles of the 1890s. The stereotypical association
between Jewishness and an innate materialism was reflected, for
instance, in an essay on 'The Jewish Community' (1889) by the
Fabian Beatrice Webb who argued, in much the same terms as Shaw,
that the 'Jewish immigrant' was the embodiment of Ricardo's *homo
economicus* who 'ignores all social obligations' outside of the 'main-
tenance of his own family'. The radical J. A. Hobson, in his *Problems
of Poverty* (1891), also echoed this account of the 'Jewish Community'
by describing the immigrant Jew as 'a terrible competitor' because
his behaviour is 'the nearest approach to the ideal "economic" man,
the "fittest" person to survive in trade competition. Admirable in
domestic morality and an orderly citizen, he is almost devoid of social
morality'. Even the socialist novelist Margaret Harkness, who lived
in the East End of London and staunchly defended the rights of
Jewish immigrants, utilized this semitic discourse. In her *In Darkest
London* (1889), she was to maintain, for instance, that compared to
'the down-trodden Gentiles' Jews knew 'how to grow rich. [They]
leave the East End to settle in Bayswater'.[4] Such was the supposed
innate ability of 'the Jew' to 'get on'.

These widespread associations between Jews and capitalism made
Jansenius and his daughter potent symbols of the overly Hebraic
liberal society that Trefusis was to reject. It is in this racialized
context that Trefusis's callous attitude to Henrietta's death can be
understood: 'she had a warm room and a luxurious bed to die in ...
Plenty of people are starving and freezing today that we have the
means to die fashionably' (126). The distaste aroused by this episode
resulted in Shaw's 'Letter to the Author' in the book's second edition
where 'Trefusis' defended himself from the accusation of being a
'heartless brute' (255). But, as *Man and Superman* was later to make
clear, the fierce antagonism that Trefusis had towards Jansenius –
'I thought you loved Hetty, but I see that you only love your feelings
and your respectability' (130) – is part of the wider Darwinian
struggle between Jansenius as a semitic *homo capitalisticus* and the
ordered evolutionary Life Force of socialism. Published in the same
year as Hobson's *Problems of Poverty*, George Meredith's influential

---

[4] Beatrice Webb and J. A. Hobson are discussed in Colin Holmes, *Anti-Semitism in British
Society, 1876–1939* (London, 1979) p. 20 and chapter 5 and Edmund Silberner, 'British
Socialism and the Jews', *Historia Judaica* 14 (1952), 36 and 27–52. Margaret Harkness is
cited in William J. Fishman, *East End 1888* (London, 1988) p. 161. See also, in this context,
P. D. Colbenson, 'British Socialism and Anti-Semitism, 1884–1914', unpublished Ph.D
thesis, Georgia State University (1977).

anti-capitalist *One of Our Conquerors* (1891) was particularly compelling in its vision of the 'Dominant Jew' as an 'anarchic' consequence of a pseudo-Darwinian 'Law of the stronger':

– Ay, but brain beats muscle, and what if the Jew should prove to have superior power of brain? A dreaded hypothesis! Why, then you see the insurgent Saxon sea-men...in the criminal box: and presently the Jew smoking a giant regalia cigar on a balcony giving view of a gallows-tree. But we will try that: on our side to back a native pugnacity, is morality, humanity, fraternity – nature's rights, aha! and who withstands them? on his, a troop of mercenaries![5]

Many popular novels followed Meredith and constructed a future world ruled over by a 'Jewish aristocracy' which, in the words of one of these novels, was a 'triumphant proof of the survival of the fittest'. Meredith would also have been familiar with an indigenous 'socialism of fools' from his fifty-year long friendship with H. M. Hyndman. In his book *Commercial Crises of the Nineteenth Century* (1892), Hyndman thought that the financial crisis of 1890 – an important reference point for *One of Our Conquerors* – was caused by 'German Jews [who] held the leading place in nearly every great Continental city'.[6] But whereas Hyndman's journal *Justice* in the 1890s was to utilize a crude semitic discourse to argue that an 'Imperialist Judaism' was the reason for the British intervention in Southern Africa, Shaw began to question and play with the binary opposition between 'socialism' and 'Judaism'. In the last page of *An Unsocial Socialist*, for instance, Trefusis meets Jansenius after a long absence and asks:

'Have you ever made up your mind, Jansenius, whether I am an unusually honest man, or one of the worst products of the social organization I spend all my energy assailing – an infernal scoundrel, in short?' (253)

The interconnectedness between the bereaved Jansenius and the 'monstrous' (125) Trefusis at the novel's denouement clearly points

---

[5] George Meredith, *One of Our Conquerors*, ed. Margaret Harris, University of Queensland Press edition (Queensland, 1975), p. 9. Further references to this edition will be in the body of the text. Richard Newby, 'George Meredith and the *Ipswich Journal*', *Forum* 28 (Winter 1987), 37 and *passim* discusses an earlier aspect of Meredith's construction of 'the Jew'.

[6] Jack Lindsay, *George Meredith: His Life and Work* (London, 1956) p. 298 cites Hyndman and J. A. Garrard, *The English and Immigration 1880–1910* (Oxford, 1971) p. 9 and p. 18 argues that social Darwinism 'provided a major part of the intellectual framework' for the debate surrounding mass Jewish immigration into Britain. For examples of the use of these theories in popular fiction to justify Jewish 'dominance' see Lucy Kane-Clifford, *Mr. Keith's Crime* (London, 1885) p. 20 and, especially, Ignatius Donnelly, *Caesar's Column* (London, 1890).

to a 'higher' synthesis between opposites which is prefigured in
Culture and Anarchy and more fully worked out in *Man and Superman*.[7]
Given their common backgrounds as recipients of inherited wealth
and Trefusis's short-lived marriage to Henrietta, the complicity
between Jansenius and Trefusis is worth emphasizing. This shared
destiny is reinforced by Trefusis's eventual marriage to Agatha
Wylie, Jansenius's seventeen-year-old ward, which also points to the
paradoxical Shavian requirement that Trefusis be a part of Jansenius's Hebraic capitalist world in order to fulfil his role as the
Christ-like 'saviour of mankind' (104). The necessary complicity of
Shavian virtue with calculation and deceit was to become a central
feature, in Shaw's Edwardian plays, of the dramatization of his
evolutionary socialism. Shaw, in particular, recognized at an early
stage that he needed 'the Jew' in order to articulate exactly those
forces which had to be transfigured in the future. In turning to *Man
and Superman*, it will be possible to see the extent to which Shaw's
radical transfiguration of capitalist society has an important semitic
dimension which is carried over, especially, from *An Unsocial Socialist*.[8]

Beatrice Webb's diary entry was the first recorded response to *Man
and Superman: A Comedy and Philosophy* (1903). Her description of its
form as a 'play which is not a play; but only a combination of essay,
treatise, interlude, lyric' remains a useful starting point for any
consideration of this work. The complex relations between Shaw's
comedy and philosophy mean that the reader is constantly aware of
the implosive possibilities within *Man and Superman*. Webb maintained
that all of these 'different forms' expressed a 'central idea' within
Shaw's work, but such certainty might well have been a result of the
mischievous polemicist in *The Revolutionist's Handbook*.[9] This 'treatise',
written as an addendum to *Man and Superman*, articulates Shaw's
evolutionary socialism and his eugenic construction of social progress.
But the dominant voice in this 'handbook' is John Tanner, Shaw's
unreliable Superman:

---

[7] J. L. Wisenthal, *The Marriage of Contraries: Bernard Shaw's Middle Plays* (Cambridge, Mass.,
   1974) pp. 8–12 for the argument that Shaw's plays often contain a range of oppositions
   which are encompassed dialectically in a higher synthesis.
[8] Margery Morgan, *The Shavian Playground: An Exploration of the Art of George Bernard Shaw*
   (London, 1972) p. 14 and *passim* for this reading of Shaw. See also Dietrich, *Portrait of the
   Artist*, pp. 54–70.
[9] Wisenthal, *The Marriage of Contraries*, pp. 22–4 cites Webb and discusses the form of *Man and
   Superman* in the light of this quotation. I will be referring to the Penguin edition of *Man and
   Superman* (London, 1981) in the body of this work.

The only fundamental and possible Socialism is the socialization of the selective breeding of Man: in other terms, of human evolution. We must eliminate the Yahoo, or his vote will wreck the commonwealth. (245)

Tanner's problematic advocacy of 'evolving' Man into Superman was echoed in a controversial talk to the Eugenic Education Society in March 1910 where Shaw claimed with inexact irony that 'a part of eugenic politics would finally land us in an extensive use of the lethal chamber. A great many people have to be put out of existence simply because it wastes other people's time to look after them'. Such eugenic theories of social and racial engineering, which were taken up by H. G. Wells, were reflected in Beatrice Webb's reaction in her diary to the 'central idea' of 'human breeding' in *Man and Superman*. This 'idea', she argued, was a subject that the Fabians 'cannot touch' even though she thought it was 'the most important of all questions, this breeding of the right sort of man'.[10] Tanner similarly states in his *The Revolutionist's Handbook* that the evolutionary Life Force entailed the replacement of 'man by the superman' which is the 'only hope' for humanity (244). In the context of a socially and biologically ordered future world of socialism, Tanner invokes Caesar, Cromwell and Napoleon as great world leaders who, by refusing to change the 'nature' of man, left the world essentially unchanged. To cap this point Tanner maintains that:

Even the Jews, who, from Moses to Marx to Lassalle, have inspired all the revolutions, have had to confess that, after all, the dog will return to his vomit and the sow that has washed to her wallowing in the mire; and we may as well make up our minds that Man will return to his idols and his cupidities, in spite of all 'movements' and all revolutions until his nature is changed. (234)

Tanner's representation of Jews as unchanging and essentially a part of the material world, relates to Ibsen's construction of the Jewish Messiah as being outside of the ideal synthesis of the 'spirit' and the 'flesh' in Act Three of *Emperor and Galilean* (1873). In this passage, which Shaw quoted at length in his *The Quintessence of Ibsenism* (1891), Julian argues that the 'Messiah of the two empires, the spirit and the world' was 'not the Jews' Messiah'. In a 1909 interview with the Russian Hebrew playwright, Reuben Brainin, entitled 'Superman and Jew', Shaw was to reinforce this perception of Jews as worldly 'messiahs' who 'play a big part in all revolutionary movements' but,

[10] G. R. Searle, *Eugenics and Politics in Britain 1900–1914* (Leiden, 1976) cites Webb and Shaw.

at the same time, fail to make the leap into a higher synthesis and thus remain aloof from the 'new race, a race of supermen'.[11] Shaw was to dramatize this simultaneous radical and reactionary doubleness in 'the Jew' in *Man and Superman*.

The inability of even *bona fide* 'Jewish revolutionaries' to transcend their own 'nature' as 'Jews' and evolve into a 'new race', meant that Shaw was able to construct 'the Jew' as a sign of the limits of a confused worldliness which remained untransformed by the Life Force. This use of a semitic discourse, however, resulted in Shaw's ambivalent representation of Jews as a 'race' which encompass both 'all the revolutions' as well as humanity's incapacity for authentic revolutionary change. Nothing fundamentally was altered, Tanner maintains, by the Puritan revolutionaries who were 'inflamed by the masterpieces of Jewish revolutionary literature' (234). In a lecture on 'Ruskin's Politics' (1919), Shaw was to single out the uselessness, among others, of Karl Marx's 'invective' when compared to Ruskin: 'Karl Marx was a Jew who had, like Jeremiah, a great power of invective. ... Yet when you read these invectives of Marx ... somehow or other you feel that Ruskin beats them hollow'. Unsurprisingly, in terms of this construction of 'the Jew', Mendoza becomes the symbolic opposite of the 'superman' John Tanner in the third act of *Man and Superman* in much the same way that Trefusis and Jansenius are ideologically opposed in *An Unsocial Socialist*. Trefusis has been rightly described by Margery Morgan as 'the first of Shaw's Don Juan figures' who prefigures Tanner in *Man and Superman*. I would go further and argue that the semitic Jansenius is also the prototype of Mendoza in the same play and, with the anachronistic Victorian Liberalism of Erskine in *An Unsocial Socialist* anticipating Roebuck Ramsden in *Man and Superman*, there are extensive parallels between these two texts.[12]

---

[11] *Jewish Chronicle*, 5 February 1909, p. 20. I have used the Penguin edition of *The Quintessence of Ibsenism* which is collected in Shaw's *Major Critical Essays* (London, 1986) pp. 78–9. For an important discussion of this passage see Wisenthal, *The Marriage of Contraries*, pp. 1–4 and his introduction to *Shaw and Ibsen: Bernard Shaw's 'Quintessence of Ibsenism' and Related Writings*, ed. J. L. Wisenthal (Toronto, 1979). George Meredith in his *The Tragic Comedians* (1880), p. 20, also emphasized this doubleness in his fictionalized portrayal of Ferdinand Lassalle – the German-Jewish leader of the revolutionary Social Democrats in Germany – as both a racialized 'Jew' and as part of a messianic 'new order of god-like men'.

[12] 'Ruskin's Politics' (1919) is anthologized in Stanley Weintraub (ed.), *Bernard Shaw's Nondramatic Literary Criticism* (Lincoln, 1972) p. 193. See also Dietrich, *Portrait of the Artist*, *passim* for an exhaustive treatment of these parallels and Morgan, *The Shavian Playground*, p. 13.

Apart from the textual connection between *Man and Superman* and *An Unsocial Socialist*, the immediate catalyst for the semitic discourse in *Man and Superman* stems from Shaw's reaction to the use of the 'socialism of fools' by H. M. Hyndman's British Social Democratic Federation during the Boer War. Hyndman, in particular, wrote to Shaw in April 1900 in a bid to persuade him to end the Fabian Society's officially neutral stance on the Boer War and form a united socialist front against the war. In his opening letter to Shaw on this subject, Hyndman referred to 'the whole series of blackguardian acts resorted to by Chamberlain, Milner, Rhodes and the German Jews ... ' and, following up this letter, Hyndman told Shaw that 'these big Jew capitalists want to reduce the cost of living [in South Africa] at the expense of the miners, White and Black'. Shaw, significantly, replied to Hyndman with distancing irony that he preferred 'your wretched Barnatos and Rothschilds' to the 'prurient, self righteous and racially arrogant Boers'. A few weeks after this exchange, in May 1900, Shaw wrote in Robert Blatchford's *The Clarion* that 'few socialists seem to share my scruples' with regard to an unqualified support of the South African Boers: 'with most of us it is "Down with equality! Down with Federation! Down with the Jews!"'[13]

Shaw's refusal to conform to Hyndman's crude 'socialism of fools' is echoed in *Man and Superman* when a 'rowdy social-democrat' turns against Mendoza telling him that 'You ain't no Christian. Youre a Sheeny, you are' (112). The ironic use of Hyndman as a 'model' for Tanner in part confirms the binary opposition in *The Revolutionist's Handbook* between Superman and Jew. At the same time, the ever-playful Shaw recognizes the ambivalence inherent in the 'socialism of fools' which can also associate the disappearance of 'Judaism' with the attainment of a messianic new age of socialism. Shaw thus explodes Hyndman's blunt distinction between 'socialism' and 'the Jews' when, at the beginning of Act Three of *Man and Superman*, Mendoza and Tanner first meet and immediately become mirror-images of each other.[14] In a sparkling opening exchange,

---

[13] Shaw's correspondence to H. M. Hyndman dated 13 and 28 April 1900 and his article in *The Clarion* are quoted in Colbenson, 'British Socialism and Anti-Semitism', pp. 370–1 and p. 373. Seven years later in the *Jewish Chronicle*, 20 December 1907, p. 18, Shaw was to quip that 'during the Boer War it was much more advisable to be a Jew than a typical Englishman. All typical Englishmen were on the side of the Boers. All the Jews were on the side of the British, except the declared revolutionary Jews'.

[14] Louis Crompton, *Shaw the Dramatist* (Lincoln, 1969) pp. 82–3 makes out a case for Hyndman as a 'model' for Tanner in *Man and Superman*. The ambivalence of the 'socialism of fools' can be seen, for instance, in the case of Charles Fourier, an early French utopian Socialist, who

the stylized dialogue of Mendoza and Tanner represents an interrelatedness similar to that of Roeback Ramsden and Tanner in Act One or Trefusis and Jansenius at the end of *An Unsocial Socialist*:

MENDOZA: § [*Posing loftily*] I am a brigand: I live by robbing the rich.
TANNER: [*Promptly*] I am a gentleman: I live by robbing the poor. Shake hands. (114)

Margery Morgan has long since argued that this initial exchange indicates the extent to which Mendoza's band of brigands 'caricatures capitalist society' which is dramatized by the top-hats worn by the revolutionaries of Mendoza's 'parliament', a costume that was more commonly employed by Shaw as the 'badge of capitalist respectability'.[15] The brigands are, after all, first encountered in the middle of a stultifying three-day political debate on the question: 'Have Anarchists or Social Democrats the most political courage?' which indicates the fractious and sterile nature of revolutionary socialism. It is the inability of this version of socialism to confront the reality of the evolutionary Life Force that meant that the brigand's revolutionary posturing – which was not unlike the politics of Hyndman's Social Democratic Federation – was depicted by Shaw as a form of romantic obfuscation which, in effect, helped capitalist society to continue. Mendoza, with his '*Mephistophelean affectation*' and '*imposing*' presence (110), embodies the dangerous unreality of revolutionary socialism.[16] This can be seen especially in Mendoza's initial representation as a mock-Disraelian hero whose impassioned Zionism and rousing oratory unites the rancorous social democrats. After being called a 'Sheeny' by the 'rowdy social-democrat' Mendoza replies with '*crushing magnanimity*':

Katz, *From Prejudice to Destruction*, p. 122 has noted represented 'the Jew' as both an 'unproductive and deceitful' capitalist who had, simultaneously, 'a pioneering role in carrying through [a] social programme'.

[15] Morgan, *The Shavian Playground*, p. 117 and Alfred Turco, *Shaw's Moral Vision: The Self and Salvation* (Ithaca, 1976) p. 148 discusses usefully the ironic 'implied equivalence between Jack [Tanner] and his *bête noire*' Roebuck Ramsden in terms that clearly prefigure the 'implied equivalence' between Mendoza and Tanner.

[16] A. M. Gibbs, *The Art and Mind of Shaw: Essays in Criticism* (London, 1983), pp. 131–3, cautiously discusses *Man and Superman* in terms of Shaw's Fabian politics. In his *Essays in Fabian Socialism*, pp. 129–130 Shaw, significantly, argues that the Tories secretly sponsored Hyndman's Marxist SDF in the 1885 General Election to serve unwittingly reactionary interests.

My friend: *I* am the exception to all rules. It is true that I have the honour to be a Jew; and when the Zionists need a leader to reassemble our race on its historic soil of Palestine, Mendoza will not be the last to volunteer [*sympathetic applause* – Hear, Hear, &c.]. But I am not a slave to any superstition. I have swallowed all the formulas, even that of Socialism; though, in a sense, once a Socialist, always a Socialist. (112)

The qualification of Mendoza's racial particularism – 'I am not a slave to any superstition' – and his rejection of all of the 'formulas' is, nonetheless, still a product of his 'Jewish' romantic individualism which is epitomized by his overly sentimental love for Louisa Straker. Even though Tanner mocks Shaw's 'evolutionary' Fabianism for its 'respectability' in *The Revolutionist's Handbook*, it is clear from Shaw's writing in general that he was vehemently opposed to a revolutionary socialism whose other-worldly idealism was deemed to be outside of the Life Force.[17] Mendoza's 'revolutionary' autobiography, in particular, exemplifies the materialistic life-denying forces which are obfuscated by his romantic illusions. After being rejected by Louisa, Mendoza recalls his time in America:

In America I went out west and fell in with a man who was wanted by the police for holding up trains. It was he who had the idea of holding up motor cars in the South of Europe: a welcome idea to a desperate and disappointed man. He gave me some valuable introductions to capitalists of the right sort. I formed a syndicate; and the present enterprise is the result. I became leader, as the Jew always becomes leader, by his brains and imagination. (119)

Anticipating his role as the Devil in the dream sequence which quickly follows this speech, Mendoza becomes the 'leader' of this world precisely because he cannot transcend his evolutionary 'nature' as a 'Jew'. Mendoza's Jewishness, in other words, signifies the all-important limits of worldly achievement. Shaw plays with the indeterminacy and inclusiveness of 'the Jew' to represent Mendoza as a 'socialist', 'cosmopolitan' (117), 'capitalist' and 'Zionist' but, at the same time, ambivalently emphasizes Mendoza's lack of material transcendence which is embodied in his racial particularism. Thus, by the fourth act of the play, the 'financier of [the] brigands' (192) is discovered to be the plutocratic Hector Malone senior and Tanner deems Mendoza's 'principles' to be 'thoroughly commercial'

17 For a discussion of Shaw's politics in these terms see Stephen Ingle, *Socialist Thought in Imaginative Literature* (London, 1979) pp. 108–14.

(192). Tanner manages to 'dispose' of Malone by introducing him to
Mendoza, and they are last seen as 'two brigands together' (197)
discussing the worth of 'Mendoza, Limited' (197). Both figures, at
this rather didactic point in the play, are firmly identified with the
regressive forces which Tanner attempts to transcend by his marriage
to Ann Whitefield. The reduction of Mendoza's maverick individualism to a 'thoroughly commercial' fixed identity in the last
pages of the play is signified by Malone's description of him as
'Mendoza, Limited': 'a mine, or a steamboat line, or a bank, or a
patent article' (192). Mendoza's untransfigured materialism is
anticipated elsewhere in *Man and Superman* by Shaw's exclusivist
construction of his racial difference. Act Three had already provided
an extraordinary limiting set of reasons for Mendoza's failure to
marry Louisa Straker:

TANNER: And did she respond to your love?
MENDOZA: Should I be here if she did? She objected to marrying a
    Jew.
TANNER: On religious grounds?
MENDOZA: No: she was a freethinker. She said that every Jew considers in
    his heart that English people are dirty in their habits.
TANNER: [*surprised*] Dirty!
MENDOZA: It shewed her extraordinary knowledge of the world; for it was
    undoubtedly true. Our elaborate sanitary code make us unduly
    contemptuous of the Gentile. (118)

To be sure, Mendoza's racial fixity is expressed in terms of a
characteristically Shavian paradox, but Louisa soon reinforces the
exclusivity of this construction of Mendoza's Jewishness by suggesting
that he marry a 'barmaid named Rebecca Lazarus' (119). The name
'Lazarus' was first used by Shaw in his novel *Love Among the Artists*
(1881) when a 'Mrs Cohen' uses the stage name 'Miss Lafitte', a
'Gentile abbreviation of Lazarus'. For all of his semitic 'pride
of race' Mendoza, rather like Miss Lafitte, tells Louisa's brother
that he 'would give everything I possess to be an Englishman'
(119). In his interview with Reuben Brainin, Shaw similarly argued
that he had not 'noticed any signs of Jews in England adapting
themselves to their environment in recent years' although Shaw, as
an 'Irishman', thought that in Edwardian England 'one gets popular by pluming oneself on one's nationality'.[18] The inability of

---

[18] 'Superman and Jew', *Jewish Chronicle*, 5 February 1909, 20. I owe the reference to *Love
    Among the Artists* (London, 1881), pp. 112–13, to Stanley Weintraub.

Jews to transcend their own 'nationality' is reinforced in *The Revolutionist's Handbook* where both the plot of *An Unsocial Socialist* and Mendoza's infatuation with Louisa are implicitly referred to:

... the son a robust, cheerful, eupeptic British country squire, with the tastes and range of his class, and of a clever, imaginative, intellectual, highly civilized Jewess, might be very superior to both his parents; but it is not likely that the Jewess would find the squire an interesting companion, or his habits, his friends, his place and mode of life congenial to her. Therefore marriage, whilst it is made an indispensable condition of mating, will delay the advent of the Superman as effectually as Property, and will be modified by the impulse towards him just as effectually. (219)

J. L. Wisenthal has read this passage as an example of a progressive 'union' between opposites – the 'philistine' and 'intellectual acuteness' – which, he argues, prefigures the eugenically sound marriage between Ann and Tanner.[19] But Tanner here surely assumes that a marriage between an anonymous 'British country squire' and a 'civilized Jewess' would, by definition, 'delay the advent of the Superman as effectually as Property' because it represents a disorderly and unscientific evolution. Just as 'Property' disguises the real relations between people and eschews the evolutionary Life Force, the 'wrong' kind of marriage opposes a planned 'socialized' future. Trefusis's short-lived marriage to Henrietta illustrates this point as does the rejection of Mendoza by the sufficiently futuristic Louisa Straker. In both cases 'the Jew' signifies exactly those disorderly 'romanticized' forces that are preventing the 'advent of the Superman'.

The binary opposition between the Superman and Jew is made explicit in the play's dream sequence 'Don Juan in Hell', which follows Mendoza's unbearably sentimental love-song to Louisa. Here the fundamental differences between Tanner and Mendoza – reimagined as Don Juan and the Devil – are emphasized by Shaw's construction of Heaven and Hell as merely a matter of 'temperament' (137). Hell, in these terms, is 'the home of the unreal and of the seekers of happiness' compared to Heaven which is 'the home of the masters of reality' (139). In Hell 'you have nothing to do but amuse yourself'. Romantics like Mendoza or Henrietta become deluded with 'joy, love, happiness and beauty' (133–4) and thus eschew

---

[19] Wisenthal, *The Marriage of Contraries*, p. 51.

'Life: the force that ever strives to attain greater power of contemplating itself' (141). Because the Devil cannot 'conceive something better than [himself]' (165), he naturally becomes the 'leader of the best society' in a Hell which 'is a city much like Seville' (126–7). 'Hell' is thus the place where the Devil tempts man away from his 'great central purpose' which is the 'breeding of the race: ay, breeding it to new heights now deemed superhuman', a purpose which the forces of evil hide 'in a mephitic cloud of love and romance' (160). While such distinctions relate 'Don Juan in Hell' directly to the eugenics of *The Revolutionist's Handbook*, Tanner's dream-vision is immediately undermined in the conscious world. Dona Ana's rather programmatic conversion to the Life Force: 'I believe in the Life to Come. [*Crying to the universe*] A father! a father for the Superman!' (173) contrasts starkly with Ann's amusing dismissal of the 'Life Force' as the 'Life Guards' (203) in the last act of the play. By giving the Devil the final devastating critique of Don Juan – 'Beware the pursuit of the Superhuman: it leads to an indiscriminate contempt for the Human' (171) – Shaw points to the anxiety in his construction of an other-worldly Superman at the expense of Man. This tension is exemplified in the structural split between Don Juan's unreal ideals and Tanner's comic reality.[20] As well as signifying the limits of worldly transformation, Mendoza as the Devil, most importantly, also articulates the boundaries of Shaw's own transfiguring ideals.

Immediately after the dream-vision has opened up a 'philo-sophical' gulf between Don Juan and the Devil, Tanner saves Mendoza's brigand's from the Spanish police and, in so doing, describes Mendoza as the only man on his journey 'capable of reasonable conversation' (177). This act of complicity, which is greeted by Mendoza with a '*Mephistophelean smile*', points to the contradictory necessity for the Hebraic forces of this world (which Mendoza and Ann exemplify) to be allied to the Hellenic Superman. In Tanner's dream, Don Juan explains that the universality of the Life Force only makes sense if it transcends issues of class and nationality as seen in his example of a couple who are:

[U]tter strangers to one another, speaking different languages, differing in race and color, in age and disposition, with no bond between them but a

---

[20] Turco, *Shaw's Moral Vision*, p. 170 and chapter 5 and Dietrich, *Portrait of the Artist*, pp. 54–64 are a good account of this Shavian anxiety.

possibility of the fecundity for the sake of which the Life Force throws them into one another's arms at the exchange of a glance. (161)

But, in reality, Mendoza's racial difference signifies his failure to transcend his materialist and romanticized 'nature' and become a part of the Life Force. Nonetheless, because Shaw's ideals are conceived in a dream vision that is divorced from the play's conscious world, those like Mendoza who stand in the way of evolutionary progress toward the Superman have a considerable dramatic appeal.[21] This is especially noticeable when Mendoza's playful indeterminacy and comic inclusivity are eventually reduced to a programmatic materialism in the last act of *Man and Superman* where, in general, Shaw's 'philosophy' and 'comedy' become uneasily intertwined. But this inclusion of Mendoza in Act Three only to exclude him in Act Four points to a wider structural ambivalence in Shaw's semitic representations. This can now be seen with reference to his *Major Barbara* (1905).

Major Barbara was the last of a 'group of three plays' which began with *Man and Superman* and *John Bull's Other Island* (1904) and which continued to concern themselves with the duality of opposing forces in relation to the goal of an evolutionary Superman.[22] *Major Barbara*, as many commentators have noted, superficially juxtaposes Barbara with her estranged father, Andrew Undershaft, in a bid to dramatize the Devil's contention in *Man and Superman* that the Life Force can also be the 'force of Death; Man measures his strength by his destructiveness' (143). As Undershaft is an 'unashamed' armaments manufacturer and his daughter an erstwhile member of the Salvation Army, the manichaean contrast between them is obvious enough. But Shaw's achievement in *Major Barbara* is that his play endeavours to break down these over-simple moral oppositions, especially in the trinitarian last act when Undershaft's factory is inherited by Barbara and her fiancé Adolphus Cusins. Shaw is at pains to encompass Undershaft within the evolutionary Life Force because, as Barbara

---

[21] W. S. Smith, *Bernard Shaw and the Life Force* (Pennsylvania, 1982) pp. 38–40 and chapter 2 for this argument.

[22] Turco, *Shaw's Moral Vision*, p. 175 quotes a programme note written in 1915 where Shaw describes *Man and Superman*, *John Bull's Other Island* and *Major Barbara* as 'a group of three plays of exceptional weight and magnitude on which the reputation of the author as a serious dramatist was first established and still mainly rests'. I will be referring to the Penguin edition of *Major Barbara* (London, 1984) and the Bodley Head collected edition of *John Bull's Other Island* (Toronto, 1971).

says, there is 'no wicked side [of life]: life is all one' (151). If God and
the Devil are 'all one', Undershaft is clearly an essential part of the
Life Force.[23]

Undershaft's inclusion within the Life Force does not, however,
apply to his business partner Lazarus, who, although he does not
actually appear on the stage, is an integral presence within Shaw's
text. For one thing, it is Lazarus who generates the crisis of succession
in the play and insists that Undershaft's successor be 'settled one way
or the other' (119). Lazarus's name is particularly associated with
Undershaft when the diabolical nature of Undershaft's power is
emphasized. Stephen reminds us that his Bible was defaced by
another student with the words: 'Son and heir to Undershaft and
Lazarus, Death and Destruction Dealers: address Christendom and
Judea' (55). Lady Britomart significantly echoes her son when she
notes that, as well as making cannons, Lazarus arranges 'war loans
... under cover of giving credit for the cannons'. After this statement,
Undershaft and Lazarus are deemed by Lady Britomart to 'have
Europe under their thumbs' (55). Later on in the play, Undershaft
evokes his partner's name when he recounts to Stephen 'with a touch
of brutality' the reality of the plutocratic power of Undershaft and
Lazarus when compared to the spurious status of the Houses of
Parliament:

I am the government of your country: I, and Lazarus. Do you suppose that
half a dozen amateurs like you, sitting in that foolish gabble shop, can
govern Undershaft and Lazarus? No, my friend: you will do what pays us.
You will make war when it suits us, and keep peace when it doesnt. You will
find out that trade requires certain measures when we have decided on those
measures. When I want anything to keep my dividends up, you will discover
that my want is a national need. (124)

In his preface to *Major Barbara*, Shaw compares Lazarus to Peter
Shirley who, by moralizing his poverty, fails 'the Kantian test' which
results in the 'misery of the world' because 'the great mass of men act
and believe as Peter Shirley' (19). Shaw argues that if the masses,
unlike Lazarus and Shirley, 'acted and believed as Undershaft acts
and believes' the 'immediate result would be a revolution of
incalculable beneficence' (19). Lazarus fails 'the Kantian test'
because, in stark contrast to Undershaft, he denies his considerable

[23] Michael Holroyd, *Bernard Shaw: The Pursuit of Power* (London, 1989), p. 110 and pp. 100–16,
summarizes recent accounts of *Major Barbara* along these lines.

power. Shaw underlines this point after Cusins, as Undershaft's
successor, asks if Lazarus should be consulted about his appointment.
Undershaft's reply to Cusins is significant:

Lazarus is a gentle romantic Jew who cares for nothing but string quartets
and stalls at fashionable theatres. He will be blamed for your rapacity in
money matters, poor fellow! as he has hitherto been blamed for mine. You
are a shark of the first order Euripides. So much the better for the firm! (138)

The relationship between Lazarus and Undershaft is not dissimilar to
that of Mendoza and Malone at the end of *Man and Superman*.
Lazarus, like Mendoza (who was encouraged to marry a 'Rebecca
Lazarus') is a 'romantic Jew' who mystifies his worldly power and
makes it 'unreal' just as Shirley moralizes his poverty. Undershaft,
like Malone before him, understands and articulates his plutocratic
power and is thus able to evolve within the Life Force and be a
potential force for good. Lazarus, on the other hand, remains aloof
from the Life Force and, in an important contrast with Undershaft,
is fundamentally unable to change, conforming to Shaw's definition
of Hell as 'the home of the unreal and of the seekers of happiness'.
With telling irony Lazarus, like the Devil, is literally unable to come
back from the dead. In contrast to Lazarus's Hebraic fixity, Cusins's
Hellenism, combined with Barbara's Christian spiritualism, indicates
the potential transformation of the Life Force as it has been defined
by Undershaft. Because Lazarus is physically absent from the stage,
Shaw makes him the structural embodiment of a 'Jewish' worldly
power which is ultimately irrelevant to the higher organization of
Socialism and is merely 'blamed' for trying to 'romanticize' a
disorderly life-denying capitalism.[24]

The 'blame' attached to Lazarus in *Major Barbara* is reflected in
John Bull's Other Island when Tom Broadbent speaks of the 'modern
hybrids that now monopolize England. Hypocrites, humbugs,
Germans, Jews, Yankees, foreigners, Park Laners, cosmopolitan
riffraff' who belong not to the 'dear old island' but to 'their
confounded new empire' (908). In his 1906 Preface to *John Bull's
Other Island*, Shaw notes that Broadbent is 'out of date' in a 'modern'
England where 'the successful Englishman of today ... often turns out
on investigation to be ... an American, or an Italian, or a Jew' (810).
Shaw goes on to point to the source of the success of these 'foreigners'

---

[24] Wisenthal, *The Marriage of Contraries*, p. 9 is wrong to regard Lazarus as 'insignificant' in
terms of his contrast with Undershaft.

as being a 'freedom from romantic illusions' (810). But this 'freedom' does not prevent 'most English patriotic sentiment' from being written by 'German Jews' (997) as Larry Doyle cynically maintains at the end of the play. In another of his reversals of the dominant representations of England and Ireland, Doyle had earlier identified Ireland with 'the Jews': 'the Almighty gave us brains, and bid us farm them and leave the clay and the worms alone' (964). The mythical association between Ireland and 'the Jews' was taken to its apogee in James Joyce's *Ulysses* (1922). This allegiance is, however, qualified in *John Bull's Other Island* by the universalizing 'Catholicism' (a word associated with the Superman in *Man and Superman*) of Doyle and Father Keegan.[25] The trinity of Broadbent, Doyle and Keegan point to an Ireland of the future which, in its idealized unity of the secular and the divine, transcends a moribund Hebraic modernity.

That Shaw's semitic constructions are outside of a higher progressive synthesis is also an aspect of *The Doctor's Dilemma* (1911) where the wealthy General Practitioner, Leo Schutzmacher, is distinguished from the other doctors in the play by his refusal to give money to the charlatan artist, Louis Dubedat. Schutzmacher justifies himself in a speech that Shaw was to repeat in many other contexts:

... when an Englishman borrows, all he knows or cares is that he wants money; and he'll sign anything to get it, without in the least understanding it, or intending to carry out the agreement if it turns out badly for him. In fact, he thinks you a cad if you ask him to carry it out in such circumstances. Just like the Merchant of Venice, you know. But if a Jew makes an agreement, he means to keep it and expects you to keep it. (131)

In an incident widely believed to have been the catalyst for *The Doctor's Dilemma*, Shaw intervened during a dispute between the British-Jewish novelist Julia Frankau and the well-known sculptor Sir Alfred Gilbert after Gilbert, not unlike Dubedat, refused to complete a commissioned sculpture of Frankau's late husband. Expressing the same sentiments as Schutzmacher, Shaw argues in his letter to Gilbert's 'admirer', Countess Feodora Gleichen, that 'it is the best virtue of the Jew that when he makes an agreement he means it'. It also might not have been a coincidence, in relation to *The Doctor's Dilemma*, that Julia Frankau had previously published a

---

[25] Wisenthal, *The Marriage of Contraries*, p. 99. See also his *Shaw's Sense of History*, (Oxford, 1988), p. 95 for opposing Shavian constructions of Catholicism. For further parallels between Ireland and 'the Jews' see the discussion of *Ulysses* in chapter 6.

novel about a homicidal doctor called *Dr Phillips* (1887). Elsewhere, Shaw repeats Schutzmacher's reading of *The Merchant of Venice* as a testament to 'the Jew's' honest business dealings when compared to the 'sentimental Englishman'.[26] Along with his innate materialism, Schutzmacher panders to the romanticized view of the medical profession by having as his motto 'Cure Guaranteed' (93–4), which is adopted by the murderous Sir Colenso Ridgeon. While Schutzmacher's spurious medical cure-alls are no less dangerous than those of the other doctors in the play, he is distinguished from them as a 'foreign' Jew (131) both in his reaction to Dubedat and in his subsequent exclusion from Ridgeon's decision to kill Dubedat. Schutzmacher's absence from Ridgeon's discussion concerning the moral worth of Dubedat points once again to a wider absence of 'the Jew' from Shaw's construction of the Life Force and the ordered evolution of the Superman. As with Henrietta, Mendoza and Lazarus before him, Schutzmacher is unable to transcend his Hebraic fixity and thus evolve beyond his romanticized worldliness.

By the time of his religious play *Androcles and the Lion* (1912) Shaw, in his Preface, was able to construct Jesus Christ as an evolutionary Superman who, rather like Trefusis, opposed the materialism of a respectable 'established Jewry':

Jesus entered as a man of thirty (Luke says) into the religious life of his time by going to John the Baptist and demanding baptism from him, much as certain well-to-do young gentlemen forty years ago 'joined the Socialists.' As far as established Jewry was concerned, he burnt his boats by this action, and cut himself off from the routine of wealth, respectability, and orthodoxy.[27]

Throughout his Preface to this play Shaw contrasts the universalist world of 'baptism' with the particularist world of 'circumcision' which reinforces the binary opposition between a socialist Jesus and a materialist Jewry or, as he puts it elsewhere in the Preface, 'God and Mammon'. Shaw defines a 'Christian' as someone who 'to this

[26] D. H. Laurence (ed.), *Bernard Shaw: Collected Letters 1898–1910* (London, 1972) pp. 609–11 for Shaw's letter to Countess Feodora Gleichen. See also the *Jewish Chronicle*, 2 June 1911, 26 for Shaw's comments on the *Merchant of Venice* and 'the Jew's business ability and honesty' and see my 'The Other Self: Anglo-Jewish Fiction and the Representation of Jews in England, 1875–1905' in David Cesarani (ed.), *The Making of Modern Anglo-Jewry* (Oxford, 1990), pp. 97–111, for an account of Julia Frankau's *Dr Phillips* (1887).
[27] Wisenthal, *Shaw's Sense of History*, chapter 5, is an excellent discussion of Shaw's use of 'present history' in his plays. See also Holroyd, *The Pursuit of Power*, pp. 282–9 for a discussion of *Androcles and the Lion* in this context. I have referred to volume IV of the Bodley Head edition of *Androcles and the Lion* (London, 1972) p. 480.

day' is 'in religion a Jew initiated in baptism instead of circumcision'
(483) and, at the same time, points to the need to 'make Christ a
Christian' and 'melt the Jew out of him' (487). According to Shaw,
Paul 'had no intention of surrendering his Judaism to the new moral
world ... of Communism and Jesuism [sic]' which he compares 'in
our own time' (548) to Karl Marx's failure to transcend his own
Jewishness. Shaw, therefore, needs to include semitic difference, as a
representation of the disorderly racial and economic evolution of
contemporary society, so that 'the Jew' can be excluded or 'baptised'
in the 'new era' of an ordered and scientific socialism. But, this
semitic discourse, which signifies those worldly forces that needed to
be transcended by the Superman, made Shaw's Jewish representations peculiarly ambivalent. Even when racially constructed 'Jews'
such as Christ, Paul or Marx brought about a worldly revolution,
they still could not transcend their disorderly Jewish 'nature'. Shaw's
radically divided view of historical progress meant that he could
construct 'the Jew' to represent both the greatest possible progress of
'mankind' as well as the ultimate limitations of such progress because
'Jews' do not, by definition, encompass a 'biologically' ordered
future.[28]

By situating the semitic 'other' at the indeterminate point at which
he would wish to transform 'mankind', Shaw, because of his ever-
present doubts at the possibilities of such a transformation, was to
identify ambivalently with the protean 'Jew' as an embodiment of
this confusion. In a letter written in 1917, Shaw began playing with
the idea that 'the Irish were the lost tribes of Izrael [sic]' and this
parallel came to its imaginative climax in *Back to Methuselah* (1921),
which was given its first public performance, coincidentally, a year
later when Joyce's *Ulysses* (making similar comparisons) was published. In the 'Tragedy of an Elderly Gentleman', the fourth part of
the *Back to Methuselah* cycle, the 'Elderly Gentleman' elaborates in a
long speech on the historic Irish claim to the 'city of Jerusalem, on the
ground that they were the lost tribes of Israel'. Regaining their 'lost
prestige' the 'Irish', in a form of mock-Zionism, march on Jerusalem
and force 'the Jews' to abandon the city and 'redistribute themselves
throughout Europe'. After Palestine proves to be barren, 'the Irish'
eventually flee to England and 'vanish from human knowledge'. In

---

[28] For Shaw's radically divided view of history see Wisenthal's *Shaw and History*, and *The
Marriage of Contraries*, p. 42 which usefully postulates a Shavian distinction between 'human
history' which is 'cyclical' and 'biological evolution' which is 'purposeful and progressive'.

similar fashion, 'the dispersed Jews [disappear] lest they should be sent back to Palestine': 'Since then the world, bereft of its Jews and Irish, has been a tame dull place'. 'The Irish', like 'the Jews', have lost 'all of their political faculties... except that of nationalist agitation' and the 'Elderly Gentleman's' comic parable against the false attraction of modern nationalism applies equally to both peoples whom Shaw regarded as 'oppressed but never conquered'. In *Arthur and the Acetone*, a three-act playlet published posthumously, Shaw went on to further debunk Jewish national aspirations in terms of Irish history by describing Palestine as 'another Ulster'.[29] Such were the dangers inherent in any form of Jewish 'national' identification.

Although his post-war sense of chaos and disorder was often tempered with a doctrinaire optimism, the apocalyptic mood of Shaw's *Heartbreak House* (1919) and *Back to Methuselah* dominated much of his writing during the inter-war years. Writing in this mood Shaw, in his later plays, both stressed the pernicious nature of non-universal racial, national or religious particularisms and continued, with added stridency, to suggest 'eugenic' means of ending such differences. His Preface to *On the Rocks* (1933), in this regard, was to state blandly that 'extermination must be put on a scientific basis if it is ever to be carried out humanely and apologetically as well as thoroughly' (574). Shaw, just as problematically, was to apply this Edwardian eugenicism to the rise of Nazi Germany. In a letter to Beatrice Webb in 1938, Shaw declared that:

We ought to tackle the Jewish question by admitting the right of States to make eugenic experiments by weeding out any strains that they think undesirable, but insisting that they should do it as humanely as they can afford to, and not shock civilization by such misdemeanors as the expulsion and robbery of Einstein.[30]

Shaw's letter, rather worryingly, constructs Jews as a potentially 'undesirable' 'strain' who might, at any time, be thought to be

---

[29] I have referred to volume v of the Bodley Head *Collected Plays with Their Prefaces*, ed. D. H. Laurence, for *Back to Methuselah* (London, 1972) pp. 509–10. *Arthur and the Acetone* has been collected in Shaw's *Complete Plays with Prefaces* (New York, 1963) and is his most concise critique of the Zionist movement in the inter-war years. For Shaw's change of perspective on Zionism see Joseph Leftwich, 'Some Side-Lights on Bernard Shaw: The Great Dramatist's Attitude to Jews and Judaism', *South African Jewish Times*, 15 December 1950. Further references to Shaw's plays and prefaces written in the inter-war years will be to the Bodley Head edition and will be cited in the body of the text.

[30] D. H. Laurence (ed.), *Bernard Shaw: Collected Letters 1926–1950* (London, 1988) p. 493 for Shaw's letter to Beatrice Webb.

outside of established nation-states. In a letter to Siegfried Trebitsch, his friend and German translator of long standing, Shaw, after returning from a trip to Germany in May 1933, expresses a temptation to bring 'all my guns to bear on Hitler's stupid mistake in trying to make political capital out of the Judenhetze'. But, in a note attached to this letter, he instead argues that 'the Germans had as much right to exclude non-Germans from governmental posts as the Americans to reserve the presidency for Americans, but [I] insisted [to the German press] that displaced Jews should be compensated and not driven out penniless by hounding the mob to attack them'. The assumption, in this letter, that German-Jews are, by definition, 'non-Germans' points to an inherent racialized exclusivism at the heart of Shaw's perception of the 'Jewish question'. At the same time, in August 1938, Shaw was to write to *The Observer* complaining that their Berlin correspondent had described Trebitsch as a 'Jew':

Herr Trebitsch is an uncircumcised and baptised Lutheran German who has never, as far as I know, set foot in a synagogue in his life, [and who is] married to a lady of unquestioned Christian authenticity. He may have a Jewish ancestor; but which of us has not; ... every person now living must be descended not only from Adam and Eve, but from everyone who was alive in the days of Abraham, including Abraham himself. Christianity has absorbed many millions of Jews since it was founded by a Jew; and it has very completely absorbed Siegfried Trebitsch. The observing circumcised Jew from the Ghetto may still present a problem to Gentile States; but an absorbed Jew presents no problem at all, and must be classed as a citizen of the State under which he was born. It is really misleading to call Herr Trebitsch a Jew in any separate sense.[31]

This is Shaw at his most ambivalently inclusivist relying on the opposition between 'observing' Jews who 'may still present a problem to Gentile States' and assimilated or 'absorbed' Jews whom Shaw would wish to see 'classed as a citizen of the State under which [they were] born'. This distinction could operate with merely unpleasant consequences for British Jewry in the context of a liberal democracy, but was to be tragically inappropriate when applied to Nazi Germany. With understandable naïveté, given these essentially late Victorian assumptions, Shaw was to argue that 'nothing should be said about concentration camps, because it was we who invented

[31] Laurence, *Bernard Shaw: Collected Letters 1926–1950*, p. 336, contains Shaw's letter to Siegfried Trebitsch. For a more detailed account of Shaw's relationship with Trebitsch see Samuel Weiss (ed.), *Bernard Shaw's Letters to Siegfried Trebitsch* (Stanford, 1986).

them'. Even after expressing 'disgust' at the 'lynchings' at Bergen-Belsen death camp after the War, he was to maintain that 'Belsen was obviously produced by the breakdown of the military command ... the result is always the same more or less'.[32] Such bland certainty clearly throws into relief the staggeringly inapt discourse through which the octogenarian Shaw articulated his views on the War.

Shaw's time-bound vocabulary, however inappropriate, did also mean that his pronounced 'Irish' self-identification with 'the Jews', a theme taken from *John Bull's Other Island*, was to continue during the inter-war period. This sense of affinity was especially reflected in the letter to *The Observer* where he laid claim to everyone having a 'Jewish ancestor' and being descended from 'Abraham'. Shaw's self-identification with the descendants of Abraham also meant that he was to stress the need for Jews, among other 'races', to inter-marry with their supposed racial 'opposite'. The integration of 'East with West' and 'Black with White' was a major Shavian theme in plays such as *The Simpleton of the Unexpected Isles* (1934), *The Millionairess* (1935) and, his last full-length play, *The Buoyant Billions: A Comedy of No Manners* (1947). This motif was given a specifically semitic context in an unpublished typescript entitled 'Further Meditations on Shaw's *Geneva*' where he wished to 'teach Herr Hitler that the vigor of his nation and ours is due to the fact that we are nations of arrant mongrels'. Shaw goes on to hope that Hitler will 'follow my advice and not only invite the Jews back to Germany but make it punishable incest for a Jew to marry anyone but an Aryan'. Wisenthal has read this passage as a culmination of the Shavian 'marriage of contraries' which he traces throughout Shaw's 'middle plays'. But this is to once again underestimate the ambivalence, continued from the Edwardian period, caused by Shaw operating within a semitic discourse which continues to differentiate between 'Jews' and 'Aryans', among others, as racial 'opposites'.[33]

---

[32] Laurence, *Bernard Shaw: Collected Letters 1926–1950*, p. 540 and p. 752 for Shaw's letters. As late as *Everybody's Political What's What?* (London, 1944) p. 290 Shaw was to state that 'even Adolf Hitler, whose anti-semite phobia out-does Joshua's anti-Canaanite phobia or the reciprocal rage of the Crusaders and the Saracens, stops short of a general order to kill all the Jewish women and not bother about the men'. See Tony Kushner, *The Persistence of Prejudice: Antisemitism in British Society During the Second World War* (Manchester, 1989) for the impact of 'liberal' antisemitism in Britain as opposed to its Nazi counterpart.

[33] Wisenthal, *The Marriage of Contraries*, pp. 6–7 and Gibbs, *The Art and Mind of Shaw*, chapter 15 is a succinct summary of Shaw's later plays in these terms and *Bernard Shaw: Collected Plays with their Prefaces*, VII, (London, 1974) pp. 172–6 contains Shaw's 'Further Meditations on Shaw's "Geneva"'.

In *Geneva* (1939), his most explicit play about the 'Jewish question' in the inter-war years, Shaw constructs the unnamed 'Jew' in the play as the opposite of the 'superman' Hitler-figure called 'Battler' and, at the same time, emphasizes the need for these two opposing forces to merge in a higher synthesis. But in stark contrast to *Man and Superman*, which should be related to *Geneva*, Shaw was writing in an historical period which made his aim of a progressive synthesis between 'the Jew' and a Hitlerite Superman seem, at best, wildly optimistic. The glaring conflict between Shaw's sanguine evolutionary philosophy and the menacing events leading up to the Second World War certainly accounted for the changes of mood in the six drafts of *Geneva* (which was radically rewritten between 1938 and 1946).[34] Throughout the inter-war years, Shaw was to construct Hitler along with Mussolini and, especially, Stalin as one of a series of 'Great Men' who had the power as individuals to transform mankind. In his 1945 Preface to *Geneva*, Shaw defined 'Great Men' as 'apparent freaks of nature [that] mark not human attainment but human possibility and hope': 'They prove that though we in the mass are only child Yahoos it is possible for creatures built exactly like us, bred from the unions and developed from our seeds, to reach the heights of these towering heads' (41). After his tour of Germany in 1933 Shaw wrote to Trebitsch, a victim of Hitlerite antisemitism, that:

Though I may have expressed the greatest contempt for the Judenhetze I have been the first to applaud Hitler's two great steps as to compulsory labor and the trade unions when the whole British press are denouncing them savagely, exactly as I supported Mussolini when he too was being denounced as the most infamous of usurpers and tyrants.[35]

During the 1930s, Shaw was also to publish celebratory articles concerning Hitler's acquisition of power in Germany describing him, in an article published in 1938, as 'no raging lunatic to deal with. He is a very able ruler, and on most subjects a very sane one. But a man may be very able and still have a bee in his bonnet. Herr Hitler's bee is a phobia against the Jews'. To some extent, these laudatory

---

[34] Gerard Anthony Pilecki, *Shaw's 'Geneva': A Critical Study of the Evolution of the Text in Relation to Shaw's Political Thought and Dramatic Practice* (The Hague, 1965) is a good account of the six drafts of this play and Shaw's constant qualification, in the light of historical changes, of his 'hopeful' evolutionary philosophy.

[35] Laurence, *Bernard Shaw: Collected Letters 1926–1950*, p. 337 for Shaw's letter to Trebitsch.

comments on Hitler were, as Wisenthal states, an example of Shaw's delight in 'assuming unpopular positions in order to attract attention to his utterances and to make his readers think' although, clearly, this argument does not apply to Shaw's private correspondence (particulary with victims of Nazi Germany). Nonetheless, when Shaw describes himself in a radio talk in 1940 as a 'National Socialist before Mr Hitler was born' one cannot discount the element of deliberate provocation in his public pronouncements. But simply to dismiss Shaw's manifold statements on Hitler (in his journalism and the Prefaces to his plays), as the attention-seeking provocations of an octogenarian playwright, is to do a disservice to the Shavian philosophy which lay behind these statements.[36] The importance of this philosophy was underlined by Shaw when, in the third version of *Geneva*, written at the end of 1938, he added a major speech by Battler to reinforce his status as a product, rather like the diabolical Undershaft, of the Life Force:

My support is no dead Jew, but a mighty movement in the history of the world. Impelled by it I have stretched out my hand and lifted my country from the gutter into which you and your allies were trampling it, and made it once more the terror of Europe, though the danger is in your own guilty souls and not any malice of mine. And mark you, the vision does not stop at my frontiers, nor at any frontier. Do not mistake me: I am no soldier dreaming of military conquests: I am what I am, and have done what I have done, without winning a single battle. Why is this? Because I have snapped my fingers in the face of all your Jewish beliefs and Roman traditions ... You must all come my way, because I march with the times, and march as a pioneer, not as a camp follower. As a pioneer I know that the real obstacle to human progress is the sort of mind that has formed in its infancy by the Jewish Scriptures. That obstacle I must smash through at all costs ... (143)

While this speech projects onto Battler Shaw's hopes for the rational progress of history, it is also undermined in the final version of *Geneva*. Battler's romantic illusions about the all-conquering power of the 'Aryan race' and his general sentimentality – epitomized by his

[36] Wisenthal, *Shaw's Sense of History*, p. 67. For the political and philosophical context of *Geneva* see Pilecki, *Shaw's 'Geneva'*, chapters 3–5. Pilecki also notes that in the early versions of *Geneva* Bombardone criticizes the antisemitic 'bee in Battler's bonnet' (p. 36) and R. F. Rattray, *Bernard Shaw: A Chronicle* (London, 1951) p. 128 cites Shaw as saying that 'It is always necessary to overstate a case startingly to make people sit up and listen and to frighten them into acting on it. I do this habitually and deliberately'. Allan Chappelow, *Shaw: 'The Chucker Out'* (London, 1969) p. 197 and p. 199 cites Shaw's laudatory comments on Hitler which are also repeated in the Preface to *The Millionairess* (1935).

tearful reaction to the death of his dog – makes Battler, as Gerard
Pilecki maintains, a 'superman manqué' or 'travesty of the superman'. *Geneva*, in this sense, needs to be distinguished from Shaw's
journalism at this time which consistently argued that Hitler's
National Socialism was a marked improvement on Britain's corrupt
'plutocracy'. As late as *Everybody's Political What's What?* (1944),
Shaw claimed that Britain was not 'fighting for democracy' in its
War against Nazi Germany as Britain's 'democracy' was 'nothing
but Anglo-Semitic plutocracy' in Adolf Hitler's 'unanswerable
retort' (351).[37] If Hitler had not had a pathological 'phobia' about
'the Jews', and if he had not acquired a Hebraic Messiah complex,
he may, according to Shaw, have helped evolve a more rational
future.

Whereas Undershaft could articulate the diabolical Life Force
with enormous clarity, Hitler/Battler let their minds become
confused by fixating on 'the Jews' who were, at best, a monumental
irrelevance when placed next to the overall progress of mankind. In
Shaw's final version of *Geneva* (which is repeated in the 1945 Preface),
Hitler, to his detriment, has become a 'mad Messiah who, as lord of
the Chosen Race, was destined to establish the Kingdom of God on
earth – a German kingdom of a German God' (35). What is
significant about this dismissal of Hitler as a potential Superman is
the semitic discourse which is utilized to 'understand' his 'pathological antisemitism'. It is precisely because Hitler's National
Socialism has been Hebraized that he is no longer able to contribute
to 'human progress' in general. Echoing Wells's journalism at this
time Shaw, in his *Everybody's Political What's What?*, compares Hitler
with the Biblical Joshua and elaborates on the 'paradox' that Hitler
is, in fact, a 'semitic' figure:

Joshua Hitler, born in comparative poverty into the bitter strife of petty
commerce in which the successful competition of the Jews is specially
dreaded and resented, and for which he is himself unfitted by his gifts, hates
the Jews, and yet is so saturated by his early schooling with the Judaism of
the Bible that he now persecutes the Jews even to extermination just as the

[37] In a similar vein, Chappelow, *Shaw*: '*The Chucker Out*', p. 199 quotes Shaw as arguing in
1940 that '...nine-tenths of what Mr Hitler says is true. Nine-tenths of what Sir Oswald
Mosley says is true. Quite often nine-tenths of what our parliamentary favourites say to
please us is emotional brag, bunk and nonsense.' See also Shaw's 'Notes by the Way', *Time
and Tide*, 12 October 1940 (no. 12) collected in Alfred Turco (ed.), *Shaw: The Neglected Plays*:
The Annual of Bernard Shaw Studies, VII, (Pennsylvania, 1987) pp. 327–8 and Pilecki, *Shaw's
'Geneva'*, pp. 162–3 and chapter 5 for these arguments in Shaw's journalism.

first Joshua persecuted the Canaanites, and is leading his country to ruin not through anti-semitism, but through Bible Semitism with its head turned. (358)[38]

In the Preface to *On the Rocks*, Shaw argues that the Jews of Jerusalem and the Roman Governor had as much right to 'exterminate Jesus' as 'to exterminate the two thieves who perished with him' (588). And, towards the end of the play, Hipney repeats Shaw's own conception of 'Great Men' by calling for 'any Napoleon or Mussolini or Lenin or Chavender that has the stuff in him to take both the people and the spoilers and oppressors by the scruffs of their silly necks...' (719). In this context, Hipney quotes the example of 'the Jews': 'The Jews didnt elect Moses: he just told them what to do and they did it. Look at the way they went wrong the minute his back was turned!' (720). Such was the tenacity of Shaw's semitic discourse that it both accounts for the decline of Hitler as a 'Great Man' and the potential salvation of 'the Jews'.

The Hebraization of Shaw's 'National Socialism' is taken a stage further in *Geneva*, where the dramatic equivalence of all 'Chosen Races', including both 'the Jew' and 'Battler', is an important motif of the Shavian Secretary of the League of Nations. In the earlier unpublished versions of *Geneva*, as Pilecki has shown, Shaw was to especially stress 'the Jew's' sense of his racial superiority and chosenness as a model which Battler, especially, was to emulate. 'The Secretary', as he is known, expresses the play's main theme in the following terms: 'You all come here to push your own countries without the faintest notion of what the League is for; and I have to sit here listening to foreign ministers explaining to me that their countries are the greatest countries in the world and their people God's chosen race' (90). Before this speech, which emphasizes the Hebraic particularism of the national representatives in Geneva, the Secretary had called for 'something higher than nationalism: a genuine political and social Catholicism' (83). At the heart of *Geneva*, in other words, is the binary opposition between a Judaic par-

[38] Pilecki, *Shaw's 'Geneva'*, pp. 94–5 and p. 131 quotes further examples of this 'paradox' but justifies Shaw's belief in Hitler's 'Bible Semitism' with this rather unpleasant apology: 'In the face of the thousands [sic] of Jews who were exterminated under Hitler, Shaw can see only the bitter humour of their being persecuted by a man who had taken their own racist theories to heart.' Wisenthal, *Shaw's Sense of History*, p. 137 argues more convincingly that, for Shaw, 'the present loses its special place in history, and becomes just another point in the historical continuum. This attitude of Shaw's partly (but not entirely) explains some of his notorious remarks about Fascist dictators.'

ticularism and a Catholic universality. It is the attempted transformation of this essentially Hebraic nationalism into the higher
'spirit' of Geneva that starkly replicates the antagonism between
Superman and Jew in *Man and Superman*. But, by this stage in his
writing, Shaw lacked the kind of self-conscious irony which enabled
him to play with these binary oppositions in his earlier work.

By the end of *Geneva* 'the Jew', like Mendoza, is an irredeemable
materialist who is last said to be 'instructing his stockbroker to sell
gilt-edged in any quantity, at any price', which will make him 'a
millionaire until the icecap overtakes him' (158–9) while the world is
on the brink of another war. Shaw, in *Geneva*, was to make 'the Jew's'
sense of racial superiority and untranscendent materialism equivalent
to other forms of rabid nationalism, including that of their Nazi
persecutors. In this play, to say the least, Shaw was to discount the
absolute inability of 'the Jews' in the 1930s to chart their own
'higher' future. By representing materialistic Jews in 1938 as selfishly
making money while the world believed itself to be heading for a
Second World War, as Lawrence Langner pointed out at the time,
Shaw 'lightly dismissed' the extreme powerlessness of Jews in
Germany.[39] Notwithstanding these strictures, *Geneva* still emphasizes
that 'the whole human race must be descended from Abraham'
(136), echoing Shaw's published letters at this time, which once
again points to the potential universality of 'the Jews'. But this
hypothetical inclusiveness by the 1930s was to be increasingly
tenuous. When, in 1933, performances of Shaw's *Too True to be Good*
(1932) were marred in Germany by Nazi taunts of 'Jew Shaw', Shaw
reacted to these taunts with the following letter:

As the Nazis are shouting 'Down with the Jew Shaw' in the German
theatres, and as a protest against the persecution would have much less
value from a Jew, it is necessary for me to emphasize the fact that I am a
Gentile, and an Irish Gentile at that, to clear myself of any suspicion of pro-
Jewish bias. I even claim a pro-Nazi, or at least a pro-Fascist bias, to give
greater weight to my protest. Otherwise I should seem to be only using the
Jew as a stick to beat Hitler, as some of our papers are obviously doing.[40]

[39] Lawrence Langner, *The Magic Curtain* (London, 1951), Appendix 2, contains his letters to
Shaw and Laurence, *Bernard Shaw: Collected Letters 1926–1950*, p. 511 includes Shaw's reply
to Langner where he describes 'the Jew' in *Geneva* as a 'bear speculator'. In *Geneva*, 'the Jew'
is last seen 'instructing his stockbroker to sell gilt-edged in any quantity, at any price' which
will make him 'a millionaire until the icecap overtakes him' (pp. 158 9).

[40] For the letters describing the attacks on the 'Jew Shaw' in Nazi Germany see Laurence,
Bernard Shaw: Collected Letters 1926–1950, pp. 342–3 and pp. 347–8. In this context Shaw also
described himself as a 'Gentile of the Gentiles' as opposed to Langer's ironic rejoinder that

Such were the limits on Shaw's 'Irish' self-identification with 'the Jews'. In the end, Shaw was to represent an all-encompassing Hebraic irrationality as, ultimately, a threat to the rational organization of the world. Even Shaw's playful reworking of this binary opposition meant that the semitic constructions in his literary works were, in the final resort, still estranged from the Life Force as racial 'others' and unreal romantics whose massive worldly presence was a monumental irrelevance. Whether it be the figure of Mendoza in the third act of *Man and Superman*, or Henrietta's ludicrous marriage of five weeks, or Schutzmacher's marginalization in the debate over Dubedat, or Lazarus's structural ambivalence, Shaw's 'Jews' had a peculiarly transient quality which indicated their ultimate insignificance in relation to a future eugenically sound, rationally ordered world state. And yet, the very persistence for over six decades of 'the Jew' in Shaw's texts highlights paradoxically the Shavian need to identify with that which, ideally, needed to be transcended. For this reason, Jews were peculiarly divided in Shaw's work and, not unlike their author, they stood on the sidelines smiling their 'Mephistophelean smile', reminding everyone of the Faustian pact with the Devil which is made when one tries to transform debased 'man' into a Superman. Where Shaw, however, could be playful and complex in constructing Jewish racial difference as a sign of a philosophical and economic materialism, H. G. Wells was not afraid, in both his fiction and journalism, to apply 'scientifically' the logic of this semitic discourse.

H. G. WELLS: TOWARDS THE WORLD STATE

The Shavian opposition between 'the Jew' and the uncertain ideal of the 'Superman' is less ironically articulated in Wells's rather dogmatic view of the world. For Wells, 'the fundamental idea of socialism' was the 'scientific' replacement of 'order by disorder'. In

---

Shaw was himself a 'Jew'. Ironically enough, Shaw's definitions of Jewishness grew increasingly all-embracing in the 1920s and 1930s. See, for instance, his *The Intelligent Woman's Guide to Socialism and Capitalism* (London, 1928) p. 465 where he constructs the nineteenth-century economist Ricardo as a 'Jewish Stockbroker'. In a letter to Matthew Forsyth, with reference to the casting of *The Millionairess*, Shaw was also to argue that a pair of cockney speakers would 'ordinarily be Jews; but you must carefully avoid any suggestion of this at present as it would drag in current politics'. Such was the inevitable political 'problem' caused by *any* form of Jewish representation at this time. For this letter see Laurence, *ibid.*, pp. 444–5.

his *New Worlds for Old: A Plain Account of Modern Socialism* (1908), one of the most influential accounts of Edwardian socialism, Wells argued that 'while Science gathers knowledge, Socialism in an entirely harmonious spirit criticizes and develops a general plan of social life'. The 'rational' planning of society as if it were a 'garden' that needed 'weeding' is made chillingly explicit in Wells's *Anticipations* (1902), a work whose title announces the attempt to chart the impact of 'mechanical and scientific progress on human life and thought'.[41] In the impending world state which is envisaged by Wells in this volume, future citizens of the 'New Republic' will not be 'squeamish ... in facing or inflicting death, because they will have a fuller sense of the potentialities of life than we possess' (300). Like Abraham, Wells argues, the New Republicans will 'have the faith to kill' and will have 'an ideal which will make killing worth the while' which will, in turn, eschew any 'superstitions about death' (300). Thus, in the last three chapters of *Anticipations*, Wells was to advocate, like Shaw, a form of 'positive' eugenics which would enable humankind to rise above the 'brutish level' (300) of their present condition.

The most extreme version of Wells's eugenics is to be found towards the end of *Anticipations* when he was to consider how 'the New Republic [will] treat the inferior races' and concludes that they will be treated 'not as races at all'. In a 'world-state with a common language and common rule ... efficiency will be the test' of citizenship, notwithstanding whether a person is 'white, black, red or brown' (315–16). But Wells was to end on an ominous note when determining the fate of 'those swarms of black, and brown, and dirty-white and yellow people, who do not come into the new needs of efficiency' in the New Republic (317). His conclusion was unequivocal:

Well, the world is a world and not a charitable institution, and I take it that they will have to go. The whole tenor and meaning of the world, as I see it, is that they have to go. So far as they fail to develop sane, vigorous and distinctive personalities for the great world of the future, it is their portion to die out and disappear. (317)

It is in this general context of the 'treatment of inferior races' that Wells points to 'that alleged termite in the civilized woodwork, the

---

[41] Further references to contemporary editions of *New Worlds for Old: A Plain Account of Modern Socialism* (1908) p. 23 and *Anticipations* will be in the body of the text. See also Zygmunt Bauman, *Modernity and Ambivalence* (Oxford, 1991), p. 34 and chapter 1 for a discussion of the Wellsian 'gardening ambitions of the state'.

Jew' and notes that although 'many Jews are intensely vulgar in dress and bearing, materialistic in thought, and cunning and base in method, [they are] no more so than many gentiles' (316). As with the other 'inferior races' Wells, in the New Republic, did not envisage the treatment of Jews as a separate 'race'. 'The Jew' will not be 'abolished' for being racially inferior but only insofar as they are 'parasitic' on the 'social body':

It is said that the Jew is incurably a parasite on the apparatus of credit. If there are parasites on the apparatus of credit, that is a reason for the legislative cleaning of the apparatus of credit, but it is no reason for the special treatment of the Jew. If the Jew has a certain incurable tendency to social parasitism, and we make social parasitism impossible, we shall abolish the Jew, and if he has not, there is no need to abolish the Jew. We are much more likely to find that we have abolished the Caucasian solicitor. (316)

While the other 'inferior races' have a stark choice between 'efficiency' and 'abolition', Wells is more ambivalent in relation to 'the Jews'. In a 'century or so', he argues, Jewish racial 'particularism' will have disappeared and they will 'intermarry with Gentiles, and cease to be a physically distinct element in human affairs'. But such assimilationism is tempered by Wells's hope that 'much of [the Jews'] moral tradition will ... never die' (317). As with the more general ambivalence of the 'socialism of fools', which Shaw especially exploited, Wells was to construct a utopian future in relation to the transcendence of a worldly semitic 'particularism'. Wells's 'kinetic' view of utopia (which was defined as 'a hopeful state, leading to a long ascent of stages'), meant that the ordered scientific evolution of even 'the Jew' was possible in the New Republic and would eradicate the dangers of semitic racial difference while still retaining the Jewish 'moral tradition'.[42] Far from the 'dread or dislike' of 'the Jew' of his Edwardian contemporaries Wells, in this optimistic context, believed that 'the Jew' is:

... a remnant and legacy of medievalism, a sentimentalist, perhaps, but no furtive plotter against the present progress of things. He was the medieval Liberal; his persistent existence gives the lie to Catholic pretensions all through the days of their ascendancy, and to-day he gives the lie to all our yapping 'nationalisms', and sketches in his dispersed sympathies the coming of the world-state. He has never been known to burke a school. (317)

---

[42] Richard Gerber *Utopian Fantasy* (London, 1955) p. 10 discusses Wells's ideal of utopia in these terms. See also Wells's *A Modern Utopia* (London, 1905) chapter 10, 'Race in Utopia'.

The association between the 'dispersed sympathies' of 'the Jews' and the 'coming of the world-state' again points to the inclusivist potential within the 'socialism of fools'. Here, the Jewish diaspora could be constructed as prefiguring a universalist world-state. Such benevolently Judaized visions of the future were anticipated by Samuel Butler's *Erewhon* (1872), a utopian work which had an important influence on Shaw and Wells.[43] Butler, in particular, ironically utilized the mythology of the Second Coming – which related the Jewish return to Palestine with the messianic era – to speculate on whether his utopian Erewhon was made up of the 'lost ten tribes of Israel awaiting the final return to Palestine' (75). In his 'business prospectus' to pay for his trip to Erewhon, Butler's narrator confirms that the '*Erewhonians* are the lost tribes' which is 'of absorbing interest to myself, but it is of a sentimental rather than a commercial value, and business is business' (256). Unlike *Anticipations*, where the assimilation of 'the Jew' into the body politic of the world-state signified Wells's utopian ideals, Butler in *Erewhon* argued that 'none but millionaires possessed the full complement of limbs with which mankind could become fully incorporate' (224). For this reason, as Basil Willey notes, Butler could speak of the Rothschilds as 'the most astonishing organisms the world has ever seen'.[44] This is in stark contrast to Wells's dismissal in *Anticipations* of Jewish particularism along with 'social parasitism' or Stock Exchange 'usury' (144).

What is clear from *Anticipations*, is that Wells's rational 'order' is constructed in opposition to racial difference but that 'the Jews', unlike the other 'inferior races', can be represented as both anticipating the rationality of the 'new world' and as a feature of the irrational present. This ambivalence was also an aspect of the thinking of T. H. Huxley, the foremost champion of Victorian orthodox Darwinism and Wells's scientific mentor, who described the racial indeterminacy of 'the Jew' in the following terms:

Even in the time of the first Caesars the Jew appears to have become for good and evil exactly what he is now – marvellously vigorous and tenacious

---

[43] I will be referring to the Penguin edition of *Erewhon* in the body of the text.

[44] Cited in Basil Willey, *Darwin and Butler* (London, 1960) p. 70. See also Butler's *Alps and Sanctuaries* (London, 1881) chapter 9 for further references to the lost ten tribes of Israel. But Butler's notebooks have a long entry on 'Matthew Arnold on Righteousness' where Butler emphasizes the 'righteousness' of 'the Greeks' as opposed to 'the Jews' and states that he does not 'care twopence whether the Rothschilds went back to Palestine or not' (pp. 103–18).

physically and morally; of an acute and broad intelligence; at its best a noble and gracious embodiment of as high ideal as men ever set before themselves; at its worst, monstrously, shamelessly base and cruel.[45]

It is precisely this Darwinian indeterminacy – which constitutes 'the Jew' as a force for either 'regeneration' or 'degeneration' – that is at play in Wells's fiction and later journalism. Instead of prefiguring the 'coming of the world-state', *New Worlds for Old* speaks of 'the developing British Plutocracy' as being, like the Carthaginian, 'largely Semitic in blood'. This 'inevitable' semitic plutocracy (178) – the opposite of a progressive 'Jewish' internationalism – was to be scrutinized by Wells in his Edwardian novels written immediately after this account of modern socialism.[46]

Tono-Bungay (1909), the most important of Wells's Edwardian novels, especially concerns itself with the recent replacement of a 'distinctively British' (12) aristocracy by an 'alien, unsympathetic and irresponsible' plutocracy (82). Dystopian fears concerning an 'alien' invasion were, in stark contrast to his proclaimed optimism as a prophet of the coming world state, a central feature of Wells's earlier science fiction. The location of these fears in a naturalistic social context in *Tono-Bungay* was anticipated, to some extent, in George Du Maurier's *The Martian* (1897) and Ford's *The Inheritors: An Extravagant Story* (1901). In both of these novels, there is a slippage from a non-human to a semitic 'alien' invader as in Du Maurier's 'vague, mysterious, exotically poetic' Martian-Jewess and the anti-heroine from another 'dimension' in Ford's novel who is ' ... of some race, perhaps Semitic, perhaps Sclav – of some incomprehensible race'.[47] Following on from these novels, George Ponderevo, the hero of *Tono-Bungay*, is quite explicit about the 'semitic' nature of the 'alien' plutocracy that is seen to be threatening 'all that is spacious, dignified, pretentious, and truly conservative in English life ... ' (51).

[45] *The Huxley Papers*, XLVII, 146–7 cited in Charles Blinderman, 'Thomas Henry Huxley on the Jews', *Jewish Social Studies* 25 (1963), 60 and 57–61.
[46] G. R. Searle, *Corruption in British Politics: 1895–1930* (Oxford, 1987), notes especially that the rise of a specifically 'semitic' plutocracy was a common political perception in Edwardian Britain. I will be referring to the Pan Classic edition of *Tono-Bungay* (London, 1978) in the body of the text.
[47] George Du Maurier, *The Martian* (London, 1897) p. 144 and Ford Madox Ford, *The Inheritors: An Extravagant Story* (London, 1901) p. 7. The latter novel also bears the name of Joseph Conrad who contributed the last twenty pages to *The Inheritors* as well as helping revise it. See also Bernard Bergonzi, *The Early H. G. Wells* (Manchester, 1961), Michael Draper, *H. G. Wells* (London, 1987) and J. R. Hammond, *H. G. Wells and the Modern Novel* (London, 1988) for the split between Wells's dystopian imagination and wildly optimistic social thought.

In the opening pages of the novel, George recalls a visit to Bladesover House, where his mother had been the house-keeper, and notes that 'the old shapes, the old attitudes remain, subtly changed and changing still, sheltering strange tenants' (9):

Bladesover House is now let furnished to Sir Reuben Lichtenstein, and has been since old Lady Drew died; ... It was curious to notice then the little differences that had come to things with this substitution. To borrow an image from my mineralogical days, these Jews were not so much a new British gentry as 'pseudomorphous' after the gentry. They are a very clever people, the Jews, but not clever enough to suppress their cleverness. (9)[48]

Soon after this observation, George walks through Bladesover village and an 'old village labourer touched his hat convulsively' (9) as he passed him by. George, however, refrains from asking the labourer whether he still remembers his poor mother as neither his 'uncle or old Lichtenstein' would have been 'man enough to stand being given away like that' (9). The complicity, at this early stage in the novel, between Sir Reuben Lichtenstein and Edward Ponderevo, George's uncle, is worth noting. As well as emphasizing the stark racial 'differences' between a historic Englishness and the 'pseudo-morphous' Jews, Edward's plutocratic history as the inventor of Tono-Bungay, a fraudulent medical cure-all, directly relates him to Lichtenstein. George's repeated emphasis on Bladesover as 'essentially England' (35), specifically points to the 'alien' otherness of the plutocracy which both he and Edward help to promote. After visiting London in his early twenties, George speaks of 'the presence of great new forces, blind forces of invasion, of growth' which are overwhelming the 'system of Bladesover' (81).[49] These invading 'new forces', which are opposed to Bladesover, are embodied for George in the 'smallness' of the Lichtensteins which, on his last visit to Bladesover, had merely 'replaced the large dullness of the old gentry' with a 'more enterprising and intensely undignified variety of stupidity' (51):

These Lichtensteins and their like seem to have no promise in them at all of any fresh vitality for the kingdom. I do not believe in their intelligence or their power – they have nothing new about them at all, nothing creative or

---

[48] 'Pseudomorphous', as defined by the *Oxford English Dictionary*, literally means a 'false or deceptive form; a crystal or other body consisting of one mineral and having the form of another'.

[49] David Lodge, '*Tono-Bungay* and the Condition of England' in Bernard Bergonzi (ed.), *H. G. Wells: A Collection of Critical Essays* (London, 1976) p. 121 and *passim* is a useful account of Wells's novel in these terms.

rejuvenescent, no more than a disorderly instinct of acquisition; and the prevalence of them and their kind is but a phase in the broad slow decay of the great social organism of England. They could not have made Bladesover, they cannot replace it; they just happen to break out over it – saprophytically. (52)

The Lichtensteins, in these terms, ambivalently represent both the false modernity of a 'disorderly' capitalism which is, nonetheless, rooted in their medieval 'instinct of acquisition' and their biological role as 'saprophytes'.[50] There is an obvious contrast between the 'hopeful' futuristic Wells of *Anticipations* – who located 'the Jew' in an ordered, scientifically based utopia – and the ancient newness of the prevailing, parasitic Lichtensteins in *Tono-Bungay*. Far from adumbrating the future, the Lichtensteins are 'but a phase in the broad slow decay in the social organism of England'. When George visits London, which is at the heart of this 'unorganised ... tumorous growth-process' (82), he notes that 'east of Temple Bar' London has 'morbidly expanded, without plan or intention' and has now become 'dark and sinister' moving ominously 'toward the clean, clear assurance of the West End' (81–2). George asks whether the poverty-stricken East Enders will ever 'shape into anything new' or whether they will remain 'cancerous' on the body politic. He goes on to note that 'together with this hypertrophy there is an immigration of elements that have never understood and never will understand the great tradition' (82):

[There are] wedges of foreign settlement embedded in the heart of this yeasty English Expansion. One day I remember wandering eastward out of pure curiosity ... and discovering a shabbily bright foreign quarter, shops displaying Hebrew placards and weird, unfamiliar commodities, and a concourse of bright-eyed, eagle-nosed people talking some incomprehensible gibberish between the shops and the barrows. And soon I became quite familiar with the devious, dirtily-pleasant exoticism of Soho. (82)

In Soho, George gets his 'first inkling of the factor of replacement that is so important in the English and American process' (82). That is, while the 'yeasty English Expansion' might have the potential to turn into something 'new', the 'exotic' Jewish 'immigration' into London's East End complicates England's 'hypertrophy'. Like the

---

[50] Defined by the *Oxford English Dictionary* as 'an organism which lives on decayed matter'. Wells's *Anticipations* (London, 1902) emphasizes the 'medieval' nature of Jewish 'social parasitism'. The influence of Wells's symbolism in *Tono-Bungay* on T. S. Eliot's poetry is discussed in chapter 6.

Lichtensteins, East End Jewish immigrants are supposedly unable to evolve within 'the great [English] tradition'. The foregrounding of these semitic 'foreign' invaders who are destroying England's capacity for rational evolution, a common theme in Edwardian England, comes to its climax when George thinks of 'his uncle's frayed cuff' proudly pointing to a London devoid of its 'old aristocratic dignity' (82).[51] The England that Edward points out is made up of 'actors and actresses, moneylenders and Jews, bold financial adventurers':

A city of Bladesovers, the capital of a kingdom of Bladesovers, all much shaken and many altogether in decay, parasitically occupied, insidiously replaced by alien, unsympathetic and irresponsible elements; – and withal ruling an adventitious and miscellaneous empire of a quarter of this daedal earth. (82–3)

Edward Ponderevo's superimposed 'frayed cuff' on London's 'parasitically occupied' West End highlights the double narrative within *Tono-Bungay*. The novel, up until this point, has used the form of a *bildungsroman* to concentrate on George's shocked account of the alien semitic nature of the 'developing British plutocracy'. For George, Bladesover has thus far provided the 'key' (71) to understanding the modernization of England since the 1870s and the dire 'condition of England' that has made it possible for his uncle to become a millionaire by selling a fraudulent medical cure-all. But, as J. R. Hammond has shown, *Tono-Bungay* is an ironic pastiche of the nineteenth-century *bildungsroman* as, by the end of the novel, George's narrative is far from discovering the 'key' to his uncle's rise to power and Edward is hardly the replacement father that George seeks.[52]

Part of *Tono-Bungay*'s ability to self-consciously parody itself and question its own authorial voice, can be found in its juxtaposition of the semitic discourse in the novel's opening chapters with the story of Edward Ponderevo who, at the height of his degeneration, becomes

---

[51] Garrard, *The English and Immigration, passim* notes the general fear of eastern European Jewish immigrants 'swamping' East London and Ford Madox Ford, *The Spirit of the People: An Analysis of the English Mind* (London, 1907) p. 45 and *Memories and Impressions* (New York, 1911) p. 171 speaks, in similar terms to Wells, of 'an east of London population which is small, dark, vigorous and gentle. In the natural course of things this eastern population will rise in scale, will cross London, will besiege the palaces, will attain to the very frames of mind of these tranquil giants'. See H. R. Huntley, *The Alien Protagonist of Ford Madox Ford* (Michigan, 1970) pp. 13–14 and p. 30 for these references.

[52] Hammond, *H. G. Wells and the Modern Novel*, chapter 6 suggestively argues that *Tono-Bungay* is a modernist pastiche of the nineteenth-century *bildungsroman* and John Batchelor, *H. G. Wells* (Cambridge, 1985), pp. 68–80 also discusses the double narrative in *Tono-Bungay*.

an increasingly Hebraic figure. After moving into the Elizabethan Lady Grove, George meets the local vicar who, as an 'Oxford man', is described as 'one of the Greeks of our plutocratic empire' who maintains a 'general air of accommodation to the new order of things' (211). George explains that although he and Edward were known to the vicar as 'pill vendors', a far worse 'strain on a good man's tact' would have arisen if 'some polygamous Indian rajah ... or some Jew with an inherited expression of contempt' had moved into Lady Grove. In the circumstances, the vicar was prepared to accept the 'substitution of new lords for old' who were at least 'English and neither Dissenters nor Socialists' (211). This disavowal of the Ponderevo's racial otherness is soon displaced by Edward's growing obsession with colonizing Palestine which is described as 'the most romantic quest in history' (210), an ironic rewriting of Edward's often repeated belief in the 'Romance of Commerce'. In a parody of Butler's *Erewhon*, Edward is associated not with the messianic return to Palestine of the 'lost tribes of Israel' but with the commercial exploitation of the Holy Land via the Suez Canal:

'There's that Palestine canal affair. Marvellous idea! Suppose we take that up, suppose we let ourselves in for it, us and others, and run that water sluice from the Mediterranean into the Dead Sea Valley – think of the difference it will make! All the desert blooming like a rose, Jericho lost for ever, all the Holy Places under water. ... Very likely destroy Christianity.' (220)

Popular Edwardian novelists such as Guy Thorne and Marie Corelli had long since associated the rise of a dominant 'Jewish plutocracy' with the end of Christianity. Thorne's *When it was Dark* (1903), his best-selling novel, was explicitly constructed around this theme. There is an oblique reference to this popular tradition in Edward's megalomanical threat to 'destroy Christianity' and in George's belief that Tono-Bungay had become a false form of Christian 'salvation' (167).[53] Edward Ponderevo whose deranged vision of the future – 'Cuttin' canals ... Making tunnels ... New countries ... New centres ... Zzzz ... Finance ... Not only Palestine' (220) – is not unlike the 'semitic' dystopia imagined in the first chapter of Meredith's *One of*

---

[53] Batchelor, *H. G. Wells*, pp. 72–3 and Draper, *H. G. Wells*, pp. 93–7 refer to the religious imagery in *Tono-Bungay*. For a discussion of Guy Thorne in these terms see Gina Mitchell, 'In His Image: A Study of Jews in the Literature of Guy Thorne', *Patterns of Prejudice* 9 (January–February, 1975), 18–24. Relevant novels by Marie Corelli include *Barabbas: A Dream of the World's Tragedy* (London, 1894) and *Temporal Power: A Study in Supremacy* (London, 1902).

Our Conquerors where the capitalist Radnor fears his 'absorption into Jewry' (10). As well as being a Hebraic plutocrat, Edward's name, 'fatty' appearance and lechery were also an unflattering tribute to Edward the Seventh whose 'Court Jews' and general decadence were themselves taken as an indictment of the Judaized Edwardian age.[54] Thus, the racialized discourse in the opening chapters of *Tono-Bungay* concerning the Lichtensteins is transformed into a wider cultural discourse concerning the Hebraization of the emblematic Edward Ponderevo.

After the premature bankruptcy of Edward's financial empire, George's narrative increasingly lacks any rational Bladesoverian 'key' to understand the world. At the same time as George dons the Wellsian mantle and becomes a science-based socialist, the Quap episode intervenes to finally demonstrate the irrationality and 'waste' of the present. The overwhelming anarchy which is caused by a semitic plutocracy is signified in this episode by the captain of the *Maud Mary*, a 'Roumanian Jew' who learnt 'English out of a book' and wanted to impress George with 'the notion that he was a gentleman of good family'. This drives George 'into a reluctant and uncongenial patriotism' because of the captain's 'everlasting carping about things English' (271). But, as well as racializing the unnamed captain, Wells also constructs him as a moral check on George's outlandish plans to transport the 'cancerous' Quap back to England (in a bid to save the 'Tono-Bungay' empire). Thus, the 'Roumanian Jew' embodies both the racial exclusivism and moral inclusivism of Wells's semitic discourse. For this reason, the captain repeats many of George's own criticisms with regard to a 'plutocratic' England which is dominated by the 'bourgeoisie' (272). Nonetheless, in a reference to the crude xenophobia of such 'sailor's tales' as Kipling's 'Bread Upon the Waters' (1898), George overcomes the captain's apprehensions by appealing to the 'taciturn' first mate who nods 'darkly and almost forbiddingly' when George notes that the captain is a

---

[54] Batchelor, *H. G. Wells*, p. 78 and Searle, *Corruption in British Politics*, pp. 21–4 has many contemporary references to the 'semitized' monarch. See also Anthony Allfrey, *Edward VII and his Jewish Court* (London, 1991). The Wellsian hero Richard Remington, in Wells's *The New Machiavelli* (1911), Penguin edition (London, 1978), p. 103 significantly described Meredith's *One of Our Conquerors* (1891) as 'one of the books that has made me' which he 'forced' upon his 'companions'. For the general impact of Meredith on Edwardian Fabianism see Graham Wallas, *Human Nature in Politics* (London, 1916) and Ian Britain, *Fabianism and Culture: A Study in British Socialism and the Arts* (Cambridge, 1982). Further references to *The New Machiavelli* will be in the body of the text.

'Roumanian Jew'. George does not say another word to the first mate after this and comments that 'more would have been too much. The thing was said. But from that time forth I knew that I could depend on him and that he and I were friends' (273). The Englishness of George and the first mate especially holds sway and undermines the captain's Jewish 'moral' authority which Wells had previously located in a future world state. That the 'Roumanian Jew' is meant to be a parody of Joseph Conrad, moreover, points to a set of authentic values that supposedly opposed Conrad's foreignness.[55]

After the Quap episode, which echoes the racialized opening chapters of *Tono-Bungay*, Wells ends on a playful note of extreme ambivalence. In a calculated break with the nineteenth-century 'Condition of England' novel, George is finally unable to control or order the 'crumbling and confusion, ... change and seemingly aimless swelling' (328–9) of contemporary England. Instead of offering any 'truths' based on his 'scientific' training, George eventually succumbs to a Hebraized England by building a 'destroyer'. By the end of *Tono-Bungay*, he can only be distinguished from the Lichtensteins and 'their kind' by his self-consciousness at his betrayal of 'England'. In stark contrast to Wells's more didactic later fiction, the last chapters of *Tono-Bungay* do not easily differentiate between the 'scientific' Wellsian persona and the racial 'other'.

The binary opposition between a futuristic 'semitic' England and scientific progress, which Wells plays with in *Tono-Bungay*, was first adumbrated in his *The Invisible Man* (1897). Towards the end of this book Griffin, the over-reaching scientist who becomes the invisible man, is confronted by his Polish-Jewish landlord at the point when he is just about to turn himself invisible. Wearing 'German silver spectacles', a 'long grey coat' and 'greasy slippers', the unnamed landlord becomes suspicious of Griffin and, with his two 'polyglot' Yiddish-speaking stepsons, threatens to evict him. Rather like the 'Roumanian Jew' in the Quap episode of *Tono-Bungay*, Wells's most unEnglish of landlords represents a moral check on Griffin's frightening scientific advance. By setting fire to his landlord's house, Griffin also finally cuts himself off from society as a whole. But, if Wells's Polish-Jewish landlord is a peculiarly ambivalent representation of society's limits on scientific advance, Griffin's self-destructive

---

[55] Hammond, *H. G. Wells and the Modern Novel*, pp. 90–5 offers an important rereading of the 'Quap episode' in *Tono-Bungay* and Batchelor, *H. G. Wells*, pp. 75–7 discusses the role of Conrad in this episode.

'science' is equally ambiguous.[56] *Tono-Bungay* is predicated on such complexities but, as with Wells's fiction as a whole, the novel is something of a watershed in this regard.

By the time of *Marriage* (1912), a 'discussion novel' designed to show the 'inevitable waste' involved in a marriage of two people who are motivated by conflicting forces, Wells seemed to be less concerned with ambiguity than with juxtaposing symbolic opposites. George Orwell's rather acidic comments that Wells's writings are consistently built around a 'supposed antithesis between the man of science who is working towards a planned world state and the reactionary who is trying to restore a disorderly past' holds true, to a large extent, for Wells's novels after *Tono-Bungay*.[57]

In *Marriage* the 'man of science', Richard Trafford, literally 'fell out of the sky' to save his future wife, Marjorie Pope, from what is later acknowledged as her 'silly upbringing' (215). The excessive Hebraism of her background is particularly emphasized by the pronounced Protestantism of the Vicarage – with its 'Jerusalem lithographs' and 'monogram' prints of the 'Mosaic law' (15–16) – where, as the novel opens, the Pope family are spending their summer holidays. Critics have rightly shown that Wells crudely associates Marjorie's extravagant consumerism with her femininity, but Marjorie is also a product of a peculiarly matriarchal Hebraism. From the beginning of the novel, Marjorie is seen to have succumbed to the seductive influence of the Carmel family which has resulted in her 'mind [being] strung up with Carmel standards' (11). At 'Oxbridge University' we learn that it was Kitty Carmel who taught Marjorie to run up extravagant debts and that, in general, the 'shockingly well off' (7) Carmels had fostered Marjorie's sense of inadequacy at her relative poverty (hence the foolishly expensive train journey which introduces Marjorie) and her 'innate hunger for good fine things' (49). Even as an adult, Marjorie still needs to

---

[56] H. G. Wells, *The Invisible Man* (London, 1897), Fontana edition, (London, 1959) p. 147. Bergonzi, *The Early H. G. Wells*, p. 120 usefully places Griffin in the 'romantic scientist' tradition of Frankenstein and Hammond, *H. G. Wells and the Modern Novel*, p. 20 emphasizes the ambiguity of the name 'Griffin'.

[57] George Orwell, 'Wells, Hitler and the World State', *Horizon* (August, 1941) collected in Sonia Orwell and Ian Angus (eds.), *The Collected Essays, Journalism and Letters of George Orwell* 4 vols. (London, 1970), II p. 169. Both Hammond, *H. G. Wells and the Modern Novel*, and Batchelor, *H. G. Wells*, defend Wells's later fiction from Orwell's criticisms. Wells's description of *Marriage* can be found in the Preface to the Atlantic edition of this novel. It is not insignificant that *Marriage* was the catalyst for the famous debate on the nature of fiction to begin in earnest between Wells and Henry James. I will refer to the Hogarth Press edition of *Marriage* (London, 1986) in the body of the text.

'impress' the Carmels because of 'their racial trick of acute appraisement' which meant that they 'were only to be won by the very highest quality all round' (160). This 'racial' dimension to Marjorie's unrestrained consumerism, which destroys Trafford's career as an exemplary research scientist, is central to the novel. As with Edward Ponderevo, Marjorie is seen to have acquiesced to the excessive Hebraism of the age – which needs to be transfigured by a 'higher' set of values – and which is promoted especially by plutocratic 'Jews'. It is not insignificant that when Trafford leaps out of the sky to save Marjorie from a disastrous marriage, he is in an aeroplane with his friend Sir Rupert Solomonson. While the aeroplane in Wells's fiction is 'associated with science, courage and freedom', its future import in *Marriage* is symbolically divided between the two opposing worlds of Trafford and Solomonson.[58]

Unlike the Carmels, who are subtly racialized as the novel progresses, Solomonson is 'manifestly a Jew' who, as he lies injured on the ground, is described crudely as a 'square-rigged Jew (you have remarked, of course, that there are square-rigged Jews, whose noses are within bounds, and fore-and-aft Jews, whose noses aren't)' (84). As a result of Marjorie's lavish over-spending, Trafford is forced to sacrifice his scientific research to the commercial interests of Solomonson who suggests that Trafford '"make money" for a brief strenuous time, and then come back [to research] when Marjorie's pride and comfort were secured' (238). Commenting on Solomonson's proposal, Trafford particularly notes the 'enormous gulf between his [own] attitudes towards women and those of... Solomonson' (235). When she stays with the Solomonsons in Geneva, their 'alien' mood is said to be 'closely akin to latent factors in Marjorie's composition' (228). In other words, the disorderly Hebraism of Solomonson, and the other Jewish families in the novel, is displaced onto the perceived irrationality of women in general, as Victoria Glendinning has noted, who are represented by Marjorie. This is, one supposes, the 'reasoning' behind Marjorie's formative attachment to the 'Carmel girls'. Just as women in general refuse to conform to the 'higher' values of scientific order, Jews also follow their own selfish designs and ignore the general good of 'mankind'.[59]

---

[58] Batchelor, *H. G. Wells*, p. 103 and Orwell, 'Wells, Hitler and the World State', both note the importance of the aeroplane in Wells's world-view.

[59] Victoria Glendinning's 'Introduction' to the Hogarth Press edition of *Marriage* includes a feminist reading of Marjorie Pope and Patrick Parrinder, *H. G. Wells* (Edinburgh, 1970) pp. 95–7 makes out a case for the 'spiritual rootlessness' of the Pope family which is perhaps the

After reluctantly joining ranks with Solomonson, Trafford sees before him 'enormous vistas of dark philoprogenitive parents and healthy little Jews and Jewesses... hygienically reared, exquisitely trained and educated' and he comments that 'he wasn't above the normal human vanity of esteeming his own race and type the best, and certain vulgar aspects of what nowadays one calls Eugenics crossed his mind' (234). *The New Machiavelli* (1911), following on from *Anticipations*, had already confirmed this belief in the Eugenic ordering of 'the race' in the guise of Richard Remington, the Wellsian hero, who believed, along with Shaw in *Man and Superman*, that 'every improvement is provisional except the improvement of the race' (306). In *The New Machiavelli*, Wells had represented the Jewish-born Liberal Cabinet Minister, Herbert Samuel, as the 'excessively correct' Lewis who speaks with a '"mandate" from the Country' which is 'sacred to his system of pretences' (225). Remington quickly becomes disillusioned with the Liberal Party and rejects Lewis's 'system of pretences' for a 'practical form of Eugenics' (337). Not unlike Trafford in relation to the 'philoprogenitive' Solomonsons, Remington's vision of a Eugenically ordered future is starkly contrasted in *The New Machiavelli* with Lewis's randomly proliferating cousins:

> Then there was Lewis, further towards Kensington, where his cousins the Solomons and Hartsteins lived, a brilliant representative of his race, able, industrious and invariably uninspired, with a wife a little in revolt against the racial tradition of feminine servitude and inclined to the suffragette point of view. (193)

The main butt of Wells's political satire in *Marriage*, in a continuation of *The New Machiavelli*, is Marjorie's Aunt Plessington's Fabian-like 'Movement' to help relieve poverty. This Movement, Wells emphasizes, is full of well-meaning but ineffectual Jews who once again signify the inadequacy of a liberal Hebraism which does not really get to the root of England's problems: '[Aunt Plessington] had been staying with the Mastersteins, who were keenly interested in [the Movement] and after she had polished off Lady Pletchworth she was to visit Lady Rosenbaum. It was all going swimmingly, these newer English gentry were eager to learn all she had to teach in the art of breaking in the Anglo-Saxon villagers' (53). At times, *Marriage* reads

corollary of their excessive Hebraism. See also Patricia Stubbs, *Women and Fiction: Feminism and the Novel 1880–1920* (Brighton, 1979) pp. 175–194 for the limits of Wells's 'feminism'.

as if England had become almost totally 'semitic', with the luxuriant opulence of Solomonson's Jewish friends creating an Eastern other-world full of 'fine fabrics, agreeable sounds, noiseless unlimited service, and ample untroubled living' which had the Svengali-like 'effect of enchantment' (226) on the Traffords.[60] Trafford tries to maintain a view of the world based on scientific objectivity, which has 'as such no concern with personal consequences', but he finally loses his 'honour as a scientific man' (247) and yields to the ruthless animalistic individualism of Solomonson who believed that:

Civilisation's just a fight ... just as savagery is a fight, and being a wild beast is a fight – only you have paddeder gloves on and there's more rules. We aren't out for everybody, we're out for ourselves – and a few friends perhaps – within limits. It's no good hurrying ahead and pretending civilisation's something else when it isn't. That's where all these Socialists and people come a howler. (243)

At one point in the novel, Solomonson transforms himself into a 'turbaned Oriental' who 'might have come out of a picture by Capaccio' (230) and, when persuading Trafford to join him, Wells observes that 'for all his public school and university training' Solomonson had 'lapsed undisguisedly into the Oriental' and 'squealed' at Trafford (246). Beneath the bourgeois 'sanity of comfort' – which is meant to be the 'unquestioning belief' of the Jewish 'race' (225) – there lies a rudimentary particularism (sig-nified by Solomonson's 'squeal') which threatens, in a beast-like fashion, merely to take care of its own kind. By the end of the novel, Trafford realizes that he has 'wasted' (347) his potential contribution to science and that he has been feminized by Solomonson's materialistic Hebraism:

'I've got into this stupid struggle for winning money ... and I feel like a woman must feel who's made a success of prostitution. I've been prostituted. I feel like some one fallen and diseased. ... Business and prostitution, they're the same thing. All business is a sort of prostitution, all prostitution is a form of business. Why should one sell one's brains any more than one sells one's body?' (297)

After a year in Labrador with Marjorie, away from a degenerate England, Trafford eventually feels that he and his wife might now

---

[60] For the enormous impact of George Du Maurier's *Trilby* (London, 1894) during the turn of the century see L. Edward Purcell, 'Trilby and Trilby-Mania: The Beginning of the Best-Seller System', *Journal of Popular Culture* 11 (Summer 1977), 62–77. Wells read a great deal of popular literature of this kind for his book reviews of the 1890s.

together be able to contribute to the 'salvation' (341) of England by
releasing 'the human spirit from the individualist struggle' (360). In
a reference to the virtues of biblical Jewry, when compared to their
contemporary plutocratic counterparts, Trafford tells Marjorie that
she is 'going to be a non-shopping woman now. You've to come out
of Bond Street, you and your kind, like Israel leaving the Egyptian
flesh-pots' (362). Here, interestingly, the Hebraic moral tradition is
once again evoked to counter the rampant Hebraic individualism
that Wells located in Edwardian England. But this latter tradition
was to be increasingly ineffective in the light of an all-powerful
'semitic plutocracy'.

In the years leading up to the First World War, England was
perceived by Wells as a nation that had grown gradually corrupt.
The 'Marconi Scandal' (1911–14), in particular, was a 'Jewish'
financial scandal which deeply disillusioned Wells in terms of the
prospect of any kind of progress within a liberal consensus. Wells
stated as much in an article on the 'Marconi Scandal' in the *Daily
Mail*, which was republished in pamphlet form as *Liberalism and its
Party: What are we Liberals to do?* (1913). The semitic representations
in his Edwardian novels were not, therefore, a product of 'one
particular Jew who was annoying him during this period' but were
related to this more general disillusionment with a Hebraized
individualistic liberalism. It would thus be wrong simply to dismiss
these representations as a peculiarly 'antisemitic' phase in Wells's
fictional output which had very little to do with the rest of his
oeuvre.[61]

Wells's general sense of a semitic Edwardian plutocracy, which
both Edward Ponderevo and Marjorie Pope succumb to, is not
unlike Marx's identification in his 'On the Jewish Question' of
'Judaism' with 'capitalism'. That the rise of a modern plutocracy is
signified by an alien 'race' needs, however, to be put in the context
of Wells's dismissal of any biological validation of racial categories. In
Marriage, to be sure, Trafford points out with reference to Aunt
Plessington's Movement that those who distinguish between the
'"Anglo-Saxon" and "Teuton" [or] the "white race" and the
"yellow race"' are engaging in the 'cackle of some larger kind of

---

[61] Batchelor, *H. G. Wells*, p. 105 raises the issue of Wells's 'antisemitism' in these terms. The
'Marconi Scandal' will be discussed in detail in chapter 5 of this book. For its effect on Wells
see David Smith, *H. G. Wells: Desperately Mortal* (New Haven, 1986) p. 133 and p. 256 and
Wells's *Liberalism and its Party: What Are We Liberals to Do?* (London, 1913).

hen' (178).[62] Rather like Arnold's indeterminate use of Hebraism, which lies ambivalently between the cultural and the racial, Wells shows that the Hebraization of the Ponderevos and of Marjorie need not be reduced biologically to the Jewish 'race'. By the end of *Marriage*, Marjorie has successfully transcended her semitic predilections, unlike George who has finally capitulated to them at the end of *Tono-Bungay*. Nonetheless, Wells in *Marriage* does point to the racial susceptibility of 'the Jew', as the embodiment of a widespread Hebraism, to pointlessly acquire wealth. Solomonson, for instance, is said to have had 'that explicit alchemy of mind which distils gold from the commerce of the world; ... he accumulated wealth as one grows a beard' (228–9). In *Joan and Peter* (1918), one of Wells's most didactic novels, Joan even speculates that 'all Jews ... ought to grow beards. At least after they are over thirty. They are too dark to shave, and besides there is a sort of indignity about their clean shaven faces. A bearded old Jew can look noble, a moustached old Jew always looks like an imitation of a Norman gentleman done in cheaper material. But that of course was exactly what he was' (320). Joan's simultaneous need to differentiate 'the Jew' and, at the same time, her lack of a racial distinction between 'a moustached old Jew' and a 'Norman gentleman' gives something of the flavour of Wells's ambivalence towards 'the Jews'. This ambivalence is particularly acute in *Joan and Peter* given Peter's previous representations of 'the full peculiarity' of his school-friend Winterbaum. Wells comments:

The differences in form and gesture of the two boys were only the outward and visible signs of profound differences between their imaginations. For example, the heroes of Peter's were wonderful humorous persons, Nobbys and Bungo Peters, and his themes adventures, struggles, quests that left them neither richer or poorer than before in a limitless, undisciplined delightful world, but young Winterbaum's hero was himself, and he thought in terms of achievement and acquisition. (109)

Winterbaum, significantly, regarded himself as 'one of the conquerors of England' (109) which echoes both Meredith's *One of Our Conquerors* and C. F. G. Masterman's not unrelated social category of

---

[62] Wells in works such as *Anticipations, A Modern Utopia*, and *The Outline of History* (London, 1920) consistently denied the efficacy of race-thinking as opposed to the Webbs, whom Wells is parodying in *Marriage*. For an example of the Webbs' race-thinking see J. M. Winter, 'The Webbs and the Non-White World: A Case of Socialist Racialism', *Journal of Contemporary History* 9 (1974), 181–92. I will be referring to contemporary editions of *The Outline of History* and *Joan and Peter* (London, 1918) in the body of the text.

'conqueror' in *The Condition of England* (1909). Wells did not make a straightforward conflation between the broad Arnoldian grouping of 'conqueror' and a biologically determined Jewish 'race'. In *The Wife of Isaac Harman* (1914), for instance, Wells's Isaac Harman is too easily regarded as a 'grasping, sneaking, socially inept and sexually insufficient Jew' when he is not, in fact, marked racially as a 'Jew' in the novel.[63] But this reading is understandable. The name 'Isaac Harman', and his involvement in the Liberal Party, directly relates him to the protaganists of the Marconi Scandal such as Rufus Isaacs (who had previously been portrayed as Lewis in *The New Machiavelli*). Harman is also introduced in terms that relate him directly to Wells's previously unequivocal Jewish representations: 'Sir Isaac was one of those men whom modern England delights to honour, a man of unpretentious acquisitiveness, devoted to business, and distracted by no aesthetic or intellectual interests' (63). His nose, moreover, is 'pointed ... to an extreme efficiency' and he did not possess 'any broader interests than [his] shop' nor did he 'trouble to think about the nation or the race or any deeper mysteries of life' (64). These are statements that were earlier applied to the Lichtensteins or Solomonson. Later on in the novel, Harman's increasingly estranged wife regards herself as a 'captured alien in [Harman's] household – a girl he had taken' (267). For all his sexual 'insufficiency', Harman can still be construed as a sexually rapacious 'alien', a long-standing semitic representation that had been popularized by George du Maurier's *Trilby* (1894).[64] Nonetheless, Wells, in the last resort, does not signify Harman as a 'Jew' but, instead, emphasizes a more generally applicable non-racial Hebraism. Thus, Harman's '"International" organisation' is:

[W]hat we all of us see everywhere about us, the work of the base, energetic mind, raw and untrained, in possession of the keen instruments of civilisation, the peasant mind allied and blended with the Ghetto mind, grasping and acquisitive, clever as a Norman peasant or a Jew pedlar is clever, and beyond that outrageously stupid and ugly. (119)

---

[63] Batchelor, *H. G. Wells*, p. 105 wrongly describes the 'fact' that Sir Isaac Harman is a 'Jew' as being 'crucial' to *The Wife of Isaac Harman*. For the importance of C. F. G. Masterman's *The Condition of England* (London, 1909) to Wells's fiction see Lodge, '*Tono-Bungay* and the Condition of England', and for Meredith see note 42.

[64] Purcell, 'Trilby and Trilby-Mania', pp. 62–77 notes the popular impact of Du Maurier's *Trilby* and see also Edward Bristow, *Prostitution and Prejudice: The Jewish Fight Against White Slavery* (Oxford, 1982) for widespread representations of the sexually rapacious Jewish male at this time.

In *The Outline of History* (1920), Wells was to characterize the early Normans as a racial group who, as they 'grew powerful, discovered themselves [to be] such rapacious and vigorous robbers that they forced the Eastern Emperor and the Pope into a feeble and ineffective alliance against them' (350). It might not be too uncharitable to suspect that the analogy between the 'rapacious and vigorous' Normans of medieval history and the contemporary acquisitive 'semitic plutocracy' was present in *Joan and Peter* and *The Wife of Isaac Harman*. Once again, Wells is concerned with what he perceived as the historical deformation of a moralistic biblical Hebraism into a degenerate capitalist individualism. It is this potential for good or evil within 'the Jews' that Wells was to chart in his 'outline' of history.

Once removed from the darker world of his fiction, as has been seen with reference to *Anticipations*, *The Outline of History* was to make apparent Wells's divided construction of 'the Jews'. In his 'outline' of the role of Judaism in the early Christian era, for instance, Wells argues that: 'The Jewish idea was *and is* a curious combination of theological breadth and an intense racial patriotism. The Jews looked for a special saviour, a Messiah, who was to redeem mankind … and bring the whole world at last under the benevolent but firm Jewish heel' (281). I have emphasized the shift to the present tense in this statement because it is worth noting the contemporary relevance for Wells of his 'history'.[65] Just as Wells in *The Outline of History* was to differentiate in general terms between progressive and reactionary traditions among specific nations and religious groups, he was also to repeatedly distinguish between the 'broad' and 'narrow' Jewish traditions. It is the Sadducees, in this view, who are the carriers of this 'broad' Jewish tradition and who are therefore 'disposed to assimilate themselves … and so share God and his promise with all mankind' (282). In stark contrast to this tradition, the Pharisees are the 'high and narrow Jews, very orthodox … intensely patriotic and exclusive' (282) who eventually 'made a racial hoard of God' (326). Wells ascribes the 'financial and commercial tradition of the Jews' to the 'Semitic' Phoenician peoples (281) and emphasizes throughout *The Outline of History* the world-wide 'religious and educational organizations' which, from the Babylonian Captivity onwards, kept such 'commercial' Jews 'in touch' with each other throughout the world (281). Such statements, represented by Wells as historical fact,

---

[65] There is an important Wellsian parallel here with Shaw's sense of 'present history'. For the latter see note 27.

were to have a particular resonance for Wells's contemporary readers given the popularization of Jewish conspiracy theories in the early 1920s. In this context, Wells was reading back into history his fears concerning a dominant Edwardian 'semitic plutocracy'.

At the same time as constructing this 'narrow' tradition of Jewish individualism, Wells also echoed Shaw's Preface to *Androcles and the Lion*, and noted that the 'Jews of the left', the universalist Sadducees, were disposed to 'assimilate themselves to the Greeks and Hellenized peoples about them' and so 'share God and his promise with all mankind'. The Sadducees were opposed to the particularist Pharisaic Jews of the 'right' who remained 'greedy and exclusive' (282). In comparing the Hebraic and Hellenic traditions, Wells argues that 'the Jews' have merely 'persisted as a people' whereas 'hellenism has become a universal light for mankind' (281). The 'great universal religion of Christianity' (146) is, especially, deemed to have partly liberated 'the Jewish idea' from its racial 'narrowness' and refocused the 'broad' aspects of the Jewish tradition onto humanity as a whole. Such is the contemporary import from this construction of Judaism. As with *Anticipations*, those Jews that physically assimilate are able to transmit the universalist moral tradition of Judaism and those that retain their Jewishness are bigoted, Pharisaic and selfish and persist to this day in this racially particularist form.[66]

As with Shaw, Wells could both associate a universalist tradition of Judaism with a future socialist world-state and represent the wholly assimilated Karl Marx, for instance, in terms of his 'racial Jewish commercialism' (516). But, unlike Shaw in his Prefaces, Wells in *The Outline of History* had some pretensions as a scientific 'historian' (146) who was demonstrating his thesis that there will eventually be 'world-wide political and social unity' (608). If 'the Jew' could signify both a more rational future and, at the same time, a degenerate, contemporary world that was preventing the attainment of that future, Wells, by the inter-war years, was to be much less certain about the utopian possibilities of a universalist 'Jewish' tradition. In *The Research Magnificent* (1915), Wells's spokesman, for instance, gives a meeting of Russian-Jews the choice between financially controlling the whole of Southern Russia or making a 'fresh beginning' for the betterment of world peace. But he is lynched when he tries to force these curiously bestial Jews to give up their

---

[66] Steven Bayme, 'Jewish Leadership and Anti-Semitism in Britain, 1898–1918', unpublished Ph.D thesis, Columbia University (1977), p. 107 usefully discusses Wells in these terms.

financial strangle-hold on Southern Russia. Just before he is assaulted, he tells his Russian-Jewish audience that 'it does not follow that because your race has supreme financial genius that you must always follow its dictates to the exclusion of other considerations'.[67] In the next three decades, Wells was to reinforce this representation of irrational, particularist Jews who have eschewed any possibility of a more enlightened future because of the dictates of their animalistic 'race instincts'.

After the First World War Wells, not unlike Shaw, grew increasingly disillusioned with the belief in the inevitable progress of civilization and continued to repudiate liberal democracy in emphatic terms. This rejection of the very possibility of liberal progress also entailed a darker construction of 'the Jew' as a prevalent symbol of the fruits of contemporary liberalism. There is a radical change, in particular, in Wells's position towards the future of Zionism which he had placed on the side of progress before the War. In a letter written in 1906, he had given qualified support to Zangwill's Jewish Territorial Organization (ITO) stating that: 'the ITO has my sympathy – in the abstract – and the project seems altogether sane and practicable. But it's not my doorstep, and I can offer you neither help nor advice. Your people are rich enough, able enough, and potent enough to save themselves'. By the inter-war years, however, Wells was not as sanguine in his response either to Zangwill's Zionism or the supposed 'potency' of British Jewry. In a series of inter-war texts Wells maintained that, with the Balfour Declaration of 1917, 'Zangwill and the Jewish spokesmen were most elaborately and energetically demonstrating that they cared not a rap for the troubles ... of any other people but their own' or that Zionists take 'no thought for the common danger and common welfare of the race. The rest of the world may go hang. In these matters these Zionists are not showing themselves to be citizens of the world but are behaving like infuriated creditors'. Wells's last major novel *You Can't Be Too Careful* (1941) repeats this argument in a fictional context although during the First World War, as David Smith has shown, Wells was himself urging Zangwill to 'restore a real Judea' and let 'the Jews have Palestine'.[68]

[67] Wells, *The Research Magnificent* (London, 1915) p. 474.
[68] Wells's letter to Israel Zangwill was published in the *Jewish Chronicle*, 30 March 1906, p. 33 under the heading 'Interesting Letters from Distinguished Writers' and Smith, *H. G. Wells: Desperately Mortal*, pp. 230, 236–7, 548 and 550 refers interestingly to Wells's relationship

To gauge the darkness of Wells's construction of 'the Jew' during the inter-war years, one need only compare Wells's *The Shape of Things to Come: The Ultimate Revolution* (1933) with *Anticipations*, his previous work of prediction. Unlike the rational evolution towards a world state in *Anticipations, The Shape of Things to Come* prophesies a World War of twenty-five years duration which began in 1940 and which plunges the world into barbarism. A world state, in this later work, only begins to emerge after a century of turmoil and is primarily in reaction to the forces of evil. In line with this relative pessimism, the dispersion of 'the Jews' does not prefigure a world state in *The Shape of Things to Come* but, instead, Wells argues that in the years leading up to the predicted World War:

It might have been supposed that a people so widely dispersed would have developed a cosmopolitan mentality and formed a convenient linking organization for many world purposes, but their special culture of isolation was so intense that this they neither did nor seemed anxious to attempt. After the World War the orthodox Jews played but a poor part in the early attempts to formulate the Modern State, being far more preoccupied with a dream called Zionism... Only a psycho-analyst could begin to tell for what they wanted this Zionist state. It emphasized their traditional wilful separation from the main body of mankind. It irritated the world against them, subtly and incurably. (298)

This construction, which is repeated throughout Wells's later journalism, contrasts starkly with *Anticipations*. By keeping themselves a 'people apart', Jews are represented in *The Shape of Things to Come* as being a 'perpetual irritant to statesmen, a breach in the collective solidarity everywhere... One could never tell whether a Jew was being a citizen or just a Jew. They married, they traded preferentially. They had their own standards of behaviour. Wherever they abounded their peculiarities aroused bitter resentment' (298). At the same time, something of the doubleness of *The Outline of History* is reflected in Wells's prognostication that, in the years between 1940 and 2059, this 'antiquated, obdurate culture disappeared. It and its Zionist state, its kosher food, the Law and all the rest of its paraphernalia, were completely merged in the human community. The Jews... were educated out of their racial egotism in less than

with Zangwill at this time. The examples of Wells's extreme anti-Zionism are taken from *In Search of Hot Water: Travels of a Republican Radical* (London, 1939) pp. 54–5 and *The Fate of Homo Sapiens* (London, 1939) p. 139 which will be discussed in detail below. Further references to contemporary editions of Wells's inter-war journalism will be in the body of the text.

three generations' (299). Wells describes the complete assimilation of 'the Jews' as a 'success' which 'the people of the nineteenth century would have deemed a miracle' and which points to his 'revolution' having 'ploughed deeper than any previous revolution' (299). In the decades leading up to the world state, the 'family group had ceased to be the effective nucleus in either economic or cultural life' which meant that the 'odd exclusiveness of the Jew [that] had been engendered in his close and guarded prolific home' (299) had also been expunged.[69] Wells's rationally organized, universalist world state is both challenged by a virulent Jewish particularism and vindicated by the 'disappearance' of 'Jewish peculiarity'. But, the 'bitter resentment' supposedly caused by the racial difference of 'the Jews' did not go away after the publication of *The Shape of Things to Come*. It was to be a dominant theme in Wells's journalism leading up to and including the Second World War.

Wells, in his *The Anatomy of Frustration* (1936), was to expand on his representation of an unassimilable Jewish particularity – a conflation of Pharisaism, Zionism and racial exclusivity – as being specifically responsible for the growth of European antisemitism. Based on Robert Burton's seventeenth-century philosophical text *The Anatomy of Melancholy*, Wells's *The Anatomy of Frustration* utilizes the pseudo-diary of a Wellsian persona, William Burroughs Steel, who examines the reasons for the persecution of contemporary Jewry in Nazi Germany. Once again, the Jewish 'tradition of acquisitiveness' (176), the 'essential parasitism of the Jewish mycelium upon the social and cultural organisms in which it lives' (178) and, above all, 'Zionism and cultural particularism', are characterized as a 'blunder and misfortune for [Jews] and mankind' (181). It was these factors, Wells concludes, that had brought about the Nazi assault on 'the Jews'. Furthermore, Wells cites a 'surprising passage' (181) from Steele's diaries which he was to repeat in several subsequent books published during the War. That is, according to Steele:

[T]he German National Socialist Movement is essentially Jewish in spirit and origin, it is Bible-born, an imitation of Old Testament nationalism. The Jews have been taxed with most sins but never before with begetting the Nazi. But Steele writes of it as if it were self-evident. National Socialism, he

---

[69] Wells, in his post-script to *Experiment in Autobiography* (London, 1934), published as *H. G. Wells in Love* (London, 1984), pp. 115–16 makes clear the connection between the 'family group' and the 'exclusiveness of the Jew': 'I have always been disposed to despise people who cluster close in families, gangs, clans and nations. That is my main objection to Jews... It is my theory that a world socialism means a bolder more fearless individualism.'

declares, is inverted Judaism, which has retained the form of the Old Testament and turned it inside out. Hitler never made a speech yet that could not be rephrased in Bible language. (182)

In his *In Search of Hot Water: Travels of a Republican Radical* (1939) Wells, as part of his anti-Zionism, was to put forward the extraordinary argument that 'no people in the world have caught the fever of irrational nationalism, that has been epidemic in the world since 1918, so badly as the Jews'. But, by this time, Wells was to concur with Steele that 'the current Nazi gospel is actually and traceably the Old Testament turned inside out' (60). What is most disturbing about Wells's statements at this time is that in his *In Search of Hot Water*, for instance, he accurately foresaw the 'systematic attempt to exterminate' the 'Jew' – 'to exterminate him brutally and cruelly' (56) – while, at the same time, arguing that this was a logical consequence of the refusal of 'the Jews' to 'assimilate' and give themselves to 'the service of mankind' (59). This argument was once again made explicit in his *The Fate of Homo Sapiens* (1939) which was reprinted in *The Outlook for Homo Sapiens* (1942) during the War. In this work Wells vigorously condemns Nazism, as he did throughout his life, but he also notes that:

[Nazism] is a horrible recrudescence of primordial human reactions, but that is no reason why we should shut our eyes to the role of the alien nationalism of the Chosen People in exposing them first and foremost before any other people to this outbreak of hatred, cruelty, bestiality and every sort of human ugliness. They are first to suffer in the social dissolution of our epoch, because they have stood out most conspicuously. (148)

Wells's belief that the refusal of the Jews to 'assimilate' caused antisemitism in both England and Nazi Germany was often cited during the War years by a wide variety of sources including Arnold Leese in *The Fascist* and Walter Holmes in the Communist *Daily Worker*. Mass Observation Sources, in particular, indicate popular support for Wells's representations of Jewish particularism. A survey on the 'means of overcoming antisemitism' in April 1943, for instance, has many references to Wells and concludes in general terms that 'it was up to the Jews themselves to combat antisemitism' by mixing 'freely with the inhabitants of the country of their adoption'. Wells was also quoted by General Sikorski, the exiled Polish Government's Commander-in-Chief, who justified his government's refusal to refer specifically to the persecution of European Jewry in 1942 by claiming that this would be 'equivalent to an implicit recognition of the racial theories which we all reject'.[70] At the end of his chapter on 'The Jewish Influence' in *The Fate of Homo Sapiens*, Wells was to maintain, in rather garbled fashion, that there is 'no other destiny for orthodox Judaism and those who are involved in its obloquy, unless that enormous effort to reconstruct human mentality for which I have been pleading arrives in time to arrest their march to destruction' (149). When faced with Jan Karski's eye-witness account of Belzec death camp in November 1942, Wells could only ask why 'in every country where Jews reside, sooner or later antisemitism emerges'. By this time, however, it is clear that both 'the Jew' and Nazism were cast in the same transient role as forces of 'irrationality' *par excellence* which, like the 'inferior races' in *Anticipations*, would 'have to go' in the context of the 'inevitable' drive towards a rationally ordered world state.[71]

By the 1940s, any form of Jewish difference was conflated by Wells into a Nazi-like unassimilable 'orthodoxy'. In Wells's *The New World Order* (1940) (which was also reprinted in *The Outlook for Homo Sapiens* during the War), Karl Marx is finally metamorphosized into a 'son of a rabbi' who, in the *Communist Manifesto*, is 'shrewd enough to use hate and bitter enough to hate' the Bourgeoisie:

Let anyone read over the Communist Manifesto and consider who might have shared the hate or even have got it all, if Marx had not been the son of a rabbi. Read Jews for Bourgeoisie and the Manifesto is pure Nazi teaching of the 1933–8 vintage. (48)

With Karl Marx reduced to a Nazi-like Pharasaic Jew, what hope was there for the 'assimilation' into 'mankind' of the rest of European Jewry? Such was the logic, taken to its bitter end, of Wells's semitic discourse. But this was Wells at his most 'bullying' and far removed from his 'comic' Edwardian fiction. After *Tono-Bungay*, Wells was to increasingly represent the semitic racial 'other' as being outside rational thought or behaviour. Unlike Shaw's playful sense of identification (however limited) with 'the Jew', Wells's increasingly impatient dismissal of any public expression of Jewish particularism helped to reinforce a narrowly defined Englishness which can also be

[70] General Sikorski is quoted in Bernard Wasserstein, *Britain and the Jews of Europe* 1939–1945 (Oxford, 1979) p. 165. See also Kushner, *The Persistence of Prejudice*, pp. 92–3 who cites usefully Mass Observation Sources and newspapers which refer to Wells.
[71] Jan Karski, 'The Message that was Delivered, But Not Heard', in Marcia Littell, Richard Libowitz and Evelyn Bodek Rosen (eds.), *The Holocaust Forty Years After* (New York, 1989) pp. 34 and 29–35. I am referring here to Wells's *Anticipations*, pp. 315–17 discussed above.

located in his fiction.[72] In the end, a fragile Hebraic 'moral' tradition and the internationalism of the diaspora proved to be an inadequate counterbalance, as Wells saw it, against a rampant and selfish 'Jewish' particularism.

CONCLUSION

To a large extent, the writings of Shaw and Wells can be seen as an extreme reworking of Matthew Arnold's *Culture and Anarchy*. Just as Arnold thought of England as overly Hebraic and in need of greater Hellenization, Shaw and Wells similarly wished to radically transcend a Hebraic individualism which they situated at the heart of capitalist society. But, unlike Arnold, Shaw and Wells had a much more doctrinaire view of the future development of liberal England and thus discounted completely any form of 'Jewish' difference. Arnold's ideal of 'culture', when compared to the socialist transformation of society, was an inclusive enough category to allow acculturated Jews into its pantheon. An ordered 'scientific' socialism, however, left little room for the expression of one's cultural particularism. By deploying the universalizing language of 'reason' and 'order', Jews were constructed as an irrational and disorderly force which were finally deemed to be standing in the way of world progress.

The imaginative works of Shaw and Wells can be said, at their best, to implicitly question the authoritarian potential within their politics. Shaw's ideal of the evolutionary Superman, by transcending ordinary humankind, was an uncertain exemplar in *Man and Superman* and was challenged dramatically by Mendoza. The complicity between Jansenius and Trefusis in Shaw's *An Unsocial Socialist* also pointedly undermined the binary opposition between Socialism and Judaism which constituted the 'socialism of fools' at the turn of the century. Wells, to be sure, utilized the racial category of 'the Jew' in his fiction to represent a dominant Edwardian semitic plutocracy. But, at the same time, his fiction could also represent a more general sense of a Hebraized plutocracy that was not merely reduced to the question of 'race'. Because of the transfiguring ideals at the centre of their politics, both Shaw and Wells were to locate in 'the Jew' the

[72] Batchelor, *H. G. Wells*, p. 29 and Richard Brown, 'Little England: On Triviality in the Naive Comic Fictions of H. G. Wells', *Cahiers, Victoriens and Edouardiens* 30 (October, 1989), 55–65.

potential for progressive change. In Shaw's case, this was the 'Jewish' ability to be at the forefront of worldly revolution and, in Wells's case, it was the internationalism of the Jewish diaspora and the efficacy of the Hebraic moral tradition. Both of these inclusive narratives were located in their imaginative works and, in their most complex writing, seriously disrupted the racial fixity of 'the Jew'. But, by the inter-war years, as the politics of Shaw and Wells became increasingly rigid and authoritarian, this alternative construction of 'the Jew' became less and less tenable. Any space for change in their post-war writings had little to do with the free play of complex narratives and was, at best, limited and programmatic.

The structural ambivalence in the socialist use of a semitic discourse – which fixed that which it wished to change – is also apparent in radical liberal thought in the Edwardian period. G. K. Chesterton and Hilaire Belloc, in the next chapter, both employ in an extreme form the language of reason and racial difference which are, in their works, in severe tension. Both writers operate within a Catholic, pro-Boer, anti-Capitalist politics but, at the same time, foreground 'race' in terms that were compatible with far right 'conservative' thought. In this way, Chesterton and Belloc embody, in an explosive configuration, the contradiction between 'race' and 'culture' in late Victorian liberal society.

CHAPTER 5

The limits of liberalism: Hilaire Belloc and G. K. Chesterton

[T]here is no such thing as a Catholic 'aspect' of European history. There is a Protestant aspect, a Jewish aspect, a Mohammedan aspect, a Japanese aspect, and so forth. For all of these look on Europe from without. The Catholic sees Europe from within. There is no more a Catholic 'aspect' of European history than there is a man's 'aspect' of himself.

Hilaire Belloc, *Europe and the Faith* (London, 1920), p. 3

There is an attitude for which my friends and I were for a long period rebuked and even reviled; and of which at the present period we are less likely than ever to repent. It was always called Anti-Semitism; but it was always much more true to call it Zionism. ... [M]y friends and I had in some general sense a policy in the matter; and it was in substance the desire to give Jews the dignity and status of a separate nation. We desired that in some fashion, and so far as possible, Jews should be represented by Jews, should live in a society of Jews, should be judged by Jews and ruled by Jews. I am an Anti-Semite if that is Anti-Semitism. It would seem more rational to call it Semitism.

G. K. Chesterton, *The New Jerusalem* (London, 1920), pp. 264–5

INTRODUCTION

The fiction and social criticism of Hilaire Belloc and G. K. Chesterton can be said to accentuate many of the contradictions and ambivalences within Edwardian liberalism. Both are radical Catholic authors whose maverick 'distributist' philosophy rejected a Tory Anglican capitalism as well as a secular socialism. The Anglo-French Belloc, who became a Liberal Member of Parliament, believed in the fundamental redistribution of wealth and, at the same time, in a return to a homogeneous medieval Christendom. A supporter of the French Revolution, he was also one of the few public figures in England who was convinced of Dreyfus's guilt. This mixture of a

radical and reactionary politics characterized his use of an anti-
capitalist racial discourse during the Boer War and his more general
construction of 'Jewish' financial scandals in Britain and France.
What Belloc gave with one hand, in terms of the transformation of
capitalist society, he took away with the other, by claiming the
ascendancy of an essentialist European Catholicism that had existed
throughout time.

Belloc's first novel was published in the wake of the Boer War and
foregrounded the 'cosmopolitan Jewish financier' as an alien,
unassimilable force which was destroying Britain. In a series of three
subsequent novels, Belloc anticipated the idiosyncratic politics of *The
Eye-Witness* and *The New Witness* groupings which constructed the
'Marconi Scandal' (1912–14) – concerning the financial impro-
prieties of 'Jewish' Liberal Cabinet Ministers – as the beginning of
the end for parliamentary democracy in Britain. Belloc's fiction,
written before the 'Marconi Scandal', self-consciously 'balanced' its
narrative between a violently 'antisemitic' response to the domination of an 'Anglo-Judaic plutocracy' and a more rational
explanation of 'the facts' behind such alien power. The inclusion of
a rational element within his heavily racialized semitic discourse was
to characterize Belloc's political practice throughout his lifetime.
Belloc thus attempted to test the limits of liberalism from the left – by
maintaining a rabid anti-capitalism – and from the right – by
positioning at the heart of his politics an exclusivist vocabulary
around 'race' and nation.

Unlike Belloc, who spent his early years in France, G. K.
Chesterton belonged to an indigenous Arnoldian liberal tradition
whose early writings incorporated the culturally differentiating terms
of 'Hebraism and Hellenism' alongside the vocabulary of racial
difference. Chesterton's gradual acceptance of an insuperable opposition between 'Jew and Christian', 'East and West' and 'Aryan and
Semite', however, became a means of defining the boundaries of a
small uniform 'English nation' and his ideal of an uncorrupted
Christendom. The 'Marconi Scandal', in this regard, was viewed by
Chesterton as a turning point in world history which threatened the
God-given identity of the English *patria*. But, even before this
'scandal', Chesterton's fiction and journalism had constructed the
assimilated or 'cosmopolitan Jew' as the embodiment of exactly the
kind of 'heretical' spiritual confusion which it was necessary for him
to combat. The pernicious influence of Belloc on Chesterton's use of

an increasingly racialized discourse is, thus, not as straightforward as
is often assumed. Much of Chesterton's Edwardian fiction will be
seen to have constructed 'the Jew' in terms of a specifically
Chestertonian 'Christian dogma'. There was, in other words, a good
deal of continuity between Chesterton's 'pre-Marconi' and 'post-
Marconi' fiction which contrasts markedly with the discontinuity
between his 'pro-Zionism' as compared to Belloc's 'anti-Zionism'.

HILAIRE BELLOC AND THE RATIONALITY OF 'RACE'

In one of his earliest published texts, *Essays in Liberalism by Six Oxford
Men* (1897), Hilaire Belloc argued that 'free trade has come; it has
enormously increased the prosperity of England, but it has been
accompanied by a flood of population not wholly beneficial'. The
qualification of the hitherto unchallenged liberal verity of 'free
trade' by the fear of 'not wholly beneficial' foreign populations was
to characterize the doubleness of Belloc's 'liberal' politics throughout
his lifetime. With his Anglo-French parentage, Belloc has been read
by his biographers as both a figure in a long line of British radicals as
well as an 'exotic' French 'antisemite' and zealous nationalist who
imported a peculiar Catholic version of anti-Tory Anglicanism to the
shores of a shocked England.[1] But instead of separating the
'reactionary' and 'radical' aspects of Belloc, as many critics have
done, it is worth emphasizing the Janus-faced nature of his social
criticism. It was this ambiguity, after all, which enabled Belloc to
make important interventions in Edwardian and post-war political
life as a novelist, journalist and Member of Parliament (1906–10).

Much of Belloc's rewriting of the 'liberal tradition' in both 'left-
wing' and 'right-wing' terms was anticipated in his *Essays in
Liberalism*. His opening chapter in this volume emphasized the failure
of Victorian liberalism to prevent the financial acquisition of land
from the peasantry – 'this eminently English force ... in the national
life' – who were pitted against the 'economic absolutism of the
landlords' (19–20). The incorporation of a racialized view of the

[1] Hilaire Belloc and J. L. Hammond (eds.), *Essays in Liberalism by Six Oxford Men* (London,
1897) p. 15. I will be referring to this collection and, unless stated otherwise, to first editions
of Belloc's and G. K. Chesterton's works in the body of the text. Robert Speaight, *The Life
of Hilaire Belloc* (New York, 1957) p. 97 emphasizes Belloc's 'strident, exotic antisemitism'
and John P. McCarthy, *Hilaire Belloc: Edwardian Radical* (Indiana, 1978) p. 15 his place as
a 'radical-liberal in the tradition of Bright, Cobden, Morley, and the younger Joseph
Chamberlain'.

'English nation' into a radical anti-capitalism characterized much of Belloc's politics. For Belloc, the 'history of England since the Middle Ages' was:

the slow and successful usurpation of the rights of the people on the one hand, and of the Crown upon the other, by a large territorial class. Until the period of that industrial revolution which has so signally increased the wealth, the population, and the perils of England, this class was supreme. (25)

Belloc called for the the redistribution of 'the land' to a 'yeoman class' in England as a means of ensuring that 'the people' do not become 'semi-servile...wage-earners' (29) under capitalism. His greatest fear was that the 'large territorial [aristocratic] class' was being replaced by the 'conquest' (4) of a newly formed plutocracy. These arguments were to be developed by Belloc at great length in a series of books on the history of England, the key role of the peasantry, and the dangers inherent in the control of government and the 'servile state' by a rapacious plutocracy. Such were the principal features of his Catholic, anti-socialist, anti-capitalist 'distributism', as it was known in the inter-war years. Belloc, along with other distributists, wished to reconstitute an idealized medieval Christendom where peasant proprietors, organized into guilds, were able to prevent the 'growth of an economic oligarchy which could exploit the rest of the community'.[2] His politics therefore challenged the radical right – who located all virtue in a unified past – and those universalist left-liberals who wished to construct an equitable future for all 'races' within the British nation-state.

In Belloc's reading of English history, the Reformation was understood as a 'largely Judaic' fall from Grace and was deemed to have resulted in the growth of a dominant 'English landlord-mercantile plutocracy' and a 'Capitalist State' which threatened to turn the masses into economically determined 'slaves'. As Jay Corrin has shown, although Belloc did not necessarily wish to return to the exemplary medieval 'Distributist State', his sense of an harmonious middle ages, where 'human relationships had not been destroyed by

[2] Hilaire Belloc, *The Servile State* (London, 1912) p. 50 which is a useful early account of Belloc's 'distributism'. I am grateful to Jay P. Corrin, *G. K. Chesterton and Hilaire Belloc: The Battle Against Modernity* (Ohio, 1981) p. 41 for this reference and *passim* for his account of Belloc's 'distributism'. See also Belloc's *A History of England*, 5 vols. (London, 1925–31), *The Place of a Peasantry in Modern Civilization* (London, 1910) and, with Cecil Chesterton, *The Party System: A Criticism* (London, 1911) for an elaboration of Belloc's views.

the cash nexus', was an attractive alternative to the contemporary plutocratic 'Servile State'. Most importantly, the reintegration of Protestant England and Northern Germany into the Catholic Church represented, for Belloc, the possibility of a revitalized, homogeneous Christendom. The organic unification of spirituality and materiality within Christendom would end the alien Judaic or spiritless materialism which was dominating modern Europe. European culture and stability, in this reading, were synonymous with Catholicism. But this did not mean that Belloc merely echoed the French 'Christian Conservatives' and dismissed the fruits of the Enlightenment. On the contrary, the French Revolution, according to Belloc's book on the subject, demonstrated the necessity of bringing down the present economic system before the Church could once again assume its rightful place at the centre of social and political life. The French Revolution and Belloc's medieval backward-looking Catholicism were, in short, the two extremes of his Janus-faced politics.[3]

Belloc's ever-present sense of a once ordered and harmonious Europe – which was being threatened to destruction by a soulless, Protestant-inspired money-power – incorporated 'the Jew' as a means of signifying the alien, catastrophic capitalism of the contemporary world. To be sure, as many commentators have noted, Belloc was particularly isolated as an Oxford undergraduate by his militant anti-Dreyfusard stance and the illiberal stridency of his constructions of semitic difference. Thus, at Oxford, Belloc was 'incredulous that one of his closest [non-Jewish] friends should have been in love with a Jewess'. He also initially declined to meet G. K. Chesterton in London because he was told that Chesterton's 'handwriting was that of a Jew'. Belloc had a French father and, before going up to Oxford, served as a volunteer in the French army where he came to identify with the 'ninety-nine Frenchmen out of a hundred' who, he contended, thought Dreyfus guilty. During the agitation for Dreyfus's retrial in France in 1898, Belloc visited Paul Déroulède and joined the *Ligue des Patriotes* which was formed by Déroulède to oppose the efforts of those defending Dreyfus. Déroulède was 'a very old family friend' and his brand of radical French

---

[3] I owe this discussion to Corrin, *G. K. Chesterton and Hilaire Belloc*, pp. 41–6. See also Ernst Nolte, 'Christian Conservatism', in his *Three Faces of Fascism: Action Française, Italian Fascism, National Socialism* (Munich, 1963) pp. 57–61, and Hilaire Belloc, 'The Jewish Question: The Historical Aspect' in *The Eye-Witness* (14 September 1911), 395 for Belloc's description of the 'largely Judaic spiritual origin[s]' of the Reformation.

nationalism was clearly akin to Belloc's own 'curious left-right revolutionary amalgam'.[4]

As with T. S. Eliot, Belloc was an avid reader of the journal of Charles Maurras's *Action Française* which, along with Eduard Drumont's immensely successful compendium *La France juive: Essai d'histoire contemporaine* (1886), constructed what has been described as an 'abstract concept of Judaism, represented by the Jewish economic elite and intelligentsia' which had supposedly made French society 'absolutely corrupt'. By the time of his *The Cruise of the 'Nona'* (1925), Belloc was to argue that the Dreyfus Affair had caused 'the four years of war, 1914–1918: for it destroyed the French Intelligence Bureau and so permitted the German surprise on Mons and Charleroi'. It was, Belloc was to remark towards the end of his life, the Dreyfus case which 'opened my eyes to the Jew question'. But, if Belloc's militant anti-Dreyfusard opinions were a contributing factor to his isolation at Oxford, his radical liberalism was no less a factor. After the publication of *Essays in Liberalism*, the journal *Isis* wrote that Belloc's anti-capitalist ideal of liberalism, especially his call for the fundamental redistribution of wealth, did not correspond to any recognized section of the Liberal Party. It was Belloc's passionate Jacobinism, as much as his unpopular anti-Dreyfusard stance, that forced him into the harsh world of metropolitan letters and prevented him from attaining the History Fellowship at All Souls which he so desired.[5]

Belloc thus positioned himself to the left of liberalism with regard to his anti-capitalism and to the right of liberalism with regard to his extreme racial discourse. He was not to strike the 'native note', with regard to English liberal opinion, until he began to rail fiercely against 'money-power' during the Boer War (1900–2). Along with Drumont and Maurras, Belloc had for many years situated mainly 'Jewish plutocrats' at the centre of French financial scandals such as the Panama Scandal of 1892–3. By the time of the Boer War, this

[4] McCarthy, *Hilaire Belloc*, p. 41 and Speaight, *The Life of Hilaire Belloc*, pp. 97–8, 120–1 and 147 for the extremes of Belloc's 'antisemitism'. These examples belie the rather vacuous claim in A. N. Wilson's *Hilaire Belloc* (London, 1984) p. 43 that 'Belloc had not come from an antisemitic home'.

[5] McCarthy, *Hilaire Belloc*, p. 18 and Corrin, *G. K. Chesterton and Hilaire Belloc*, p. 14 for references to Belloc's radicalism while he was at Oxford. See also Belloc, *The Cruise of the 'Nona'* (London, 1925) p. 215, Hesketh Pearson and Hugh Kingsmill, *Talking of Dick Whittington* (London, 1947) for Belloc's views on the Dreyfus Affair and Jacob Katz, *From Prejudice to Destruction: Antisemitism 1700–1933* (Cambridge, Mass., 1980) pp. 296 and 300 and chapter 24 for the French context.

discourse of semitic corruption had gained widespread appeal in Britain. With the publication of his *The Jews* (1922), Belloc was to associate the Dreyfus Affair with the Boer War in terms of the growth of interest in the 'Jewish Question' on the 'part of the average citizen'. The Boer War, he believed, was 'openly and undeniably provoked and promoted by Jewish interests in South Africa' and the Dreyfus Affair was, similarly, one of a 'series of direct international actions undertaken by Jewish finance' at the turn of the century.[6] Along with this later emphasis on the 'Jewish Question' there was also, as G. R. Searle has shown, an indigenous politics of 'corruption' – which included increasingly vociferous objections to the rise of an 'unEnglish' plutocracy – which could be endorsed without necessarily referring to French antisemitism. In fact, it was precisely the alien, corrupt 'other' that was to define an exclusivist 'English nation'. For this reason, those who utilized the politics of 'corruption', many of whom were known aptly enough as Little Englanders, were to include racialized constructions of 'Jews' as a central element in their opposition to the Boer War. The influential radical J. A. Hobson, for instance, in his *The War in South Africa* (1900), was to write a chapter called 'For whom are we fighting?' Hobson claimed in this chapter that resources in Southern Africa were largely under the direction of 'a small group of international financiers, chiefly German in origin and Jewish in race'. In terms that Belloc was to repeat *ad nauseam*, Hobson went on to describe the war as a 'Jew-Imperialist design':

The Jews are par excellence the international financiers ... They fastened on the Rand ... as they are prepared to fasten upon any other part of the globe ... Primarily they are financial speculators, taking their gains not out of the genuine fruits of industry, even the industry of others, but out of the construction, promotion and financial manipulation of companies.[7]

---

[6] Belloc, *The Jews* (London, 1922) p. 50 for this argument. This book was anticipated by Belloc's series of eight articles on 'The Jewish Question' in *The Eye-Witness* (7 September–26 October 1911), 365–589 and, especially, 'The Peril', 458–9. Kenneth Lunn, 'Political Antisemitism Before 1914: Fascism's Heritage?' in Kenneth Lunn and Richard Thurlow (eds.), *British Fascism* (London, 1980) p. 28 has rightly stressed that the 'pattern of thought' in *The Jews* had been established in these articles by 1911. Corrin, *G. K. Chesterton and Hilaire Belloc*, p. 63, amongst many others, wrongly reads *The Jews* as a post-First World War work. For Belloc's 'native note' during the Boer War see J. H. Grainger, *Patriotisms: Britain 1900–1939* (London, 1986) p. 121 and chapter 7.

[7] J. A. Hobson, 'Capitalism and Imperialism in South Africa', *Contemporary Review* 77 (1900), 4–5 and *The War in South Africa* (London, 1900) p. 226, cited in Colin Holmes, *Anti-Semitism in British Society 1876–1939* (London, 1979) p. 67. For a broader discussion of the politics of 'corruption' see G. R. Searle, *Corruption in British Politics: 1895–1930* (Oxford, 1987).

This widespread radical representation of a 'semitic plutocracy', as part of an anti-imperialist and anti-capitalist opposition to the Boer War, was utilized by Belloc to Judaize the 'international financiers' which, so the argument went, had initiated the Boer War to protect their own 'alien' interests. In this way, Jews were constructed as unassimilable cosmopolitans who possessed an international wealth which eroded national boundaries and traditions. As Hobson states, 'the Jews' could threaten Britain's national productivity by living parasitically on the 'genuine fruits of industry'.[8] The binary opposition between an 'English' citizenry and a rootless, degenerate 'Jew' was central to Belloc's semitic discourse and his response to the Boer War. Such was his challenge to a universalist liberalism that wished to grant citizenship to all within its borders. A racially defined Englishness, which opposed this universalizing impulse, can be seen especially in his poem 'To the Balliol Men Still in Africa' (1910). Here, Belloc laments the loss of his college friends who had since been killed in the Boer War:

> I have said it before and I say it again,
>   There was treason done, and a false word spoken,
> And England under the dregs of men,
>   And bribes about, and a treaty broken:
> But angry, lonely, hating it still,
>   I wished to be there in spite of the wrong.
>
> Oh! they have wasted you over the sea!
> The only brothers ever I knew,
>   The men that laughed and quarrelled with me.

Belloc's sense of the loss of his 'brothers' during the Boer War reflects, as J. H. Grainger has argued, his larger awareness of the destruction of a familial English *patria*. This perception is at its apogee in 'Ha'nacker Mill' (1923), written after the First World War, where there are 'Spirits that call and no one answers; / Ha'nacker's down and England's done'. What helped cause the deaths of good 'Balliol men' (the backbone of Englishness) during the Boer War were the international plutocrats, the 'dregs of men' who, it was supposed, were the main beneficiaries of the War. The necessary corollary to Belloc's poem 'To the Balliol Men Still in Africa' is, thus, 'Verses to a Lord who, in the House of Lords, said that those who opposed the

---

[8] See chapters 3 and 4 for further examples of this kind of race-thinking in the context of a radical anti-imperialism and anti-capitalism.

South African Adventure confused Soldiers with Money-Grubbers'
(1910). In this satire, the heroic English *patria* and the semitic
'money-grubbers' are grotesquely interchanged with one another:

> You thought because we held, my lord,
> An ancient cause and strong,
> That therefore we maligned the sword:
> My lord, you did us wrong.
>
> We also know the sacred height
> Up on Tugela side,
> Where those three hundred fought with Beit
> And fair young Wernher died.
>
> The little mound where Eckstein stood
> And gallant Albu fell,
> And Oppenheim, half blind with blood,
> Went fording through the rising flood –
> My Lord, we know them well.
>
> The little empty homes forlorn,
> The ruined synagogues that mourn,
> In Frankfort and Berlin;
> We knew them when the peace was torn –
> We of nobler lineage born –
> And now by all the gods of scorn
> We mean to rub them in.

Such were the dire consequences of disregarding an insuperable
opposition between the 'English nation' and international 'Jewish'
financiers. The popular verse at the time of the Boer War, as has been
seen with reference to T. W. H. Crosland, similarly reconstructed
Kiplingesque patriotic heroism in terms of semitic degeneracy.
Martin van Wyk Smith's account of the poetry of the Boer War
contains many examples of this juxtaposition, such as the following:

> Oh, Tommy, Tommy Atkins,
> My heart beats sure for you,
> To be made the bloomin' catspaw
> of the all pervading Jew.
> And when you're back in England
> Invalided, full of care,
> You'll find you've drawn the chestnuts
> For the multi-millionaire.[9]

---

[9] Martin Van Wyk Smith, *Drummer Hodge: The Poetry of the Anglo-Boer War* (1899–1902)
(Oxford, 1978) p. 63 and Grainger, *Patriotisms*, p. 116.

The construction of patriotic fervour during the Boer War in opposition to 'the Jews' reflects, as historians have recently argued, the 'double movement' leading up to the introduction of the 1905 Aliens Act. This immigration act both incorporated elements of the urban working class into a racial-Imperial 'Englishness' and, at the same time, excluded 'undesirable' Jewish 'aliens' from the shores of Britain and, thereby, severely narrowed the liberal 'idea of the nation'. Such doubleness was reflected in Belloc's 'distributist' politics which, on the one hand, proposed to financially empower the lower classes but which also intended to 'segregate' Jews and other 'foreigners' from the English *patria*.[10]

As well as his political campaigns and journalism on the subject Belloc also represented the 'Jewish Question' in his novels. He initially published in April 1900 a brief extract of his first work of fiction, *Emmanuel Burden: A Novel* (1904), in *The Speaker* (a journal on the radical wing of the Liberal Party). In these early drafts, Belloc concentrated on the figure of Emmanuel Burden as the embodiment of a defunct Anglicanism and English Whiggism that needed to be spiritually reinvigorated and radically transformed. But these published extracts, it should be said, bore little or no relation to the eventual novel which was written in the aftermath of the Boer War and included the 'cosmopolitan financier', Mr I. Z. Barnett. Burden and Barnett are, nonetheless, closely associated with each other. The exploitative worldliness of Barnett, a 'German Jew', flourishes precisely because Burden's Englishness is so ineffectual. As his biographers have noted, Belloc had great difficulty in completing *Emmanuel Burden* which, unusually for him, took many years to write. It was not until the end of October 1903 that Belloc wrote to his friend Reginald Butler to say that he had, at last, made considerable progress on this work. As Corrin has shown, the main reason for the delay in finishing this novel is that Belloc's intended publishers, after reading the original manuscript of *Emmanuel Burden* in July 1903, feared that they would be accused of publishing a 'Jew-baiting' book. The revision of certain 'objectionable sections' of this work to

---

[10] Belloc's separatist or apartheid solution to 'The Jewish Question' is the 'thesis' of his *The Jews*, chapters 1 and 12. Daniel Pick, *Faces of Degeneration: A European Disorder 1848–1918* (Cambridge, 1989) p. 215 and David Feldman, 'The Importance of Being English: Jewish Immigration and the Decay of Liberal England' in David Feldman and Gareth Stedman Jones, *Metropolis London: Histories and Representations since 1800* (London, 1989) p. 78 and chapter 3 both usefully emphasize the ambivalence surrounding discourses of 'the nation' in Britain at the turn of the century.

fit in with the concerns of his publisher was, in later years, to be a
salutary lesson for Belloc. He had been shown the acceptable limits of
his racial discourse and was to learn to champion discussions of the
'Jewish Question' using the language of reason. In *Emmanuel Burden*,
Belloc was to adopt a narrative voice of 'aggrieved astonishment', as
if anyone could have the temerity to 'question the excellence of Mr I.
Z. Barnett's motives'. This tone of blanket irony was to please his
eventual publishers, A. M. S. Methuen, who found Belloc's novel
'subtle, restrained and continuous'.[11]

To be sure, *Emmanuel Burden* is the subtlest and most restrained of
the quartet of novels – which also includes *Mr Clutterbuck's Election*
(1908), *A Change in the Cabinet* (1909) and *Pongo and the Bull* (1910) –
that chart the stupendous rise of Mr I. Z. Barnett. The central thrust
of *Emmanuel Burden* is an examination of the all too fragile Englishness
of Burden who eventually succumbs to 'those forces of the modern
world ... which proved fatal' to him (21). Written as a mock-
biography, a 'record of [the] lineage, speculations, last days and
death' of Emmanuel Burden, Belloc begins his novel by charting, in
some detail, Burden's ancestors from the seventeenth century
onwards. Burden, we are told, comes from a long line of rather
shallow Protestants who, as honest 'merchants', increased their
wealth and social standing through the years in line with England's
growing prosperity. As minor characters in the history of England, it
is the bovine stability and longevity of the Burdens, as opposed to
their 'public fame', that point to their 'influence upon the fortunes of
our great empire' (2). By corrupting this staid, centuries-old
merchant tradition, it is implied, something of 'England' is irre-
trievably lost. Belloc's narrator only slightly exaggerates when he
observes that 'to see [Burden] open his umbrella was to comprehend
England from the Reform Bill to Home Rule' (80) and this English
'patriotism' is said to be 'like a perennial spring; it was the deepest
thing in the man' (81).

But Burden is not simply an unquestioned emblem of the English
patria. In 'knowing nothing but his country', Burden's 'patriotism' is
also a weakness as his narrow Protestant 'religion was in some odd
way muddled up with her vices, her spirit' (81). This conflicting

---

[11] Cited in Wilson, *Hilaire Belloc*, p. 128. See also Corrin, *G. K. Chesterton and Hilaire Belloc*, p.
24 and Speaight, *The Life of Hilaire Belloc*, p. 181. Speaight, however, is wrong to argue that
'much of [*Emmanuel Burden*] had already appeared in *The Speaker*' before it was published in
book form.

depiction of Burden's Englishness remains an unresolved tension in Belloc's fiction. Burden is both the embodiment of England's history and, also, a 'burden' on the future development of England. His lack of recognition of his own patriotic 'influence' especially enables Barnett to manipulate him and gain undeserved power. At one point in the novel, Belloc's narrator complains that Burden 'never really got it into his mind that *he* was an actor in the drama; that *he*, as a citizen, was making the new world' (83). Burden, in other words, represents a passive parochial Englishness which allows more aggressive outsiders to dominate.

For the most part, however, the narrator coyly refrains from directly commenting on Burden's inherited lack of spiritual ambition and his dearth of political idealism. Instead, there are mischievous fissures in his dull mercantile heritage when, for instance, one of Burden's overly Hebraized relatives declares himself to be the Messiah 'at some time between April and June 1684' (4). Even when filial relations become strained in the nineteenth century, because Burden's father was a supporter of Disraeli in stark contrast to his son who was a committed Gladstonian, the Burdens were still incapable of voicing their political differences (11). Thus, when 'Mr Disraeli was promoted to the peerage and offered a golden wreath by a co-religionist', Burden's most extreme reaction was to go 'so far as to take Mrs Burden to the seaside for a week, until the storm should have blown over' (12). The anonymous 'co-religionist' was presumably Lord Rothschild, notwithstanding Disraeli's baptism into the Anglican church at the age of thirteen. And yet, Emmanuel Burden's comically mild reaction to the political 'storm', caused by the elevation of Disraeli to the peerage, anticipates his subsequent inability to deal with Mr I. Z. Barnett, another 'semitic' threat to 'England' that is not dissimilar to that of Disraeli. As with other texts that have dealt with the 'Condition of England', the 'semitic' conquest of England is made possible, in the first place, by an inadequate and declining Englishness which is in urgent need of spiritual regeneration.

It is through his son, the appropriately named Cosmo, that Burden eventually comes into contact with the Judaic 'forces of the modern world' that finally defeat him. Cosmo, especially, reinforces Belloc's sense of historical regression and lack of a national purpose. His features are 'devoid of meaning' (19) and he shows himself to be morally and financially bankrupt at university where his over-

spending as an undergraduate, rather like that of Marjorie Pope's in
H. G. Wells's *Marriage* (1912), leads him into the world of 'Cosmopolitan Finance'. In particular, it is the 'Levantine' (42) figure of Mr
Harbury, a 'man such as our manifold Empire alone produces' (40),
who introduces Cosmo to Mr Barnett via a money-lender. Belloc's
narrator bitterly contrasts the 'deep roots which our English families
strike into the soil' (24) with Harbury's extra-territorial Empire-
building and self-aggrandizement which, not unlike Anthony Trollope's Lopez, uses the vestiges of a false Englishness to undermine 'the
nation'. Harbury's foreignness signifies the capitalist detachment from
the 'deep roots' of the 'English soil' which, Belloc makes explicit in
The Servile State (1912), is the unwitting consequence of even Burden's
mercantile capitalism. By aligning himself with the international
finance capitalism of Harbury and Mr Barnett, Cosmo simply
continues this process of detachment from 'the soil' in its most
extreme form.[12] Compared to the racial fixity of the 'English nation',
Barnett was born in Frankfurt 'somewhere between June 1840 and
March 1845' (66). His indeterminate origins, which echo Trollope's
Melmotte, make him the model of national confusion as opposed to
the spiritual rootedness which Belloc seeks. Even with his acknowledged German origins, 'full pendulous' nose and lisping, foreign
accent, a timid and restrained Englishness allows Barnett to be one of
the 'men who direct no small part of our national fortunes' (2):

It is an impression – a conviction rather – that this man is in some
inscrutable way linked with the fate of England. Such an assertion in cold
print means little; made in the presence of the man or his emblem, it has the
force of prophecy. (66–7)

Just as Burden becomes a rather too obvious representative of an
ineffectual Gladstonian Whiggism, Barnett's scheme to discover gold
beneath the 'marshes' of the M'Korio Delta in West Africa embodies
a corrupt Imperialism. Critics have described Barnett in contrary
fashion as part of a preposterous 'caricature of reality' and as a
'recognisable type', with present-day counterparts, who is one of
Belloc's 'most amusing creations'.[13] What is clear from the political

---

[12] Belloc, *The Servile State*, is the most succinct account of this process of historical detachment
from 'the soil' or the 'soul' of 'the nation' and into a Protestant-inspired, extra-territorial
capitalism.

[13] Wilson, *Hilaire Belloc*, p. 126 contends outrageously that 'Mr Barnett is a recognisable type;
perhaps cruder than his Rothschild or Oppenheimer Edwardian originals, infinitely less so
than his modern equivalents, like "Lord" [sic] Kagan or Sir James Goldsmith'. For the

contexts of *Emmanuel Burden* is that Barnett's M'Korio Delta scheme helped to reinforce a semitic discourse that was utilized during the Boer War and which helped to create a host of 'Jewish' financial scandals at this time. In Belloc's mock defence of Barnett he itemizes, in great detail, the eighteen newspapers that he owns to 'prove' (91) that Barnett has no influence over the press whatsoever. With similar bludgeoning irony, the lisping, 'alien' (69) Barnett is increasingly identified with 'the spirit of England' (97) and the 'builder of the new world' (95) whose 'singular depth and power...immense tenacity...organising ability and staying-power' (66) are more than a match for Burden's innocent Old England. Burden, through his son, is used to represent the M'Korio Delta scheme as an act of commendable Empire-building in an indigenous merchant tradition of a 'people born to Empire' (83). The novel revolves around Burden's growing realization of the semitic financial corruption at the heart of the spurious hunt for gold in West Africa:

[Burden] would have maintained, in a kind of abstract way, that the connection between finance and politics was dangerous...he would have felt a very genuine horror at hearing that a Cabinet minister had held, or had been given, such and such shares in a company connected with our Imperial development.... He refused to follow the logical consequences of his creed. (84)

The extent of Barnett's growing influence can be gauged from the fact that the M'Korio Delta became 'a touchstone for the future of England' (84–5). Fearing Barnett's motives, Burden felt 'something old in his blood' and 'thirsted...for the presence of the British statesman', Lord Blenthorpe (138). Blenthorpe is not unlike one of the deracinated aristocrats, such as Lord Longstaffe, who surround Melmotte in *The Way We Live Now*. In other words, Blenthorpe crudely embodies the impotence of the aristocracy in the face of a rising plutocracy. After the agricultural depression in the 1870s, we are told that 'He borrowed' (112); a two word sentence which sums

---

stereotypical originals out of which Belloc constructed Barnett's lisping, greasy Jewishness see M. J. Landau, *The Jew In Drama* (London, 1926) and also G. K. Chesterton's illustrations to *Emmanuel Burden*. J. A. V. Chapple, *Documentary and Imaginative Literature 1880–1920* (London, 1970) pp. 209–10 reads *Emmanuel Burden* as a 'fable designed to bear an application to real life' which fails because the author has not 'hit upon some strong prevailing tendency in human nature or society'. But this is also to ignore the racial discourse out of which *Emmanuel Burden* was constructed.

up his loss of heritage and integrity. Like Cosmo and Harbury, Blenthorpe represents the outward signs of Englishness, devoid of content, which is manipulated by the unscrupulous Barnett for his own gain. They are 'England, and not England' (219) and it is an inner, racialized Englishness which is associated with the 'Anglo-Saxon' tradition of Empire, as opposed to its modern 'cosmopolitan' sham.[14]

It is Charles Abbott, Burden's long-standing business partner and the chief proprietor of the Abbott line of steamers, who symbolizes this 'Anglo-Saxon' tradition of Empire and attempts to expose Barnett's fraudulent machinations. Unlike anyone else in the novel, Abbott had 'about him something of the explosive radicalism which was often to be discovered in the older sort of English officials and business men' (85). As his name indicates Abbott reflects the legacy of Victorian radicalism, which was epitomized by William Cobbett, whom Belloc admired. But, not unlike Burden, Abbott is also a deeply ambiguous figure. To be sure, the 'anachronistic' (85) Abbott, as Grainger notes, does attempt to put 'sand in the bearings' (197) of modern England. He is 'sound' on Free Trade and, most importantly, embodies the 'soil, the air, the habit' (198) of the English *patria*. Nonetheless, Grainger is wrong to assume that Abbott's 'rash political indignation' is unproblematically equivalent to Belloc's.[15] Abbott's 'explosive radicalism' is, I would argue, qualified by Belloc's narrator in one important respect:

There are men who hate the successful or the rich, but whose hatred is not quite dishonest, though it is wildly unjust. They see conspiracies upon every side, they scowl at every new fortune, but they do so in good faith, for they are haunted by a nightmare of Cosmopolitan Finance – pitiless, destructive of all national ideals, obscene, and eating out the heart of our European tradition. (90)

While the 'good faith' of Abbott's 'political indignation' is empha-sized in this quotation, so is its 'wildly unjust' rashness. It is precisely the 'violence' of Abbott's reaction to his partner's unwitting involvement with Barnett and, above all, his appeal to Burden's 'heart' and not his 'reason' (205), that confuse Burden and makes

---

[14] Grainger, *Patriotisms*, p. 116 and Speaight, *The Life of Hilaire Belloc*, pp. 202–3 both emphasize Belloc's belief that Imperialism had its 'noble side'.

[15] Grainger, *Patriotisms*, p. 118. Grainger's chapter on Belloc and G. K. Chesterton is, significantly, entitled 'rash, political indignation' (Belloc's description of Abbott in *Emmanuel Burden*) which reinforces the supposed equivalence between Abbott and Belloc.

him unable to confront the implications of his interest in the M'Korio Delta scheme. Although there is a great deal of rather too obvious irony in the 'moral' (202) critique of Abbott in the novel – given that his worst fears are proved to be entirely correct – there is still a strong sense in which the very irrationality of Abbott's behaviour is counter-productive. Towards the end of *Emmanuel Burden*, a hopelessly perplexed Burden visits Abbott only to be severely abused by his life-long friend. The ferocity of Abbott's 'temper' causes Burden to have a fatal breakdown. At this stage in the novel, it is hard not to agree that the 'blundering hand' (271) of Abbott has done an enormous disservice to his cause:

It will be perceived that, with a man of Mr Abbott's temper, the great forces of modern England would breed, not only a reactionary hatred, but a mania of suspicion. The man was for ever putting two and two together. He was perpetually seeing conspiracies where no conspiracy existed, nay where no conspiracy could, in the nature of things, exist. He would smell out the secret influences of what he called 'cosmopolitan finance', in the actions of the dullest and most ordinary civil servants. He had dropped one newspaper after another, proceeding on a scale, as it were, from the fairly sane to the hopelessly fanatical. At last he had come to reading none, with the exception of a weekly sheet which not only floundered into a mare's nest of politics, but was largely supported by subscriptions from Mr Abbott himself. (272)

It was significant that Belloc was to similarly chastise those conspiracy-obsessed 'fanatics' that wrote for his own 'weekly sheet' *The New Witness* and who, like Abbott, spoke loosely about 'greasy German Jews' (275) and appealed not to 'reason' but to 'violent emotion'.[16] The dangers, for Belloc, in Abbott's 'rash political indignation' should not be underestimated given the fact that Abbott inadvertently causes Burden's death and thereby allows Barnett to succeed. By the end of the novel Cabinet Ministers, deceived by Barnett's newspapers, have bought the spurious M'Korio Delta Company which enables Barnett to achieve 'more than fortune – true political power, a thing to him worth all the effort of a life' (287). At the same time as he is implicitly condemned, however, Abbott's paranoid vision of the world is confirmed as Burden succumbs to 'the massed forces of the new world surging against him' (296) and the narrator cannot 'quite see who there is to take [the] place' of this 'honest Englishman' (312). Rather like H. G. Wells's *Tono-Bungay*

---

[16] Letter to Maurice Baring, 30 October 1913. Cited in Speaight, *The Life of Hilaire Belloc*, p. 363. Belloc, here, was referring specifically to Cecil Chesterton and F. Hugh O'Donnell.

(1909), the final apocalyptic vision of London in *Emmanuel Burden* is of a city dominated by the semitic 'East': 'The dirty light grew in the east of the world, and lit without hope the labour and despair of the city' (310). Such is the nature of an alien, international capitalism detached from the roots of 'Anglo-Saxon' England.

Belloc buries Burden in Norwood cemetry, 'just beyond the sections consecrated to the Roman Catholics and the Jews' (311) and, interestingly, associates the otherness of his own Catholicism with that of 'the Jews'. By situating his narrator ambivalently in opposition to both Abbott's antisemitic 'fanaticism' and Barnett's Jewish 'cosmopolitan finance', Belloc attempts to negotiate rationally between the 'fact' of semitic power and the irrationality of the 'antisemitic' response to it. This supposedly 'balanced' narrative position prefigures Belloc's self-proclaimed 'rational' political response to the 'Jewish Question'. At one point in *Emmanuel Burden*, when discussing the history of Barnett, it is noted that the failure of one of Barnett's previous enterprises was caused by a journalist who pointed out that Barnett could not afford to pay the interest on his borrowings (71). It is precisely this kind of rational exposure of the inequities of Barnett and his like that caused Belloc, eventually, to set up *The Eye-Witness* journal. Thus, on the one hand, Belloc was to continually challenge a timid Whiggism by incorporating into his 'liberal' politics the language of 'race' and nation and a vehement anti-capitalism. At the same time, however, he was to use strategically the language of 'reason' and facticity, as opposed to 'violent emotion', as the best means of exposing the semitic threat to an indigenous Englishness.

Belloc's next three novels concerning Barnett, written during his time as an Independent Liberal Member of Parliament, replicate, with less subtlety, the structure of *Emmanuel Burden*. The best of these subsequent works, *Mr Clutterbuck's Election*, concerns the 'revolutions of fortune' of Mr Clutterbuck, a Burden-like middle-class merchant who passes 'from ease to affluence' and is 'launched on public life' (2) after accidentally buying a large share-holding in a Company which owns a million eggs (intended for the troops stationed in South Africa). Much to Clutterbuck's astonishment, this company is launched on the Stock Exchange during the Boer War and makes him a fortune. Like Cosmo, Clutterbuck is a 'complete blank' (9), a *tabula rasa* who succumbs to the debased machinations of Barnett after his windfall is invested in 'Barnett and Sons' Bank':

The story [of Clutterbuck's success] rose beneath him like a tide; it floated him out of his suburb into a new and great world; it floated him at last into the majestic councils of the nation. It all but bestowed him an imperishable name among the Statesmen of England. (68)

Clutterbuck's stock rises 'like a balloon' (68), which reflects his insubstantial character and his all too 'perishable' good name. His newly found financial wherewithal enables him to be elected as a Member of Parliament and join the 'majestic councils' of Mary Smith, an 'intimate friend' of the Prime Minister and the sister-in-law of the leader of the opposition (75). Such is the corrupt nature of political power in Edwardian England.

Whereas the shadowy world of Barnett's M'Korio Delta scheme was on the margins of society in *Emmanuel Burden*, the nepotistic world of Mary Smith, 'a power in both Political parties' (77), places Barnett at the heart of the Front Bench parliamentary conspiracy which Belloc and Cecil Chesterton were to elaborate in their *The Party System* (1911). Her social gatherings at The Plâs demonstrate the extent that Barnett's world of financial corruption and her own political nepotism reinforced each other. Thus, there is a 'warm understanding' between Mary Smith and Barnett, who has recently been made the Duke of Battersea, and the 'devotion' of the 'aged Duke' was said to be the 'summit' of her 'achievement' (76). As with Burden, it is Clutterbuck's painful realization that the Duke of Battersea is not what he seems that makes him begin to question the nature and purpose of his plutocratic wealth. On hearing that Barnett is known as the 'Peabody Yid', Clutterbuck turns to Mary Smith's brother, William Bailey, who had 'gone mad upon the Hebrew race' (214). Like Abbott in relation to Burden, Bailey attempts to educate the naïve but honest Clutterbuck in the sordid realities of modern-day international capitalism. Four years after the publication of *Emmanuel Burden*, Belloc is clearly more confident about discussing explicitly the 'Jewish Question' in his fiction. Bailey's preoccupations pointedly concern 'the Jews' as opposed to a racially unspecified 'cosmopolitan finance'. Belloc is once again concerned with how best to deploy the language of corruption in relation to a figure such as Barnett. Bailey clearly fails in this regard:

[Bailey] saw Jews everywhere: he not only saw them everywhere, but he saw them all in conspiracy. He would not perhaps have told you that the conspiracy was conscious, but its effects he would have discovered all the same ... The disease advanced with his advancing age; soon all the great families of Arnold were Jews; half the English aristocracy had Jewish blood; for a little he would have accused the Pope of Rome or the Royal Family itself; and I need hardly say that every widespread influence, from Freemasonry to the international finance of Europe, was Israelite in his eyes; while our Colonial policy, and especially the gigantic and successful struggle in South Africa, he twisted into a sort of petty huckstering, dependent upon Petticoat Lane. (214–15)

Like Abbott, Bailey is a peculiarly ambiguous figure in Belloc's text as he has access to the sordid truth behind Barnett's motives and, at the same time, is represented as an irrational 'diseased' figure who appeals to the heart and not the head of the hapless Clutterbuck. Belloc's distancing irony, and references to the potential Jewishness of the Pope and the Royal Family, reinforce Bailey's crankiness. And yet, like Belloc, Bailey is elected as an Independent Liberal Member of Parliament who, filled with disgust at what he had witnessed as an MP, refused to stand again. Bailey's manifold statements on the 'Jewish Question' are, moreover, not dissimilar to those of Belloc even though Bailey, contrary to his author, is too much of a 'fanatic' to be able to influence events. The fact that Bailey is the sister of Mary Smith also points to his complicity in prolonging a system that he would wish to bring down. That he drips with the 'antisemitic virus' (216) means that he not only defeats himself but, as Belloc was to consistently argue, those that would wish to rationally 'solve' the 'Jewish Question'.[17] Whereas the language of 'reason' can bring the 'Jewish Question' to the centre of British politics, Bailey continues to marginalize that most important of contemporary issues. Nonetheless, Bailey does point Clutterbuck in the direction of the 'Anapootra Ruby Mines Scandal' and also appeals to Clutterbuck's sense of patriotic outrage concerning the connections between Barnett's company (which own the Anapootra Ruby Mines) and the government. But, instead of enlightening Clutterbuck, he only succeeds in increasing Clutterbuck's heightened emotions:

'D'you suppose old Battersea can't make 'em dance? Why, the Peabody Yid's only got to wink and it's like a red-hot poker to the politicians... You must go on pressing and pressing. It's the only way – it's the only way in which anything gets done. Besides which, it's enough to make any man – '

[17] See Belloc's *The Jews, passim* for the similarity between Bailey and Belloc on the issue of the conspiratorial secrecy of 'the Jews' and the Jewishness of Freemasonry, the Arnold family, the aristocracy, international finance, and 'the empire' (especially in South Africa). *The Jews*, chapter 7, also attempts to distance Belloc from the unproductive 'hatred' of the antisemite.

Interestingly enough, this passage was added by Belloc to the second edition of *Mr Clutterbuck's Election*, presumably to reinforce the reader's sense of Bailey's 'fanaticism'.[18] Although Clutterbuck is spurred into action by this outburst, his inability to discuss calmly the political corruption behind Barnett's company means that he is easily suppressed and, eventually, reappears as Lord Methlinghamhurst in *A Change in the Cabinet* (1909). In this novel, Clutterbuck is one of five Peers who are 'concerned with the Anapootra mines' (299) and, in effect, a paid hireling of the Duke of Battersea in the House of Lords. Once again, Barnett's success is reliant upon an Englishness that is either weak and ineffectual or unthinking in its irrationality.

By the time of *Pongo and the Bull* (1910), Belloc has dispensed with his 'fanatical' intermediary and ironic narrator and, instead, uses an unmediated voice to point directly to the disastrous consequences of a future where the Duke of Battersea is 'the very centre' of the Prime Minister's world and 'the chief and the most respected of British financiers' (17) whose 'name alone could support the credit of the country' (18). The overweening plutocratic power of the eighty-five-year-old Duke is made crudely apparent when it is noted that Battersea House has long since replaced St James's Palace and dominates 'every other building in the neighbourhood' (62). Belloc, at his most disillusioned with Parliamentary democracy, sets his novel in 1925 and portrays a country devoid of the means of raising capital which, at the same time, it urgently needs to finance its troubled Imperial presence in India.

Left with no other choice, 'Dolly', the Prime Minister, who is in cahoots with 'Pongo', the Leader of the Opposition, is forced to ask the Duke of Battersea for a loan. As soon as he does, he is 'shocked' to note a mysterious 'change in the financier's manner' (68) which 'other men ... in more than one capital in Europe had witnessed' (69). The lisping Duke, who speaks three languages in his household, begins to outline the difficulty of the government's position with 'one allusion after another ... to the gradual decline of the borrowing power of the government' – a decline, it is implied, which Battersea had helped to create (70). He then starts to lay down the conditions of the loan and the need for the inclusion, in particular, of his various relations: '"there iss my brodher Chames ... You know Chames?

---

[18] This quotation was added to the Eveleigh Nash edition of *Mr Clutterbuck's Election* (London, 1908) and is missing from the T. Nelson and Sons edition (London, 1908). I am referring to the Eveleigh Nash edition in the body of the text.

Well, he would no doubt not say as I say ... my brodher Chames ...
and his sohn also. Well! Each most know!" [sic]' (70). Battersea, we
are told, 'bore a very different aspect according to whether one
happened to be above or below him' (72) and, even though the
Prime Minister had known the Duke for many decades, it was clear
that 'the lender of money must ever be the master – even of a
sovereign State' (73). For the first time, the alien 'racial' (72) nature
of Battersea's 'old usurer's heart' (74) is articulated by Belloc without
an 'antisemitic' mediator:

... the Duke of Battersea ... lay in Battersea House not yet asleep. He was
feeding internally and nourishing his soul upon Dolly [the Prime Minister]
and the Indian Loan. He held Dolly between his spatulated forefinger and
his gross thumb. But then he did not understand blood that was not his own,
nor what sympathies might arise between men of one race and one society
... (90)

It is at this point that the main theme of *Pongo and the Bull* emerges.
Even though Battersea had been a citizen of England for over half a
century, he is of a different 'blood' and, by 'feeding internally' off
the British government, he maintains a parasitic relationship with his
adopted country. Bram Stoker's *Dracula* (1897) had long since
associated Jews with the 'image of the parasite' and the 'alien
invasion' of Jews into the East End of London who, according to
Arnold White, were also 'feeding off' and 'poisoning' the blood of
the Londoner. A year after publishing *Pongo and the Bull*, Belloc was
to reinforce these constructions in an article on the 'anti-Jewish riots
in South Wales':

To attack Jews as Jews would be flagrantly unjust; nevertheless it is an
unfortunate but unquestionable fact that everywhere a sort of Jew presents
himself to the public view, not only as an oppressor of the poor, but, what
is much more intolerable, an alien oppressor – an oppressor incapable of
understanding the feelings of those he oppresses. That impossibility of
understanding is the real root of anti-semitism and many worse things.[19]

Battersea, in *Pongo and the Bull*, also does 'not understand blood that
is not his own' and it is this racial lack of 'understanding' that
threatens to turn even the Prime Minister of England into a 'fanatic':
'Sixty-six is late in life for a man to become a man, and the mood of
anger will not last long at such an age. But Dolly was certainly
extremely angry. ... Leaders of every other people in Christendom

[19] *The Eye-Witness*, 31 August 1911. Pick, *Faces of Degeneration*, p. 173 cites Arnold White in this
context and discusses Bram Stoker's *Dracula* (London, 1897).

save his had drunk deep of that cup at one time or another. He was being bullied by the money-lenders' (76–7). Such was the rational cause of the 'fanaticism' of even the Prime Minister of England. More importantly, such was the necessity for honest Englishmen everywhere to confront the alien threat in their midst.

Unsurprisingly, the rest of Belloc's novel is concerned with replacing Battersea with an 'Anglo-Saxon' multi-millionaire who can undertake the Indian Loan. This racially acceptable financier turns out to be George Quinlan Smith, an eccentric long-lost American uncle of Mary Smith. Although Mary was 'almost the adopted daughter' (7) of Battersea, she is quick to recognize his 'alien' unscrupulous nature and, therefore, persuades her uncle to finance Britain's debt without any preconditions. Interestingly enough, much of the tension in Belloc's novel is generated by Quinlan Smith's hunt in France for a spoon used by Disraeli – as he 'loved to collect objects connected with the life of the late ... Prime Minister' (58). Disraeli's name is continually evoked in this context as a relic of the past which prevents Quinlan Smith from arranging the Indian Loan for the British government. By the end of *Pongo and the Bull*, the newly found but 'very real patriotism' (224) of Dolly and Mary Smith meant that Battersea also becomes a 'semitic' relic of the past who lost 'a good deal more money' because, the narrator adds ominously, Battersea had gained an appreciation of 'certain things in the English character which had hitherto escaped him' (288). The needs of the Burdens and Clutterbucks of this world to assert their superior heritage is made explicit in this novel. After a decade of writing fiction, Belloc was now able to forcefully assert the authoritarian import of his politics.

All of Belloc's Barnett novels utilize the crude racial distinctions that are made explicit in *Pongo and the Bull*. In emphasizing that Clutterbuck is an 'honest man', for instance, Belloc argues in *Mr Clutterbuck's Election* that 'the occasions on which it is possible to bring against a man of *English lineage* the grave accusation of tampering with political morals are very, very rare' (242, my emphasis). The plot of *A Change in the Cabinet* is also predicated on a Cabinet Minister 'of English lineage' being turned insane – not unlike Edward Ponderevo in *Tono-Bungay* or Victor Radnor in *One of Our Conquerors* – by the 'immoral' way in which he makes money. It is the semitic discourse at the heart of this racially differentiating 'Englishness' that, above all, undermines Belloc's rationalist pretensions when examining the 'Jewish Question'. And yet, many historical and biographical studies of Belloc have deferred to him in this matter and, like Belloc, have rationalized a semitic racial discourse by arguing, for instance, that 'Jewish financial power did, very often, cut a repellent figure'; or that Barnett is a 'recognisable type' and that there is a 'measure of truth in Belloc's caricatures'; or that Belloc's novels are the 'best guide' to an understanding of 'Edwardian politics'.[20]

This reading of Belloc's novels in a 'realist' mode can be explained by the fact that his Barnett quartet culminated in the 'Marconi Scandal' (1912–14), a supposedly 'Jewish' financial scandal which, to many literary critics and historians, seems to have confirmed the 'truth' of Belloc's fiction. Even historians of British antisemitism, such as Colin Holmes, have naturalized the 'Marconi Scandal' and claimed that there is an 'irreducible core of Jewish involvement' which caused the 'scandal' and have, in this way, reinforced Belloc's reasoning. In an otherwise exemplary article David Lodge, with reference to the 'Marconi affair', avows that 'Belloc indeed might have been forgiven for thinking that life had imitated the art of his own novels'. William Empson demonstrates this confusion between 'life' and 'art' with regard to Belloc's fiction by claiming that 'an early stage in the revolt against Parliamentary democracy can be seen in the comic novels of Belloc, written around 1910, largely inspired by the Marconi Scandal'. Empson is right to relate Belloc's fiction to the later 'revolt against Parliamentary democracy' by D. H. Lawrence, T. S. Eliot, Ezra Pound and Wyndham Lewis. But the 'Marconi Scandal' was hardly Belloc's source of 'inspiration' as his 'comic novels' were all written before the 'scandal' began.[21] Empson's muddling of his chronology, and his assumption that there is a causal relationship between Belloc's fiction and historical 'reality', is, however, understandable when we note that the semitic

[20] A. J. P. Taylor, 'Introduction', Donald Read (ed.), *Edwardian England* (London, 1982) p. 12 makes this extraordinary claim. See also Speaight, *The Life of Hilaire Belloc*, p. 184 and Wilson, *Hilaire Belloc*, p. 130.

[21] William Empson, 'Preface', John Harrison, *The Reactionaries: A Study of the Anti-Democratic Intelligentsia* (London, 1966) p. 9 and David Lodge, 'The Chesterbelloc and the Jews', *The Novelist at the Crossroads* (London, 1971) p. 153. See also Holmes, *Anti-Semitism in British Society*, p. 81 and Bryan Cheyette, 'Hilaire Belloc and the "Marconi Scandal" 1900–1914: A Reassessment of the Interactionist Model of Racial Hatred' in Tony Kushner and Kenneth Lunn (eds.), *The Politics of Marginality: Race, the Radical Right and Minorities in Twentieth Century Britain* (London, 1990) pp. 131–42 for a fuller critique of those historians that have naturalized a semitic racial discourse in a supposedly 'rational' framework.

discourse at the heart of the 'Marconi Scandal' was prefigured in the fictional financial scandals of Belloc's 'comic novels'.

As Kenneth Lunn and G. R. Searle have shown, there was a large element of self-fulfilment in the racial representations which were drawn upon in the context of the 'Marconi Scandal'. That is, many of the assumptions behind the 'scandal' had been a part of the politics of 'corruption' for over a decade. *The Eye-Witness* journal, which was launched in June 1911 by Belloc, was specifically intended to oppose political 'corruption' and saw the 'scandal' as the culmination of a long history of semitic venality. In a series of eight articles on the 'Jewish Question', published three months after *The Eye-Witness* was established, Belloc constructed a timeless 'Jewish financial power' that, since the eighteenth century and for the third time in world history, had dominated Europe. Due to the 'largely Judaic' Reformation there was, according to Belloc, 'no better instrument than the English Government' for the expression of this 'Jewish cosmopolitan financial power'. A year before writing these articles, Belloc had described the House of Lords, in a parliamentary debate, as a 'Committee for the protection of the Anglo-Judaic plutocracy under which they lived'. In a subsequent letter, Belloc had justified these remarks by maintaining that:

The existence of the Anglo-Judaic plutocracy seems to me a fact as obvious as the existence of the French Army, or the House of Commons, or of St. Paul's Cathedral. All the main parts of our policy are, it is notorious, conducted in the interests of and by the advice of small groups of rich men, and part of the dominating influence of those groups is Jewish, while part is English, or rather, British. This is notoriously the case in Egypt; it was notoriously the case before the outbreak of the infamous South African War; it is notoriously the case in connection with Indian trade, and it is notoriously the case in connection with the new movement in Turkey.[22]

The 'Marconi Scandal' can be dated from the time when the Marconi tender to provide wireless stations throughout the Empire was provisionally accepted by Herbert Samuel, the Postmaster General, in March 1912. The tender also involved an exchange of shares in the American Marconi Company between Lloyd George, Asquith's Chancellor of the Exchequer, Alec Murray, the Liberal

[22] Letter to Oswald John Simon, 2 March 1910 cited in the *Jewish Chronicle*, 11 March 1910, 14. See also *The Eye-Witness*, 14 September 1911, 395 and 21 September 1911, 427 for two of Belloc's articles on 'The Jewish Question' that are relevant in this context. See also Lunn, 'Political Antisemitism Before 1914', and Searle, *Corruption in British Politics*, chapter 8 for the long-standing racial assumptions that lay behind the 'Scandal'.

Party Chief Whip, Godfrey Isaacs, Marconi's Managing Director, and his brother Rufus Isaacs, the Attorney-General. As Belloc's articles on the 'Jewish Question' had long since postulated a fundamental conflict between 'Jewish cosmopolitan finance' and the English 'national interest', it is not surprising, in these circumstances, that Belloc and *The New Witness* coterie – which replaced Belloc's *The Eye-Witness* in November 1912 – saw the 'Marconi Scandal' as conclusive evidence of an 'Anglo-Judaic plutocracy' running Parliament. Belloc also described the issue of importing cheap Chinese labour in South Africa, the subject of his maiden speech in Parliament, as a policy that was 'not English, but Jewish'. It is in terms of these racial constructions that Belloc's fictional representations and rhetorical strategies in his novels were replicated in the political arena.[23]

Like Bailey, in *Mr Clutterbuck's Election*, who published an encyclopaedia of European-sounding Jewish names next to their 'original' semitic counterparts, Belloc believed that Jews were, above all, an unassimilable 'foreign body' in the European 'organism'. And yet, as with Bailey and Abbott in the Barnett quartet, Belloc distanced himself from the 'fanatical' antisemitism of F. Hugh O'Donnell under Cecil Chesterton's reckless editorship of *The New Witness*:

> The irritation against Jewish power in Western Europe is partly the friction between two races, but much more the annoyance of feeling that non-national financial power can restrict our information and affect our lives in all sorts of ways. It is legitimate to point out, if one does not grow wearisome, the fact that Jewish financial power has prevented people from knowing the truth about the most famous foreign trials where Jews were concerned. But just because these matters so nearly verge upon violent emotion, it is essential to avoid anything like the suspicion of fanaticism. It destroys one's case and weakens all one's efforts ... [24]

Belloc, in his articles and book on 'the Jews', consistently distinguished himself from the 'liberal' policy of 'absorption', which he

---

[23] The best account of the 'Marconi Scandal' is Kenneth Lunn, 'The Marconi Scandal and Related Aspects of British Antisemitism, 1911–1914', Ph.D thesis, University of Sheffield, (1978), which, sadly, remains unpublished and has therefore not yet replaced Frances Donaldson, *The Marconi Scandal* (London, 1962). Lunn also emphasizes that the 'Marconi Scandal' was 'part of a much wider campaign [in *The New Witness*] against Jews, and, in particular, against Jewish wealth and power' (p. 200). For examples of this see *The Eye-Witness*, 21 September 1911, 427 and 28 September 1911, 459.

[24] Letter to Maurice Baring, 27 August 1913. Cited in Speaight, *The Life of Hilaire Belloc*, p. 363. Lunn, 'The Marconi Scandal', chapters 5 and 6 has an exhaustive amount of material on Belloc's attempts to curb the worst excesses of F. Hugh O'Donnell and Cecil Chesterton. See also *The Eye-Witness*, 28 September 1911, 458–9 and 12 October 1911, 522.

thought unworkable, and the 'antisemitic' policy of 'exclusion', which led only to an unChristian 'negative' hatred and did not offer a 'solution' to the 'Jewish Question'. Mediating between these two positions, Belloc called for the return of the 'medieval' notion of 'privilege' or 'private law' where the 'Jewish race' would be 'legally recognised' throughout Europe. This was a euphemism for all Jews being required to give up their national citizenship and to enrol in separate 'Jewish' institutions. As with his fictional narrators, Belloc presented himself as an intermediary between the 'fact' of 'Jewish cosmopolitan financial power' and the irrational 'hatred' of the antisemite. Thus, as well as chiding O'Donnell and Cecil Chesterton for being 'fanatical' and not presenting their case in a rational manner (which could only help the 'other side'), Belloc also addressed many Edwardian Anglo-Jewish societies on his 'solution' to the 'Jewish Question'. Jews were urged in these meetings to voluntarily adopt Belloc's 'medieval solution' and 'develop their corporate traditions as a separate community' which, he believed, would end the 'friction' between the 'Jewish race' and the 'Europeans'. It was, Belloc believed, 'not only impossible, but most harmful' for Jew and Gentile to 'merge'. The *Jewish Chronicle*, with a surprising lack of irony, unintentionally mocked Belloc's position by writing, in an editorial, that:

Mr. Belloc's antisemitism, it must be admitted, is not of a very rabid order, and such prejudice as exists in his mind is probably derived from an imperfect knowledge of the facts of the case, or too implicit reliance on doubtful testimony.[25]

The assumption in the *Jewish Chronicle* editorial – that if Belloc were to gain a more accurate 'knowledge' of Jewish behaviour then he would, somehow, cease to be 'antisemitic' – neatly exposes the powerful ambivalences at the heart of Belloc's 'liberal' race-thinking. By negotiating between a supposedly rational world based on 'facts', 'testimony' and 'the truth', and a supra-rational world based on unchanging racial distinctions, the Janus-faced Belloc managed to face in two fundamentally opposed directions at the same time. The illusory nature of this position was especially exposed when Belloc

---

[25] 'Some Words from an Antisemite', the *Jewish Chronicle*, 12 August 1910, 5. See also 'Interview with Mr Hilaire Belloc, MP', the *Jewish Chronicle*, 12 August 1910, 14, 'Mr. Hilaire Belloc, MP, on "Antisemitism"', 6 March 1908, 19, 'Mr Hilaire Belloc on "Jews in Modern Journalism"', 9 December 1910, 19, '"The Antisemite": Mr Hilare Belloc Defines the Term', 13 December 1912, 25 and 'The Marconi Inquiry: Mr Hilaire Belloc's Explanation', 2 May 1913, 10.

failed to curb the unremitting racial outbursts of F. Hugh O'Donnell and Cecil Chesterton in *The New Witness* by appealing to their sense of reason.

Nonetheless, historians and biographers of Belloc have tended to accept the 'factual' basis of Bellocian 'antisemitism' at its face value. A. N. Wilson, Belloc's most influential apologist, argues that the 'Marconi Scandal' 'stinks' but that Cecil Chesterton 'phrased his accusations in hysterical anti-Jewish language; he did not bother to check his facts; he spoilt, forever, an investigation which needed making and which could, with more subtlety, have toppled his enemies'.[26] But Cecil Chesterton's mock-defence of Rufus Isaacs as someone who is from a 'racial tradition wholly alien from ours' and who should, therefore, not be prosecuted in England, reflects the bludgeoning irony of Belloc's own fiction. The title of F. Hugh O'Donnell's rabidly Judeophobic column in *The New Witness*, 'Twenty Years On', takes its timescale and nightmare vision of a 'semitic' future from *Pongo and the Bull*. Most importantly, the 'plot' of the 'Marconi Scandal' – with its emphasis on fringe political meetings and 'independent liberal' journals attempting to expose the conspiratorial machinations of a dominant 'Jewish cosmopolitan finance' – is not dissimilar from Bailey's attempted exposure of the 'Anapootra Ruby Mines Scandal' in *Mr Clutterbuck's Election*. Both Bailey and *The New Witness* circle carried placards outside the offices of their enemies to further their cause and *The New Witness*-inspired 'National League for Clean Government' campaigned for 'clean government' in much the same way as Bailey did in Belloc's fiction. Even the final eclipse of Barnett's power in *Pongo and the Bull* is 'explained' as the inevitable decline of a cyclical 'Jewish financial power' which, according to Belloc, had reached the peak of its influence in the early twentieth century and was, thus, unable to prevent an 'antisemitic' backlash and the exposure of its worst excesses.[27]

The difference between Belloc's understated *Emmanuel Burden* and the crudely racialized *Pongo and the Bull* undoubtedly points to the

---

[26] Wilson, *Hilaire Belloc*, p. 199 and pp. 195–200 for a recent apologetic account of Belloc's position during the 'Marconi Scandal'. See also Cheyette, 'Hilaire Belloc and the "Marconi Scandal"', for further examples of this reasoning.

[27] *The Eye-Witness*, 12 October 1911, 522–3 and 4 July 1912, cited in Corrin, *G. K. Chesterton and Hilaire Belloc*, p. 58 and *The New Witness*, 3 April 1913. See also Lunn, 'The Marconi Scandal', chapter 7 and 'Political Antisemitism Before 1914', for the importance of the 'National League for Clean Government' in the history of British Fascism.

growing influence and utilization of a semitic discourse in all spheres of Edwardian society from 1900 to 1914. In the years leading up to the First World War, the 'Marconi Scandal' became a common aspect of established politics and seriously threatened to bring down Asquith's government. Furthermore, it succeeded in disillusioning influential figures on the 'left' and the 'right', such as H. G. Wells and Rudyard Kipling, against the liberal consensus and parliamentary democracy. With the publication of *The Free Press* (1918), Belloc could write that if he wanted to know 'what was happening in France' he would read a 'Jewish Socialist paper' or Drumont's 'antisemitic "Libre Parole"' (62). The liberal mainstream was, after the 'Marconi Scandal', no longer a suitable avenue for 'the truth'.

By the inter-war years, Belloc was able to confidently reformulate his semitic discourse in *The Jews* and, in the light of the Bolshevik revolution of 1917, point to the 'half alliance which you find throughout the world between the Jewish financiers on the one hand and the Jewish control of the Russian revolution on the other' (61). Belloc was clearly emboldened in his 'illiberal' conspiratorial thinking by the general discussion of the 'Jewish Question' in England at the time – a far cry from his anti-Dreyfusard days. The language of a Bailey or an Abbott, in other words, was now part of the political mainstream. Looking back to the turn of the century in his *An Essay on the Nature of Contemporary England* (1937), Belloc remembers his isolation in England during the Dreyfus Affair, 'Englishmen were determined, almost to a man, that Dreyfus was innocent... and they were convinced that he was martyred because he was a Jew' (69). Even to this day, because of England's shared 'Commercial Spirit' with 'Israel', he 'still finds in England not only a warm friend, nor even only a permanent ally, but an enthusiastic supporter' of 'Israel' (68). The reasons for this enthusiastic support are made clear by Belloc in the *Weekly Review*, the final and most extreme metamorphosis of *The Eye-Witness*:

The whole of English life is interwoven with Jewry. Our leading families are intermarried with it, our universities, our legal system, our financial system of course and, most important of all, the moral tradition of our society is inseparable from the Jewish money power throughout the world.[28]

---

[28] Belloc, *Weekly Review*, 1 September 1938, cited in Lunn, 'Political Antisemitism Before 1914', p. 35. Corrin, *G. K. Chesterton and Hilaire Belloc*, p. 191 describes the *Weekly Review*, founded in March 1938, as having a 'palpably pro-fascist outlook'.

To demonstrate the extent that England was 'interwoven with Jewry', Belloc even rewrote the 'Marconi Scandal' in *The Postmaster-General* (1932), one of his few inter-war novels, as if it were now the norm of British political life. As a consequence of such thinking Belloc, in the years leading up to the Second World War, became convinced increasingly that 'Cosmopolitan Jewish' bankers were trying to cause a war with Germany so that they might profiteer by financing, at usurious rates, the manufacture of armaments.[29]

By the late 1930s, however, Belloc's interpolation of the language of 'reason' into his discussions of the 'Jewish Question' were to become increasingly fantastic. In a lengthy additional 'Introductory Chapter' to his 1937 edition of *The Jews*, Belloc concentrated on the Spanish Civil War, the rise of Nazism and the nascent State of Israel as three events that had 'accentuated the Jewish question' (xxiv) since 1922, when he had first published his 'admirable Yid book' (as he was to dub *The Jews*). The 'conflict in Spain', according to Belloc, was a 'branch of that general revolutionary movement called Jewish Communism... as expressed by Mordacai himself (Marx)' (xxvii-xxviii). He also hardened his general anti-Zionist position in this chapter and emphasized, in this context, what he called the interwoven strands of Jewish racial feeling and German racial feeling' (xlix) which echoed Shaw and Wells at this time. When it came to the 'German Reich', which he condemned generally for being 'Prussianized' (xli), he was to ask in his 'balanced' fashion whether 'the Nazi attack was sincere. There is no doubt that *in the eyes of its authors* it was provoked by a situation which *they* thought intolerable. But can it be fruitful? ... The attack made upon the Jews is neither thorough nor final' (xl-xli, his emphasis). Later on, he was to reinforce this point with 'the Nazi attack upon the Jewish race... [is] not thorough, not final, but incomplete, and I think soon to prove abortive' (xliii). This is a far cry from Wilson's tendentious claim that we should welcome Belloc's *The Jews* because it 'prophesied what would happen to European Jewry with such eery accuracy'.[30]

[29] Corrin, *G. K. Chesterton and Hilaire Belloc*, pp. 191–2 and chapter 9. Wilson, *Hilaire Belloc*, pp. 357 and 362 also discusses Belloc's Jewish conspiracy theories at this time and Tony Kushner, *The Persistence of Prejudice: Antisemitism in British Society During the Second World War* (Manchester, 1989) p. 38 notes that the *Weekly Review* was to offer lukewarm support to the war effort because it believed Catholic Poland was under threat from a combination of 'Jewish Bolshevism-Nazism' as well as Hitler. For a similar view to this see Oswald Mosley's contemporary speech on the 'Jewish policy of war' in his *My Life* (London, 1968) p. 339.

[30] Wilson, *Hilaire Belloc*, pp. 259–60 and 383 makes facile claims for Belloc's powers of 'prophecy' with regard to 'the Jews' which were mistakenly taken up by most journalistic

On the contrary, Belloc's criticisms of the Nazi's lack of 'thorough-ness' in succumbing temporarily to violent antisemitic emotion could not have been further from the prophetic mark. It was, so he thought, his own apartheid system of 'Privilege' – or separate 'Jewish' and 'Christian' development within European nation-states – that was a more lasting and reasonable 'solution' to the 'Jewish question'. But such was the vacuous unreality of Belloc's simultaneous 'rational' and 'racial' understanding of 'the Jews'. G. K. Chesterton, unlike his life-long friend, was unable to hold in place the extreme contra-dictions of this Janus-faced view of the world. It is to this other half of the 'chesterbelloc' that we shall now turn.

G. K. CHESTERTON: TOWARDS THE NEW JERUSALEM

In his posthumous *Autobiography* (1936), G. K. Chesterton described the 'Marconi Scandal' as 'one of the turning-points in the whole history of England and the world' and, in so doing, divided recent history into 'Pre-Marconi and Post-Marconi days': 'It was during the agitations upon that affair that the ordinary English citizen lost his invincible ignorance; or, in ordinary language, his innocence' (202). Comparing the naïve Whiggish optimism of the Victorian Age with the widespread 'political corruption' (201) of Edwardian England, Chesterton went on to associate the 'Marconi Scandal' with the cynical acceptance by 'the ordinary English citizen' of a parliamentary democracy which was bereft of the last vestiges of liberal idealism.

This extraordinary emphasis on the 'Marconi Scandal' as a turning point in world history has led many of his critics and biographers to regard Chesterton's 'antisemitism' as an 'aberration' brought about by the prosecution in 1913 of his brother, Cecil Chesterton, for criminal libel. During this trial Cecil was received into the Catholic Church and this act of sanctification, juxtaposed with the ignominy of Godfrey Isaacs winning his case, is said to have been the catalyst for G. K.'s severe nervous and physical breakdown in 1914. According to this argument, G. K. was 'not noticeably antisemitic' until after the 'Marconi Scandal' when, under the pernicious influence of Belloc's 'exotic' unEnglish 'antisemitism', G. K. assumed the mantle of Cecil's fanaticism and began editing *The*

reviews of his biography. But it is a sign of the weakness of Wilson's position that, as well as emphasizing Belloc's prophetic powers, he also argues tamely that much of what Belloc had to say about 'the Jews, or the Rich, or the Dons ... remained jokes' (p. 373).

New Witness.[31] G.K.'s impassioned 'Open Letter to Lord Reading', published in *The New Witness* soon after Cecil's untimely death at the end of the First World War, is often cited as evidence of this irrational 'antisemitism' which supposedly contrasts starkly with G. K.'s declarations on 'the Jews' before the war. Chesterton is reacting against Rufus Isaacs, the Lord Chief Justice of England, being chosen as one of the British representatives at the Versailles Peace Conference:

Are we to lose the War which we have already won? That and nothing else is involved in losing the full satisfaction of the national claim of Poland. Is there any man who doubts that the Jewish International is unsympathetic with that full national demand? And is there any man who doubts that you will be sympathetic with the Jewish International? No man who knows anything of the interior facts of modern Europe has the faintest doubt on either point. ... Are we to set up as the standing representative of England a man who is a standing joke against England? That and nothing else is involved in setting up the chief Marconi Minister as our chief Foreign Minister.[32]

The 'Open Letter' begins by referring to the end of 'the great Marconi duel' in which Lord Reading and Chesterton 'played the part of seconds' but which had ended, tragically, with Cecil Chesterton 'found dead in the trenches'. Throughout the letter, Chesterton juxtaposed the 'strange private loyalty' of the Isaacs family with the 'public honour' of the 'English nation' and, it is implied, the Chesterton family. Unlike Chesterton's early novel *The Ball and the Cross* (1910), which was published serially between 1905 and 1906, the antagonistic 'duelists' are far from united by a spiritless world. With rather less imagination, Chesterton merely reinforces the binary opposition between a rooted Englishness and a rootless 'Jewish International' which is predicated on the ambiguous sin of 'private loyalty'.

It is, however, a mistake to narrowly situate Chesterton's acknowl-

---

[31] Maisie Ward, *Gilbert Keith Chesterton* (London, 1944) has been influential in this regard. See also John Coates, *Chesterton and the Edwardian Cultural Crisis* (Hull, 1984) p. 9 and Corrin, *G. K. Chesterton and Hilaire Belloc*, p. 61. By far the most detailed account of Chesterton's literary 'antisemitism' is Owen Edwards, 'Chesterton and Tribalism', *The Chesterton Review* 6 (Number 1, 1979–80), 33–69 and his 'The Innocence of Rufus Isaacs', *The Chesterton Review* 9 (Numbers 3–4, 1985), 339–76 and 496–519. These articles contrast favourably with the many apologetic discussions of Chesterton's 'antisemitism' in the pages of *The Chesterton Review*.

[32] 'The Sign of the World's End: An Open Letter to Lord Reading' is usefully reproduced in Frances Donaldson, *The Marconi Scandal*, Appendix A, pp. 256–9.

edged 'semitism' in the bitter aftermath of the 'Marconi Scandal'. In the years leading up to the 'Open Letter', it is quite possible to trace an equivalent set of semitic racial constructions in Chesterton's Edwardian writings and public pronouncements. Towards the beginning of *The Ball and the Cross*, for instance, MacIan and Turnbull attempt to duel in the back garden of a Dickensian 'old curiosity shop' but are prevented by the shop-keeper, Henry Gordon, whom they tie up and gag. Chesterton's narrator is clear about his low opinion of Gordon and, by the end of the novel, he is known as the 'Jew shopkeeper' (392):

I have suggested that the sunset light made everything lovely. To say that it made the keeper of the curiosity shop lovely would be a tribute perhaps too extreme. It would easily have made him beautiful if he had been merely squalid; if he had been a Jew of the Fagin type. But he was a Jew of another and much less admirable type; a Jew with a very well sounding name. For though there are no hard tests for separating the tares and wheat of any people; one rude but efficient guide is that the nice Jew is called Moses Solomon, and the nasty Jew is called Thornton Percy. The keeper of the curiosity shop was of the Thornton Percy branch of the chosen people; he belonged to those Lost Tribes whose industrious object is to lose themselves. (50–1)

Chesterton, in his *Charles Dickens* (1906), had already accused Dickens of attempting in a 'double sense' to 'judge Israel' by introducing 'the kind old Jew' in *Our Mutual Friend* as a public recompense for the 'bad old Jew' in *Oliver Twist* (209). Five years later, in his *Appreciations and Criticisms of the Works of Dickens* (1911), he went on to state in his introduction that 'to anyone who knows a low Jew by sight or hearing, the story called *Our Mutual Friend* is literally full of Jews' (xi-xii). This description of assimilated 'low Jews' was elaborated on by Chesterton in a talk to the West End Jewish Literary Society in 1911. In this talk, Chesterton continued to echo *The Ball and the Cross* and distinguished between 'two kinds of Jews, rich and poor' and concluded that 'the poor were nice and the rich were nasty' which was a life-long axiom of his semitic discourse:

[T]he broad-minded Jew was a difficulty and an offense in Europe; the narrow-minded Jew was an excellent fellow, whom one admired and regarded with an amount of veneration as one did any other great relic of antiquity, such as the pyramids.[33]

---

[33] Cited in the *Jewish Chronicle*, 1 December 1911, 20. A decade later, in 'The Trees of Pride', collected in *The Man Who Knew Too Much* (London, 1922) p. 165, Chesterton went on to

This deliberately 'nasty' construction of the 'broad-minded Jew' is, most importantly, of a piece with Chesterton's more widespread fear of a loss of a 'sense of limits' – 'all my life I have loved edges, and the boundary line that brings one thing sharply against another'. The need for an orthodox 'dogma' to oppose the 'vagueness and drift' of the modern world meant that the 'narrow-minded Jew' was to be venerated by Chesterton precisely because he maintained a distinct 'boundary line' between his Jewishness and Christendom. His racial counterparts, on the other hand, were to cause 'offense' by attempting, industriously, 'to lose themselves' in their supposedly 'adopted' European nation. In his attempt to 'assimilate', the 'broad-minded Jew' thus lacks any sense of 'limitation'. It was, above all, this specifically Chestertonian inflection to his semitic discourse that distinguished it from Hilaire Belloc.

In *The Ball and the Cross* the 'Jew shopkeeper', Henry Gordon, opposes MacIan and Turnbull's life-and-death struggle over the importance of religion with a wishy-washy 'little respect for humanity'. Turnbull, in response to this superficial humanism, points out that Gordon is a 'pornographic bookseller' and deserves to be 'ruled like a dog or killed like a cockroach' (53–4). Gordon's denial of 'human limitation' is, as Lynette Hunter has pointed out, the 'root of madness' in *The Ball and the Cross*. Chesterton's sense of religious virtue is rightly described by Hunter as a 'limiting structure' through which it is possible briefly to glimpse the absolute. I would argue that Chesterton's sense of religious 'boundaries' is central both to his model of Christian individualism and his national construction of a 'small oppugnant' English *patria*.[34] This can be seen, especially, in Chesterton's *Heretics* (1905), published in the year that *The Ball and the Cross* was completed. In *Heretics*, 'nationality' is separated from 'race' and is defined as being akin to 'a church or a secret society; it is a product of the human soul and will; it is a spiritual product' (174). Rudyard Kipling's Imperialism, in contrast to this spiritualized 'nationalism', is specifically attacked in this context as a form of 'cosmopolitanism' (50):

---

describe 'the Jew... as a venerable and historic relic', echoing his talk of a decade before. This recycling of significant phrases, across decades, is a common feature of Chesterton's writing.

[34] Grainger, *Patriotisms*, p. 104. See Lynette Hunter, *G. K. Chesterton: Explorations in Allegory* (London, 1979) p. 10 and p. 62 and Corrin, *G. K. Chesterton and Hilaire Belloc*, p. 9 for Chesterton's need for 'limiting structures'.

Mr Kipling is a man of the world, with all the narrowness that belongs to those imprisoned in that planet. He knows England as an intelligent Englishman knows Venice. He has been to England a great many times; he has stopped there for long visits. But he does not belong to it, or to any place; and the proof of it is that he thinks of England as a place. The moment we are rooted in a place, the place vanishes. We live like a tree with the whole strength of the universe. (49)

Grainger has aptly described Chesterton's England as an 'occluded country, occluded by its governing classes, its press magnates, its art, culture and science and, above all, by its Empire'. This sense of occlusion, which necessitated 'the recovery of a lost *patria*', under-pinned Chesterton's unique anti-Imperial romanticization of the Boers. In his early poem 'Africa', Chesterton even described the Boers as a 'sleepy people, without priest or kings' living in a land that 'is free and smells of honour and English things'. During the Boer War, as he was to state in his *Autobiography*, Chesterton 'emphatically' supported the right of the small Boer nation to patriotically defend 'their little farming commonwealth' (115). This extreme pro-Boer position was to inspire Chesterton's first novel, *Napoleon of Notting Hill* (1904). In this work, Adam Wayne's 'passionate loyalty' to Notting Hill, and his opposition to an impersonal bureaucracy, is comically privileged in much the same way as Chesterton had supported the refusal of the Boers to sublimate their patriotism to the 'cosmo-politan' British Empire.[35]

Chesterton's 'Zionism' was similarly intended to release a Jewish 'narrow-minded' dogma and sense of patriotism which would neutralize the 'broad-minded Jew' who, apparently, had no sense of national limits. Both Chesterton's pro-Boerism and pro-Zionism, as Christopher Hollis has observed, can be distinguished from Belloc's politics at this time. Whereas Chesterton accentuated a spiritual, bounded Englishness, Belloc chose to emphasize the other side of this national particularism and foregrounded, instead, the international 'Jewish financier'. On the issue of Zionism, Belloc told the *Jewish Chronicle* in a 1910 interview that he did not support the creation of a Jewish State in Palestine as 'the Jew' was 'too much a part of Europe ever to be satisfied and successful apart from Europe'. In contrast to Belloc, Chesterton, also in a *Jewish Chronicle* interview, maintained a year later that:

---

[35] Grainger, *Patriotisms*, p. 108. See also Margaret Canovan, *G. K. Chesterton: Radical Populist* (London, 1977) p. 104.

Zionism would bring to the Jew territorial patriotism, which he now lacks. It would assuredly allow him to develop his own culture in arts, in literature, in science, and it would put an end to the eternal entanglement of mutual wrong of which he is the unhappy cause between himself and the nations among whom he lives.[36]

These differences in emphasis point to a specifically Chestertonian inflection in his use of a semitic discourse which qualifies the supposedly 'implacable' influence which the 'antisemitic' Belloc was meant to have had on the innocent Chesterton. Unlike Belloc, who attempted to interpolate a semitic discourse within a tradition of liberal rationalism, none was more aware of the limits of this tradition than Chesterton. Before meeting Belloc, as his biographers have noted, Chesterton would specify 'no Jews' at certain gatherings or would offer, with 'semitic jocularity', to walk to the 'gates of the Ghetto' with his well-to-do Anglo-Jewish friends. This commonplace construction of Jewish racial difference was also central to Chesterton's 'Zionism' which was predicated on the basis that 'the Jew is not an Englishman, because his nationality is not English'. Whereas 'the Jew' in Belloc's writings epitomized an alien tradition of capitalism, Chesterton still believed in the potential for Jews to change for the better. Nonetheless, any improvement of 'the Jew' was to take place outside the borders of England. Chesterton's Zionism, therefore, was predicated on the belief that 'the Jew' will not be able to develop a 'nationality' which 'he now lacks' until 'he discovers he is of a separate race, with a history of his own, and a future which to be worthy he must make his own'. Such is the confusion generated by the unbounded, nationless 'Jew'.[37]

It was in relation to this sense of a fixed, national absolutism – 'the moment we are rooted in a place, the place vanishes. We live like a tree with the whole strength of the universe' – that Chesterton was to represent 'the orthodox Jewish theory' as a replication of his

[36] 'Interview with Mr Hilaire Belloc, MP', the *Jewish Chronicle*, 12 August 1910, 14 and 'G. K.C: Interview for the *Jewish Chronicle*', the *Jewish Chronicle*, 28 April 1911, 18. See also Christopher Hollis, *The Mind of Chesterton* (London, 1970) pp. 106–7. Chesterton's interview in the *Jewish Chronicle* has been reprinted in *The Chesterton Review* 13 (Number 2, May 1987), 152–9 and his 'Zionism' has been usefully compared with Belloc's 'anti-Zionism' in Kevin Morris, 'Reflections on Chesterton's Zionism', *The Chesterton Review* 13 (Number 2, May 1987), 163–75.
[37] Hunter, *G. K. Chesterton*, chapters 1 and 4 is an excellent account of Chesterton's awareness of the limits of liberalism. See also Dudley Barker, *G. K. Chesterton: A Biography* (London, 1973) pp. 36–7 for his youthful 'antisemitism'. For Chesterton's early 'Zionism' see his *Jewish Chronicle* interview, 28 April 1911, 18 which can also be found in *The Chesterton Review* 13 (Number 2, May 1987), 157.

boundary-ridden 'orthodox Christian theory'. The 'broad-minded' or heretic 'Jew', in this construction, was to embody the worst excesses of a 'cosmopolitan' lack of rootedness. Thus, in a 1908 article in *Albany Review*, Chesterton was to speak of England's 'open servility to the strong international Jew' and, three years later, he was to refer in the *Nation* to the 'spirit' of Jewish 'international finance' as being a 'contempt for nationality'. The need for 'the Jew' to gain 'a centrum' – or a sense of national and personal limitation – was articulated at length by Chesterton in the *Nation* and in his 1911 *Jewish Chronicle* interview. The *Nation*, a Liberal journal, had criticized a provision in Lord Swaythling's will which 'bound his children to the profession of the Jewish religion [and] forbade them to marry anyone who was non-Jewish'. Chesterton's defence of Swaythling is significant:

[T]he central and singular point is this. Many Englishmen, and I am one of them, do seriously think that the international and largely secret power of the great Jewish houses is a problem and a peril. To all this, however, you are indifferent. You allow Jews to be monopolists and wire-pullers, war-makers and strife-breakers, buyers of national honours and sellers of national honour. The one thing apparently, that you won't allow Jews to be is Jews. You don't mind their managing our affairs; it is when they manage their own affairs that you interfere with them. ... The wealthy Semite sits in the inmost chamber of the State; he controls it by a million filaments of politics and finance. But the only pebble you throw at the poor old man, you throw at his most honourable moment, when the schemes are over and his riches vain, and with a gesture, momentarily sublime, he bears witness to the God of his fathers. This does not strike me as respecting a religion – or even tolerating it.[38]

This uncompromising racial division of 'the Jew' into perilous 'international' financiers and 'orthodox' emblems of religious virtue, however short-lived, was not to be sustained in Chesterton's fiction published shortly after this correspondence. In *Manalive* (1912), the figure of Moses Gould conforms, on one level, to Chesterton's 'nice Jew'. As with the imaginary 'Moses Solomon' in *The Ball and the Cross*, Gould's healthy lack of assimilation means that he does not attempt to 'lose himself' in an 'alien' English nationality. The Cockney Gould is introduced initially in terms of his racial

[38] The *Nation*, 18 March 1911, cited in *The Chesterton Review* 13 (Number 2, May 1987), 146–7. This correspondence is reproduced and discussed in *The Chesterton Review* 13 (Number 2, May 1987), 143–52 and in the *Jewish Chronicle*, 16 June 1911, 26. See also the *Albany Review* 2 (1907–8), 188.

explicitness as a 'small resilient Jew', a lodger in Beacon House, whose 'negro vitality and vulgarity amused Michael [Moon] so much that he went round with him from bar to bar, like the owner of a performing monkey' (19). But his 'negro' race also disallows Chesterton's class and national distinctions between wealthy Jewish cosmopolitans and poor 'orthodox' Jews.[39]

Gould's racial difference, in other words, also prevents him from conforming to Chesterton's construction of the 'good' nationalist Jew. Thus, as Michael Moon's 'comic crony', Gould's 'dark eyes' dominate and point to the semitic depths that underlie his godless bestiality: 'swaggering on short legs with a preposterous purple tie, he was the gayest of godless little dogs; but like a dog also in this, that however he danced and wagged with delight, the two dark eyes on each side of his protuberant nose glistened gloomily like black buttons' (32). Far from situating him in an exemplary nationalism, it is the 'shameless rationality of another race' (43) that prevents him from attaining the spiritual transfiguration that he so desperately needs. At one point in the novel, Moon stands in Gould's 'tall crooked shadow' (39) as if to highlight the overly Hebraic English Puritan tradition which Moon initially embodies and which he must transcend as a Catholic Irish 'Christian mystic'.[40] While the other tenants of 'Beacon House' succumb to a Christian 'state of submission and assent', and so reinforce Moon's conversion, Gould, in stark contrast, remains the 'disinterested' Jew (143):

> The instant [Moses Gould] had spoken all the rest knew they had been in an almost religious state of submission and assent. Something had bound them all together; something in the sacred tradition. ... Moses Gould was as good a fellow in his way as ever lived; far kinder to his family than more refined men of pleasure, simple and steadfast in his admirations, a thoroughly genuine character. But wherever there is conflict, crises come in which any soul, personal or racial, unconsciously turns on the world the most hateful of its hundred faces. English reverence, Irish mysticism, American idealism, looked up and saw on the face of Moses a certain smile. It was that smile of the Cynic Triumphant, which has been the tocsin for many a cruel riot in Russian villages or medieval towns. (215–16)

Although Gould is 'ill-adapted both physically and morally for the purposes of permanent sculpture' (145), it is precisely his racial fixity

---

[39] Sander Gilman, *Difference and Pathology: Stereotypes of Sexuality, Race and Madness* (Ithaca, 1985) *passim* usefully relates constructions of 'the Jew' as 'black' to more general racial representations based on colour.   [40] Hunter, *G. K. Chesterton*, p. 101.

which prevents him from going beyond his worldly 'common sense' (139) so that he, too, can become spiritually 'alive'. While 'little nosey Gould' (135) is a 'nice Jew' who is 'kind to his family', his cynical smile, the 'most hateful of [his] hundred faces', provides the spurious 'tocsin' or Bellocian rationale for the Russian or medieval pogroms. At the same time, it is Gould's inability to transcend the merely rational and enter the 'beacon' of Christendom in *Manalive* which is the necessary racial, religious and philosophical counterpoint to the novel's privileged supra-rational 'Christian' sphere. The racially determined Gould is mitigated neither by his class nor his obvious Jewish 'nationality'. By evoking the 'hundred faces' which Gould might potentially wear Chesterton, in the end, prefigures the dangerous lack of 'permanence' that will be seen to define Chesterton's indeterminate 'semites' in his later fiction.

Written just before the 'Marconi Scandal', the focal point for Chesterton's story 'The Queer Feet', collected in *The Innocence of Father Brown* (1911), is the Vernon Hotel. It is in this hotel that the false apostles of capitalism, 'The Twelve True Fishermen', hold their annual dinner. This abode is the obverse of Beacon House as it caters not for those distinguished by a Christian 'state of submission and assent' but for an 'oligarchical society which has gone almost mad on good manners' (58). It is only possible to make meaningful distinctions in this reductive 'commercial' world because at the 'heart of a plutocracy tradesmen become cunning enough to be more fastidious than their customers' (58). The owner of this emblematically Edwardian 'hotel' is a 'Jew named Lever' who made a 'million out of it, by making it difficult to get into' and this 'limitation in the scope of his enterprise' is made possible by 'the most careful polish in its performance' (59). In other words, the 'madness' of Lever's 'good manners' abolishes the most profound of spiritual relations with a 'higher' world and sets up, instead, a series of false material 'limitations'. Once again, 'the Jew' signifies the confusion which arises when false or wordly distinctions blur the timeless boundary between God and man.

When Father Brown comes to administer the last rites to an Italian waiter, Lever is embarrassed by his rather dingy appearance and locks Father Brown into a small room which he can use as a makeshift confessional. The room, we are told, was normally used by Lever 'for delicate and important matters, such as lending a duke a thousand pounds or declining to lend him a sixpence' (61–2). There are echoes here of Arnold Bennett's *The Grand Babylon Hotel* (1902) where the Jewish millionaire, Sampson Levi, arranges loans for the 'Princes and Courts of Europe' and, in turn, is known as 'the Court Pawnbroker'.[41] Continuing this commonplace reference to the feared control of a European aristocracy by a semitic plutocracy, Chesterton's narrator notes with conspicuous irony the inversion of religious values inherent in the Vernon Hotel:

It is a mark of the magnificent tolerance of Mr Lever that he permitted this holy place to be profaned by a mere priest, scribbling away on a piece of paper. The story which Father Brown was writing down was very much a better story than this one, only it will never be known. (62)

Father Brown's confessional enabled the thief Flambeau to tell him his unknown 'story' and so restore a set of spiritual boundaries to the Vernon Hotel. Flambeau had stolen the hotel's silver cutlery by 'appearing' simultaneously as both a waiter and a plutocrat and is persuaded by Father Brown to confess his crime. He is able to obtain this confession as Flambeau had been given away by the differing sounds which his 'queer feet' had made when they passed the confessional. Father Brown's 'Christian reasoning', in short, had allowed him to make the key distinctions between various superficial disguises. The residents of the Vernon Hotel, on the other hand, were unable to see such differences in a world defined by the unbounded 'madness' of 'good manners'.[42] Flambeau's super-human skills of assimilation exploit this spurious lack of difference between human beings. He is, however, a pale reflection of the assimilated Lever, the main benefactor of this spiritual confusion. By confessing his crimes in 'The Queer Feet', Flambeau is allowed to enter the spiritual realm of Christendom in the rest of *The Innocence of Father Brown*. In stark contrast, Lever reverts to his racial type and, as the story progresses, is known as 'the Jew' (74) who speaks with a 'deepening accent' (74) and his skin, a 'genial copperbrown', is turned into a 'sickly yellow' (73). As in *Manalive* Chesterton attempts to re-establish the 'orthodox' boundaries of Christianity by differentiating racially between gentile and Jew. Flambeau, after this story, becomes Father Brown's trusted aid whereas 'the Jew' in the later Father Brown stories becomes increasingly the embodiment of spiritual confusion.

---

[41] Arnold Bennett's *The Grand Babylon Hotel* (London, 1902), Penguin edition, p. 90.
[42] See Hunter, *G. K. Chesterton*, p. 157 for this useful reading of 'The Queer Feet'.

A decade earlier, in a 1901 article in *The Speaker* called 'Jews Old and New', Chesterton had similarly associated Jews in general with an untranscendent worldliness:

It is the formidable normality that constitutes the real power of the Jew. ... It is no mere accident that the most brilliant Jew of this age is Dr Max Nordau; a man with whom, to speak paradoxically, sanity has become a madness. He spares nothing in his application of the religion of common sense, the law that is written in men's bones. Neither the hardness of Tolstoi nor the fragility of Maeterlinck; neither the bitter simplicity of Ibsen nor the drunken glory of Whitman can lure this old Hebrew from the strait path of judgement.[43]

Chesterton, in this article, also refers to the 'Jewish plutocratic problem' and the 'internal disease' of 'Jewish commerce' – citing Max Nordau's disdain for the 'Semitic plutocrats' – which gives the lie to those that situate Chesterton's use of a semitic racial discourse after the 'Marconi Scandal'. One should not underestimate the continuity of Chesterton's construction of 'the Jew'. In his *Four Faultless Felons* (1930), for instance, Chesterton could reiterate the 'formidable normality' of 'the Jews' by describing as 'absolutely characteristic' for a 'little Jew to have a little champagne, but very expensive; and to have black coffee, the proper digestive, after it' (260). Having said that, Chesterton's emphasis in this early piece on the 'weird domesticity' and 'terrible contentment' of 'the Jews' also has its origins in Matthew Arnold's non-racial construction of a complacent bourgeois Hebraism.[44] That Chesterton could utilize this Arnoldian vocabulary of 'culture' – along side that of 'race' – can be seen from *Heretics* where H. G. Wells's Utopia and Kipling's Imperialism are said to be forms of 'cosmopolitanism' as they both have abolished 'all patriotic boundaries' (80). By the time of *The Victorian Age in Literature* (1913), Kipling's poetry is read as having concentrated 'on the purely Hebraic parts of the Bible' (60) and this 'cosmopolitan' Hebraism is second only to George Bernard Shaw's ideal of the Superman in its denial of mankind's rootedness and innate spirituality. This Arnoldian 'cultural' discourse can also be

---

[43] Chesterton, 'Jews Old and New', *The Speaker* (2 March 1901) reprinted in *The Chesterton Review* 9 (Number 1, February 1983), 9 and 6–11. Chesterton is referring here to Max Nordau's *Degeneration* (1895) which made a considerable impact in Britain in the late 1890s.

[44] Chesterton, 'Jews Old and New', 9–11. Chesterton's *Eugenics and Other Evils* (London, 1922) has a chapter entitled 'The Anarchy from Above' to characterize a society devoid of Christian values. See also the discussion of George Bernard Shaw's *An Unsocial Socialist* (1884) for equivalent representations of 'Jewish' worldliness.

applied to *The Man Who was Thursday* (1908) which Owen Edwards
has argued suggestively is the 'nightmare of a man who fears
Christians are really Jews, or *vice versa*'. Michael Coren is wrong to
conclude from Edwards's reading that this novel is an 'antisemitic'
text because 'Sunday's right-hand men' are 'South African and
American millionaires' who 'got hold of all the communications'. By
posing this sense of indeterminacy and conspiratorial power in non-
racial terms, Chesterton is true in *The Man Who was Thursday* to his
Arnoldian 'cultural' legacy.[45]

The tension between this 'cultural' legacy, and the racial discourse
underpinning it, can be seen in Chesterton's earliest writings. A year
before meeting Belloc, a rather youthful Chesterton had published a
poem, 'To a Certain Nation' (1899), in *The Wild Knight* (1900),
which reflected the horror of mainstream liberal English opinion at
the persecution of Dreyfus:

> Thou hast a right to rule thyself; to be
>   The thing thou wilt; to grin, to fawn, to creep;
> To crown these clumsy liars; ay, and we
>   Who knew thee once, we have a right to weep.

In a letter to Ethel Smyth, published in 1900, Chesterton wrote that
'I wish we were all *born* Roman Catholics. I believe in their spirit and
refuse to acknowledge the Exclusive Supremacy of their church; just
as I am an anti-Dreyfusard and refuse to acknowledge – and should
refuse on a rack – the guilt, or even the probable guilt, of the
Captain'. Chesterton, in this letter, identifies interestingly with
Dreyfus as an individual victim (as opposed to the Dreyfusards who
campaigned on his behalf) just as, at this stage, he accepted the
'spirit' of Catholicism but not its institutional 'supremacy'. There is
a parallel here with Chesterton's sense of outrage in the 1890s at the
pogroms in Eastern Europe. In an early poem, Chesterton referred to
the 'Persecution of the Jews in Russia' and wrote that 'a brave and
tortured people cry the shame of men to God'. On hearing the news
of a particularly vicious pogrom, Chesterton wanted to 'knock
someone down, but refrained'. Writing in the liberal tradition of
Arnold, George Eliot and Robert Browning, Chesterton could
identify in this early period with 'the Jew' as victim. But, even when
utilizing this Arnoldian cultural discourse, he could still racially

---

[45] Michael Coren, *Gilbert: The Man Who Was G. K. Chesterton* (London, 1989) p. 205 and
Edwards, 'Chesterton and Tribalism', 57.

define 'continental anti-Semitism' in 1901 as a phenomenon that 'flourish[es] tauntingly the image of a martyred Jew upon an Aryan gibbet'.[46] In Chesterton's book on *Robert Browning* (1903), there is a similar confusion of a racial and cultural terminology in his examination of the 'theory' that Browning was 'of Jewish blood'. Chesterton notes that this suggestion was a 'perfectly conceivable' view which Browning 'would have been the last to have thought derogatory, but for which, as a matter of fact, there is exceedingly little evidence':

> The chief reason assigned by his contemporaries for the belief [in Browning's 'Jewish blood'] was the fact that he was, without doubt, specially and profoundly interested in Jewish matters. This suggestion, worthless in any case, would, if anything, tell the other way. For while an Englishman may be enthusiastic about England, or indignant about England, it never occurred to any living Englishman to be interested in England. Browning was, like every other intelligent Aryan, interested in the Jews; but if he was related to every people in which he was interested, he must have been of extraordinarily mixed extraction.[47]

Along with his reference to Browning as an 'Aryan', Chesterton goes on to contend, with a commendable lack of racial determinism, that 'Browning's descent from barons, or Jews, or lackeys, or black men, is not the main point touching his family. If the Brownings were of mixed origin, they were so much the more like the great majority of English middle-class people' (7). But this generous assessment of Browning's racial heritage was to be rewritten in the 1905 edition of *The Wild Knight*, which contained 'To a Certain Nation'. Writing in a conspiratorial mode, Chesterton attached a note to this new edition saying that he has not 'been able to reach my final verdict on the individual' at the centre of the Dreyfus Affair because of the 'acrid and irrational unanimity of the English press'. He 'roughly states' his new-found 'position' as follows: 'There may have been a fog of injustice in the French courts; I know that there was a fog of injustice in the English newspapers.' Maisie Ward is obviously right to point her finger at the influence of Belloc with regard to Chesterton's change of 'position' on the Dreyfus Affair and his 'To a Certain

[46] Chesterton, 'Jews Old and New', p. 11. Barker, *G. K. Chesterton*, p. 16 cites Chesterton's letter to Ethel Smyth and Coren, *Gilbert*, pp. 35–6 cites Chesterton's reaction to the Russian pogroms.

[47] Chesterton, *Robert Browning* (London, 1903) p. 4. Further references to this book will be in parentheses in the body of the text.

Nation'. Nonetheless, the 'fog' surrounding the Dreyfus Affair is in line with Chesterton's fictional construction of 'the Jew' as a site for spiritual confusion.[48] His early representation of Moses Gould as an innocent victim of the pogroms in *Manalive* is similarly undermined when Gould's racial failure to go beyond his 'cynical' rationality is said to have acted as a 'tocsin for many a cruel riot in Russia'. The replacement of the liberal view of 'the Jew' as a victim with the 'fog' of conspiratorial uncertainty can be seen especially in Chesterton's story, 'The Duel of Dr Hirsch', which was collected in *The Wisdom of Father Brown* (1914).

'The Duel of Dr Hirsch' is the culmination of Chesterton's reassessment of the Dreyfus Affair which was begun in the second edition of *The Wild Knight*. It also demonstrates the extent that Chesterton eventually came to privilege a racial discourse over Arnold's ideal of 'culture'. Unlike his earlier writings, Chesterton could no longer identify with the Jewish 'victim' or recognize the potential for change within 'the Jew'. Father Brown explicitly describes 'The Duel of Dr Hirsch' as 'another Dreyfus case' (343) which might also be said to refer back to the Marconi 'duel' and *The Ball and the Cross*. This story concerns the supposedly traitorous acts of a French Jewish scientist, Dr Paul Hirsch, who is accused of passing military secrets to 'the Prussians'. Hirsch, 'although born in France and covered with the most triumphant favours of French education' is said to be 'more like a German than a Frenchman' (342). A note written in German is found in his pocket betraying his scientific discoveries and France, as with the Dreyfus Affair, is divided between the 'atheist' left and the 'nationalist' right (348) about whether the note is a forgery or not. In discussing the 'Hirsch affair' with Flambeau, Father Brown admits to being morally confused over whether Hirsch is guilty and compares it with his 'puzzle' over the 'Dreyfus case':

[W]hat puzzled me was the *sincerity* of both parties. I don't mean the political parties; the rank and file are always roughly honest, and often duped. I mean the persons of the play. I mean the conspirators, if they were

---

[48] *The Collected Poems of G. K. Chesterton* (London, 1927) p. 318 contains the 'note' to the second edition of *The Wild Knight* written in 1905. Ward, *Gilbert Keith Chesterton*, pp. 117–18 discusses this in her biography of Chesterton which more recent biographies have echoed. It should be noted, however, that Ward shares many of Chesterton's racial assumptions about 'the Jews'. In her 1944 biography, *Gilbert Keith Chesterton*, she argues that *The New Witness* was correct to point out that 'a Jew might not be specially pro-German in feeling, yet his actions might help Germany by being pro-Jewish' (p. 354).

conspirators. I mean the men who *must* have known the truth. Now Dreyfus went on like a man who *knew* he was a wronged man. And yet the French statesmen and soldiers went on as if they *knew* he wasn't a wronged man, but simply a wrong 'un. I don't mean they behaved well; I mean they behaved as if they were sure. I can't describe these things; I know what I mean. (351–2)

Father Brown's inability to say what he 'means' and to distinguish between good and evil leaves him admitting, with regard to the 'Hirsch affair', that he doubts 'everything that has happened today' (354). After postulating that Dreyfus was both innocent *and* guilty, Father Brown, in a characteristic moment of revelation, begins to understand Hirsch's 'contradictory position' (352). Hirsch, Father Brown discovers, has doubled as his most savage accuser and, like Dreyfus, is worse than 'guilty' as his actions have knowingly divided France. Encouraged by Father Brown to follow Hirsch's supposed accuser to his house, Flambeau finally stumbles on the frightening 'truth' underlining the 'Hirsch affair':

Seen thus in the glass the white face looked like the face of Judas laughing horribly and surrounded by capering flames of hell. For a spasm Flambeau saw the fierce, red-brown eyes dancing, then they were covered with a pair of blue spectacles. Slipping on a loose black coat, the figure vanished towards the front of the house. A few minutes later a roar of popular applause from the street beyond announced that Dr Hirsch had once more appeared upon the balcony. (361)

Hirsch's one-man conspiracy to devilishly gain personal 'glory' (355) at the expense of France is contrasted in particular with his intellectual ascendancy as a cross between 'Darwin doubled with the position of Tolstoy' (342). It is, presumably, Hirsch's Judas-like egotism that is prepared to betray France in a bid to gain the necessary power to fulfil his superficially humanitarian ideals. Just as the Isaacs brothers were motivated by a 'strange private loyalty' which, in Chesterton's view, undermined British parliamentary democracy, Hirsch's personal beliefs also threaten to inflict untold damage on France. The 'truth' that lies behind both Hirsch and the Isaacs brothers is that they have not accepted any limits on their beliefs or actions and that they, therefore, play any role to achieve their ends at the expense of 'the nation'. Such, finally, are the dangers inherent in this semitic lack of limitation and the resulting uncertainty that surrounds the moral worth of even the most obvious Jewish victim.

Written on the eve of Chesterton's mental and physical breakdown, *The Flying Inn* (1914) is Chesterton's most comprehensive construction of semitic confusion in his fiction. It has been described as both 'jovial and light-hearted' and a 'bitter ... post-Marconi book' and this ambiguity of tone is reflected in its starkly manichaean form. John Coates has usefully emphasized the intellectual coherence of *The Flying Inn* which, he argues, goes beyond the common reading of this novel as a 'rambling extravaganza'. In this reading, *The Flying Inn* is structured around a series of binary oppositions which enables the novel to operate 'on many levels, social, political, philosophical and religious'.[49] Chesterton's perennial bugbears are embodied crudely in the contrast between Lord Philip Ivywood's all-embracing futuristic Nietzscheanism which, in attempting to close down the traditional public house and turn Britain into a Moslem country, threatens a distinctive English past. Ivywood, as with Michael Moon in *Manalive*, is an overly Hebraic Puritan who, unlike Moon, retains his unChristian Nietzschean ideal of 'man' as God or 'superman' (281). Ivywood's insane lack of a sense of human, national, religious or cultural boundaries is symbolized by his blurring of 'East' and 'West', 'Europe' and 'Asia' and, especially, by his aim of replacing Christianity with a Judaized Islam:

The East and the West are one. The East is no longer East nor the West West; for a small isthmus has been broken; and the Atlantic and the Pacific are a single sea. ... I have long been increasingly convinced that underneath a certain mask of stiffness which the Mahomedan religion has worn through certain centuries, as a somewhat similar mask has been worn by the religion of the Jews, Islam has in its potentialities of being the most progressive of all religions; so that in a century or two to come we may see the cause of peace, of science, and of reform everywhere supported by Islam as it is everywhere supported by Israel. (70)

Rather like Dr Hirsch, who attempts to sacrifice the French nation on the altar of his supposedly progressive ideals, Ivywood is similarly prepared to destroy England's European roots and cultural traditions for the greater 'cause of peace, of science, and of reform everywhere'. Ivywood is, significantly, surrounded by Jews as well as Moslems whom he consistently conflates, not unlike Disraeli, as 'Semites': 'in

---

[49] Coates, *Chesterton and the Edwardian Cultural Crisis*, p. 87 and p. 95. See also Ian Boyd, *The Novels of G. K. Chesterton* (London, 1975) p. 65 and Hollis, *The Mind of Chesterton*, p. 143. I am referring to the 1919 Methuen edition of *The Flying Inn*.

the gradual emergence of mankind from a gross and sanguinary mode of sustenance, the Semite has led the way' (113). The Moslem Misyra Ammon has 'the Jewish nose and the Persian beard' (72) and Dr Gluck, the caricature lisping German-Jewish financier, enthusiastically endorses Islam and the Turkish invasion of England as does Leveson, Ivywood's Jewish secretary, who is renowned for his 'organizing power' (106). Chesterton in *The Everlasting Man* (1925), as Hollis has noted, constructed an oriental Judaism and 'Mahomedanism' as 'inhuman' religions which had more in common with each other than a 'wholly European' Christianity. Misyra Ammon, as well as being a shallow pun on 'mammon', also refers to the 'pagan god called Jupiter-Ammon' in *The Everlasting Man* which, according to Chesterton, prefigured the 'jealous God' of the 'secretive' and 'nomadic people' of the Old Testament. In his *The New Jerusalem* (1920), Chesterton even called for a law which would ensure that in England 'every Jew must be dressed like an Arab' confirming the spuriously 'eastern' origins of Britain's Jews.[50] Moslems and Jews are also brought together in the novel by their mutual 'veto on Pork' which Leveson believed had been the 'origin of Vegetarianism' (115). Hence the unpleasant 'song' for Dr Gluck:

> Oh, I knew a Doctor Gluck,
>   And his nose it had a hook,
> And his attitudes were anything but Aryan;
>   So I gave him all the pork
>   That I had, upon a fork;
> Because I am myself a Vegetarian. (121)

Coates has rightly argued that the threatened Turkish invasion, and Ivywood's absurdly eclectic political agenda, should not just be read for their historical verisimilitude but, instead, for their internal symbolic resonance.[51] Ivywood's aim of making Britain more 'oriental' or 'Turkish' cannot simply be dismissed for its lack of 'realism' as it is positioned in opposition to those, like Lady Joan Brett, who privilege 'the truth' of 'English history and literature' (111). Ivywood is a 'naked fanatic' precisely because he can 'feed on nothing but the future' (194). This is in stark contrast to Humphrey Pump, rooted in past culture and tradition, who intuitively represents

---

[50] Chesterton, *The New Jerusalem* (London, 1920) p. 272 and Hollis, *The Mind of Chesterton*, p. 136 and p. 141 who cites Chesterton's *The Everlasting Man* (London, 1925) in this context.
[51] Coates, *Chesterton and the Edwardian Cultural Crisis*, chapter 4 and pp. 111–15 has a useful reading of *The Flying Inn* in these terms.

'the English boundaries' (164) and 'that incorruptible kindness which was at the root of his Englishry, and yet may save the soul of the English' (80–1). Along with Patrick Dalroy (who is a product of a pre-modern, Catholic Ireland), Pump challenges Ivywood's 'mighty work of unity' (70) which threatens to expunge a distinct Englishness. It is in these terms that a bounded, historically determined 'English nation' is defined in opposition to a boundless, racially differentiated 'semitic' East.

At the conclusion of *The Flying Inn*, when Pump and Dalroy are fighting for 'the soul of the English', Chesterton comments on Joan's fear of being 'crushed by the weapons of brown men and yellow' which 'had made the English what they had not been for centuries' (281). In the end, the philosophical differences between those that promote a problematical creed of worldly perfection – which denies human and national limitations – is reduced to the issue of the racial difference between 'East' and 'West' or 'Europe' and 'Asia'. The 'brown men and yellow' that are trying to swamp Britain – and dilute the 'brave Christian blood' (281) of 'the English' – include the 'swarthy' (71) or 'dark' (75) Leveson as well as the cosmopolitan Gluck. Although Gluck had worn the 'Prussian, Austrian, or Turkish Orders', he still had 'unanswering almond eyes [which] had no more changed than the face of a wax figure in a barber's shop window' (107). This Gluck-like fixity of 'race' lies behind the myriad of 'eastern' nations and religions that are evoked in *The Flying Inn* in opposition to 'the English boundaries'. Chesterton's snide 'Song of the Quoodle' (with its references to 'The park a Jew encloses, / Where even the Law of Moses / Will let you steal a smell') is not merely an example of 'school-boy antisemitism' but points to the necessity in the novel as a whole for semitic difference to be the racial counterpoint to Chesterton's 'Christian dogma'. The spiritual and national confusion generated by 'the Jew' is, in this way, opposed to a boundary-ridden Englishness which was threatened by an increasingly intricate and expansive set of conspiracies.[52]

The Hebraism of Ivywood, which Chesterton had found previously inherent in Shaw's Nietzschean ideal of 'man' as a God-like 'superman', or Wells's 'cosmopolitan' ideal of Utopia, was to be crudely racialized in *The Flying Inn*. This reduction of an Arnoldian cultural tradition to vulgar racial differentiations clearly signalled

[52] Boyd, *The Novels of G. K. Chesterton*, p. 72.

Chesterton's 'literary decline' in the inter-war years. Ian Boyd has rightly emphasized that this decline was especially marked by the publication of *The Man Who Knew Too Much* (1922) which had an 'almost parasitic dependence on the political concerns of the earlier fiction'.[53] This backward-looking novel, in particular, refers directly to the political programme of *The New Witness* circle, as outlined by Belloc and Cecil Chesterton in their *The Party System*, with its emphasis on the irredeemable corruption of British government and an all-embracing front bench parliamentary conspiracy. Originally a collection of eight magazine stories written around a central character, Horne Fisher, each story in *The Man Who Knew Too Much* describes a crime where the criminal cannot be sent to jail because of his political connections. To his detriment, Chesterton's fiction at this time seems to be unduly influenced by Belloc's Barnett quartet with its constant reference to all-powerful Jewish plutocrats such as 'nosey Zimmern [who] lent money to half the Cabinet' (89) and post-Marconi fears that Britain had 'yielded to foreign financiers' (147). Not unlike Bailey in Belloc's fiction, Fisher resigns from parliament in disgust soon after he is elected. He then, predictably, goes on to oppose 'cosmopolitan moneylenders' such as Sir Isaac Hook or Sir Francis Verner (who is otherwise known as 'Franz Werner'). In an explicit reference to *Pongo and the Bull* and the 'Marconi Scandal', Verner uses the Exchequer to gain access to 'the Egyptian Loan and Lord knows what else' (142).

Oddly enough, as Boyd has noted, even though *The Man Who Knew Too Much* was published soon after Chesterton formally converted to Roman Catholicism, there is a striking lack of a spiritual dimension in this work. After 1925, the political agenda of *The New Witness* circle continued with the formation of *G. K.'s Weekly*, edited by Chesterton until his death in 1936, and the Distributist League which helped fund this journal. The 'Marconi Scandal' also continued to loom large in these circles and it is not surprising, therefore, that much of Chesterton's fiction was 'set in an indetermined period of the past and [was] concerned with the politics of Edwardian rather than contemporary times'.[54]

The importance of Chesterton's pre-war political agenda can be gauged from the fact that he chose 'The Five of Swords' from *The*

---

[53] Boyd, 'Philosophy in Fiction' in John Sullivan (ed.), *G. K. Chesterton: A Centenary Appraisal* (London, 1974) p. 55 which is a useful supplement to his book, *The Novels of G. K. Chesterton*.

[54] Boyd, *The Novels of G. K. Chesterton*, p. 84 and 'Philosophy in Fiction', p. 55.

Man Who Knew Too Much for an anthology entitled *My Best Story*
(1929). Although the choice of this story, as Edwards has noted,
shows an acute lack of self-criticism – as it is far from being one of his
'best' – it is certainly characteristic of much of his inter-war fiction.[55]
The story revolves around the murderous intentions of a group of
Jewish plutocrats who fake a duel in France so as to murder a young
man who refused to take part in their nefarious activities. Chesterton's
conspirators with 'swords and hateful faces' are described as being
'Messrs. Miller, Moss and Hartman, one of the first firms in the
civilized world, as big as the Bank of England' (278). The innocent
victims of their conspiracy have a look of 'stupefaction' after being
told this and Chesterton's rather obvious French spokesman goes on
to explain this connection:

Oh, how little you ... know of the modern world! What do you know about
Miller, Moss and Hartman, *except* that they have branches all over the world
and are as big as the Bank of England? You know they go to the ends of the
earth, but where do they come from? Is there any check on businesses
changing hands or men changing names? Miller may be twenty years dead,
if he was ever alive Miller may stand for Muller, or Muller for Moses. The
back-doors of every business to-day are open to such new-comers, and do
you ever ask from what gutters they come? ... Their real names were not
Lorraine, Le Caron, etc., any more than they were Miller, Moss, etc.,
though they went by the first in society and the second in business. Just now
we need not trouble about their real names; I'm sure that they never did.
They were cosmopolitan moneylenders mostly; I was in their power ...
[and] they would no more have thought of fighting a duel than of going on
a crusade. (278–9)

It is precisely the impermanent origins of the 'cosmopolitan
moneylenders' that make their financial machinations such a threat
to the fixed national boundaries of European countries, such as
Catholic France. Behind the spiritual and national confusion caused
by 'cosmopolitan moneylenders', there still lurks the undeniable fact
of 'the Jew'. Hence the certainty with which Chesterton's narrator
'knows' that these conspirators would not have 'thought' of 'going
on a crusade'. By the time of *Four Faultless Felons* (1930), Chesterton
can refer to a presumably Yiddish 'tongue that was not English, nor
wholly German, but which shrieked and chattered in all the ghettoes
of the world'. In such a boundary-less world of ever-changing names

---

[55] Edwards, 'Chesterton and Tribalism', pp. 42–4. See also *My Best Story: An Anthology of Stories
Chosen by Their Own Authors* (London, 1929) pp. 108–39.

and national and racial identities, it is possible for a duke in 'The Purple Wig' (1914) to be a Jewish solicitor who was 'a guttersnipe ... a pettifogger and a pawnbroker not twelve years ago'.[56]

The extent of the semitic uncertainty spread by these all-powerful conspiracies can be found in a great many stories by Chesterton whose plot often turns, as in 'The Duel of Dr Hirsch', on the fateful indeterminacy surrounding supposedly humanitarian, assimilated Jews. This paranoid construction of 'the Jew' reached its apotheosis in 'The Resurrection of Father Brown', collected in *The Incredulity of Father Brown* (1926). In this story, Father Brown is the victim of a scheme by South American Jewish revolutionaries to disprove the power of miracles and, thus, the spiritual efficacy of Christianity. Mendoza and Alvarez are the instigators of 'the most huge and horrible scandal ever launched against [the Catholic Church] since the last lie was choked in the throat of Titus Oates' (23). Given the enormous power and the pernicious influence behind these Marconi-style bids to undermine Christendom, it is not surprising that 'the Jew', in the inter-war years, had a great deal of difficulty in retaining his earlier role, in Chesterton's liberal pantheon, as a 'victim'. This was made explicit in his *A Short History of England* (1917), where Chesterton reads Medieval history backwards from the point of view of a contemporary, post-Marconi perspective. Such was the 'Semitic trouble in all times':

The Jews in the middle ages were as powerful as they were unpopular. They were the capitalists of the age, the men with wealth banked ready for use. ... But the real unfairness of the Jews' position was deeper and more distressing to a sensitive and highly civilised people. They might reasonably say that Christian kings and nobles, and even Christian popes and bishops, used for Christian purposes (such as the crusades and cathedrals) the money that could only be accumulated in such mountains by a usury they inconsistently denounced as unChristian; and then, when worse times came, gave up the Jew to the fury of the poor, whom that useful usury had ruined. That was the real case for the Jew; and no doubt he really felt himself oppressed.

Unfortunately it was the case for the Christians that they, with at least equal reason, felt him the oppressor; and that mutual charge of tyranny is the Semitic trouble in all times.[57]

---

[56] This Father Brown story is collected in *The Wisdom of Father Brown* and is cited in Edwards, 'Chesterton and Tribalism', p. 40. I am also grateful to Edwards (p. 45) for the reference to *Four Faultless Felons* (London, 1930).

[57] Cited in Coren, *Gilbert*, pp. 203–4 who emphasizes this as 'an example of selective history: no mention of the infamous blood libels which plagued the Jewish community at the time'.

Even when 'the Jews' in their medieval ghettoes conformed to Chesterton's ideals – and were a distinct and unequivocal orthodox religious 'civilisation' – they could not simply be a victim of the medieval pogroms. Their supposed financial power meant that they were also one of the main instigators of 'oppression'. Here a Bellocian sense of 'balance' prevails between 'the Jew' as a tyrannous usurer and 'the Christians' as the true victims of usury.

After the First World War, Chesterton did not retain even a spurious sense of 'balance' in his fictional constructions of the victimized Jew. In 'The Ghost of the Golden Cross' (1926), Father Brown makes a point of denying that 'Jews were persecuted in the Middle Ages' and goes on to say that, 'if you want to satirize medievalism, you could make a good case by saying that some poor Christian might be burned alive for making a mistake about the Homoousion, while a rich Jew might walk down the street openly sneering at Christ and the Mother of God' (118). The earlier distinctions between 'rich and poor' or 'orthodox and broad' Jews are, by this time, elided in the all-embracing context of 'Semitic trouble'. In 'The Resurrection of Father Brown' and 'The Ghost of Gideon Wise' (1926), both collected in the same volume, it is the racial inter-connection between poor Jewish communists and rich Jewish capitalists that is of paramount importance and transcends all class and religious differences. 'The Ghost of Gideon Wise', especially, constructs a conspiracy between three Jewish millionaires and three Jewish Bolsheviks who Father Brown discovers are not opposed to each other, as most think, but are in cahoots. This story was anticipated by Chesterton's *What I Saw in America* (1922) where he argued in relation to America and revolutionary Russia that, 'the cosmopolitan Jews who are the Communists in the East will not find it so very hard to make a bargain with the cosmopolitan Jews who are Capitalists in the West. The Western Jews would be willing to admit a nominal Socialism. The Eastern Jews have already admitted that their Socialism is nominal' (247). Any subtleties in Chesterton's thinking on these matters had, clearly, long since past.

By the time of his posthumously published *The Paradoxes of Mr Pond* (1937), Chesterton was similarly able to blame the victim for the rise of Nazism as he had previously done in relation to medieval 'oppression' and the expulsion of Jews from England in the twelfth century. As opposed to Mussolini's Fascism which he defended in his *The Resurrection of Rome* (1930), Chesterton condemned Nazism in general terms as an example of the worst kind of Prussianism. This, moreover, had been vehemently denounced in his anti-German *The Barbarism of Berlin* (1914) and *The Crimes of England* (1915). While a 'Prussian' Nazism genuinely appalled Chesterton, so did the all-powerful 'Semite'. The point of 'A Tall Story', collected in *The Paradoxes of Mr Pond*, was to resolve this conflict between two equally pernicious forces.

'A Tall Story' opens with the Chestertonian Gahagan agreeing that it is 'a damned shame' that 'hundreds and thousands of poor little fiddlers and actors and chess-players ... should be kicked out' of Nazi Germany. But he quickly goes on to qualify his sympathy for the Jewish 'fiddlers, actors and chess-players' by averring that 'I fancy they must be kicking themselves, for having been so faithful to Germany and even, everywhere else, pretty generally pro-German' (232). It is not, as in the Middle Ages, Jewish financial power that causes 'antisemitism' but, instead, a Jewish national and diasporic loyalty to Germany. Later on, when 'A Tall Story' looks back to the hunt for German spies in a British resort during the First World War, a German-Jew called Levy is warned by Mr Pond against calling himself 'C. Schiller'. This change of name causes Levy's neighbours to wrongly suspect him of being a spy and Pond confronts Levy with this information:

Why the dickens do you people do it? It will be more than half your own fault if there's a row of some kind and a Jingo mob comes here and breaks your windows for your absurd German name. I know very well this is no quarrel of yours. I am well aware ... that you never invaded Belgium. I am fully conscious that your national tastes do not lie in that direction. I know you had nothing to do with burning the Louvain Library or sinking the *Lusitania*. Then why the devil can't you call yourself Levy, like your fathers before you – your fathers who go back to the most ancient priesthood of the world? And you'll get into trouble with the Germans, too, someday, if you go about calling yourself Schiller. You might as well go and live in Stratford-on-Avon and call yourself Shakespeare. (243)

Pond, following on from Gahagan, is quite explicit about the role of Jewish assimilation as the main cause of 'antisemitism' during the First World War in Britain and, as he predicts, in Germany 'someday'. This is the exact reversal of H. G. Wells's and George Bernard Shaw's position during the inter-war years. Both of these writers, we remember, asserted forcefully that it was the *failure* of Jewish assimilation that resulted in the Nazi persecution of the Jews

and British 'antisemitism'. When Levy, with a stage-Jew lisp, replies
to Pond that, 'there'th a lot of prejudith againth my rathe', Pond
clinches his 'advice' to Levy with 'there'll be a lot more' if he insists
on changing his name (243). This position, to be sure, is entirely
consistent with Chesterton's championing of distinctly identifiable
Jews, as opposed to indistinct Jewish 'cosmopolitans'. In Chesterton's
The New Jerusalem, written nearly two decades earlier, he even
prefigures exactly the plot of 'A Tall Story' by maintaining that the
anti-Jewish riots during the First World War were 'partly at least the
fault of the Jew himself, and of the whole of that futile and unworthy
policy which had led him to call himself Bernstein when his name was
Benjamin'. The conclusion that acculturated Jews, who change their
names as a 'policy', thereby caused their own persecution is not a
particularly new aspect of his thinking. Chesterton's 'anti-Nazism',
in this context, is not as straightforward as is often claimed and
remained absolutely in line with his more general racial constructions.[58]

At one point in 'A Tall Story', Pond becomes 'dreamily conscious
of the chasm between Christendom and that great other half of
human civilization' and thinks of Levy who, he imagines, gives him
'a whiff of the strange smell of the East' (245). It was in the last
chapter of *The New Jerusalem* that Chesterton was to argue comprehensively that 'the Jew... came from the East' and thus 'we must
treat the Jew as an oriental; we must dress him as an oriental'
(268–70). In an analogy with British perceptions of Germany,
Chesterton claims that 'for years we were told that the Germans
were a sort of Englishman because they were teutons; but it was all
the worse for us when we found out what Teutons really were. For
years we were told that Jews were a sort of Englishman because they
were British subjects' (266). But these confusions, in Chesterton's
terms, were the dire consequences of a failure to distinguish between
'Jews' and 'Englishmen' which would have been achieved by dress-
ing Jews in the 'gorgeous and trailing robes' of 'an Arab' (272). By
letting Jews assimilate as 'British subjects' they will, like the
Germans during the First World War, one day act surreptitiously in
their own 'national' interests – as they did during the 'Marconi

[58] Chesterton, *The New Jerusalem*, pp. 272–3, although Chesterton, rather eccentrically, must
have imagined that Benjamin was distinctly 'Jewish' and Bernstein distinctly 'German'.
Coren, *Gilbert*, pp. 210–12 makes extravagant claims for Chesterton's 'anti-Nazism' but has
been misled in this regard by Ward's biography, *Gilbert Keith Chesterton*, p. 265.

Affair' – and cause untold ruin. This was clearly the import of much of Chesterton's inter-war fiction concerning 'the Jews'. In the end, the reason why 'Jews' could never become 'Englishmen' rests on Chesterton's quasi-religious 'patriotism', outlined in *The New Jerusalem*, which encompasses an ideal spiritual and national unification after death:

Patriotism is not merely dying for the nation. It is dying with the nation. It is regarding the fatherland not merely as a real resting-place like an inn, but as a final resting place, like a house or a grave. Even the most Jingo of the Jews do not feel like this about their adopted country; and I doubt if the most intelligent of the Jews would pretend that they did. Even if we can bring ourselves to believe that Disraeli lived for England, we cannot think that he would have died for her. If England had sunk in the Atlantic he would not have sunk with her, but easily floated over to America to stand for the Presidency. (284–5)

This racialized reading of Disraeli certainly harks back to the 1870s and to those that challenged the limits of an 'English nation' that would allow even converted Jews to become 'British subjects' and, worst of all, a Tory Prime Minister. Not insignificantly, however, this last chapter of *The New Jerusalem*, originally intended for the *Daily Telegraph*, was considered 'antisemitic' and not published in this Conservative newspaper. Questioning the 'patriotism' of Disraeli, after all, usually came from maverick Chestertonian Liberals who feared the universalist outcome of their supposedly 'liberal' creed. Such was the reason for Chesterton's construction of insuperable differences between 'Jew and Christian', 'East and West' and 'Aryan and Semite' which became, eventually, an iron wall in his thinking to deny any possibility of British-Jewish citizenship.

CONCLUSION

It is usual to think of Belloc and Chesterton as peculiarly 'antisemitic' and, thus, as outside of mainstream English liberal culture. Their strident Roman Catholicism and idiosyncratic 'distributist' politics reinforce this sense of the 'chesterbelloc' as exotic figures on the margins of Edwardian society. But what is clear from our discussion in this chapter is the extent to which both writers use a vocabulary that was a commonplace in many different political contexts. Belloc could thus draw on a radical anti-capitalist and anti-imperial discourse as well as his sense of a superior Anglo-Saxon Englishness. Not unlike Trollope's fiction, Belloc positioned himself as a 'balanced' or impartial narrator who could comment objectively on the influence of alien outsiders on an English nation, formed in the past, that was now under threat. The reason that 'honest Englishmen' are turned into fanatics is caused specifically by the impersonal and devastating economic power of those that do not conform to the spiritual values of Old England. Belloc's politics replicated this narrative position by, initially at least, mediating between the supposed 'fact' of 'Jewish plutocratic power' and the excessive response generated by this power.

If Belloc followed the reactionary 'liberalism' of an Anthony Trollope, Chesterton, on the other hand, initially used the ambivalent language of Matthew Arnold. The tension between Arnold's inclusive and exclusive vocabularies was apparent in Chesterton's early liberalism which combined both the language of racial determinism with a more generous cultural expansiveness. Chesterton, however, increasingly constructed 'the Jew' as the opposite of both a familial Englishness and a homogeneous European Christendom. It was precisely the assimilationist 'cultural' ideal of Arnoldian liberalism that, in the end, threatened to unleash spiritual confusion on a small, bounded English nation. Chesterton, in theory, divided 'the Jew' into those 'Zionists' that made explicit their racial difference and those indeterminate 'citizens' that attempted dangerously to hide their Jewishness. In his fiction and post-war journalism, however, such distinctions between 'good' and 'bad' Jews were invariably undermined by a more prevalent racialized vocabulary. Chesterton was especially concerned with the indeterminacy generated by Jews who could not, racially, assimilate into a 'higher' spiritual world. As with Belloc, he began to associate the confusion of national and religious boundaries with Jewish conspiracy theories that were also a dark double of the Roman Catholic Church. Such race-thinking was not, however, caused by the 'Marconi Scandal' (1912–14), as is often thought, but was implicit in much of Chesterton's imaginative writing and social criticism before this period.

By turning now to the modernist writings of James Joyce and T. S. Eliot, it will be possible to see that it was exactly Chesterton's sense of spiritual confusion and national uncertainty, embodied in 'the Jew', that positioned a semitic discourse at the heart of much of their literature. Whereas Joyce, in *Ulysses* (1922), made a virtue out of the ambivalence generated by an indeterminate 'Jewishness', T. S. Eliot constructed such semitic imprecision as a significant force preventing any understanding of the all-important relationship between the modern world and past tradition.

CHAPTER 6

Modernism and ambivalence: James Joyce and T. S. Eliot

Ulysses is a highly romantic self-portrait of the mature Joyce (disguised as a Jew) and of his adolescent self – of Bloom and Stephen.

Wyndham Lewis, *Time and Western Man* (London, 1927), pp. 75–113

Every nation, every race, has not only its own creative, but its own critical turn of mind; and is even more oblivious of the shortcomings and limitations of its critical habits than those of its creative genius.

T. S. Eliot, 'Tradition and the Individual Talent' (1919), *The Sacred Wood* (London, 1920), p. 47

INTRODUCTION

From radically differing perspectives the modernist writers, James Joyce and T. S. Eliot, both undertook a comprehensive critique of the late Victorian modernizing assumptions behind Matthew Arnold's *Culture and Anarchy*. Joyce's *Ulysses* (1922) includes a cluster of 'Hebraic and Hellenic' representations and employs them to explode any notions that an Arnoldian grand synthesis of these oppositions is equivalent to the progress of civilization. The modernist techniques at the heart of Joyce's novel constructs an indeterminate 'Jewgreek' – Leopold Bloom, a modern-day Odysseus – who cannot be 'known', unproblematically, by any received set of criteria. In this way, Joyce makes him the site on which to challenge the reader's faith in a literary text to order 'reality'. It is precisely the instability of 'the Jew' as a racial and cultural signifier that Joyce, throughout his novel, exploits to undermine any dominant discourse whether it be religion, nationalism, or Arnoldian liberalism. Bloom's ambivalent 'racial difference' is thus utilized by Joyce as a means of subverting the cultural certainties surrounding Jewish assimilation or Irish national and Catholic religious superiority. Two of Joyce's earlier texts, *Dubliners* (1914) and *Giacomo Joyce* (1914), will also be discussed to see the extent to which they anticipated the sophisticated narrative and representational concerns in *Ulysses*.

As with Joyce, Eliot's poetry constructed 'the Jew' as a site for confusion and uncertainty. But instead of deploying this uncertainty to break down the binary opposition between Gentile and Jew, Eliot reinforced these distinctions so as to privilege the Classical or Hellenic aspect of his categorizing modernism. The 'Jew', in this regard, became a necessary 'objective correlative' in his poetry for that which is inexact and uncategorizable. Rather like G. K. Chesterton's 'orthodox' construction of 'the Jew', many of Eliot's 1920 *Poems* included a semitic discourse to signify a deep-seated spiritual confusion. Unlike Bloom/Ulysses, who provided an essential conduit between a spiritually empty modernity and the past, Eliot's racialized 'Jews' are a force which prevent a specifically 'European' understanding of its 'own' history and tradition. Eliot, for this reason, concluded that 'free-thinking Jews' needed to be placed within distinct religious, racial and national boundaries. Such are the libertarian and authoritarian potentialities within the modernist construction of the indeterminate 'Jew'.

JAMES JOYCE: 'JEWGREEK IS GREEKJEW'

Ulysses begins with that great tempter, Buck Mulligan, endeavouring to seduce Stephen Dedalus with, among much else, the power of Matthew Arnold's rhetoric. Within the first few pages of 'Telemachus', Mulligan has emphasized both the absurdity of Dedalus's name, 'an ancient Greek' (1:34), as well as the 'Hellenic ring' of his own double-dactyled 'Malachi Mulligan' (1:41–2). By fixing their names in this Hellenic mould, Mulligan tries to tempt Stephen into taking a trip with him to Athens, encourages him to learn ancient Greek (1:79–80) and to work with him so as to 'hellenize' Ireland (1:158). This latter call especially echoes Arnold's *Culture and Anarchy* as well as the influence of Oscar Wilde whom Stephen paraphrases a good deal at this point in the novel. As Don Gifford and Robert Seidman have pointed out, 'Stephen' is named after the first Christian martyr, St Stephen Protomartyr, an important first-century Christianized Jew educated in Greek.[1] Malachi, literally 'my messenger' in Hebrew, is an Old Testament prophet who foretold the second coming of Elijah; a messianic transfigurer who, in Bloomian guise, threatens to appear throughout *Ulysses*. Mulligan's first name also recalls the tenth-century High King of Ireland, Malachy the Great, as well as St Malachy, who was commonly believed to have had the gift of prophecy. The one-eyed call for the 'hellenization' of Ireland, in other words, excludes the seminal hybridity of both Mulligan and Stephen's prophetic 'greekjewish' names. Mulligan's empty paganized Hellenism, above all, lacks Hebraic seriousness and the tragic pain of the inner transformation which Stephen seeks.[2] This buckish Hellenism is particularly invoked during the noisy debagging of Clive Kempthorpe in an Oxford College:

Shouts from the open window startling evening in the quadrangle. A deaf gardener, aproned, masked with Matthew Arnold's face, pushes his mower on the sombre lawn watching narrowly the dancing motes of grasshalms. (1:172–5)

The importance of 'Matthew Arnold's face' (1:173) in this context does not merely suggest, as Theoharis Constantine Theoharis has argued, the fixed 'dramatization' of *Culture and Anarchy* in *Ulysses*. By superimposing an Oxonian locale onto an Irish colonial setting Joyce is radically challenging Arnoldian liberal Celticism and the Victorian promise of modernity. As Seamus Deane has noted, the deaf Oxford gardener's refusal to accept the freakish anarchy, bred within the walls of a supposedly 'hellenized' Oxford, points to a wider failure of Arnoldian liberalism to acknowledge those 'anarchic' forces which it is meant to contain. Deane rightly regards Arnold's simultaneous and equally influential calls for the 'Celticization of Ireland' and the 'Hellenization of England' as one and the same 'movement'. Both movements, that is, are equally necessary to redeem an overly Hebraic English bourgeoisie.[3] Given such parochialism, it is no

---

[1] Don Gifford and Robert Seidman, *Notes for Joyce, An Annotation of James Joyce's 'Ulysses'* (New York, 1974) pp. 7–8 and Robert Scholes and Richard Kain (eds.), *The Workshop of Daedalus* (Evanston, 1965) pp. 264–66 for a detailed account of the Hellenized Jewish background of St Stephen Protomartyr. I am referring throughout to the chapter and line number of the Penguin student edition of Joyces's *Ulysses*, ed. Hans Walter Gabler (London, 1986).

[2] Gifford and Seidman, *Notes for Joyce*, p. 7 for the various etymologies of Malachi and Beryl Schlossman, *Joyce's Catholic Comedy of Language* (Wisconsin, 1985) pp. 7–9 for the theological significance of Stephen's rejection of Mulligan.

[3] Theoharis Constantine Theoharis, *Joyce's 'Ulysses': An Anatomy of the Soul* (Chapel Hill, 1988) pp. 142–4 and chapter 4 is the most comprehensive, if unsophisticated, comparison to

wonder that 'Arnold's face' masks an 'Oxford gardener' who, like Arnold, tends his own little patch (not unlike 'Lawn Tennyson, gentleman poet' (3:492) in 'Proteus') and ignores the anarchy around him. By reconstructing Arnold's ideals from the margins, Joyce exposes their irrelevance and their spurious universality. Arnoldian Celticism and Hellenism are both rejected by Stephen who views their proponents, not just Mulligan, as 'usurpers'. The confidence that modern society can be ordered and planned like a 'garden' – taken to its apogee in the thought of such twentieth-century modernizers as H. G. Wells – is cleverly undermined in Joyce's own 'gardening' analogy which places 'anarchy' at the centre.[4] What is of supposedly universal significance for English civilization, the assimilation of the bourgeoisie into 'culture', is of peripheral concern when applied to a colonial Ireland. For this reason Stephen, in a continuation of his satanic depiction of the artist-hero in *A Portrait of the Artist as a Young Man* (1916), identifies with the dark underside of modernity which cannot be contained by the cosy certainties of Arnold's *Culture and Anarchy*.

Throughout these opening chapters, the dark 'anarchic' forces which threaten the unifying potential of either Celticism or Hellenism are explicitly Judaized. Haines in 'Telemachus' believes that the 'national problem' of England is that it has fallen 'into the hands of German jews' (1:667–8). From the other end of the Irish political spectrum, Deasy in 'Nestor' similarly speaks about England being in the 'hands of the jews. In all the highest places: her finance, her press. And they are the signs of a nation's decay. ... Old England is dying' (2:346–50). As Jeffrey Perl has shown, Stephen is clearly attracted to those dark, semitic powers which are said to be undermining Britain. In 'Nestor' Stephen thinks of Moses Maimonides, a medieval rabbinical philosopher who was said to have synthesized Aristotelian rationalism with orthodox Judaism. For Stephen, Maimonides was, along with the Spanish-Arabian philosopher Averroës, one of the 'dark men in mien and movement, flashing in their mocking mirrors the obscure soul of the world, a darkness shining in brightness which brightness could not comprehend' (2:157–60). There is a similar

date of Joyce and Arnold. See also Seamus Deane, '"Masked with Matthew Arnold's Face": Joyce and Liberalism' in Morris Beja (ed.), *James Joyce: The Centennial Symposium* (Urbana, 1986) pp. 12–13 and p. 20.

[4] Zygmunt Bauman, *Modernity and Ambivalence* (Oxford, 1991) p. 34 and chapter 1 for the relationship between the 'gardening state' and the 'spirit of modernity'.

artist-satanic identification with Deasy's dark-eyed wanderers (anticipating Leopold Bloom) who 'sinned against the light' and who are, in Perl's words, 'under-world creatures – creatures of depth'. Perl rightly relates Deasy's antisemitism to Stephen's own 'mind's darkness' at the beginning of 'Nestor', 'a sloth of the underworld, reluctant, shy of brightness, shifting her dragon scaly folds' (2:73–4). But Perl goes on to conclude rather reductively that, for Joyce, 'consciousness would seem to be Gentile; the unconscious, Semitic'.[5] As well as Stephen's crucial recognition of Europe's Judaic 'unconscious', he also registers the need for Europe to be associated with a conscious, ordering, Arnoldian liberalism which is similarly implicated in the 'semitic'. Thus, Stephen's oft-quoted response to Deasy's antisemitism – 'History … is a nightmare from which I am trying to awake' (2:376) – both evokes and challenges the liberal ideal of order and progress which has not necessarily succeeded in taming the 'nightmare' of past hatreds. As many have previously noted, this plea for the transcendence of hatred is echoed by Bloom in 'Cyclops' and, according to Richard Ellmann, is the ethical core of *Ulysses*.[6]

The transfiguring morality of *Ulysses*, however, is constantly unsettled by the racial discourse which fixes Bloom as an untranscendent 'other'. Stephen's disavowal of antisemitism, as part of a modernizing discourse, therefore stands in an uneasy relation with the construction of 'the Jew' as the dark creative 'unconscious' of European civilisation. Stephen replies to Deasy's statement that 'their eyes knew the years of wandering and … knew the dishonours of their flesh' with the question 'who has not?' (2:371–3) which universalizes the racial 'other' as a modern everyman. Stephen's economic category of 'merchant' – 'A merchant … is one who buys cheap and sells dear, jew or gentile, is he not?' (2:359–60) – also opposes Deasy's racial particularizations with a universal language. And yet, it is precisely the inadequacy of this transcendent vocabulary that leads Stephen and Joyce back to a semitic particularity. Stephen, in 'Proteus', mocks any attempt at an Arnoldian grand synthesis with his telephone call to the source of all knowledge – 'Aleph, alpha: nought, nought, one' (3:39–40) – which ironically combines the Hebrew and Greek alphabets. Unlike Arnold, Joyce in *Ulysses*

---

[5] Jeffrey Perl, *The Tradition of Return: The Implicit History of Modern Literature* (Princeton, 1984) p. 205 and chapter 6 for this argument.

[6] Richard Ellmann, *Ulysses on the Liffey* (London, 1974) p. xiii and p. 116 for this argument.

does not attempt to synthesize 'Hebraism with Hellenism' but deploys Hebraism as a means of disrupting the certainties implied in a unifying Hellenism. Bloom, as a 'Jewgreek', is ambivalently constructed as *both* a universal 'everyman' – the embodiment of modernity – and, at the same time, as a dark 'other', repressed in the unconscious, who can not be assimilated into the grand narrative of modernity. Those that have been unduly influenced by T. S. Eliot's acclaimed review, and have read *Ulysses* merely as a parallel to the 'myth' of Odysseus, do the novel a disservice by ignoring the unsettling potential of the Hebraic unconscious which shadows Joyce's rewriting of the *Odyssey*. Far from being a way 'of controlling, of ordering, of giving shape and a significance to the immense panorama of futility and anarchy which is contemporary history', the Homeric context of *Ulysses* self-consciously fails in its impossibly Arnoldian task of 'ordering' the 'anarchy' of 'contemporary history'.[7] It is, especially, the indeterminately Judaized figure of Bloom that embodies this failure.

Stephen's troubled self-identification with Europe's supposedly semitic 'unconscious' clearly anticipates Bloom but also introduces an important problem for Joyce to try to overcome. If Bloom is fixed racially as a 'Jew', in what way can he represent something other than the 'Hebraic' or 'Israelite' aspects of European civilization? At the end of 'Proteus' Stephen remembers 'Monsieur Drumont, gentleman journalist' (3:493–4), the doyen of modern French antisemitism and author of the immensely popular compendium *La France juive: Essai d'histoire contemporaine* (1886), which became an antisemitic bestseller during the Dreyfus Affair. Drumont's description of Queen Victoria as an 'old hag with yellow teeth' is recalled by Stephen and associated with his own 'bad' teeth, 'toothless Kinch the superman' (3:496). Taken to its extreme, the idea of a dark semitic European 'unconscious' leads to the antisemitism of a Drumont with its concomitant Nietzschean 'superman' which is needed to rid Europe of its Judaic 'other'.[8] Even when

[7] T. S. Eliot, '*Ulysses*, Order and Myth', *The Dial* 75 (November, 1923), 480–3 collected in R. H. Deming, *James Joyce: The Critical Heritage, 1902–1927* (London, 1970), p. 270 and Morton P. Levitt, 'A Hero for Our Time: Leopold Bloom and the Myth of *Ulysses*', *James Joyce Quarterly* 10 (Fall 1972), 132–46 for a recent reworking of Eliot's position.
[8] Michael F. Duffy and Willard Mittleman, 'Nietzsche's Attitude Toward the Jews', *Journal of the History of Ideas* 49, (April–June, 1988), 301–317 for this argument. See also Joyce's letter to Carlo Linati, Richard Ellmann (ed.), *Selected Letters of James Joyce* (London, 1975) p. 271 for Joyce's well-known description of *Ulysses* as an 'epic of two races (Israel-Ireland)'.

Stephen is an ironically 'toothless' or impotent 'superman', he is still placed in racial opposition to Bloom's Jewishness and, in 'Ithaca', this results in Stephen singing an antisemitic song in response to Bloom's Zionist anthem. Frank Budgen, in his seminal *James Joyce and the Making of 'Ulysses'* (1934), has been especially influential in this reductive reading of *Ulysses* as a novel of racial opposites:

> There is a sudden break with Stephen after the end of the third episode.... A man of different race, age and character comes into the foreground of the book and almost without a break stays there till the end. He is Joyce's Ulysses, the Jew, Leopold Bloom. Bloom and Stephen are opposites. Bloom *is* while Stephen is becoming. He leans to the sciences, Stephen to the arts. He is by race a Jew, is equable in temper, humane and just, whereas Stephen, the Gentile, is egotistical, embittered, denies his social obligations and can be generous but is rarely just. But there is a difference of dimension and substance as well as character. Stephen is a self-portrait, and therefore one-sided. Bloom is seen from all angles, as no self-portrait can be seen. He is as plastic as Stephen is pictorial.[9]

Speaking with the assumed authority of his friendship with Joyce, Budgen, throughout his book, persists in representing Bloom as an 'unchanging Jew' (175) whose 'difference of race' (261) makes him Stephen's insuperable 'opposite'. In a significant lapse Budgen, unlike Wyndham Lewis, finds it impossible to conceive that Joyce can represent his 'self-portrait' as a 'Jew'. But he also maintains, in contradictory fashion, that the racially fixed Bloom is a 'plastic' or protean figure. As we have long since argued, racial constructions are rhetorically ambivalent precisely because they constitute an 'other' which is 'already known' and, yet, must be 'anxiously repeated'.[10] No one is more aware of this ambivalence than Joyce who, throughout *Ulysses*, deploys repeatedly an encyclopaedic knowledge of semitic representations to racially fix Bloom as a 'Jew' and, simultaneously, universalizes Bloom as an Hellenic everyman. The inability of the 'Jewgreek' Bloom to be confined by an ordered set of criteria makes him the site on which *Ulysses* challenges the reader's faith in the capacity of a literary text to order 'reality'. Those that attempt to find an answer to the one-eyed question in 'Cyclops' – 'Is he a jew or a gentile or a holy Roman or a swaddler or what the hell is he?' (12:1631–2) – miss the point when they argue that Bloom 'is'

[9] Frank Budgen, *James Joyce and the Making of 'Ulysses'* (Oxford, 1972 edition) p. 60. Further references to this edition will be cited in parentheses in the main text.

[10] For this see Homi Bhabha, 'The Other Question: Stereotype and Colonial Discourse', *Screen* 24 (Number 6, November–December, 1983), 18 and 18–35.

(or 'is not') a 'Jew' according to a predetermined religious, historical, sociological or ethnic framework.[11] Far from adhering to such received thinking, Joyce is playing relentlessly with the rampant instability of the signifier 'Jew'.

That Bloom cannot be confined by such 'scientific' knowledge, above all, defines his indeterminate, uncertain Jewishness. As Fritz Senn has shown, Bloom's heated reply to the Citizen in 'Cyclops' that 'Christ was a jew like me' (3:1808–9) is far from being a definitive statement as the phrase 'like me' begs the question and makes absurd Christ's Bloom-like Jewishness. Later on, in 'Eumaeus', Bloom compounds the absurdity of this response and, in recalling his clash with the Citizen, tells Stephen 'without deviating from the plain facts' that ' ... his God, I mean Christ, was a jew too, and all his family, like me, though in reality I'm not' (16:1083–5) which, similarly, pre-empts what is meant by 'in reality'.[12] Before examining in more detail how Bloom's sceptical, displacing semitism disturbs the reader's sense of 'reality' in *Ulysses*, it is worth looking at some of Joyce's earlier writing to see the extent to which, from the very beginning, he was to imaginatively challenge the binary oppositions between 'East and West' or 'Jew and Gentile'.

Not unlike George Bernard Shaw's work at about this time, Joyce's *Dubliners* (1914) attempted to break down Budgen's sense of an insurmountable difference between an unchanging semitic 'other' and a 'gentile' Irish self. To be sure, as Ira Nadel has shown, *Dubliners* did associate 'the Jew' with a feminized orientalism and a transcendent otherness. Moreover, these racialized differences were superficially evoked as an exotic counterpoint to the cold sterility of Ireland.[13] But Joyce, even in his earliest stories in *Dubliners*, also undermined such distinctions. In his opening story, 'The Sisters', an Oriental other-world is linked with the perverse Catholicism of Father James Flynn. As the boy (often read as a prototype Daedalus) dreams of Flynn lying on his death bed he 'felt that I had been very far away, in some land where the customs were strange – in Persia, I

---

[11] For a recent nonsensical article along these lines see Erwin Steinberg, 'Reading Leopold Bloom/1904 in 1989', *James Joyce Quarterly* 26 (Spring 1989), 397–416. See also Daniel Schwartz, *Reading Joyce's 'Ulysses'* (London, 1987) chapter 5 and Ira Nadel, *Joyce and the Jews* (London, 1989) which is a comprehensive source of information on these matters.

[12] Fritz Senn, *Joyce's Dislocations: Essays on Reading in Translation* (Baltimore, 1984) p. 67 and p. 107.

[13] Nadel, *Joyce and the Jews*, pp. 159–160. I will be referring to the Penguin edition of *Dubliners* in the body of the text.

thought ... But I could not remember the end of the dream' (11). The dead body of Flynn in part represents Joyce's description of Dublin as the centre of Ireland's moral 'paralysis' but it is, also, uneasily juxtaposed with the possibility of escape from 'paralysis' which is signified by the far-away dream-land of Persia. This doubleness is introduced in the opening paragraph of the story as the boy-author is captivated by the word 'paralysis' which 'filled me with fear, and yet I longed to be nearer to it and to look upon its deadly work' (7). Father Flynn offers the prospect of going beyond the sordidness of Dublin but is in the end, in William Johnsen's words, 'bound more firmly to the tyranny of the family' as the dominating 'sisters' grotesquely minister to his corpse. As Vicki Mahaffey contends, Flynn and the boy are not just two conflicting versions of Joyce ('empty faith' or 'faithful rebellion'), as is often thought, but are reciprocal figures who supplement each other.[14] Even at this early stage in Joyce's writings, the father-figure who is associated with the otherness of the East and the 'son', trapped in the nets of Dublin, are not merely defined by their differences but are aspects of the same 'paralysis'.

In 'A Little Cloud', Little Chandler understands his own sense of familial entrapment in relation to the 'thousands of rich Germans and Jews, rotten with money, that'd only be too glad ... ' (79) to marry his friend Ignatius Gallaher. In the epiphanic moment when he thinks of himself as a 'prisoner' (81), in comparison to the legendary freedom of Gallaher (a successful London journalist), he makes a painful contrast between his wife and Gallaher's orientalized women:

He looked into the eyes of [his wife's] photograph and they answered coldly. Certainly they were pretty and the face itself was pretty. But he found something mean in it. Why was it so conscious and lady-like? The composure of the eyes irritated him. They repelled him and defied him: there was no passion in them, no rapture. He thought of what Gallaher had said about rich Jewesses. Those dark oriental eyes, he thought, how full they are of passion, of voluptuous longing! Why had he married the eyes in the photograph? (80)

---

14 William Johnsen, 'Joyce's "Dubliners" and the Futility of Modernism' in W. J. McCormack and Alistair Stead (eds.), *James Joyce and Modern Literature* (London, 1982) p. 11 and Vicki Mahaffey, *Reauthorizing Joyce* (Cambridge, 1988) pp. 26–32. Richard Ellmann (ed.), *Letters of James Joyce*, 3 vols. (London, 1966), II, p. 134 contains a well-known letter to Constance Curran where Joyce described *Dubliners* as a series of stories which would 'betray the soul of that hemiplegia or paralysis which many consider a city'.

Chandler's sense of an unassailable difference between his world and that of the exotic 'other' is further emphasized when he tries to read Byron. A Byronic sexual and imaginative potency – which is derived from Byron's links with the Orient – is, once again, starkly compared with Chandler's inability to add to the Celtic Twilight. This connection between an unobtainable Orient and Irish impotency was to be the playful subject of 'Araby'. In this story, Joyce was to evoke his boy narrator's overwrought musings over Mangan's 'brown' skinned (28) sister at the Araby penny bazaar. Instead of the literary impotence of Little Chandler, 'Araby' is overdetermined with textual references, such as *The Arab's Farewell to his Steed*, which heightens the boy's unreal expectations surrounding Mangan's sister. The erotic commotion caused by these expectations is given a parodic oriental air, 'the syllables of the word *Araby* were called to me through the silence in which my soul luxuriated and cast an Eastern enchantment over me' (30). This exotic vision, which turns Mangan's sister into an amorous possession from the East, is starkly undercut as the boy is humiliated at a stall in the bazaar by two Englishmen. Joyce here substitutes the boy's fantasized sense of power over the silent eastern 'other' with the brute realities of Ireland's subjugation to the English. And yet, the boy's sense of impotent powerlessness at the end is still represented in the language of orientalism, 'I looked humbly at the great jars that stood like eastern guards at either side of the dark entrance to the stall... Gazing up into the darkness I saw myself as a creature driven and derided by vanity; and my eyes burned with anguish and anger' (33). Like Stephen in the Telemachiad, the 'dark' exotic East is also the inner darkness of self-realization. The 'otherness' which the boy seeks turns out to be both the possibility of eroticized escape as well as, more mundanely, an unadorned sense of the present.[15]

In an act of reconciliation with Ireland, 'The Dead' situates an Eastern otherness within a specifically Irish context. Gretta Conroy's 'grace and mystery' (207) and the 'solid rectangle of Smyrna figs' and 'pyramid of oranges' (194) at the Misses Morkans' table need no longer have a purely semitic provenance. Instead of being opposed to an oriental 'other', Ireland contains within its own borders a redemptive otherness which is, significantly, located in the 'west' of

---

[15] Suzette Henke, 'James Joyce East and Middle East: Literary Resonances of Judaism, Egyptology, and Indian Myth', *Journal of Modern Literature* 13 (1986), 307–19 is a suggestive account of these issues.

the country. When the worldly Gabriel, at the end of the story, decides to 'journey westward' it is, apart from anything else, in singular opposition to those protagonists in *Dubliners*, such as Little Chandler, who have previously looked to 'the East' for their salvation. This inner 'westward' journey is related to the final words of the story where 'the snow falling faintly through the universe' (220) symbolically elides all differences. The small epiphany caused by the 'silver and dark' snow-fall brings together Gabriel's conscious worldliness with the unspoken passions of his wife's dead lover. This search for primeval life-giving sources which unite 'the living and the dead' (220) connects Gabriel's final vision with Stephen's sense of a dark historical unconscious in the early chapters of *Ulysses*. Just as Joyce was to locate a semitic 'otherness' within Stephen, Gabriel need no longer look to the Orient for his or Ireland's renewal.

That a semitic potency can be found within the borders of Ireland, and the consciousness of its inhabitants, can be seen from Joyce's lecture, 'Ireland, Island of Saints and Sages' (1907), which was written around the same time as 'The Dead'. In this lecture, Joyce postulated that although far removed from what he called 'the centre of culture', the 'Irish nation's insistence on developing its own culture by itself is not so much the demand of a young nation that wants to make good in the European concert as the demand of a very old nation to renew under new forms the glories of past civilization'. It is precisely on these grounds of 'renewal' through the recreation of the 'glories of past civilization' – and Joyce in his essay specifically takes us back to the first century of the Christian era – that gives *Ulysses* what Perl calls, in an apt reference to T. S. Eliot, an 'associated' sensibility. Not unlike Eliot's 'Tradition and the Individual Talent' (1919) and 'Hamlet' (1919), Joyce needed to connect with the past in order to redefine a modern sense of 'culture'.[16] As both capitalist 'everyman' and timeless spiritualized Wanderer, Bloom's old-new Jewishness is, in this regard, a suitably ambivalent expression of the need to 'renew' the present through its links with the spiritual origins of Christianity. But this 'associated' sensibility is not just a comment on Bloom's 'semitic' racial origins. The young Dedalus, in conversation with his friend Cranly in *Stephen Hero*, had long since defined his sense of 'the modern spirit' in terms

[16] Richard Ellmann and Ellsworth Mason (eds.), *The Critical Writings of James Joyce* (London, 1959) p. 157. Perl, *The Tradition of Return*, p. 162 cites T. S. Eliot to good effect in this context.

of a scientific or 'vivisective... process' which was underpinned by 'magical properties' that 'transform and disfigure'.[17] Bloom's magical transformation, when juxtaposed with his 'vivisective' modern persona, is akin to Gabriel Conroy's sense in 'The Dead' of an elemental human spirit, located in the past, which is needed to supplement his worldly success. Such links between 'modernity and antiquity' are, also, a means of universalizing Bloom's indeterminate racial identity as a 'Jew'.

Budgen has quoted Joyce, with regard to 'the Jews', as saying that 'it was a heroic sacrifice on their part when they refused to accept the Christian revelation. Look at them. They are better husbands than we are, better fathers, and better sons' (346). This refusal to believe in the 'Christian revelation', paradoxically, connects Stephen with the ambivalent Jewishness of the twice baptized Bloom. At the same time as Stephen rejected the sly blandishments of Mulligan's Hellenism Bloom, in 'Calypso', repudiated the Hebraic 'enthusiasm' of Dlugacz, a 'ferreteyed porkbutcher' (4:152) of supposedly Hungarian-Jewish antecedents. Not unlike the perverse English proponents of Irish Celticism, the Zionist Dlugacz, hoping to restore Palestine as the homeland of 'the Jews', sells Bloom a pork kidney which is doubly unkosher (as eating kidney offends the Laws of Kashrut no less than eating pork). Just as that 'very old nation' Ireland cannot be 'renewed' through the rhetoric of religion and nationalism, Bloom's old-new Jewishness, from the very beginning, goes beyond these narrow means of comprehending the world. That this is a lesson which Stephen learns throughout *Ulysses* can be seen in 'Aeolus' which made use of John F. Taylor's lecture *The Language of the Outlaw*, where the 'youthful Moses', who resisted Egyptian domination, is evoked in the context of the Celtic revival. In this Irish nationalist rewriting of the biblical story, the Egyptian high priest tries to tempt the 'youthful Moses' into succumbing to a superior Egyptian civilization. When this does not work, he threatens him with the strength of Egypt's army which is compared to the abject weakness of Israel. According to Theoharis, the speech which follows is the 'centrepiece of the Mosaic analogy in *Ulysses*, aligning Ireland with Israel and England with Egypt on the issues of cultural, military and religious domination':

[17] *Stephen Hero* (London, 1944) p. 190 cited in Christopher Butler, 'Joyce, Modernism and Post-Modernism' in Derek Attridge, *The Cambridge Companion to James Joyce* (Cambridge, 1990) p. 263.

– But, ladies and gentleman, had the youthful Moses listened to and accepted that view of life, had he bowed his head and bowed his will and bowed his spirit before that arrogant admonition he would never have brought the chosen people out of their house of bondage, nor followed the pillar of the cloud by day. He would never have spoken with the Eternal amid lightnings on Sinai's mountaintop nor ever have come down with the light of inspiration shining in his countenance and bearing in his arms the tables of the law, graven in the language of the outlaw. (7:862–9)[18]

Just as the 'youthful Moses' is tempted by the fleshpots and power of Egypt, Stephen is tempted by the nationalist rhetoric and power of Taylor's lecture. Stephen's inner commentary on Taylor's words – 'Noble words coming. Look out. Could you try your hand at it yourself?' (7:836–7) – is significant given the ironic debunking of this lecture in the title of his *A Pisgah Sight of Palestine or the Parable of the Plums*. Hugh Kenner has observed that Stephen's New Testament 'parable' can be said to act as a commentary on the Old Testament 'Pisgah Sight of Palestine'. But Stephen's story of Anne Kearns and Florence MacCabe – trying in vain to see a view of Dublin from the top of Nelson's pillar – might perhaps, as has been commonly noted, have appeared in *Dubliners* along with Joyce's original account of Alfred Hunter as 'Ulysses'. The reworking of Taylor's windy rhetoric into the modern-day 'language of the outlaw' points to the relationship between what Karen Lawrence has called the 'Odyssey of style' in *Ulysses* and the Mosaic analogy.[19] Many studies have assumed that Joyce simply replicates the undoubted rhetorical power of these 'Judaic' sources. But, rather like Stephen in relation to Taylor, there is a partial or 'pisgah' identification with the Hebraic other-story which defines Stephen (who, like Joyce, carries the ashplant traditionally associated with the Wandering Jew) as much as Bloom.

The Arnoldian cultural synthesis between 'Hebraism and Hellenism', which is interrogated throughout the novel, can also be related to the 'modernist style' in *Ulysses*. Joyce certainly recognized that the acculturated Jew was an important cultural symbol of the promise of modernity. His refusal to contain 'the Jew' within a realistic narrative, therefore, should be linked to his scepticism concerning conventional, modernizing discourses. It is not insignificant that when Radnor, in George Meredith's proto-modernist *One*

---

[18] Theoharis, *Joyce's 'Ulysses'*, p. 188 and Nadel, *Joyce and the Jews, passim* for references to Mosaic analogies in *Ulysses*.

[19] Karen Lawrence, *The Odyssey of Style in 'Ulysses'* (Princeton, 1981) and Hugh Kenner, *Ulysses* (London, 1980) p. 140.

of Our Conquerors (1891), rejects Socialism as a means of redeeming a semitic England, he uses words which Bloom was to repeat in 'Calypso', 'still, there was an idea in it… '[20] During his visit to Dlugacz's, Bloom takes a leaflet asking him to purchase Agendath Netaim, 'vast sandy tracts from the Turkish government… with orangegroves and immense melonfields north of Jaffa' (4:193-4), which he carries around with him during his wanderings but immediately burns when he arrives home. This potential Zionist restoration of the 'promised land' is greeted with Radnor's words, 'Nothing doing. Still an idea behind it' (4:200). Later on these Palestinian melonfields become Molly's posterior, another 'pisgah' version of Bloom's homeland. In a less hopeful mood, the 'promised land' of 'the Jews' is quickly reconstructed not as ripe 'melonfields' but as 'the grey sunken cunt of the world' (4:228-9). This change of mood quickly undermines any utopian traces in Dlugacz's Zionism. Unlike *Daniel Deronda*, Joyce does not merely banish his transcendent ideals onto a rhetorical 'promised land'. Whereas the all-important Greek 'idea' of 'metempsychosis' enables Eliot to displace a liberal sense of progress onto another world, Bloom does not succumb to this temptation. His equally kabbalistic sense of spiritual unification is, above all, undermined by his uneasy wanderings around different versions of himself.[21] Although using similar material, the modernist writer can no longer contemplate the unproblematic transcendence of the novel form.

As a 'Jewgreek', who displaces the Homeric myth onto a Judaic double, Bloom is always more than his 'reality' at any one moment in the novel. With specific reference to 'Circe', as Marilyn Reizbaum has shown, Bloom is constructed as a messianic figure who moves through an ever-enlarging purview from domestic redemption (as Rudy's father); to become 'the world's greatest reformer' (15:1359) (as the Mayor of Dublin); as well as being the saviour of the Irish nation (as Parnell); and the symbol of universal religious salvation (as Moses and Jesus). At the same time as assuming power through these redemptive constructions, Bloom is also rendered powerless by the semitic racial representations which repeatedly confront him

---

[20] George Meredith, *One of Our Conquerors*, ed. Margaret Harris (Queensland, 1975) p. 9. For a discussion of George Eliot in these terms see chapter 2 of this book. I plan to discuss in detail the relationship between Meredith's *One of Our Conquerors* and Joyce's *Ulysses* in a forthcoming article.

[21] Jackson Cope, *Joyce's Cities: Archaeologies of the Soul* (Baltimore, 1981), chapter 4, is an important account of *Ulysses* in these terms.

throughout the novel – 'when in doubt persecute Bloom' (15:975–6)
– where Bloom is also the site for the dark, reverse side of the
'promised land of modernity'.[22] Unlike Deronda, who is eventually
fixed by his racialized vocation, the slippery Bloom always elides such
narrative resolution.

The constant play between the unchanging, mythically Wandering Bloom and his racialized 'protean' double – whose ambivalence threatens the certainties of nation and religion – exposes
the arbitrariness and power of a semitic discourse in *Ulysses*. At the
end of 'Lestrygonians', to take just one well-known example, Bloom,
with regard to Reuben J. Dodd, concludes with the following private
thought: 'Now he's really what they call a dirty jew' (8:1159). In
'Hades', Dodd had previously been stereotyped as a usurious
moneylender by the mourners at Paddy Dignam's funeral and Bloom
takes on board these assumptions. Stanley Sultan has rightly pointed
out the bitter irony of Bloom's 'really' and 'they call' which
indicates, above all, the instability at the heart of the racial
constructions in *Ulysses*. It is immaterial what 'they call' Dodd if he
is 'really' a 'dirty jew'. Given Bloom's own fixity as a 'dirty jew' in
the eyes of those around him, Dodd is a convenient recipient for those
aspects of Bloom's Jewishness which he would wish to jettison. Critics
have pointlessly argued whether Dodd 'really' is a Jew or not which,
once again, misses any sense of the haphazard designation of the word
'Jew' in the novel.[23] Whether the historical Reuben Dodd 'really'
was a Jew is irrelevant when juxtaposed with (even) Bloom's volatile
use of a semitic discourse to fix its object as a 'Jew'.

In 'Cyclops', the arbitrary power of the novel's semitism, which
had been previously applied to Reuben J. Dodd, tranforms Bloom, as
Ellmann has written, into the ultimate racial outsider. Bloom
becomes 'Virag', the name of his Hungarian-Jewish father; he is not
an Irishman but, instead, a 'Jerusalem cuckoo' (12:1571–2); and he

22 Marilyn Reizbaum, 'Joyce's Judaic "Other": Texts and Contexts', unpublished Ph.D
    thesis, University of Wisconsin (1985), p. 111 to whom I am indebted for this argument.
23 Stanley Sultan, *Eliot, Joyce and Company* (Oxford, 1987) p. 80 and pp. 77–82 for a recent
    account of the 'Reuben J. Dodd' debate. An early example of tendentious criticism on this
    matter is R. A. Adams, *Surface or Symbol* (Oxford, 1962) pp. 105–6. For the ubiquity of the
    Jewish self-hatred expressed by Bloom at this time see Sander Gilman, *Jewish Self-Hatred*:
    Antisemitism and the Hidden Language of the Jews (Baltimore, 1986). That Joyce was aware of
    this form of Jewish self-hatred can be seen from his notesheets to 'Cyclops' where he observes
    that 'the jew hates the jew in the jew' which is cited in Nadel, *Joyce and the Jews*, p. 139.
    Reizbaum, 'Joyce's Judaic "Other"', chapter 3 and her 'The Jewish Connection, Con'd'
    in Bernard Benstock (ed.), *The Seventh of Joyce* (Indiana, 1982), pp. 229–37 notes the
    influence of Otto Weininger on Joyce in this context.

is not a 'patriot' but is deemed to be 'not quite sure which country' he is supposed to 'love' (12:1628–30). Against this one-eyed nationalist reading of Bloom by the Citizen, Ellmann points to Bloom's two-eyed rejection of 'force, hatred, history, all that' for 'love, ... the opposite of hatred' (12:1481–5). Colin MacCabe has usefully added to this reading by noting that the binary opposition between 'love' and 'hatred' is left hanging by Bloom when he states that 'I must go now' and declines to elaborate on his belief that what is 'really life' is 'love' (12:1485). Bloom's refusal to define what is 'really life' points, as MacCabe argues, not to an opposite ethical system to that of the Citizen, but to a wider rejection of all 'dominant discourses' which Joyce ruthlessly parodies in 'Cyclops'.[24]

Thus Bloom is not simply a Christ-like antidote to the nationalism of the Citizen, since stereotyping him as 'a new apostle to the gentiles' (12:1489) limits Bloom no less than calling him a 'Jerusalem cuckoo'. As we have seen, Bloom's defensive evocation of 'Mendelssohn', 'Karl Marx', 'Mercadante', 'Spinoza' and 'the Saviour' (12:1805) as Jews 'like me' absurdly assumes a Bloom-like Jewishness that has existed throughout history. Far from postulating an alternative 'Jewish' history of 'persecution' to that of the Citizen's chauvinism, Bloom's uncertain Jewishness is set against the fixity of the myths of Irish nationhood which are ruthlessly parodied throughout this episode. The ending of 'Cyclops', therefore, is not merely a substitution of one discourse for another, where Bloom, according to Clive Hart, has 'something approaching Christ-like qualities' and becomes 'the potential saviour of [a] crumbling civilisation'. On the contrary, as MacCabe notes, no discourse within 'Cyclops' is 'allowed the privilege of physically ending it'.[25] Such is the debunking of the biblically prophetic language used to describe Bloom's enforced escape (from the Citizen and his dog) as he runs to catch a 'Jarvey' or horse-drawn carriage:

When, lo, there came about them all a great brightness and they beheld the chariot wherein He stood ascend to heaven. And they beheld Him in the chariot, clothed upon in the glory of the brightness, having raiment as of the sun, fair as the moon and terrible that for the awe they durst not look upon Him. And there came a voice out of heaven, calling *Elijah! Elijah!* And he

---

[24] Ellmann, *Ulysses on the Liffey*, pp. 113–14 and Colin MacCabe, *James Joyce and the Revolution of the Word* (London, 1979) pp. 101–2

[25] MacCabe, *James Joyce*, p. 101 and Clive Hart, *Ulysses* (Sydney, 1968) pp. 65–6. For a reading of 'Cyclops' in terms of the 'language of parody' see Lawrence, *The Odyssey of Style*, p. 102 and chapter 5.

answered with a main cry: *Abba! Adonai!* And they beheld Him, even Him,
ben Bloom Elijah, amid clouds of angels ascend to the glory of the brightness
at an angle of fortyfive degrees over Donohoe's in Little Green Street like a
shot of a shovel. (12:1910–18)

The transformation of Bloom's 'Jarvey' into a fiery heaven-bound
chariot, which is bathetically brought down to earth in Little Green
Street, is not merely, as MacCabe would have it, an expression of
some universal 'ceaseless interplay of relations' within 'the text'.
Throughout *Ulysses* such textual indeterminacy is, more specifically,
related to Bloom's precarious Jewishness. It is, precisely, the 'double
discourse' which constructs Bloom as *both* a messiah-figure (who
represents the potential of turning society into a 'promised land')
and as a racial 'other' (a figure beyond society) that Joyce specifically
invokes throughout *Ulysses*. Even the bathetic word 'shovel', at the
end of 'Cyclops', echoes the Hebraic sounding 'shov-el' which
simultaneously evokes and undercuts the messianic potential invested
in Bloom.[26]

The conclusion of 'Scylla and Charybdis', another important
chapter ending, is also a key example of Bloom playfully undermining
his Homeric persona. Here Mulligan, in his repressed Hebraic role as
the prophet Malachi anticipating the second coming of Elijah,
detects Bloom 'behind' Stephen (echoing the ending of 'Proteus').
Mulligan, who had previously characterized Bloom as a homosexual
'Ikey Moses' (9:607) who was 'greeker than the greeks' (9:614–15)
sees him again and comments: 'the wandering jew ... did you see his
eye? He looked upon you to lust after you. I fear thee, ancient
mariner. O, kinch, thou art in peril. Get thee a breechpad'
(9:1209–11). Bloom's 'eye' here neatly captures his 'greekjewish'
doubleness as it refers equally to his supposed 'greek' homosexual
advances to Stephen as well as the hypnotic eye (anticipating
Svengali in 'Circe') usually associated with 'Ahasuerus', the
Wandering Jew. In 'Cyclops', Bloom's cuckoldry was used to
emasculate him and this impotency enhanced his unsettling Jewishness which, in parallel fashion, was used to denationalize him. His
transexuality in 'Scylla and Charybdis' and 'Cyclops' brought
together a racial and sexual indeterminacy which were, especially, to
be mutually reinforcing in the latter half of the novel. With Stephen
in 'Scylla and Charybdis' called an 'inquisitional drunken jew jesuit'

---

[26] MacCabe, *James Joyce*, p. 101. I am indebted to Alistair Stead for pointing out to me the
Hebraic sounding 'shov-el'.

(9:1159) by Mulligan, while trying to 'prove' that Shakespeare was a 'jew' (9:763), *Ulysses* playfully refuses to acquiesce to any of the fixed racial or sexual characteristics commonly associated with its Hellenistic or Hebraic motifs.[27]

By the time of 'Circe', Joyce was able to rehearse exhaustively the gamut of 'semitic' representations which had previously been used to determine Bloom as a 'Jew'. These representations are dramatized phantasmagorically to emphasize, more than any other episode, the disturbing potential of the dark semitic unconscious which has been hitherto repressed in Bloom's conscious thoughts. The absurdly literal re-enactment of his symbolic role as a 'messianic' saviour and as a racial 'other' especially highlights the constructed, protean quality of Bloom's slippery 'Jewishness'. All of the expressions of Bloom as a 'Jew' are, in this way, contingent and hallucinatory. This effect is intensified by his extravagant transexuality as a 'new womanly man' (15:1798–9) which follows on from 'Scylla and Charybdis'. In 'Circe', the uncertainty of Bloom's gender is the sexual equivalent of his racial 'greekjewishness', both of which help to define the potentially life-giving underworld of the novel. By having Bloom enact a myriad of sexual and racial roles Joyce, in 'Circe', explodes the repressive dominant discourses in the novel in a feast of over-determination. The expectations loaded on to 'the Jews' as a group who can embody the values of a modernized 'civilization' are, for instance, outrageously parodied in Bloom who, in the 'messianic' section of 'Circe', assumes the guise of 'the world's greatest reformer' (15:1359):

BLOOM

I stand for the reform of municipal morals and the plain ten commandments. New worlds for old. Union of all, jew, moslem and gentile. Three acres and a cow for all children of nature. Saloon motor hearses. Compulsory manual labour for all. All parks open to the public day and night. Electric dishscrubbers. Tuberculosis, lunacy, war and mendicancy must now cease. General amnesty, weekly carnival, with masked licence, bonuses for all, esperanto the universal brotherhood. No more patriotism of barspongers and dropsical imposters. Free money, free love and a free lay church in a free lay state. (15:1684–93)[28]

---

[27] Jean-Michel Rabaté, 'The Portrait of the Artist as a Bogeyman' in Bernard Benstock (ed.), *James Joyce: The Augmented Ninth* (Syracuse, 1988) pp. 103–35 is an important account of 'Scylla and Charybdis' in these terms.

[28] Reizbaum, 'Joyce's Judaic "Other"', p. 109 notes that Joyce explicitly thought of this part of 'Circe' as the 'messianic' section.

The echo in this mock-Bloomian manifesto of H. G. Wells's modernizing *New Worlds for Old: A Plain Account of Modern Socialism* (1908) recalls the assimilated Jew, in Wellsian parlance, as a desirable sign of 'universal brotherhood' – 'mixed races and mixed marriages' (15:1699) – who exemplifies the 'union of all'. But, as well as representing the 'new', Bloom's Jewishness is also a part of the 'old world'. Bloomian progressivism is extravagantly undercut throughout 'Circe' as this episode compulsively locates in Bloom a residual historical Judaism. Shortly before this speech, Bloom makes a ludicrous assertion of his Judaic particularity by reciting, meaninglessly, the handful of Hebrew words which he can remember: 'Aleph Beth Ghimel Daleth Hagadah Tephilim Kosher Yom Kippur Hanukah Roschaschana Beni Brith Bar Mitzvah Mazzoth Askenazim Meshuggah Talith' (15:1623–5). As Bloom is put on 'trial for his otherness', in Reizbaum's acute phrase, it is significant that Sir Frederick Falkiner, the 'antisemitic' Judge who directs the proceedings, has 'Mosaic ramshorns' (15:1165) which later *'sound'* as the *'standard of Zion is hoisted'* (15:1619–20). Even at the extreme point of exclusion, Joyce universalizes Bloom's Hebraism to include even his most ardent persecutor. And yet, as well as being empowered by the messianic elements of his Jewishness, Bloom is both limited and trapped by his racial 'otherness' as the appearance of a quorum of 'the circumcised' (15:3226) at the height of his sexual domination by Bella Cohen graphically illustrates. In the 'Circean' hall of mirrors, his doubleness is further reflected in the figure of Bella Cohen, his female self, whose marked Jewishness and sexual indeterminacy redouble that of Bloom's.[29] Far from fixing Bloom's Jewishness, Joyce points to the infinite number of ways in which Bloom can be constructed as a 'Jew'.

It is, thus, the uninhibited variety of Bloom's 'semitic' associations in 'Circe' that is of crucial importance. The temporary, hallucinatory nature of Bloom's 'Jewish' identities exposes the impossibility of a single, unified self and this uncertainty is articulated through the unreality of his 'race'. A fragmented, manifold Bloomian self is starkly contrasted with the crude binarism of Arnold's *Culture and Anarchy*, suitably caricatured, after 'Telemachus', as *'the Siamese twins, Philip Drunk and Philip Sober, two Oxford dons with lawnmowers …*

---

[29] I owe this argument to Richard Brown (in conversation) and also to Reizbaum, 'Joyce's Judaic "Other"', p. 110.

masked with Matthew Arnold's face' (15:2512–4). This dismissal of a grand Arnoldian synthesis of opposites had already been anticipated by Lynch's cap which had earlier, with '*saturnine spleen*', repudiated Stephen's rather sterile question, 'which side is your knowledge bump?':

THE CAP

Bah! It is because it is. Woman's reason. Jewgreek is greekjew. Extremes meet. Death is the highest form of life. Bah! (15:2097–8)

Lynch's cap does not, as is often thought, affirm the coming together of Bloom as 'Jewgreek' with Stephen as 'greekjew'. The disdain of Lynch's cap for this overly formalistic sense of Arnoldian unification defines a Jewishness that cannot be facilely assimilated in this way. This can be seen at the end of 'Circe' where the final vision of Stephen as 'Rudy' reading a Hebrew text '*from right to left inaudibly, smiling, kissing the page*' (15:4959–60) might be said to represent the 'familial' reconciliation of father and son but it also anticipates, as Richard Brown has argued, the return to the beginning of *Ulysses* as it is re-read from 'right to left' from a 'Circean' point of view.[30] Joyce's refusal to allow Bloom, the Rabelaisian 'everyman', to be safely contained within a single transcendent narrative points to this restless re-reading of him as a disruptive 'Jewgreek'. By criss-crossing *Ulysses* with an unassimilable semitism, which can be read in a myriad of ways, Bloom, unlike the classical myth underlying *Ulysses*, can never, quite, be 'known'.

This 'Circean' self, which is defined in relation a semitic 'other', was, interestingly, prefigured by Joyce in *Giacomo Joyce* (1914). As Vicki Mahaffey has noted, the masochistic positioning of Giacomo with regard to that of Amalia Popper in *Giacomo Joyce* is akin to the subjugation of Bloom by Bella Cohen in 'Circe'. The feminized semitic 'other' in *Giacomo Joyce* echoes the erotic writings of Leopold von Sacher-Masoch with her 'heavy odorous furs' (1), 'high heels' (1), and, later on, 'boots laced in deft crisscross' (4). The aristocratic bearing of Amalia in *Giacomo Joyce*, imagined imperiously on horseback with the refrain '*The lady goes apace, apace, apace*' (8), is

[30] Richard Brown, *James Joyce: A Post-Culturalist Perspective* (London, 1992) p. 91 for this argument and Morton Levitt, 'The Family of Bloom' in Fritz Senn (ed.), *New Light on Joyce* (Bloomington, 1972) pp. 141–8 for a reading of Bloom's Jewishness in terms of familial relations.

significantly repeated during the high point of Bloom's sexual humiliation in 'Circe' as 'Bello', literally, rides roughshod over him (15:2947).[31] As well as writing about domineering aristocratic women dressed in furs who enslave and torture their male companions, Sacher-Masoch also wrote *Tales from the Ghetto* (1881) which Joyce had in his library and Bloom notices in 'Wandering Rocks'. Along with his novella *Sabbathai Zewy* (1874), concerning the seventeenth-century Jewish false messiah, Sacher-Masoch's 'ghetto tales' are permeated with masochistic motifs from his erotic works and revolve around racially unobtainable virginal Jewesses, not unlike the figure in *Giacomo Joyce*. Far from being racially 'opposed', Bloom and Giacomo are superimposed on each other in these two, mutually reinforcing, texts.

In fact this text can be said to proliferate throughout Joyce's writing. The masochistic definition of a masculine self in relation to life-giving Oriental Jewesses goes back, as we have seen, to *Dubliners*. The 'dark oriental eyes' which are 'full of passion' and 'voluptuous longing' at the end of 'A Little Cloud' also completely enrapture Giacomo in *Giacomo Joyce*. As *Giacomo Joyce* has been rightly described as an 'affair of the eye', it is worth remembering Mulligan's emphasis on the hypnotic 'eye' of the 'Wandering jew' at the end of 'Scylla and Charbdis' and Deasy's parallel account of 'the jew' in 'Nestor': 'their eyes knew the years of wandering' (2:371–2). Just as Bloom is ambivalently constructed through the many eyes that behold him, Amalia is a protean figure who assumes a variety of 'natural and fantastical' guises that were to reappear in 'Circe'. Most importantly, like Bloom, Amalia in *Giacomo Joyce* is both a figure of redemption – who renews the 'artist-lover' – as well as threatening to destroy those that try to possess her. She is, as Mahaffey rightly notes, represented variously as 'virgin, Virgin Mother, lover, corpse and faithless whore', which anticipates the masculine equivalent of the range of associations linked with Bloom in *Ulysses* as would-be messiah and racial 'other'.[32] By bringing Bloom and Giacomo together as

[31] Vicki Mahaffey, 'Giacomo Joyce' in Zack Bowen and James F. Carens (eds.), *A Companion to Joyce Studies* (Connecticut, 1984) p. 413 and chapter 9. See also Richard Brown, *James Joyce and Sexuality* (Cambridge, 1985) pp. 86–8 for Joyce's interest in Leopold von Sacher-Masoch. I am referring throughout to Joyce's *Giacomo Joyce*, ed. Richard Ellmann (London, 1968).

[32] Mahaffey, 'Giacomo Joyce', pp. 387–8 and p. 394 to which I am indebted for this argument. See also David Biale, 'Masochism and Philosemitism: The Strange Case of Leopold von Sacher-Masoch', *Journal of Contemporary History* 17 (1982), 305–23, Nadel, *Joyce*

compatible 'self-portraits', it is possible to show the extent that Joyce constructs a self in opposition to an 'other' that can only be known through an uncertain 'eye'. This precarious definition of the self has substantial implications for the 'homecoming' sections of *Ulysses* and the supposed 'fusion' of Bloom and Stephen.

In his comprehensive study of 'Joyce and the Jews', Ira Nadel has postulated an unproblematical Joycean identification with 'the Jews' for reasons which varied from: 'a similar sense of marginality shared by the artist and the Jew, to similar family values shared by Joyce and Jews'. For Nadel, 'the Jew' is an 'essential reflection of Joyce' and an unchanging 'cornerstone of Joyce's artistic and personal life'.[33] But this sense of 'the Jew' as a straightforward mirror-image which defines 'the self' is finally eschewed in the closing chapters of *Ulysses*. Bloom, in other words, is neither reduced to being Stephen's racial 'opposite' nor is he merely reproduced as Joyce's surrogate 'self'. In 'Ithaca', in particular, Joyce deploys semitic racial difference so as to undermine a too easy sense of narrative resolution between Stephen and Bloom:

Did he find four separating forces between his temporary guest and him? Name, age, race, creed (17:402–3)

Did either openly allude to their racial difference? Neither (17:525–6)

By not 'openly allud[ing] to their racial difference', Bloom and Stephen can be said to have mutually repressed a 'separating force' that eventually divides them. To be sure, throughout 'Ithaca' the issue of 'racial difference' helps to constitute the 'identities' of Stephen and Bloom.[34] But this ambivalent construction of identity, which utilizes 'difference' as a means of unifying 'Blephen' and 'Stoom', only takes place on the level of 'Ithaca's' modernizing vocabulary. The pseudo-scientific discourse of 'Ithaca', which attempts to comprehensively categorize the similarities and dif-

and the Jews, chapter 4 and Francis Restuccia, *Joyce and the Law of the Father* (New Haven, 1991) p. 131, p. 144 and p. 148.

[33] Nadel, *Joyce and the Jews*, p. 4, p. 14 and p. 238 and Levitt, 'The Humanity of Bloom, the Jewishness of Joyce' in Benstock, *The Seventh of Joyce*, pp. 225–8 for an earlier version of this argument. For more detailed criticism of this book see my 'Signs of Industry', *Times Literary Supplement* (Number 4527, 5–11 January, 1990), 17.

[34] Reizbaum, 'Joyce's Judaic "Other"', p. 143, p. 149 and chapter 5 *passim* for a useful reading of the 'homecoming' chapters in these terms. See also Lawrence, *The Odyssey of Style*, p. 194 and chapter 8 for a reading of 'Ithaca' in terms of 'identity and difference' which, unfortunately, excludes 'racial difference'.

ferences of its protagonists, represses that which it cannot classify. Thus, 'reduced to their simplest reciprocal form', Joyce mocks any attempt to objectify 'Bloom's thoughts about Stephen's thoughts about Bloom and Bloom's thoughts about Stephen's thoughts about Bloom's thoughts about Stephen':

He thought that he thought that he was a jew whereas he knew that he knew that he knew that he was not. (17:527–31)

The certainty of Bloom's knowledge that Stephen is not 'a jew' is in marked contrast to Bloom's equivocal identity as he moves, in Reizbaum's telling phrase, 'in and out of his Jewishness' and, thereby, undermines the pretence of scientific exactitude.[35] In 'Eumaeus', after Bloom recalls the physical attack on him by the Citizen, Stephen notes their 'two or four eyes conversing, *Christus* or Bloom his name is, or, after all, *secundum carnem*' (16:1091–3). Bloom's identity, his 'name', is always uncertain and ever-changing in its range of semitic associations. Shortly after this, Stephen 'looked up and saw the eyes that said or didn't say the words the voice he heard said...' (16:1146–7), once again dissociating the 'words' which surround Bloom from his indefinite 'eye'. It is only when Bloom places his arm on Stephen and physically joins him that Stephen 'felt a strange kind of flesh of a different man approach him, sinewless and wobbly and all that' (16:1723–4). In these 'home-coming' chapters, it is not the fixity of the 'eye' that distinguishes Bloom but his strange, wobbly, flesh which, like the 'jewie' smell linked with Bloom in 'Cyclops', is threatening precisely because it is constructed as diffuse and uncontrollable.[36] As the language of empiricism excludes that which it cannot categorize, another kind of 'olfactory' thinking is needed to represent Bloom.

It is not insignificant that the much-quoted 'analogy' in 'Eumaeus' – that 'their minds were travelling, so to speak, in one train of thought' – is qualified with the phrase, 'though they didn't see eye to eye in everything' (16:1579–81). This combination of apparent harmony and the inability to see 'eye to eye' characterizes the lack of inclusiveness in the 'homecoming' chapters. As well as travelling along 'one train of thought', both Stephen and Bloom also

[35] Reizbaum, 'Joyce's Judaic "Other"', p. 147.
[36] The nameless one in 'Cyclops' comments that 'I'm told those Jewies does have a sort of a queer odour coming off them' (12:452–3). For a recent account of the significance of this kind of 'olfactory' thinking see Zygmunt Bauman, 'The Sweet Scent of Decomposition' in Chris Rojak and Bryan Turner (eds.), *Forget Baudrillard* (London, 1993).

utilize a vocabulary which prevents them from mirroring each other. In 'Eumaeus', for instance, Bloom constructs a historical Jewishness in terms of an unchanging economic astuteness and, at the same time, identifies with the Citizen's Irish nationalist vocabulary, 'I'm... as good an Irishman as that rude person I told you about at the outset' (16:1119–32). Stephen also uses, and repudiates, the stereotypical language of the Citizen: 'Is that first epistle to the Hebrews, he asked, as soon as his bottom jaw would let him, in? Text: open thy mouth and put thy foot in it' (16:1268–70). An insurmountable difference between Irishmen and Jews is again emphasized just before Bloom invites Stephen back to Eccles Street: 'The most vulnerable point too of tender Achilles, your God was a jew, because mostly they appeared to imagine he came from Carrick-on-Shannon or somewhere about in the county Sligo' (16:1640–2). Here the assumption that a 'jew' can not come from Carrick-on-Shannon or the county Sligo casts a shadow over Bloom's 'Utopian plans' (16:1652) with regard to Stephen. Thus, while Nadel is absolutely right to note the many self-defining similarities and parallels in these chapters between Irish and Jewish history and Catholic and Judaic theology, it is equally important to recognize that an undercurrent of 'racial difference' shatters these points of connection.

This self-consciousness and playful deployment of 'racial difference' can be seen, for instance, when Stephen recounts his *A Pisgah Sight of Palestine or the Parable of the Plums* to Bloom in 'Ithaca'. Bloom's list of 'examples of postexilic eminence' (17:709–10), intended to reinforce the Mosaic analogy in the 'parable' between Irish and Jewish history, hardly achieves this task as Bloom not only excludes Irish thinkers but also doubly rebuffs Stephen by privileging a Jewish intellectual tradition.[37] Stephen's recitation of the medieval antisemitic and misogynist ballad of Little Harry Hughes in response to Bloom's Zionist anthem, 'Hatikva', similarly repeats this temporary process of differentiation. Bloom's 'mixed feelings' and 'unsmiling' response to Stephen's ballad are, interestingly, qualified by his sense of 'wonder' that a 'jew's daughter' can be 'dressed in green' (17:830–1). Here the wondrous hybridity of his Irish-Jewish daughter overcomes the supposed racial difference between Bloom and Stephen. Soon after this, their ambivalent sense of 'unification' is summarized with the question, 'in other respects were their

---

[37] Reizbaum, 'Joyce's Judaic "Other"', p. 149 for this argument.

differences similar?' (17:893). By referring explicitly in Mosaic terms to Bloom's 'homecoming', Joyce again reinforces the 'different similarities' between Stephen and Bloom which both bring together and separate his protagonists:

In what order of precedence, with what attendant ceremony was the exodus from the house of bondage to the wilderness of inhabitation effected? (17:1021–2)

Just as Bloom in 'Aeolus' mistakenly thought that 'the Jews' were led by Moses 'out of the land of Egypt and *into* the house of bondage' (7:206–9, my emphasis), the Mosaic analogy in 'Ithaca' accentuates Bloom and Stephen's unresolved 'wilderness of inhabitation'. The Mosaic analogy reinforces the incomplete 'pisgah' character of their meeting and, at the same time, positions Stephen in the role of Moses as he 'takes charge of a wandering given up too soon by Bloom'.[38] After Stephen leaves Eccles Street, Bloom, appropriately enough, hears the 'double vibration of a jew's harp in the resonant lane' (17:1243–4); looks 'in the direction of Mizrach, the east' (17:1262–3); burns Dlugacz's prospectus to Agendath Netaim (17:1325); and then goes on to dwell upon his fragile utopia, 'flowerville'. It is the tenuous, musical quality of Bloom's 'jew's harp' Jewishness that, by the end of 'Ithaca', undermines the fixity of Zion and replaces it with his delicate 'flowerville'. The 'double vibration of a jew's harp', resonating after Stephen, is as good an objective correlative as any for the 'doubling' semitic discourse which gently disrupts the Hellenistic classicism of *Ulysses*. Along with much else that had preceded it, Joyce was to redouble this semitic 'otherness' in 'Penelope'.

It should be remembered that it was 'woman's reason' in 'Circe' that, in a moment of transcendence, merged the 'Jewgreek' with the 'greekjew'. While Lynch's cap scornfully dismissed this too easy sense of Arnoldian unification, anticipating the chapters that followed 'Circe', this rejection was in the limited context of a sterile intellectual debate with Stephen. 'Woman's reason' is writ large in 'Penelope' where Molly's realm of 'darkness' at last gives voice to the silent semitic 'other' which had previously been the object of erotic desire in *Giacomo Joyce* and *Dubliners*. Molly's recognition that she is 'jewess looking after my mother' (18:1184–5) is particularly important in this regard, given Joyce's unrestrained emphasis on the semitic racial

---

[38] Rabaté, 'The Portrait of the Artist', p. 124.

origins, among others, of the 'jewess looking' Martha Fleischmann.[39] While Phillip Herring has made out a convincing case for the historical sources of Molly's Spanish-Jewish origins, it is significant that her textual Jewishness in 'Penelope' is constructed so as to deliberately reproduce and redouble the ambivalent semitism of the previous chapters. Being 'jewess looking', as Suzette Henke has pointed out, could mean that her mother's Spanish features made her 'look' like a Jew or, equally uncertainly, that she 'was' a Jew. And yet, it is of some note that Bloom is initially attracted to Molly precisely because of her perceived Jewishness:

I dont know how the first night ever we met when I was living in Rehoboth terrace we stood staring at one another for about 10 minutes as if we met somewhere I suppose on account of my being jewess looking after my mother (1181–5)[40]

Whether Bloom is captivated by Molly's Jewishness, like Giacomo Joyce, or whether he projects a semitic 'otherness' onto Molly points, once again, to the doubleness of Molly and Bloom's identities. By meeting Molly while she is living in the biblically named 'Rehoboth terrace', Joyce confirms the association of the 'promised land' of Agendath Netaim with Molly's body. In Genesis (chapter 26, verse 22), 'Rehoboth' was one of three wells dug by Isaac in the desert, a life-giving habitation out of nowhere to compare with Bloom's unremitting 'wilderness of inhabitation' in 'Ithaca'. While Molly's Oriental and 'Moorish' racial origins are referred to throughout *Ulysses*, it is clear that Joyce wished to maintain a measured indeterminacy towards her racial 'identity' by not specifically fixing her as a 'jew' in this context. If Molly becomes the embodiment of an Eastern utopianism, then she represents the fragile, imagined utopianism of 'flowerville' as opposed to the nationalist fixity of Zion. In this, as in much else, she is Bloom's double.

---

[39] Mahaffey, *Reauthorizing Joyce*, p. 19. For Joyce's letters to Martha Fleischmann see Richard Ellmann (ed.), *Letters of James Joyce*, 3 vols. (London, 1966), III, p. 433 where Joyce wrote to Martha, thinking that she was a Jewish woman, that 'Jesus Christ put on his human body: in the womb of a Jewish woman'. It is not insignificant in this regard that Molly's birthday coincides with that of the Virgin Mary. Ellmann's *Four Dubliners* (London, 1987), chapter 3, discusses Joyce's obsession with Martha in some detail and interestingly relates his letters to her to the 'Nausicaa' episode of *Ulysses*.

[40] Phillip Herring, *Joyce's Uncertainty Principle* (New Jersey, 1987) chapter 5 meticulously presents the historical evidence for the 'uncertain' Jewishness of Molly's mother, Lunito Laredo. See also Suzette Henke, *James Joyce and the Politics of Desire* (London, 1990) chapter 5 and pp. 249–50 for a sceptical reading of this passage.

Soon after her account of her 'first night ever' with Bloom, she remembers him taking her to see an 'Indian god ... one wet Sunday in the museum in Kildare street' and Bloom saying that the Indian god was 'a bigger religion then the jews and Our Lords both put together all over Asia' (18:1201–4). The domain of 'Asia', beyond that of Judeo-Christianity, is not unlike Molly's 'women's reason' in its pronounced separation from the masculine chapters that have preceded it. 'Penelope' reinstates the unconscious realm of darkness, which Stephen first identifies with in the Telemachiad, and, as Mahaffey has argued, 'gives it a specifically female character'. Stephen's misogynist and antisemitic ballad of Little Harry Hughes both draws together these sexual and racial other-worlds, that underpin the supposedly 'enlightened' conscience of Christian Europe, and points to the limits of his own received consciousness.[41] Molly similarly experiences an untransfigured Judaism as fossilized and sterile in her dismissal of 'Cohens old bed' (18:1498–9); her memory of 'the old longbearded jews in their jellibees and levites' (18:687); and in her inability to read Hebrew in the 'jews burialplace' (18:834). But, unlike Stephen, she gives full expression to the racial and sexual other-world which supplements the dominant masculine and Christian discourse which he needs to unlearn. Molly and Bloom's dark 'eyes', therefore, are able to unconsciously communicate in a way that eludes Stephen and Bloom in 'Ithaca': 'I asked him with my eyes to ask again yes and then he asked me would I yes to say yes' (18:1605–6). She thus goes beyond Bloom's protean, indeterminate 'Jewishness' and is attracted to his unique difference, his authentic 'otherness'. The image of the Indian god, in signifying the novel's other-realm, also, importantly, articulates this unsayable uniqueness: 'I suppose there isn't in all creation another man with the habits he has look at the way hes sleeping at the foot of the bed ... like that Indian god he took me to' (18:1197–1201). While a great deal of criticism has been written on the significance of the last few affirmative lines of 'Penelope', it is of some consequence that Joyce, just before Molly's last 'yes', includes a utopian reading of the plot of *Ulysses* where all differences are elided and, just for a moment, the dark 'semitic' Eastern unconscious and the Irish Christian conscious world exist happily together:

[41] Mahaffey, *Reauthorizing Joyce*, p. 117 and p. 129 for this argument. For the separateness of 'Penelope' see Brown, *James Joyce and Sexuality*, pp. 34–5 and p. 98.

I was thinking of so many things he didnt know ... the Spanish girls laughing in their shawls and their tail combs and the auctions in the morning the Greeks and the jews and the Arabs and the devil knows who else from Europe and Duke street (18:1582–9)[42]

In ending with those 'things' that Bloom 'didnt know' and that can not be 'known' in the previous chapters, Molly glimpses a time when 'Jewgreek' *is* 'greekjew' and where, eventually, Shem can be conceived in *Finnegans Wake* as a 'semi-semitic serendipitist... Europasianised Afferyank' (*FW* 191.2–4).[43]

Despite Molly's material and carnal expression of this 'most Hegelian' of ideals – the merging of 'Greek' and 'Jew' – Joyce is finally trapped in a received consciousness and must wait until *Finnegans Wake*, his fully-fledged novel of the night, before attempting to realize fully the life-giving world of the unconscious. There is a sense in which Molly is like Hermes, the 'god of sign-posts', who helped Homer's Odysseus out of Circe's den and who Joyce defined as 'the point at which roads parallel merge and roads contrary also'. But, before such points of convergence are necessary, the roads which Joyce travelled on must first be constructed as 'parallel' or 'contrary', as, in other words, Hellenic or Hebraic. Mere accumulation of detail and complexity, as Gabriel Josipovici has argued, do not break the cycle of repetition and prevent *Ulysses* from being limited by an essentially nineteenth-century discourse which, ultimately, could not be exorcized.[44] But no writer tried, with more success, to rid his fiction of the strait-jacket of semitic racial oppostions which poisoned the language of the first half of the twentieth century.

---

[42] Reizbaum, 'Joyce's Judaic "Other"', p. 163 has rightly emphasized the importance of this passage as a 'conceptual promised land'. It is worth noting, in the context of the ending of 'Penelope', that a significant number of Bloom's semitic doubles come near the end of chapters. The end of 'Nestor', 'Aeolus', 'The Lestrygonians', 'Scylla and Charbdis', 'Cyclops' and 'Circe' all utilize semitic representations and, thereby, give the illusion of closure.

[43] For two recent accounts of the 'Jewish' element in *Finnegans Wake* see John Gordon, 'The Convertshems of the Tchoose: Judaism and Jewishness in *Finnegans Wake*' in John Harty (ed.), *James Joyce's 'Finnegans Wake'*, *A Casebook* (New York, 1991) pp. 85–98 and Morton Levitt, 'The New Midrash: *Finnegans Wake*', *Joyce Studies Annual* 3 (1992), 57–76. I am referring to the page and line number of the Faber and Faber edition of Joyce's *Finnegans Wake* (London, 1939).

[44] Gabriel Josipovici, *The Mirror of Criticism: Selected Reviews 1977–1982* (Brighton, 1983) p. 83. Brown, *James Joyce: A Post-Culturalist Perspective*, p. 87 refers interestingly to the 'god of sign-posts' in relation to 'Circe'. See also Ellmann, *Selected Letters of James Joyce*, p. 272 and Jacques Derrida, 'Violence and Metaphysics' in *Writing and Difference* (London, 1978) pp. 227–8 who describes Joyce as 'the most Hegelian, *perhaps*, of modern novelists'. This essay is interestingly taken up by Rabaté, 'The Portrait of the Artist', pp. 103–8.

In this, there is still much to learn from *Ulysses*. We will now turn to
T. S. Eliot for a very different lesson in the political potential of
modernist poetics.

T. S. ELIOT: 'GENTILE OR JEW'

In 'The Approach to James Joyce', one of many radio broadcasts
that Eliot was to give during the Second World War, he argued that
the structure of *Ulysses* is realized by Joyce 'introducing himself – the
same Stephen Daedalus who is the hero of the *Portrait* – and he
creates Bloom as a counterpart, an opposite to himself'.[45] Not unlike
Budgen's account of *Ulysses*, Bloom is conceived by Eliot as Joyce's
'opposite' or 'counterpart' who throws the self into relief. While I
have tried to show that the fixed distinction between a 'self' and a
semitic 'other' is continually subverted by Joyce, it is the authoritarian use of an equivalent set of binary oppositions that is at the
heart of Eliot's poetry and social thought. Two years after his
influential review of *Ulysses* in *The Dial*, Eliot was to reinforce Joyce's
Hellenizing 'mythic method' in a 1923 *Criterion* Commentary on
'The Importance of Greek':

> [T]he study of Greek is the exact study of an exact language, a language of
> refinement and precision ... the study of Greek is part of the study of our own
> mind: Our categories of thought are largely the outcome of Greek thought;
> our categories of emotion are largely the outcome of Greek literature. One
> of the advantages of the study of a more alien language, such as one of the
> more highly developed oriental languages, is to throw this fact into bold
> relief: a mind saturated with the traditions of Indian philosophy is and must
> always remain very different from one saturated with the traditions of
> European philosophy – as is *every* European mind, even when untrained and
> unread. What analytic psychology attempts to do for the individual mind,
> the study of history – including language and literature – does for the
> collective mind. Neglect of Greek means for Europe *a relapse into un-
> consciousness*.[46]

The rigid associations, in this editorial, between Greek literature
and thought and the 'language of refinement and precision', on the
one hand, and the inexact non-European 'alien languages', on the
other, are wholly characteristic of Eliot's social thought in *The
Criterion*. Such generalizations, however, also hark back to the rather

[45] T. S. Eliot, 'The Approach to James Joyce', *The Listener* 14 October 1943, 447.
[46] T. S. Eliot, 'The Importance of Greek', *The Criterion* 3 (Number 2, April 1925, his
emphasis), 341–2.

loose references to the 'mind of Europe' in 'Tradition and the Individual Talent' (1919). In this cruder restatement of his earlier essay, Eliot fears that the collective 'European mind' might potentially be superseded by 'alien' traditions.[47] By neglecting Greek – which defines 'our own mind' – the exactness of 'our categories of thought... and emotion' are fatally undermined and threatened with 'a relapse into [oriental] unconsciousness'. Such manichaean oppositions, which threaten the fragility of the 'mind of Europe', result in what has been called a 'contagion of antitheses' in the work of Eliot. Maud Ellmann, who has recently discussed Pound and Eliot in these terms, rightly sees Eliot's modernism as unconsciously repudiating its own 'impersonal' precepts. Unlike Joyce's artful deconstruction of a semitic racial discourse in *Ulysses*, Eliot's excluded oriental 'alien languages' constantly return, in unexpected ways, to haunt his poetry. In striving for 'classical' exactitude and canonical authority, Eliot relied upon an 'other' – which could not, quite, be repressed – to represent the opposite of his 'Greek' ideals.[48]

It is in the discursive context of Eliot's attack on the disorderly '"slither" of Romantic individualism', that 'the jew' became a necessary 'objective correlative' for that which is inexact and uncategorizable. As Christopher Ricks has recently shown, Eliot's semitic 'prejudices' are not a temporary or superficial aberration that was caused by an idiosyncratic personality or a peculiar social milieu. Instead, Ricks argues that Eliot's 'antisemitism' cannot be 'isolated from the larger issues of categorizing and prejudice in Eliot's poetry'.[49] That Eliot's categorizing prejudices were at the heart of his thinking can be gauged from an early satiric prose dialogue, 'Eeldrop and Appleplex' (1917), published in *The Little Review* in two parts. This has been appropriately seen by Ricks as an important commentary on Eliot's ingrained preoccupation with 'prejudice'. Just after the dialogue opens between the Eliotian 'Eeldrop' and the Poundian 'Appleplex', the narrator announces his attempt to escape

[47] T. S. Eliot, 'Tradition and the Individual Talent' (1919) in *The Sacred Wood: Essays on Poetry and Criticism* (London, 1920) p. 51.

[48] Maud Ellmann, *The Poetics of Impersonality: T. S. Eliot and Ezra Pound* (Brighton, 1987) p. 13 for this argument.

[49] Christopher Ricks, *T. S. Eliot and Prejudice* (London, 1988) p. 61 and chapter 2 *passim* to which I am indebted and Ellmann, *The Poetics of Impersonality*, p. 4. For an example of the kind of approach to Eliot's 'antisemitism' which Ricks rightly dismisses see Melvin Wilk, *Jewish Presence in T. S. Eliot and Franz Kafka* (Atlanta, Georgia, 1986). Robert H. Canary, *T. S. Eliot: The Poet and His Critics* (Chicago, 1982) pp. 150–9 crudely annotates much of the post-war criticism on 'Eliot and Antisemitism'.

'the too well pigeon-holed, too taken-for-granted, too highly systema-
tized areas'. A welcome doubleness ensues as Eeldrop and Appleplex
self-consciously utilize fixed racial and sexual stereotypes and, at the
same time, question the implications of such reductive pigeon-holing:

> Why ... was that fat Spaniard, who sat at the table with us this evening, and
> listened to our conversation with occasional curiosity, why was he himself for
> a moment an object of interest to us? ... He was oppressively gross and
> vulgar; he belonged to a type, he could easily be classified in any town of
> provincial Spain. Yet under the circumstances – when we had been
> discussing marriage, and he suddenly leaned forward and exclaimed: 'I was
> married once myself' – we were able to detach him from his classification
> and regard him for a moment as an unique being, a soul, however
> insignificant, with a history of its own, once and for all. It is these moments
> which we prize, and which are alone revealing. For any vital truth is
> incapable of being applied to another case: the essential is unique. Perhaps
> that is why it is so neglected: because it is useless. ... With the decline of
> orthodox theology and its admirable theory of the soul, the unique
> importance of events has vanished. A man is only important as he is classed.
> (8–9)[50]

The countervailing sentiments in this passage, for a moment, detach
the 'fat Spaniard' from his 'classification' and regard him as a
'unique being'. But an interesting tension in Eliot's thinking is
exposed when the notion of individual uniqueness is immediately
qualified – 'a man is only important as he is classed' – and the 'fat
Spaniard' is reduced to his 'type'. Appleplex's explicit renunciation
of a romanticized Bergsonian individualism, soon after this part of
the dialogue, is clearly allied to the Classicist ideal of 'classification'.
And yet, Eeldrop tries to synthetically resolve the conflict between
Classicism and Romanticism by wishing for a 'moment of pure
observation' which is 'not alien to the principle of classification, but
deeper' (10). In acknowledging that 'when a man is classified
something is lost', the 'mystic' Eeldrop recognizes an 'other' sphere
of experience which goes beyond the 'materialist' classifier, Appleplex, and his comic file index, 'from A (adultery) to Y (yeggmen)'
(8).

   In the second part of 'Eeldrop and Appleplex', which has been
largely ignored by Eliot's critics, the conflict between a Hulmeian
classifying 'philosophy' and a romanticized individualism is shifted

---

[50] T. S. Eliot, 'Eeldrop and Appleplex', *The Little Review* (May, 1917), 7–11 and (September,
   1917), 16–19. Further references to this story will be in the body of the text. See also Ricks,
   T. S. Eliot and Prejudice, p. 115.

from the racial to the sexual sphere. Looking out of the window of their 'disreputable' apartment for a second night, Eeldrop wonders what happened to 'Edith', a friend of Mrs Howexdon, who had recommended to Appleplex that he read Bergson. Eeldrop thinks of Edith as 'Scheherazade', after the Arabic tales of *A Thousand and One Nights*, who was forced to tell stories so as to remain alive. After pointedly ignoring Appleplex's factual account of Edith, contained in his 'Survey of Contemporary Society' file (16), Eeldrop prefers to meditate on her romantic philosophy, '"Not pleasure, but fullness of life... to burn ever with a hard gem-like flame", these were her words' (17):

I do not like to think of her future. Scheherazade grown old! I see her grown very plump, full-bosomed, with blond hair, living in a small flat with a maid, walking in the Park with a Pekinese, motoring with a Jewish stock-broker. With a fierce appetite for food and drink, when all other appetite is gone except the insatiable increasing appetite of vanity; rolling on two wide legs, rolling in motorcars, rolling towards a diabetic end in a seaside watering place. (17)

Here Edith's rampant individualism, and her licentious but declining sexual 'appetite', is associated with the motoring 'Jewish stock-broker' who prefigures the subsequent use of a semitic discourse in many of the poems in *Ara Vos Prec* (1920) or *Poems* (1920). In a letter to Pound, written in October 1917, Eliot describes the President of the Anglo-French Society, Harry Webster Lawson, first Viscount Burnham, as 'a Jew merchant, named Lawson (sc. Levi-sohn?)'.[51] Eliot, evidently, was quite at home at this time with such race-thinking. Nonetheless, in this early prose dialogue, Eeldrop is uncertain if Edith, 'in spite of her romantic past, [pursues] steadily some hidden purpose of her own' and, later on, he thinks of her as 'an artist without the slightest artistic power' (18): 'Her material, her experience that is, is already a mental product, already digested by reason. Hence Edith (I only at this moment arrive at understanding) is really the most orderly person in existence, and the most rational. Nothing ever happens to her; everything that happens is her own doing' (19). Once again, Eliot attempts to elide the 'philosphical' opposition between a disorderly, Bergsonian individualism and a Hulmeian classical, ordered rationality. The 'romantic' Edith can also be seen, in a 'moment of pure observation', as 'the most orderly person in existence'.

[51] Valerie Eliot (ed.), *The Letters of T. S. Eliot: 1898–1922* (London, 1988) p. 206.

Such studied ambivalence, even if deliberately comic or pseudo-sophisticated, indicates the very real dangers of a too literal application of Hulme's seminal essay, 'Romanticism and Classicism' (n.d.), to Eliot's subsequent poetry. Part of the influential attack on Bergson's romantic 'subjectivism' by Lasserre, and other ideologues of L'Action française, was also an attack on Bergson's Jewishness.[52] By connecting Edith's romanticism with a 'Jewish stock-broker' driving aimlessly around London, Eliot reinforces such racial associations but then, interestingly, distances himself from them. Edith's potentially 'classical' traits makes her one of 'those people who provide material for the artist' and who have in them 'something unconscious, something which they do not fully realise or understand' (19). Eeldrop's identification with Edith and her exotic 'unconscious' world is, of course, in stark contrast to Eliot's fear, in *The Criterion*, of a descent into an alien 'unconsciousness' should the 'classical' forms disappear from Europe. But one should certainly distinguish between Eliot's doctrinaire application of Hulme's *Speculations* (1924) in *The Criterion*, and his unsettling recognition of himself – as that which is classified as 'other' – in his poetry.

Maud Ellmann has suggestively compared Eliot's critical ideals of, as he put it, using 'the right word in the right place' with his political quest to 'purify the speech community'. With particular reference to *After Strange Gods: A Primer of Modern Heresy* (1934), she rightly brings together Eliot's need to control the rhetorical boundaries of '*written* language' with his imposition of national boundaries on 'nomadic Jews who threaten the cohesion of the group'.[53] But what is startling about these analogies is the obvious dissimilarity between the classicist critic who wished to use 'the right word in the right place' and the Prufrockian poetic persona who was only too painfully aware of the impossibility of 'say[ing] just what I mean'. One of Eliot's most explicitly self-referential poems, 'Mélange Adultère de Tout', similarly represents his own contradictory disposition and cosmopolitanism, like the ambivalent 'Jew', as inexact and uncategorizable. At the end of the poem, Eliot mockingly displaces his fragmentary identities onto the African Continent, where he imagines himself a wanderer from Omaha to Damascus, celebrating his birthday at an African oasis, dressed in a giraffe's skin. It is precisely

---

[52] Ellmann, *The Poetics of Impersonality*, p. 12 and Michael H. Levenson, *A Genealogy of Modernism: A Study of English Literary Doctrine* 1908–1922 (Cambridge, 1984) chapter 3.
[53] Ellmann, *The Poetics of Impersonality*, p. 54

this spectacular lack of a sense of resolution with an 'other' world that seems to define his 1920 *Poems*.[54] In a characteristic 'quatrain' poem, 'Mr Eliot's Sunday Morning Service', the tone of enigmatic irony is continued from 'Eeldrop and Appleplex' and encompasses the playful juxtaposition of 'philosophical' and 'racial' opposites. Guided by the epigraph from Marlowe's *The Jew of Malta* – '*Look, look, here comes two religious caterpillars*' – a number of critics have particularly emphasized the '"semitic" element' in this poem which is carried over into the first stanza:

> Polyphiloprogenitive
> The sapient sutlers of the Lord
> Drift across the window-panes.
> In the beginning was the Word.[55]

With reference to Eliot's neologism, 'polyphiloprogenitive', George Montiero has noted that David Friedrich Strauss's *A New Life of Jesus* (1865), a key influence on *Daniel Deronda*, states that it was the task of 'the Jews' to 'assimilate' Jesus to the 'philoprogenitive Gods of the heathen'. The American *New International Encyclopedia* (1902) describes, similarly, one of the 'distinguishing mental and moral traits of the Jews' as 'a strong family sense and philoprogenitiveness'. Whether Eliot knew of these particular sources or not is less important than the fact that the association between Jews and 'philoprogenitiveness' was a fairly common perception. H. G. Wells's *Marriage* (1912) portrayed in racialized terms the 'enormous vistas of dark philoprogenitive parents and healthy little Jews and Jewesses ... hygienically reared, exquisitely trained and educated'. And, in general, the connection between rampant Jewish reproduction and the scale of East European immigration into Britain was well established by the time Eliot was writing his poem.[56]

---

[54] For an opposing approach to this poem and Eliot's 1920 *Poems* see Robert Crawford, *The Savage and the City in the Work of T. S. Eliot* (Oxford, 1987) p. 1 and p. 101 which will be discussed below in this chapter.

[55] George Montiero, 'Christians and Jews in "Mr Eliot's Sunday Morning Service"', *T. S. Eliot Review* 3 (1976), 20–2 and Hyam Maccoby, 'An Interpretation of "Mr Eliot's Sunday Morning Service"', *Critical Survey* (January, 1968), 159–65. The use of *The Jew of Malta* as the epigraph of *Portrait of a Lady* has not, it should be said, illicited an equivalent critical response.

[56] Montiero, 'Christians and Jews', cites Strauss and the *New International Encyclopedia* and Wells's *Marriage* is discussed in chapter 4 of this book. See Colin Holmes, *Anti-Semitism in British Society, 1876–1939* (London, 1979) in general for hostile attitudes towards Jewish 'philoprogenitiveness' and, for the eugenic racial context of these fears, see Juan Leon,

Montiero's '"semitic" element' has been reinforced by Hyam
Maccoby who has made out a rather dogmatic case for the 'sapient
sutlers of the Lord' being 'the Jews'. To be sure, the 'sapient sutlers'
do 'drift across the window-panes' not unlike 'the jew' who 'squats
on the window-sill' in 'Gerontion'. If there is an explicit continuation
with Marlowe's *The Jew of Malta* in this first stanza, then it might be
said that the 'sapient sutlers of the Lord', like Barabas and Ithamore,
are commentating satirically on the 'house' of Christendom as patent
outsiders. But, it is unnecessary to fix Eliot's materialist 'sutlers', who
trade in words, as 'Jews'. The Lord's 'sutlers' are condemned by
their Old Testament, Hebraic qualities rather than their racial
Jewishness. This is especially apparent in the next stanza when the
opening of the poem is contrasted with the overly spiritualized deity
of the Greek philosophers, τὸ ἕν, epitomized by the self-castrated
'enervate Origen'. These two contrary versions of God – either
Hebraically materialist or Hellenistically ethereal – are, as Maccoby
notes, synthesized initially in the painting of the 'Baptized God' in
the third stanza.[57] While the need to control the 'polyphiloprogenitive' reproduction of words was to be later signified by the
imposition of national boundaries on 'free-thinking Jews', it would
be reductive to read 'Mr Eliot's Sunday Morning Service' solely in
these terms. On the contrary, it is the use of an Arnoldian sense of
Hebraism in this poem, without a fixed 'Jewish' racial referent, that
is worth emphasizing. At the same time, the transfiguration of the
'sapient sutlers' into industrious worker-bees (who carry the pollen
from the 'stamen' to the 'pistil' like entrepreneurial 'middle-men')
implicitly alludes to Marlowe's parasitic 'religious caterpillars' and,
also, prefigures much of the animal-imagery used to construct 'the
jew' in Eliot's poetry.[58] Because the modern-day Church is more
concerned with 'piaculative pence' rather then 'penitence', its
accumulative materiality gives rise to Sweeney:

> Sweeney shifts from ham to ham
> Stirring the water in his bath.
> The masters of the subtle school
> Are controversial, polymath.

'"Meeting Mr Eugenides": T. S. Eliot and the Eugenic Anxiety', *Yeats Eliot Review* 9
(1988), 169–77.
[57] Maccoby, 'An Interpretation', pp. 160–1 to whom I am indebted for this reading.
[58] B. C. Southam, *A Student's Guide to 'The Selected Poems of T. S. Eliot'* (London, 1968) p. 64 and
J. A. Morris, 'T. S. Eliot and Antisemitism', *Journal of European Studies* 2 (1972), 173–82 for
Eliot's animal-imagery.

The emphatic contrast between the overly physical Sweeney shifting from 'ham to ham' in his bath and the 'unoffending feet' of the 'Baptized God' has often been noted. But the unbridgeable gap between 'the Flesh' and 'the Word' in this last stanza, as Maccoby points out, is underpinned by the polymathic 'masters of the subtle school' who echo, both literally and philosophically, the 'polyphilo-progenitive' sutlers who open the poem. Here, the empty controversies of present-day thinkers are directly related to the all-pervasive Judaic founders of the Church. The unity of 'the Word' is, in this reading, fragmented by the rampant individualism and parasitical materialism of those in the established Protestant Church who have, historically, 'dissociated' the soul from the body of Christ.[59]

There is an important distinction to be made here between the racialized Irish Sweeney and the deracialized Arnoldian vocabulary in 'Mr Eliot's Sunday Morning Service'. While Sweeney is unquestionably the antithesis of the 'Baptized God', the 'sapient sutlers' are, in contrast, inherently ambivalent as there is always the possibility that they include the overly Hebraic 'Mr T. S. Eliot' himself. Just as Eliot could represent himself as the wandering, deracinated cosmopolitan in 'Mélange Adultère de Tout', there is a sense in 'Mr Eliot's Sunday Morning Service' that he is unconsciously associating himself with that which is 'other' to his categorizing aesthetic. As Piers Gray has argued, the latter poem is a curious paradox because it, implosively, 'breeds exactly the form of exegesis which it satirizes'. With this crushing assertion in mind, it seems that one should take seriously Lyndall Gordon's suggestion that the 'Mr Eliot' in the title of the poem is not merely a self-parody but also refers to Eliot's cousin, Fred Eliot, who conducted Sunday morning services as a Unitarian minister.[60] Eliot's profound dismissal of his family's liberal, Christ-belittling, Unitarianism has been suggestively related to his 'antisemitism' by both William Empson and Christopher Ricks. Eliot, in *The Criterion*, categorized Unitarianism as 'outside the Christian Fold' and he was to reject

[59] Maccoby, 'An Interpretation', p. 164. For a reading of Eliot's theory of the 'dissociation of sensibility' in terms of contemporary American antisemitism see Jonathan Morse, *Word by Word: The Language of Memory* (Ithaca, 1990) pp. 49–50.

[60] Lyndall Gordon, *Eliot's Early Years* (Oxford, 1987) p. 70 and Piers Gray, *T. S. Eliot's Intellectual and Poetic Development 1909–1922* (Brighton, 1982) p. 197. For Sweeney as an Irish racial stereotype see Jonathan Morse, 'Sweeney, the Sties of the Irish, and *The Waste Land*' in Kinley E. Robey (ed.), *Critical Essays on T. S. Eliot: The Sweeney Motif* (Boston, 1985) pp. 135–46. A. D. Moody, *Thomas Stearns Eliot: Poet* (Cambridge, 1979), p. 60 argues vaguely that 'Sweeney has some relation to Bleistein'.

unambiguously the 'intellectual and puritanical rationalism' of his childhood. In an autobiographical aside in his 'American Literature and Language' (1953), he described the household of his childhood as if he had, himself, been one of the biblical Children of Israel:

The standard of conduct was that which my grandfather had set; our moral judgements, our decisions between duty and self-indulgence, were taken as if, like Moses, he had brought down the tables of the Law, any deviation from which would be sinful. Not the least of these laws, which included injunctions still more than prohibitions, was the law of Public Service: it is no doubt owing to the impress of this law upon my infant mind that... I have felt... an uncomfortable and very inconvenient obligation to serve upon committees.[61]

The bathetic note which gently undercuts his grandfather's Mosaic 'injunctions' to serve the public, and his recognition of being shaped by rather puritanical but well-meaning Old Testament patriarchs, clearly encourages a largely repressed identification between his Unitarian background and Judaism. Eliot was to explicitly acknowledge the possibility of this connection in a rather heated exchange of letters with J. V. Healy. In response to Healy, Eliot redefined the unwelcome 'free-thinking Jews' in *After Strange Gods* as products of 'the Jewish religion... shorn of its traditional practices, observances and Messianism [which] tends to become a mild and colourless form of Unitarianism'. This largely unacknowledged sense of his own Protestant Hebraism is reinforced by Eliot's early occupations in finance and journalism (so-called 'Jewish' professions) and his painful awareness, at this time, of his own 'foreignness' and cosmopolitan detachment from British social mores.[62] That a semitic discourse could be applied to Eliot in this distinctive context can be seen from an extraordinary outburst by C. S. Lewis:

Assuredly [Eliot] is one of the enemy: and all the more dangerous because he is sometimes disguised as a friend. And this offence is exaggerated by attendant circumstances, such as his arrogance. And (you will further

---

[61] T. S. Eliot, 'American Literature and Language' (1953) in *To Criticize the Critic and Other Writings* (London, 1965) p. 44 and *The Criterion* 10 (July 1931), 771. See also Ricks, *T. S. Eliot and Prejudice*, pp. 46–7 and William Empson, *Using Biography* (London, 1984), 'Eliot', pp. 187–200. The most comprehensive account of Eliot's Unitarian background is Eric Sigg, *The American T. S. Eliot* (Cambridge, 1989) chapter 1.

[62] J. V. Healy's correspondence with Eliot in May 1940 is quoted in Ricks, *T. S. Eliot and Prejudice*, p. 44 and Ricks also rightly argues that Eliot's poetry begins 'in pain at foreignness and at denationalized disintegration' (p. 198). This theme is taken up by Ritchie Robertson in his 'Eliot's Antisemitic Poems', *Jewish Quarterly* 37 (Number 139, Autumn 1990), 46–8.

forgive me) it is further aggravated for an Englishman by the recollection that Eliot stole upon us, a foreigner and a neutral, while we were at war – obtained, I have my wonders how, a job in the Bank of England [*sic*] – and became (am I wrong) the advance guard of the invasion since carried out by his natural friends and allies, the Steins and Pounds and *hoc genus omme*, the Parisian riff-raff of denationalised Irishmen and Americans who have perhaps given Western Europe her death wound.[63]

Here Eliot, like 'the jew', is constructed as a 'disguised' enemy who wheedles his way into key financial institutions and, with a few alien co-conspirators, helps to bring about the collapse of Western European civilization. While the irrevocably inferior Sweeney was to remain an ape-like Irishman, there was always an unarticulated possiblity that the 'denationalised' Eliot was himself a Hebraic 'master of the subtle school' who proliferated meaningless words and, thus, helped to perpetuate an all-encompassing spiritual malaise. This largely repressed fear of being contaminated by degenerate forces outside of his control helped shape Eliot's definition of Classicism, in a 1916 lecture, as 'essentially a belief in Original Sin – the necessity for austere discipline'. Eliot's disciplined search for a fixed sense of tradition and a transcendent 'order' took many forms – a fastidious Englishness; a devout Anglo-Catholicism; and a keen political authoritarianism – all of which were constructed to oppose a disorderly 'Jewish' liberal individualism. It was probably a coincidence, although Eliot did take particular care over such matters, but the explicitly 'semitic' poems which I now wish to discuss opened, and so helped define, the 1920 editions of his verse.[64]

'Gerontion' was completed as late as July, 1919, but was immediately placed at the head of Eliot's *Poems* and *Ara Vos Prec* and was soon perceived to characterize the volume as a whole in much the same way as 'Prufrock' had done in Eliot's earlier collection. Recent criticism, however, has emphasized that 'Gerontion', far from developing a Prufrockian persona, is more accurately read as a withdrawal from the very idea of 'persona'. The physical and spiritual disintegration of Gerontion, it is argued, results in a loss of

[63] Quoted in Ricks, *T. S. Eliot and Prejudice*, p. 198 who notes, interestingly, that Lewis himself was a 'denationalized Irishman' who was projecting his own 'foreignness' onto Eliot.
[64] For Eliot's early definition of Classicism see Ronald Schuchard, 'T. S. Eliot as an Extension Lecturer, 1916–1919', *Review of English Studies* 25 (Number 98, 1974), 165. Eliot decided the order of the poems in his *Poems* (1920) in a letter to John Quinn, 28 September 1919, which is published in Valerie Eliot, *The Letters of T. S. Eliot*, p. 335.

individuality and a disembodied self that is hardly fixed by the 'I' that opens the poem: 'the gap between Gerontion's name and his "I am" is the first of many "windy spaces" in the text'. The precedent for 'Gerontion' is not 'Prufrock' but, according to Piers Gray, the method suggested by 'Mr Eliot's Sunday Morning Service' which is 'a parody of exegisis'.[65] The doubleness in the title and import of this earlier poem are reflected in the semitism at the heart of 'Gerontion':

> My house is a decayed house,
> And the jew squats on the window-sill, the owner,
> Spawned in some estaminet of Antwerp,
> Blistered in Brussels, patched and peeled in London.
> The goat coughs at night in the field overhead;
> Rocks, moss, stonecrop, iron, merds.

Up until this point, the 'old man' had been distinguished precariously by what he was not – 'I was neither ... Nor ... Nor ... ' – and 'the jew' acts ostensibly as a convenient 'other' against which the fragmented Gerontion can be clearly defined. In this reading, 'the jew' is the poem's antithesis, a squatting beast or insect (foreshadowing the 'spider' or 'weevil') who is not born but 'spawned' and, because 'blistered' and 'peeled', is the embodiment of an untranscendent dryness. Rather like the haphazard energy of 'bees / with hairy bellies' who pass between the (male) 'stamen' and (female) 'pistil', 'the jew' is a natural force who, in its betrayal of vitality, anticipates the poisonous fertility of the 'flowering judas'.[66] Just as the aimless potency of bees results in confusion – the sexually indeterminate 'office of the epicene' – 'Jewish' frenetic cosmopolitan proliferation and arbitrary financial power (as 'the owner') decays national boundaries and threatens the unity of Christian Europe. There is, as many commentators have noted, an implicit contrast with the spawned 'jew' in 'some estaminet in Antwerp' and the birth of the Christ-child who emerges soon after this passage. The 'jew', in these terms, can be read as an 'anti-Christ', the ultimate antagonist, 'if the Christ-child is the symbol of Oneness and centrality, the 'jew' is the symbol of plurality and disintegration ... [as] he is not a single

[65] Gray, *T. S. Eliot's Intellectual and Poetic Development*, p. 211 and p. 214. See also Ellmann, *The Poetics of Impersonality*, p. 81 and Franco Moretti, *Signs Taken for Wonders* (London, 1988) p. 218.

[66] Southam, *Student's Guide*, p. 64, and for this reading of 'Gerontion', Hyam Maccoby, 'A Study of the "jew" in "Gerontion"', *Jewish Quarterly* 17 (Number 2, 1969), 19–22 and 39–43.

centre but one of a swarm'. To be sure, the disconnected textual landscape of Eliot's waste land – 'Rocks, moss, stonecrop, iron, merds' – is also the spiritual antithesis of what follows:[67]

> Signs are taken for wonders. 'We would see a sign!'
> The word within a word, unable to speak a word,
> Swaddled with darkness.

Instead of the atomized, 'dissociated' word of 'the jew', 'the word within a word, unable to speak a word' (taken verbatim from Lancelot Andrewes) is the Logos, the Word incarnate. In his essay on 'Lancelot Andrewes', written in 1926, just before he was baptized into the Church of England and became a British citizen, Eliot was to cite this line as one of the 'flashing phrases which never desert the memory'.[68] Andrewes's sermons are set against those of John Donne and a deluded majority who are 'fascinated by "personality" in the romantic sense of the word – for those who find "personality" an ultimate value – [and] forget that in the spiritual hierarchy there are places higher than Donne' (26). In *For Lancelot Andrewes: Essays on Style and Order* (1928), Eliot went on to famously define his 'general point of view' as 'classicist in literature, royalist in politics, and anglo-catholic in religion' (7). Despite such impersonal certainties and fixed hierarchies concerning 'style and order', it would be a mistake to confine the tentative, equivocal consciousness of 'Gerontion' to this rather comfortable retrospective restoration of 'meaning' to the poem.

As opposed to the fixed binary oppositions between the Logos and 'the jew', Christ and the anti-Christ, it is possible to think of Gerontion himself as a 'Jew' who unconsciously signifies that which has been constructed in the poem as semitically 'other'. The fragmented, disintegrating Gerontion is, after all, an 'old man driven by the Trades' and is named in a ballad, 'Geruntus', which gave rise to the character of Shylock. Not unlike Gerontion, Jews have been represented, historically, as debased old men who, in stark contrast to a youthful Christianity, lack any spiritual vigour to renew mankind.[69]

---

[67] Maccoby, 'A Study of the "jew" in "Gerontion"', p. 39. Until he was dissuaded by Ezra Pound, Eliot thought of 'Gerontion' as a possible 'Prelude' to *The Waste Land*.

[68] T. S. Eliot, *For Lancelot Andrewes: Essays on Style and Order* (London, 1928) p. 22. All further references to *For Lancelot Andrewes* will be cited in the body of the text.

[69] Maccoby, 'A Study of the "jew" in "Gerontion"', p. 20 thinks, usefully, of Gerontion as 'a Jew' but does not take on board the disturbing implications of this reading for his own account of 'the jew' in Eliot's poem.

H. G. Wells used a contemporary version of this long-standing representation in *Tono-Bungay* (1909):

These Lichtensteins and their like seem to have no promise in them at all of any fresh vitality for the kingdom. I do not believe in their intelligence or their power – they have nothing new about them at all, nothing creative or rejuvenescent, no more than a disorderly instinct of acquisition; and the prevalence of them and their kind is but a phase in the broad slow decay of the great social organism of England. They could not have made Bladesover, they cannot replace it; they just happen to break out over it – sapro-phytically.[70]

Not unlike 'the jew' in 'Gerontion', the Lichtensteins represent a 'disorderly instinct of acquisition' who live, like insects or sapro-phytes, on decayed matter and who are fundamentally old, 'they have nothing new about them at all, nothing creative or rejuvenes-cent'. All of these widespread constructions prefigure 'Gerontion', perhaps even suggesting to Eliot the neologism, 'juvescence'. Just as Edward Ponderevo became a non-racial Hebraic double of the Lichtensteins in *Tono-Bungay*, Gerontion, in this reading, can be said to redouble 'the jew' in the poem. The clearest textual evidence for this possibility has been assembled by Piers Gray who has shown that 'Gerontion' is, in part, a subversive parody of St Paul's teachings in the New Testament. That Gerontion is, from the beginning, 'being read to by a boy' points intriguingly to the prospect of the poem being an aged, spiritless 'reiteration' of, in this case, Pauline philosophy. The multiple, various consciousnesses of Gerontion, which refuse to be limited by the Christian Logos, are, to this extent, 'Jewish'. Even when the racialized 'jew' can be said to have a 'fascistically' fixed presence, the language used to describe 'him' or 'it' – 'some estaminet' – discloses an ambiguously vague precision.[71] Thus Gerontion is both an 'other' to the racialized 'jew' and, at the same time, his repressed double. Such is the instability at the heart of 'Gerontion'.

Far from simply constructing 'the jew' as a settled racial 'other', Gerontion reproduces a proliferating semitic vocabulary which he ostensibly opposes. Thus his attempted contra-baptism – 'knee deep

---

[70] *Tono-Bungay* (London, 1909) p. 52, Pan Classic edition, discussed in chapter 4 of this book.
[71] Gray, *T. S. Eliot's Intellectual and Poetic Development*, pp. 211–13 and p. 219 and Ellmann, *The Poetics of Impersonality*, p. 81 for this reading. See also Gabriel Pearson, 'Eliot: An American use of Symbolism' in Graham Martin (ed.), *Eliot in Perspective* (London, 1970) pp. 87–8.

in the salt marsh' – echoes the squatting 'jew' who gives rise to a 'slimy' excrement which unsettles that which is solid and 'known'.[72] A disconnected, rootless world dominated by 'philoprogenitive' Judaic 'masters of the subtle school' is also menacingly realized by Gerontion in his 'wilderness of mirrors', 'many cunning passages, contrived corridors', 'whispering ambitions', 'supple confusions' and 'thousand small deliberations'. The cosmopolitan residents of Gerontion's rented house, such as Mr Silvero 'with caressing hands', can be seen, in this reading, as non-racial 'jews' (mirroring Bleistein with his 'palms turned out') not unlike Gerontion. Instead of the opposition between 'the jew' and its racial 'others', all in the poem are dispossessed and 'devoured' by the 'flowering judas / to be eaten divided, to be drunk'. This inverse Communion is, above all, a betrayal ('among whispers') of the promise of the Christ-child, as the Word incarnate is negatively transfigured into the splintered remains of Gerontion's 'ghostly rhetoric'. The associative import of the word 'jew' encompasses both 'judas' and 'juvescence' and this latter neologism has been glossed, somewhat arbitrarily, to include 'jew, juice, essence, effervesence'.[73] But the indeterminacy in Eliot's use of language is reflected, in particular, in Gerontion's own inability to completely separate himself from 'the jew'.

One should not underestimate the very real terror in 'Gerontion' of being Judaized. This terror, I suspect, is an implicit allusion to *The Education of Henry Adams: An Autobiograhy* (1918), which was reviewed by Eliot while writing 'Gerontion' and which, in turn, became an intimate aspect of the poem. After lambasting Bostonian Unitarianism and Adams, as a product of this world, Eliot in his review anxiously states that 'there is nothing to indicate that Adams's senses either flowered or fruited' in this intellectual atmosphere. Seeing Adams as a prime example of 'Boston doubt', he argues that his scepticism is 'a product, or a cause, or a concomitant, of Unitarianism; it is not destructive, but it is dissolvent ... Wherever this man stepped, the ground did not simply give way, it flew into particles'.[74] Such are the 'fractured atoms' that surround Gerontion. This sense

[72] Tony Pinkney, *Women in the Poetry of T. S. Eliot: A Psychoanalytic Approach* (London, 1984) p. 134.
[73] Maccoby, 'A Study of the "jew" in "Gerontion"', p. 41. See also John Harrison, *The Reactionaries: A Study of the Anti-Democratic Intelligentsia* (London, 1966) p. 150 and Stephen Spender, *Eliot* (London, 1975) p. 64.
[74] T. S. Eliot, 'A Sceptical Patrician', *Athenaeum*, 23 May 1919, 361–2

of Bostonian dissolution was also proclaimed in a piece on American literature, written for the *Athenaeum* a month before his Adams review, where Eliot described 'the great figures of American Literature' as being 'peculiarly isolated ... Their world was thin ... Worst of all it was secondhand; it was not original and self-dependent – it was a shadow'. This sentiment is certainly reflected in Adams's autobiography where he described his Patrician world as 'dead' and compared it unfavourably with a newly arrived 'Polish Jew' who had a 'keener instinct, an intenser energy, and a freer hand' than indigenous 'Puritans and Patriots'. After a visit to Warsaw, Adams even claimed that 'the Jew and I are the only curious antiquities in [the city]. My only merit as a curiosity is antiquity, but the Jew is also a curiosity'. It is, in short, the fear of becoming a deracinated but venerable 'shadow' of another more vibrant tradition – in other words a 'jew' or a Unitarian – which is ingrained in 'Gerontion' and might be said to culminate in 'The Hollow Men' (1925).[75]

The paragraph in Adams's autobiography, that Eliot explicitly used in 'Gerontion', is worth recalling as it is a good illustration of the contradictory impulses in Eliot's poetic construction of 'the jew' as both an inhuman racial 'other' as well as a potential 'self'. Adams is comparing the richness of the spring in Washington with his bleaker memories of the same time of the year in New England:

The Potomac and its tributaries squandered beauty ... Here and there a Negro log cabin alone disturbed the dogwood and the judas-tree ... The tulip and the chestnut tree gave no sense of struggle against a stingy nature ... The brooding heat of the profligate vegetation; the cool charm of the running water; the terrific splendour of the June thundergust in the deep and solitary woods, were all sensual, animal and elemental. No European spring had shown him the same intermixture of delicate grace and passionate depravity that marked the Maryland May. He loved it too much as if it were Greek and half human.[76]

Adams's paganized sense of the 'sensual, animal and elemental' Maryland spring, in contrast with the blander 'European spring' of New England, evokes what Robert Crawford has called the 'savage' element in T. S. Eliot. The description of the Maryland spring as

---

[75] T. S. Eliot, 'American Literature', *Athenaeum*, 25 April 1919, 236–7. Adams is cited in this context in both Wilk, *Jewish Presence in T. S. Eliot*, pp. 59–60 and chapter 3 and Ricks, *T. S. Eliot and Prejudice*, pp. 67–70.

[76] This passage was first noted in F. O. Matthiessen, *The Achievement of T. S. Eliot: An Essay on the Nature of Poetry* (Oxford, 1935) p. 73.

'Greek and half human' interestingly juxtaposes 'the savage' with Eliot's 'civilising' ideals. It is precisely this kind of synthesis that Crawford has argued is at the heart of Eliot's writing. According to this interpretation, 'the savage' is an essential supplement to the modern, urban world of 'the city' and Eliot, in his poetry, constantly brought together these 'opposites'. In this way, Eliot's poetry is deemed to have united 'tradition and modernity', 'Europe and America', 'blasphemy and religion' and 'slap-stick mischief and poker-faced enthronement'.[77] Leaving aside those critics of Eliot that have emphasized in general his poetic irresolution and studied imprecision, it would seem that this sense of Hegelian unification in Eliot's poetic practice conflicts radically with his use of a semitic discourse. To be sure, 'the jew' is nothing if not a 'savage', as can be seen from his animalistic appearance in 'Gerontion' and successive 1920 *Poems*. But 'the jew' is also 'the owner', the embodiment of a failed, corrupt modernity which is rejected by Eliot. Far from 'binding together the savage and the city', the overdetermined 'jew' cannot but splinter such antitheses. Thus, in his July 1921 'London Letter' in *The Dial*, Eliot notes that 'Einstein the Great has visited England ... [and] has taken his place in the newspapers with the comet, the sun-spots, the poisonous jelly-fish and octopus at Margate, and other natural phenomena'. Even Einstein, the apogee of scientific (Jewish) modernity, is also something of a primitive, a part of the 'savage' world of 'natural phenomena'.[78] More characteristically, as in Eliot's reading of Baudelaire's 'stock of imagery' – 'his prostitutes, mulattoes, Jewesses, serpents, cats, corpses' – 'the jew' is initially conceived to be situated in a hybrid world of unmitigated savagery. Such rigid categorizations, however, even in his uncompromising 'Sweeney Among the Nightingales' (1918) and 'Burbank with a Baedeker: Bleistein with a Cigar' (1919) – poems which Eliot described as 'intensely serious, and ... among the best that I have ever done' – can hardly be said to 'explain' Eliot's contradictory and ambivalent uses of the all-encompassing 'jew'.[79] What makes 'the jew' such a threat is, precisely, the sense that it is impossible to contain in any one category.

---

[77] Crawford, *The Savage and the City*, p. 1 and *passim*.

[78] T. S. Eliot, 'London Letter', *The Dial* 71 (Number 2, August 1921), 213–17 and Crawford, *The Savage and the City*, p. 237.

[79] Letter to Henry Eliot, 15 February 1920, which is published in Valerie Eliot, *The Letters of T. S. Eliot*, pp. 363–5 and 'Baudelaire' (1930) in *Selected Essays* (London, 1966), p. 424, which will be referred to in the body of the text.

Along with 'Sweeney Erect' (1919), 'Sweeney Among the Nightingales' is Eliot's most unremitting depiction of sexual bestiality:

> Apeneck Sweeney spreads his knees
> Letting his arms down to laugh,
> The Zebra stripes along his jaw
> Swelling to maculate giraffe.

Sweeney, in this opening stanza, is both 'animalized' and, simultaneously, circumscribed by the line from the *Agamemnon* – 'Alas, I am struck deep with a mortal blow' – that acts as the poem's epigraph. As Ricks has shown, 'Sweeney Among the Nightingales' is a particularly 'unsettling' poem because it invites the reader to contemplate their own 'prejudices' while steadfastly refusing to satisfy them. Thus, critics who debate whether Sweeney's predicament is heightened or further demeaned by the allusion to the grandeur of Agamemnon miss the point of the poem.[80] Either of these narratives might be imposed on 'Sweeney' but Eliot deliberately elides such fixed meanings with his cryptic references, throughout, to 'the person in the Spanish cape', 'the silent man in mocha brown' or 'someone indistinct'. Such empty, shadowy figures disturb the comfortable juxtaposition – for good or ill – of Sweeney and Agamemnon. Using the emphatic language of *The Criterion*, Eliot's poem does not allow the reader to determine the extent to which the categories of Greek 'thought and emotion' incorporate Sweeney's unconscious animalism.

But just at the point when we are certain of the poem's uncertainties, Eliot introduces the overly specified, determinedly 'semitic' figure of 'Rachel *née* Rabinovitch' who 'tears at the grapes with murderous paws'. Ricks has gently problematized an overly reductive reading of the culturally indefinite category of 'Rachel *née* Rabinovitch'.[81] If, as many commentators have noted, 'nightingale' is slang for 'prostitute' then 'Rachel' can at least be said to embody Baudelaire's 'stock of imagery' as his 'prostitutes, mulattoes, Jewesses, serpents, cats, corpses' can all be read into her rep-

---

[80] Ricks, *T. S. Eliot and Prejudice*, p. 7 and p. 32. Martin Schofield, *T. S. Eliot: The Poems* (Cambridge, 1988) p. 93 follows J. Grover Smith, *T. S. Eliot's Poetry and Plays* (Chicago, 1974) p. 46 in his rather narrow discussion of 'Sweeney Among the Nightingales'.

[81] Ricks, *T. S. Eliot and Prejudice*, pp. 30–3 as opposed to the cruder reading of Morris, 'T. S. Eliot and Antisemitism', pp. 173–82.

resentation. Her rampant bestiality immediately refers back to Sweeney in the opening stanza but only to show the differences between the two of them. Whereas Sweeney is positioned, however inscrutably, in an historical analogy with Agamemnon, Rachel is introduced precisely because she is outside of that history. As in Eliot's disdainful reference to 'Harry Lawson Webster Lawson (sc. Levi-sohn?)', 'Rachel *née* Rabinovitch' is a category which, by definition, is pedantically precise but, on closer investigation, surprisingly vague. Such is the confusion that surrounds her that Eliot violently yokes together a racially constructed social group – present-day urban, assimilated Jews – with a timeless 'murderous' savagery. Rachel's animality, that is, is firmly situated in the melodramatic imprecision of the poem's contemporary setting:

> She and the lady in the cape
> Are suspect, thought to be in league;
> Therefore the man with heavy eyes
> Declines the gambit, shows fatigue,
>
> Leaves the room and reappears
> Outside the window, leaning in,
> Branches of wistaria
> Circumscribe a golden grin;

The cowardly 'man with heavy eyes' might be read as a non-racialized 'jew', a metallic cousin of 'Mr Silvero', especially as he echoes both 'Mr Eliot's Sunday Morning Service' and 'Gerontion' in being 'outside the window, leaning in'. Like Rachel, he is outside the 'house' of history and a Hellenic consciousness because he confounds nature with an underlying materialism (suggested by 'branches of wistaria/Circumscribe a golden grin'). Such is the 'semitic' confusion that prevents the reader from making an 'exact' assessment of Sweeney's – and by implication contemporary Europe's – relationship to their 'own' naturalized Greek myths. In a telling inexactitude, in the last verse, 'Agamemnon cried aloud/And let their liquid siftings fall/To stain the stiff dishonoured shroud'. Their 'liquid siftings' evoke both Agamemnon's 'bloody' death and, at the same time, the 'jewish' faeces (from 'Gerontion') which turn into 'slime' that which is secure and 'known'.[82]

[82] Harrison, *The Reactionaries*, p. 150 and Pinkney, *Women in the Poetry of T. S. Eliot*, p. 88. Robert Casillo, *The Genealogy of Demons: Anti-Semitism, Fascism, and the Myths of Ezra Pound* (Evanston, 1988) is a good account of Ezra Pound's use of similar imagery in his poetry.

In 'Burbank with a Baedeker: Bleistein with a Cigar', Eliot unambiguously articulates a semitic 'sliminess' when Bleistein's 'lustreless protrusive eye / Stares from the protozoic slime / At a perspective of Canaletto'. To depict this as an innocent juxtaposition of the 'repellently primitive' with the 'brilliantly sophisticated' elides the significance of Bleistein's obfuscating 'protrusive eye'.[83] The radical disjunction between his diseased 'perspective' on Venice and that of Canaletto is, in short, the subject of the poem. Bleistein, like all of Eliot's 'jews', is a hybrid creature consisting of an originary 'savage' primitivism beneath a cosmopolitan, moneyed modernity. The doubleness of Bleistein's opulent animalism is later condensed in the all too literal phrase, 'money in furs':

> But this or such was Bleistein's way:
>   A saggy bending of the knees
> And elbows, with the palms turned out,
>   Chicago Semite Viennese.

This description, just before Bleistein 'stares' at the Canaletto, has been read as a debased primitive ritual – rather like a crude version of 'Hakagawa, bowing among the Titians' – and as a racial, 'animalizing' cartoon whose 'saggy bending' dissolves its object into a welter of boundary-crossings, 'Chicago Semite Viennese'. In a letter to Eleanor Hinkley, written in 1917, Eliot describes a promising 'youth named Siegfried Sassoon (semitic) and his stuff is better politics than poetry'.[84] Instead of merely confusing poetry with politics, the 'semitic' designation, in the case of Bleistein, is at the heart of the devolution and disintegration of Venetian culture. Bleistein's cigar smoke is, in other words, an ideal figurative expression of a semitic confusion which obscures the cultural significance of the past:

> The smoky candle end of time
>
> Declines. On the Rialto once.
>   The rats are underneath the piles.

---

[83] Crawford, *The Savage and the City*, p. 2 and Pinkney, *Women in the Poetry of T. S. Eliot*, pp 81–2.

[84] Letter to Eleanor Hinkley, 31 October 1917, which is published in Valerie Eliot, *The Letters of T. S. Eliot*, pp. 205–6. See also Crawford, *The Savage and the City*, pp. 113–14 and Pinkney, *Women in the Poetry of T. S. Eliot*, p. 82.

The jew is underneath the lot.
Money in furs.

If, at this point, Bleistein (which, literally means 'leadstone') occupies the lowest rung on the evolutionary ladder, as Crawford argues, then the poem is not merely 'funny, but at everyone's expense'.[85] The location of 'the jew … underneath the lot', ravaging at the foundations of Venice, ostensibly acts as the poem's nucleus, a symbolic 'explanation' for the decline of the 'mind of Europe'. But if Bleistein's diseased, smoke-ridden eye makes it impossible to assess the centrality of Venetian culture, then the poem itself can also be said to have been infected by such 'semitic' confusion. The epigraph of 'Burbank with a Baedeker', as has been commonly noted, itself verges upon smoky incoherence – ' *Tra-la-la-la-la-la-laire – nil nisi divinum stabile est*; *caetra fumus*' – with references to six disparate accounts of Venice through the ages in almost as many lines. This kaleidoscopic, impressionistic account of Europe's crumbling centre captures, in miniature, the method of the poem as a whole, especially in its 'multiplicity of partial dramatizations'. It is, as Gray has noted, the 'elaborate irrelevance' of the poem's historical allusions that fatally undermines 'Burbank with a Baedeker'.[86]

Even the all-explaining 'jew' cannot be disparaged with any certainty as 'he' or 'it' appears at the beginning, the middle, and at the end of time in a myriad of contradictory guises: as a diseased eye, an eternal parasite, a cosmopolitan, a plutocrat, a usurer – Bleistein, Sir Ferdinand Klein, Shylock – as well as the whole of (Venetian) Jewry. Eliot's allusions, as Ricks felicitously puts it, 'conceal by exposure' and are no less 'slimy' than Bleistein. As with 'Sweeney Among the Nightingales', 'Burbank with a Baedeker' anxiously repeats history in a bid to understand the relationship between the 'collective' and the 'individual' European mind. But the latter poem self-consciously fails in its task. In the first of a series of equivocal, Sweeney-like repetitions, Burbank re-enacts the 'fall' of mankind in his sexual encounter with Princess Volupine as seen through the narrative of Shakespeare's Anthony and Cleopatra. But, as F. W. Bateson has shown, such historical precedents also contain a

---

[85] Crawford, *The Savage and the City*, pp. 115–16 and Ricks, *T. S. Eliot and Prejudice*, p. 36 who rightly takes Crawford to task for this statement by noting that 'it should be retorted that the groups, races and classes in the poem cannot equally afford the expense'.

[86] Gray, *T. S. Eliot's Intellectual and Poetic Development*, pp. 204–5 and chapter 6. See also Ricks, *T. S. Eliot and Prejudice*, p. 38 and Schofield, *T. S. Eliot*, p. 91.

contemporary reference to Eliot's review of Adams's autobiography, 'Henry Adams in 1858 and Henry James in 1870 ... land at Liverpool and descend at the same hotel':[87]

> Burbank crossed a little bridge
> Descending at a small hotel;
> Princess Volupine arrived,
> They were together, and he fell.

This textual connection between Burbank and the Bostonian patricianhood is, however, further diminished by the vulgar, popular figure of the Californian, Luther Burbank, a much discussed plant breeder who was acclaimed in 1911 as 'the most ingenious and successful of all hybridizers'. Crawford has interestingly associated Luther Burbank with 'Burbank with a Baedeker' by pointing out that Eliot's poem concerns the 'hybridization of the human plant "Chicago Semite Viennese"'. I would add that, like Adams's and Eliot's repressed identification with 'the Jew', Burbank's name also implicates him in this terminal 'semitic' process of 'hybridization'. This is born out in the poem by the re-enactment, at a future time, of Burbank's 'primeval Fall':[88]

> Princess Volupine extends
> A meagre, blue-nailed, phthisic hand
> To climb the waterstair. Lights, lights,
> She entertains Sir Ferdinand
>
> Klein. Who clipped the lion's wings
> And flea'd his rump and pared his claws?
> Thought Burbank, meditating on
> Time's ruins, and the seven laws.

Sir Ferdinand Klein's repetition of Burbank's initial fall from grace escalates the biological and cultural descent inherent in the sexual encounter which opens the poem. Placed at the beginning of a line, the ironically drooping 'Klein', meaning 'little', echoes both 'declines' and 'a little bridge / descending at a small hotel' in the first stanza. The ascendant but bestial Princess Volupine, like Bleistein, embodies the corrupting disease which, in her case, has

---

[87] Cited in F. W. Bateson, 'The Poetry of Learning' in Martin, *Eliot in Perspective*, p. 41. See also Ricks, *T. S. Eliot and Prejudice*, pp. 35–6, Moody, *Thomas Stearns Eliot*, p. 59 and Crawford, *The Savage and the City*, p. 110.

[88] Crawford, *The Savage and the City*, pp. 65–6 and p. 115 and also see Leon, 'T. S. Eliot and the Eugenic Anxiety', p. 172.

made it possible for the European aristocracy to be semitically adulterated. Along with the German-Jewish financier, Sir Alfred Mond, whom Eliot evokes as a money-lender in 'A Cooking Egg' (1919) – 'I shall not want capital in heaven / For I shall meet Sir Alfred Mond' – Sir Ferdinand Klein represents that class of Edwardian plutocrat who buttresses, racially, a Bleisteinian Jewish bourgeoisie. Together such types were commonly seen to have destroyed a traditional sense of (aristocratic) order and continuity with the past. Princess Volupine's call for 'Lights, lights' is reminiscent of Kipling's 'The House Surgeon' (1909), where a 'fortifying blaze of electric light' also represented a failed modern attempt to efface the sins of the past.[89] Not unlike Burbank's Baedeker-inspired meditations on 'Time's ruins and the seven laws', such superficial acts are unable to expunge a culture in a deep-seated spiritual crisis. What is, nonetheless, particularly ironic about 'Burbank with a Baedeker' is that not only does Burbank himself contribute to the 'ruins' (in all senses) of history, but that 'the jew' – explaining everything and nothing – ultimately reduces the authoritarian import of the poem to 'smoke'.

In 'The Bible as Scripture and Literature', an unpublished lecture which was given to the Boston Women's Alliance in 1932, Eliot argued that the influence of the Bible upon English literature in the future will be 'in direct ratio to the extent to which people read the Bible, and read it *not* as "literature"'. In an implicit defence of his use of certain kinds of biblical imagery in, especially, 'Gerontion' and *The Waste Land*, Eliot acknowledges the 'truth' that the 'world of the Old Testament is largely a world of drought' but warns against a too facile literary allusion to the Hebraic 'dry land':

The Hebrews lived in a dry land, in which water is always welcome and beneficent; we can hardly consider the Flood as an exception. ... But this is simply an illustration of the way in which the imagery of the Old Testament can strike anyone who is impressed by its spirit. You cannot effectively 'borrow' an image, unless you borrow also, or have spontaneously, something like the feeling which prompted the original image. An 'image'

---

[89] 'The House Surgeon' is collected in Andrew Rutherford (ed.), *Rudyard Kipling: Short Stories*, Penguin edition, 2 vols. (London, 1971), I, p. 201 and discussed in chapter 3 of this book. For further textual links between this story and Eliot see Hyam Maccoby, '"The Family Reunion" and Kipling's "The House Surgeon"', *Notes and Queries* (February 1968), 50 and 48–57. Crawford, *The Savage and the City*, pp. 131–8 highlights usefully the importance of Kipling for Eliot's *The Waste Land*. See also Crawford, *The Savage and the City*, p. 113 for an interesting 'evolutionary' reading of 'Burbank with a Baedeker' to which I am indebted.

in itself, like dream symbolism, is only vigorous in relation to the feelings out of which it issues, in the relation of word to flesh.[90]

Eliot begins his lecture with the premise that the Old Testament has been traditionally enjoyed as 'literature' by those who 'suspend definitely *Christian* belief' (2) and, presumably, dissociate 'the word' from 'the flesh'. Although Eliot admits that he is 'totally un-acquainted with Hebrew' (3), this does not disable him entirely from having 'something like the feeling which prompted the original [biblical] image'. This all-important Christian empathy with the Hebraic 'dry land' contrasts uneasily with the semitic 'dry season' in Eliot's 1920 poems and also helps us to understand the elusive relationship in *The Waste Land* between the unpublished 'Dirge' and 'Death by Water'. 'Dirge' has been read variously as a 'sardonic coda after the pathos of the Phlebas passage' and, although unpublished, as being 'still deeply involved in the final poetry'.[91] The decision to leave 'Dirge' unpublished is, I want to argue, an essential moment of transition between Eliot's early and later use of a semitic discourse. The poem needs to be quoted in full so that its profound 'involvement' with 'Death by Water' will become apparent:

> Full fathom five your Bleistein lies
> Under the flatfish and the squids.
> Graves' Disease in a dead jew's eyes!
> When the crabs have eat the lids.
> Lower than the wharf rats dive
> Though he suffer a sea-change
> Still expensive rich and strange
>
> That is lace that was his nose
> See upon his back he lies
> (Bones peep through the ragged toes)
> With a stare of dull surprise
> Flood tide and ebb tide
> Roll him gently side to side
> See the lips unfold unfold
> From the teeth, gold in gold
> Lobsters hourly keep close watch

[90] 'The Bible as Scripture and Literature', unpublished lecture to the Women's Alliance, King's Chapel, Boston (1 December 1932). Uncorrected typescript, Houghton Library, bms AM 1691 (26), 10–11. Page references to this typescript will be included in the body of the text.

[91] Grover Smith, *T. S. Eliot's Poetry and Plays*, p. 311 and Empson, 'Eliot', p. 196. Ricks, *T. S. Eliot and Prejudice*, p. 38 notes that Grover Smith's account of 'Dirge' makes 'no mention whatsoever of either Bleistein or Jew' and he astutely echoes Grover Smith's own verdict on the poem by noting that 'a more purifying critical effect can hardly be imagined'.

Hark! now I hear them   scratch scratch scratch.[92]

Written nearly two years after 'Burbank with a Baedeker', the reintroduction of Bleistein in 'Dirge' and the seemingly gratuitous repetition of certain motifs from this earlier poem – 'Graves' Disease in a dead jew's eyes!... Lower than the wharf rats dive' – has been said, by Ricks, to confirm it as 'the ugliest touch of antisemitism in Eliot's poetry'. Maccoby, however, is more salutary in his understanding of 'Dirge' as a poem that attempts to depict the 'purgation' of Bleistein. The victorious 'jew' in 'Burbank with a Baedeker', who has confused and infected European civilization, is, in this reading, experiencing a 'painful purgatory by water'.[93]

As opposed to the all-encompassing 'dry season' of Eliot's preceding representations, the defeated Bleistein in 'Dirge' is given a redemptive 'sea-change' as he is rolled 'gently side to side' in a perverse act of baptism (echoing Eliot's implicit pun which 'gently' transforms 'the Jews' into 'Gentiles'). Just as 'water' in the Old Testament can potentially transfigure the Hebraic 'dry land', Bleistein in this poem is no longer saggily indistinct and smoke-ridden but is, literally, reduced to his bare bones, 'see the lips unfold unfold / From the teeth, gold in gold'. There are reminders here of the 'golden grin' of the racially non-specific 'man with heavy eyes' in 'Sweeney Among the Nightingales'. But Eliot, in a significant change to his manuscript, insists on 'a dead jew's eyes' as opposed to 'a dead man's eyes'. This might well be the 'darkest variant reading in Eliot', in Ricks's words, but it also emphasizes the theological dimension in 'Dirge' which William Empson, along with Maccoby, has noted. Empson, especially, has pointed out that Ariel's original song, 'Full fathom five', in *The Tempest* concerns Prince Ferdinand's supposedly drowned father and, because of this, he sees Bleistein as a repressed substitute for Eliot's Unitarian father.[94] The baptismal redemption of the 'Judaic father' is, more generally, central to Christianity and was to become an increasingly important dimension of Eliot's later poetry and social thought. This aspect of 'Death by

[92] 'Dirge' in Valerie Eliot (ed.), *The Waste Land: A Facsimile and Transcript of the Original Drafts* (London, 1971) p. 121.

[93] Valerie Eliot, *The Waste Land: A Facsimile*, p. 131 argues that '*Dirge* was probably written in 1921' and Ricks, *T. S. Eliot and Prejudice*, p. 38, in an exceptional lapse, uses the poem merely to express his moral exasperation. For a more suggestive reading of 'Dirge' see Hyam Maccoby, 'The Anti-Semitism of T. S. Eliot', *Midstream* 19 (Number 5, May 1973), 74–7.

[94] Empson, 'Eliot', pp. 194–8 and Ricks, *T. S. Eliot and Prejudice*, p. 39. See also Valerie Eliot, *The Waste Land: A Facsimile*, p. 119 for an early draft of 'Dirge'.

Water', a version of the last seven lines of 'Dans le Restaurant' (1918), relates it back to Eliot's earlier poetry:

> Phlebas the Phoenician, a fortnight dead,
> Forgot the cry of gulls, and the deep sea swell
> And the profit and loss.
>   A current under sea
> Picked his bones in whispers. As he rose and fell
> He passed the stages of his age and youth
> Entering the whirlpool.
>   Gentile or Jew
> O you who turn the wheel and look to windward,
> Consider Phlebas, who was once handsome and tall as you.

After an 'excessively depressed' Eliot had questioned whether Phlebas should remain in *The Waste Land*, Pound reminded him that the 'drowned Phoenician Sailor' in 'The Burial of the Dead' introduces Phlebas and that he is 'needed ABSolutely where he is'. Pound realized astutely that 'Death by Water' was an 'integral' part of *The Waste Land* and his advice proved to be so effective that, as Empson has shown, the 'calm' at this point in the poem was replicated in each of the *Four Quartets* which contain 'a similar lyrical penultimate section'. The original version of 'Death by Water' was, according to Eliot, 'inspired by the Ulysses episode in the *Inferno*' and a number of commentators have also related Phlebas to Gerontion as well as to other versions of Ulysses.[95] Gerontion can be said to be one of those who 'turn the wheel and look to windward' as he is also 'driven by the Trades', an ironically punning image on the arbitrary commercial world of 'profit and loss'. Eliot had read and incorporated the occasional phrase from *Ulysses* into *The Waste Land* and was aware, while composing his poem, that Joyce had made a 'Jewish' advertising salesman the contemporary analogue of Ulysses. Influential studies such as Victor Bérard's *Les Phéniciens et L'Odyssée* (1902) had confirmed Joyce's belief in the Phoenician 'semitic roots' of the *Odyssey* and that Ulysses, prefiguring Bloom's capitalist perambulations, had 'followed established trade routes in his legendary wanderings'. Just as the 'fractured' consciousness of

---

[95] Valerie Eliot, *The Waste Land: A Facsimile*, p. 128 lists the various versions of 'Ulysses' which inspired 'Death by Water'. Crawford, *The Savage and the City*, p. 125 and Gordon, *Eliot's Early Years*, p. 111 both relate Phlebas the Phoenician to Gerontion and also note that parts of the longer version of this section of *The Waste Land* ended up in 'The Dry Salvages'. See also Empson, 'Eliot', p. 196 and Valerie Eliot, *The Letters of T. S. Eliot*, pp. 504–5 for the republication of Eliot's correspondence with Pound on the early versions of *The Waste Land*.

Gerontion was to redouble 'the jew' in 'Gerontion', it is clear that the 'death by water' undergone by Phlebas is, as Maccoby puts it, a 'muted and idealized' redoubling of Bleistein's 'purgation' in 'Dirge'.[96]

The Phoenicians, as Joyce learnt from Bérard, were a mercantile, Hebrew-speaking people who were commonly perceived as ancient equivalents of the contemporary Jewish bourgeoisie. Such 'parallels between contemporaneity and antiquity', as Eliot argued in his review of *Ulysses*, began to be exploited as early as Gustave Flaubert's *Salammbô* (1850). The popular journalism of H. G. Wells was also to utilize such ancient parallels and, in his *New Worlds for Old*, he was to speak of the 'developing British plutocracy' as being, like the Carthaginian, 'largely Semitic in blood'. This historical analogy was especially expanded in his *The Outline of History* (1920), where Wells was to ascribe the 'financial and commercial tradition of the Jews' to the 'semitic' Phoenician people. The destruction of Carthage, a 'semitic' city in Wells's terms, is implicitly referred to throughout *The Waste Land* and, according to Empson, is at the heart of Ezra Pound's understanding of the 'unity' of Eliot's poem. Before he was to so deftly edit *The Waste Land*, Pound had written that 'London has just escaped, from the First World War, but it is certain to be destroyed in the next one, because it is in the hands of international financiers. The very place of it will be sown with salt, as Carthage was, and forgotten by men; or it will be sunk under water'. The 'purgation' of Phlebas, echoing that of Gerontion in 'the Gulf' and Dante's Ulysses, is, according to this reading, also implicated in the cleansing of the Carthaginian 'Judaic father' whose all-pervading materialism and 'semitic' confusion had brought about the downfall of European civilization.[97] Eliot's *post hoc* 'notes' at the end of the poem, however, give a conflicting gloss on this argument:

Just as the one-eyed merchant, seller of currants, melts into the Phoenician Sailor, and the latter is not wholly distinct from Ferdinand Prince of Naples, so all women are one woman and the two sexes meet in Tiresias.[98]

---

[96] Maccoby, 'The Anti-Semitism of T. S. Eliot', p. 75. Ellmann, *James Joyce*, p. 521, p. 511 and p. 562 for the importance of Victor Bérard on Joyce's thinking and also Nadel, *Joyce and the Jews*, p. 16 and 27.

[97] Empson, 'Eliot', p. 191 quotes Pound's letter and reads *The Waste Land* in terms of Poundian 'antisemitism'. Wells's *New Worlds for Old: A Plain Account of Modern Socialism* (London, 1908) p. 178 and *The Outline of History* (London, 1920) p. 281 both make a popularly held parallel between the historic 'semitic' Phoenicians and the contemporary British-Jewish plutocracy.

[98] T. S. Eliot, 'Notes on *The Waste Land*' in *Collected Poems 1909–1962* (London, 1963), p. 82.

Phlebas, in this admittedly unreliable 'note', merges into Ferdinand (in an interesting echo of Sir Ferdinand Klein) as opposed to his father, Alonso. With this emphasis on the 'once handsome' Prince, 'Death by Water' inverts 'Dirge' where Bleistein is positioned as a grotesque version of Ferdinand's father. Both 'semitic' father and son are, nonetheless, taken from Ariel's equally deceptive song and the double use of the line 'those are pearls that were his eyes' from this song tends to disrupt the allusions to *The Tempest* in the poem. It would, moreover, be a mistake to fix the meaning of *The Waste Land* either in terms of Poundian Jewish conspiracy theories or Eliot's equally determining 'notes'. The inclusiveness inherent in the phrase 'Gentile or Jew' in 'Death by Water' fatally undercuts 'Dirge' largely because its imprecision cannot, merely, be reduced to the question of 'race'. By constructing Tiresias, in his 'notes' at least, as the figure who effectively contains both sexes and '*sees*' the poem as a whole, Eliot avoids the use of 'the jew' in this all-encompassing role as the embodiment of the spiritually 'dry' waste land. Critics, in rewriting Eliot's 'notes', have argued just as fixedly that Phlebas is reincarnated in 'Death by Water' and relives not only his past lives but that of all the other personages in the poem who are symbolically 'drowned' in 'the whirlpool'.[99] But it is a mistake to see Phlebas as unproblematically embodying the poem in this way. As with *Ulysses*, no one discourse – including a semitic discourse – is allowed to dominate *The Waste Land*.

While non-racially specific versions of the 'semitic' Phlebas, such as 'Mr Eugenides, the Smyrna merchant', abound in *The Waste Land* – not unlike 'De Bailhache, Fresca, Mrs Cammel' in 'Gerontion' – such readings all avoid being reduced to Eliot's fixed racial discourse surrounding 'the jew'. To be sure, it was the semite-obsessed Ezra Pound who convinced Eliot not to publish 'Dirge' by placing '??doubtful' beside the fair copy of the poem. Pound, wisely, also prevented Eliot from publishing his satirical accounts of a thinly-veiled semitic Hampstead. There is, after all, an important difference in Eliot's indeterminate fears surrounding 'those hooded hordes swarming / Over endless plains' in 'What the Thunder Said' when compared with the more racially and socially specific sentiments in 'The Cooking Egg': 'The red-eyed scavengers are creeping / From

---

[99] Cleo McNelly Kearns, *T. S. Eliot and Indic Traditions: A Study in Poetry and Belief* (Cambridge, 1987) pp. 210–12 and Moody, *Thomas Stearns Eliot*, pp. 96–7 for this argument. Eliot chose to foreground Tiresias in his 'Notes on *The Waste Land*' in *Collected Poems*, p. 82.

Kentish Town and Golder's Green; / Where are the eagles and the trumpets?'[100] *The Waste Land* opens, as B. C. Southam has shown, with a reference to Rupert Brooke's 'The Old Vicarage, Granchester' (1912), which was probably as important an influence on 'The Burial of the Dead' as Chaucer's General Prologue. Brooke's poem is a nostalgic account of his childhood memories in rural England during the Spring when compared with his miserable time in contemporary Berlin:

> Just now the lilac is in bloom,
> All before my little room.
>
> . . .
>
> Here am I, sweating, sick, and hot,
> And there the shadowed waters fresh
> Lean up to embrace the naked flesh.
> *Temperamentvoll* German Jews
> Drink beer around ... [101]

By avoiding such glib references to 'German Jews', Eliot was able to construct a poem that was not reduced to any one discourse (racial or otherwise). The biblical allusions to 'rock' and 'water' which pervade *The Waste Land* encompass both the 'dry land' of the Old Testament and the semitic 'dry season' of Eliot's 1920 poems but are not limited by these controlling mythologies. Helen Williams is right to point out the 'drowning, rotting, and corrosive' aspects of water and the Wagnerian sense of 'waste and void' inherent in the evocation of the sea in Eliot's poem. In this deliberately ambiguous reading, the 'handsome' Phlebas, under the sea, is not simply undergoing a 'purgation' but represents those passions and worldly preoccupations which, like the 'slimy' Bleistein, 'dissolves mind and sensibility'. Ironically enough, Jessie Weston's *From Ritual to Romance* (1920) – which has encouraged interpretations of *The Waste Land* based on an over-simple series of binary oppositions associated with the life-giving properties of water – also conceived of the Grail legend as the 'shadowy background of the history of our Aryan race'. Eliot

---

[100] Morris, 'T. S. Eliot and Antisemitism', p. 173 links 'The Cooking Egg' to other aspects of Eliot's 'antisemitic' animal-imagery and Morse, *Word by Word*, p. 61 thinks of the 'hooded hordes' in *The Waste Land*, like many critics, as part of the Bolshevik Revolution who come from 'the East... the direction of the exotic and the uncanny'. Ricks, *T. S. Eliot and Prejudice*, p. 73 rightly makes a plea for critical 'discriminations within antisemitism' of the kind that Eliot made in *The Waste Land*. Pound's dismissal of 'Dirge' is recorded in Valerie Eliot, *The Waste Land: A Facsimile*, p. 120–1.

[101] Southam, *Student's Guide*, pp. 73–4 usefully relates Rupert Brooke's 'The Old Vicarage, Granchester' (1912) to the opening of *The Waste Land*.

was, obviously, well aware of Weston's stress on the quest for the Holy
Grail as a restoration of 'our Aryan forefathers', but chose to
accentuate an implicitly 'semitic' Phlebas and the 'dry land' of the
Hebrew prophets as opposed to their contemporary degenerate
counterparts.[102] This decision was to have an important impact on
his poetry and social thought after *The Waste Land*.

Eliot might have been talking about his own early poetry when he
argued, in his 1930 essay, that Baudelaire's 'stock of imagery' was, in
retrospect, 'not wholly perdurable or adequate': 'his prostitutes,
mulattoes, Jewesses, serpents, cats, corpses form a machinery which
has not worn very well' (424). The search for 'perdurable' images in
his later poetry, as Ricks has shown, resulted in a marked decline in
Eliot's 'prejudicial animus'. Eliot's ideal 'Jew' in this non-Baude-
lairean context can be found in an article, 'Towards a Christian
Britain', which he published in *The Church Looks Ahead* (1941) and
which defined present-day 'Christian prophets' as 'men who have
not merely kept the faith through the dark age, but who have lived
through the mind of that dark age, and got beyond it'. His example
of a man who lived 'beyond' the 'dark age' was Charles de
Foucauld, who was 'born to wealth and social position'. Eliot
describes Foucauld as a man who had 'abandoned a life of pleasure
and dissipation, first to travel in the disguise of a humble Jewish
trader...in French Morrocco and Algeria'. He then 'made a
pilgrimage as a mendicant to the Holy Land, and finally, ordained as
a priest, became a missionary in a solitary African outpost'.[103]

Written in 1941 (and broadcast as a radio talk), Eliot's 'Towards
a Christian Britain' mentions Foucauld's peculiarly transient disguise
of a 'humble Jewish trader' in the context of the transcendence of
wealth, pleasure and dissipation which culminated in a Christ-like
association with Palestine. This, in G. K. Chesterton's terms, was
Eliot's 'orthodox' construction of 'the Jew' in the inter-war years.
Such orthodoxy accounts for Eliot's acknowledged position as a
'detached observer' of, among much else, the Jewish fate during the

---

[102] Helen Williams, *T. S. Eliot: 'The Waste Land'* (London, 1973) p. 29 and p. 41 makes out
a sound case for the 'ambivalence' of the water imagery in *The Waste Land*. This reading
is opposed to Jessie Weston's *From Ritual to Romance* (Cambridge, 1920), a text which was
privileged, misleadingly, by Eliot at the beginning of his 'Notes on *The Waste Land*', p. 80.
The semitic racial discourse in Weston's book has, as far as I know, been ignored by critics
of *The Waste Land*.

[103] T. S. Eliot, 'Towards a Christian Britain' (radio broadcast, 26 March, 1941) collected in
The Church Looks Ahead (London, 1941), pp. 115–16 and 106–17 and Ricks, *T. S. Eliot and
Prejudice*, chapters 6 and 7 for the decline of 'prejudicial animus' in Eliot's later poetry.

Second World War. His life-long and active support of Charles Maurras's authoritarian L'Action française was, as Moody notes, particularly mediated through his 'Christian philosophy'. In a letter to the *Church Times* in 1934, Eliot argued that the 'point' about Fascism is 'whether the Christian and Catholic idea and the Fascist idea are, themselves, compatible'.[104] Written a few months before this letter, Eliot's notorious references to 'free-thinking Jews' in *After Strange Gods* can certainly be read in terms of its 'compatibility' with his Christian orthodoxy:

The population should be homogenous; where two or more cultures exist in the same place they are likely either to be fiercely self-conscious or both to become adulterate. What is still more important is unity of religious backgrounds; and reasons of race and religion combine to make any large number of free-thinking Jews undesirable. There must be a proper balance between urban and rural, industrial and agricultural development. And a spirit of excessive tolerance is to be deprecated.[105]

It is precisely the opposition of heretical 'free-thinking Jews' to a 'homogenous' religious 'unity' which, as Maud Ellmann has shown, returns *After Strange Gods* to the crude racial discourse of his 1920

[104] T. S. Eliot, 'The Blackshirts', Letter to the *Church Times*, 2 February 1934, p. 116 and *The Criterion* 8 (July 1929), 682–3 where Eliot declared, teasingly, that along with 'most of his readers', 'I believe that the fascist form of unreason is less remote from my own than is that of the communists, but that my form is a more reasonable form of unreason'. Eliot's inter-war 'orthodox' Christian construction of 'the Jew' was akin to the views of G. K. Chesterton's discussed in chapter 5. It is not insignificant, in this regard, that Eliot was elected a Vice-President of the Distributist League in July 1936. For a view of Eliot in these terms see Moody, *Thomas Stearns Eliot*, p. 324 and 'Appendix C', 'The Christian philosophy and politics between the wars', pp. 319–26 and, also, William M. Chace, *The Political Identities of Ezra Pound and T. S. Eliot* (Stanford, 1973) chapter 9. As late as his 'The Literature of Politics' (1955) in *To Criticize the Critic*, pp. 136–44, Eliot was staunchly defending Charles Maurras of L'Action française as he had done for the previous five decades.

[105] T. S. Eliot, *After Strange Gods: A Primer of Modern Heresy* (London, 1934) pp. 19–20. Although Eliot refused, sensibly, to republish this volume as a whole after the Second World War he did allow various sections of it to be republished in a selection of his prose, *Points of View* (London, 1941) edited by John Haywood. Eliot also vigorously defended *After Strange Gods* in a long correspondence with Ezra Pound in the *New English Weekly*, March-May, 1934. Most contemporary critics of *After Strange Gods* thought of it as one of the 'three small books in preparation, one of which was to be about heresy in our time' which is mentioned in Eliot's pre-war Preface to *For Lancelot Andrewes*, p. 7. This Preface has been subsequently changed in the 1970 edition of *For Lancelot Andrewes* to indicate, dis-ingenuously, that 'the "three small books" referred to by the author in his Preface were unfortunately never written'. Pre-war critics, such as Yvor Winters, 'T. S. Eliot: The Illusion of Reaction (1) and (2)', *The Kenyon Review* 2 (Numbers 1 and 2, Spring and Winter, 1941), 7–30 and 221–39 certainly took Eliot at his word that *After Strange Gods* was a 're-formulation' of 'Tradition and the Individual Talent' (p. 15).

Poems. Presumably, as many apologists for Eliot's authoritarian politics have argued, 'orthodox' Jews would be perfectly acceptable to Eliot as they would be defined by the requisite spiritual and national boundaries and might be able to achieve, what was called elsewhere in *After Strange Gods*, the traditional 'blood kinship of "the same people living in the same place"'.[106] As Harold Fisch has noted, there is a good deal of veneration for the biblical prophets and heroes, who embody the Judaic sources of the Christian Saints, in Eliot's later poetry and, especially, his play *The Rock* (1934). By situating morally acceptable pre-Christian Jews in the biblical past, however, there is always the fear that their degenerate 'free-thinking' counterparts will return to 'adulterate' present-day Christendom. As late as 1948, in his Preface to Charles Williams's *All Hallows Eve* (1945), Eliot was to congratulate Williams on his portrait of the Jewish Clerk Simon who 'is defined by his function of representing the single-minded lust for unlawful and unlimited power' not unlike those Jews who have, historically, disrupted a potentially unified Christian Europe.[107] In a telling footnote to his *Notes Towards the Definition of Culture* (1948), Eliot makes explicit the limits of his 'orthodox' Christian rewriting of 'the Jew':

Since the diaspora, and the scattering of Jews amongst peoples holding the Christian Faith, it may have been unfortunate both for these peoples and for the Jews themselves, that the culture-contact between them has had to be within those neutral zones of culture in which religion could be ignored: and the effect may have been to strengthen the illusion that there can be culture without religion.[108]

[106] Eliot, *After Strange Gods*, p. 18. Ellmann, *The Poetics of Impersonality*, pp. 44–57 rightly situates *After Strange Gods* at the centre of Eliot's 'poetics of impersonality' instead of banishing from discussion its vehement attack on, what Eliot called, a 'society like ours, worm-eaten with Liberalism' (p. 13). Most apologetic accounts of Eliot's references to the desirability of 'free-thinking Jews' are led by Roger Kojecky, *T. S. Eliot's Social Criticism* (London, 1971) pp. 12–13 who argues that 'the notorious passage in *After Strange Gods* is capable of the interpretation that a community of *orthodox* Jews would be socially "desirable" because of the strong bonds established by Jewish solidarity'. But this form of special pleading which distinguishes between 'heretical' and 'orthodox' Jews ignores the racial discourse which, of necessity, elides such theological distinctions.
[107] Harold Fisch, *The Dual Image: A Study of the Jew in English Literature* (London, 1959) p. 89 and Charles Williams, *All Hallows Eve*, 'Preface' (Grand Rapids, 1981).
[108] T. S. Eliot, *Notes Towards the Definition of Culture* (London, 1948) p. 70 which was changed in the 1962 edition as Moody, *Thomas Stearns Eliot*, p. 371 has illustrated. George Steiner, *In Bluebeard's Castle: Some Notes on the Re-Definition of Culture* (London, 1971) p. 34 rightly referred to this 'oddly condescending footnote' as a sign of the 'long-standing ambiguities on the theme of the Jew in Eliot's poetry'. This contention caused a furious correspondence in the *Listener*, April-May, 1971. Interestingly enough, the Centenary Edition of Eliot's *Notes Towards the Definition of Culture* along with his *The Idea of a Christian Society* (London,

By living in Christian Europe, 'the Jews' have reinforced the 'illusion' that 'culture' can exist without 'religion' and it was this confusion, according to Eliot (writing during the Second World War), that might well have brought about the 'unfortunate' antisemitic attacks on 'the Jews'. Eliot had long since placed Matthew Arnold in the vanguard of those who had committed the fatal deception of replacing 'religion' with 'culture'. In *The Criterion*, he went so far as to say that 'any person ... who is aware of "culture" at all, will be aware that there are various cultures, and that the difference between our own culture and an alien culture is different from the difference between culture and anarchy ... ' Because of 'reasons of race and religion', 'the Jews' are a part of an 'alien culture' and Matthew Arnold's foolishly all-inclusive view of 'culture' elides the essential differences between 'Christian' and 'Jew'. The refusal of a universalist Arnoldian 'culture' to make such distinctions is, above all, the basis of Eliot's concerted attack on Arnold, over nearly three decades, which culminated in the opening chapter of his *Notes Towards the Definition of Culture*.[109]

In a later addition to his unfortunate footnote in *Notes Towards the Definition of Culture*, written in 1962, Eliot argues that 'it seems to me highly desirable that there should be close culture-contact between devout and practising Christians and devout and practising Jews' (70). This implicit refusal to countenance 'culture-contact' between 'Gentile or Jew' outside of the sphere of 'devout' religious practice, points to the authoritarian nature of Eliot's semitic discourse. Such writing also contrasts starkly with Matthew Arnold who constructed, however ambivalently, a humanitarian, liberal cultural space in which Jews could attempt to transcend their supposed racial difference. Even after the Second World War, Eliot continued to profoundly implicate 'free-thinking Jews' both in the rise of

1939), published as *Christianity and Culture* (New York, 1988), has reverted back to the original footnote (p. 144).

[109] 'The Three Senses of "Culture"' in *Notes Towards the Definition of Culture*, pp. 21–34 and editorial, *The Criterion* 3 (1924–5), 163. Eliot's initial broadside on Arnold's lack of 'critical' discrimination (Arnold spent his time merely 'attacking the uncritical') can be found in his introduction to *The Sacred Wood*, pp. xiii and xi–xvii, his first volume of essays. Many critics have discussed Eliot's quest to replace Arnold as the critic of his 'generation', such as Ian Gregor, 'Eliot and Matthew Arnold' and John Peter, 'Eliot and the *Criterion*', in Martin, *Eliot in Perspective*, pp. 252–79. See also Edward Lobb, *T. S. Eliot and the Romantic Critical Tradition* (London, 1981) and Levenson, *A Genealogy of Modernism*, chapter 2. A Freudian argument along the lines of Empson's 'Eliot' would be that Eliot's continual references to Arnold's incoherent criticism and view of 'culture' turned Arnold into yet another Judaically Puritan substitute for his own hated father.

European antisemitism as well as the near terminal spiritual malaise caused by the rampant growth of unwelcome 'neutral zones' of 'culture'. Once outside of a 'devout' religious sphere, Jews, in short, helped to replace the clarity and moral certitude of the Christian 'idea' with that of a fragmentary, indistinct, pluralistic, liberalism. In *The Idea of a Christian Society* (1939), his last and most scathing attack on a universalizing liberal democracy, Eliot could thus claim as his 'ideal' a 'Christian community' in which there is 'a unified religious-social code of behaviour' and argue that 'the tendency of totalitarianism is to reaffirm, on a lower level, the religious-social nature of society'. For this reason, Eliot continued to contend, as late as 1939, that 'a people feels at least more dignified if its hero is the statesman however unscrupulous, or the warrior however brutal, rather than the financier'. Given a choice between a valueless liberal plutocracy and a 'religious-social' totalitarianism Eliot, for the sake of his boundary-ridden Christianity, was to choose the latter.[110]

CONCLUSION

To a large extent, the construction of 'the Jew' in late Victorian and Edwardian literature culminated in the modernist fiction and poetry of James Joyce and T. S. Eliot. In all of the previous writers under discussion, 'the Jew' exceeded the discursive limits of the ideologies which attempted to represent them. The authors of a supposedly all-encompassing mode of liberal 'realism', for instance, eventually conceded an imperfect 'knowledge' of 'the Jew' even though, at one time, they believed that they had access to an absolute or balanced 'truth'. Uncontainable Jewish representations similarly challenged the political pretensions of global systems, such as Imperialism and Socialism, to manage everything within their purview. Even the 'distributist' politics of G. K. Chesterton and Hilaire Belloc – formed especially to address the 'Jewish Question' – foundered on its inability to generate an unequivocal vocabulary which could safely confine 'the Jew'. In other words, the literary texts that have been previously explored all incorporate a superabundance of 'Jewish' constructions which starkly undercuts the avowed priorities of their authors.

---

[110] 'The Idea of a Christian Society', in *Christianity and Culture*, p. 27, p. 40 and p. 34. This argument differs, obviously, from those in Chace, Moody and Kojecky who all emphasize Eliot's studied political neutrality during the inter-war years.

The modernist literature of Eliot and Joyce can be said to have consciously reproduced the excess of meaning associated with 'the Jew' in Western culture. Whereas the comprehensive explanations of late Victorian and Edwardian writers were to be thrown into disarray by an ambivalent semitic discourse, modernist writers were all too aware of the slipperiness and indeterminacy of 'the Jew'. The acceptance, within a modernist aesthetic, of the impossibility of fully 'knowing' anything, made 'the Jew' an ideal objective correlative for this lack of absolute knowledge. There is, in short, an important coincidence of interest between 'the Jew' as an unstable cultural signifier and a modernist style which refuses to be reduced to a settled narrative. Joyce, in *Ulysses*, especially made a virtue of the disruptive capacity of Leopold Bloom's unstable 'greekjewish' identity. Rather than impose a fixed reading on Bloom – either as the writer's mirror image or as Stephen Dedalus's racial opposite – Joyce constructed Bloom as a figure who could challenge all dominant discourses whether they be religious, nationalistic or bourgeois liberal.

Instead of playfully disturbing prevailing narratives, however, an equivalent 'semitic' confusion in Eliot's writing was constructed as a particularly threatening aspect of contemporary Western civilization. Unlike Joyce, who attempted to break down the binary oppositions between 'Jew and Gentile' or 'Hebrew and Hellene', Eliot was at pains to restore the boundaries between these oppositions which, he felt, had been dangerously blurred. Eliot's poetry and social criticism wished to establish a clear and unequivocal relationship with the European past which made it all the more necessary to maintain the distinction between, say, Oriental and Western culture. If, in *Ulysses*, one possible reading of Bloom was as a Joycean 'self', it was Eliot's repressed fear of being Judaized that resulted in an extreme racialization of 'the Jew' in his 1920 *Poems*. A semitic discourse is produced in Eliot's poetry at exactly the point when he wishes to distinguish himself whole-heartedly from a shocking identification with the Jewish racial 'other'. This fearful recognition of 'the Jew' within the writer, I now want to argue, places a semitic discourse at the heart of literary production in general.

CHAPTER 7

Conclusion: semitism and the crisis of representation

The history of the Chosen people is full of such *contretemps* but they survive and thrive. ... And look at them in the railway carriage now. Their faces are anxious and eloquent of past rebuffs. But they are travelling First.

E. M. Forster, *Pharos and Pharillon* (London, 1923), p. 29
(after witnessing a verbal assault on a British-Jew)

I object as much to semitism in matters of mind as in matters of commerce.

Ezra Pound, letter to Wyndham Lewis, in Timothy
Materer (ed.), *Pound/Lewis: The Letters of Ezra Pound and
Wyndham Lewis* (New York, 1985), p. 218

A central argument of this study is that the racial construction of 'the Jew' in English literature and society is far from being a fixed, mythic stereotype as is commonly thought. On the contrary, we have shown that writers do not passively draw on eternal myths of 'the Jew' but actively construct them in relation to their own literary and political concerns. This active remaking of Jewish racial difference resulted in a bewildering variety of contradictory and over-determined representations of 'the Jew' which were particularly threatening to those who would wish to exert a sense of control and order over an increasingly unmanageable 'reality'. It was in these terms that a more general crisis of representation could be reflected in a semitic discourse which constructed 'the Jew' as both within *and* without; a stranger *and* familiar; an object of esteem *and* odium; a progressive universalist *and* a racial particularist. To name just a few 'semitic' designations in this book, Jews could be represented as: 'Eastern', 'Oriental', 'European', 'Asian', 'modern', 'medieval', 'pagan', 'prophetic', 'degenerate', 'regenerate', 'proletarian', 'bourgeois','aristocratic', 'tribal', 'assimilated', 'orthodox', 'heretical', 'rational', 'deranged', 'vengeful', 'orderly'. The list could be extended endlessly but I have located this 'semitic confusion', somewhat arbitrarily, in Matthew Arnold's *Culture and Anarchy*. For one thing, his binary opposition between 'culture' and 'anarchy' was frequently evoked to distinguish between those acculturated Jews that could be accommodated within a higher 'culture' and those uncontainable 'semites' who contributed to a racialized sense of 'anarchy'. Arnold's semitic discourse, in short, was replicated in all of the literature under discussion which also moralized 'the Jew' in terms of this dual potentiality for good or evil. The stable bifurcation of 'the Jew', therefore, was to represent exactly the kind of virtuous order supposedly sought by all right-thinking people.

However, these moralized oppositions did not remain unquestioned or immutable in the imaginative and journalistic literature which is examined in this study. The over-determined representations of 'the Jew', within a semitic discourse, invariably exploded a writer's absolute hold on 'reality' which is implicit in the secure classification of Jews into 'good' and 'evil' stereotypes. Jews, in short, were constructed *at one and the same time* both as embodying the aspirations of an enlightened State and as undermining the essential characteristics of a particularist nation. Such was the disturbing ambivalence of 'the Jew' who, in the end, embodied simultaneously both 'culture' *and* 'anarchy'. This structural incoherence, within Victorian liberalism, was replicated throughout the Edwardian and post-First World War period.

Following on from Arnold, all of the twentieth-century writers explored in this work wished to incorporate 'the Jew' within a transcendent discourse. By encompassing the unruly 'Jew' – an age-old outcast from history as well as Christian theology – the efficacy of a civilizing liberalism, or an all-controlling Imperialism, or a rationalizing socialism, could be established beyond all doubt. There is, perhaps, a distinction to be made between those perspectives that actively wished to remake 'the Jew' in their own image and those, such as 'distributism' and 'modernism', which accepted as axiomatic the supposedly all-pervasive nature of 'semitic confusion'. As opposed to the transfiguring impulse which begins this study, these latter post-liberal discourses aimed to situate Jews within strict boundaries or, as in the case of James Joyce, to explicitly embrace the playful, disruptive possibilities inherent in 'Jewish' inassimilability. Joyce, especially, demonstrates the libertarian potentiality within a semitic discourse that was becoming increasingly authoritarian. To be sure, all of the writers that we have explored have constructed

Jewish racial difference as an 'other' which defined their own values. But it was precisely the impossibility of fixing the indeterminate, slippery 'Jew' as a stable 'other' that exposed the severe limitations of, even, the most exhaustive world outlook. The 'Jew', as George Bernard Shaw wrote in *Man and Superman*, was an 'exception to all rules'. Such was the instability of a semitic discourse which could always be rewritten to disprove any given representation of 'the Jew'.

The theological necessity to transfigure a 'fossilized' or 'materialist' Judaism has, as many have argued, a medieval pedigree. Nonetheless, it is the radically imprecise character of 'the Jew' – as constructed within a semitic discourse – that has been foregrounded in this work. As Harold Fisch has shown, Christianity historically had a deeply uncertain relationship with Judaism. While Jews were, on the one hand, a 'deicide nation' their longed-for Christian 'conversion' had a messianic charge which could also potentially 'redeem mankind'. This theologically endorsed split in 'the Jew' was, we have seen, replicated and reproduced in a multiplicity of 'enlightened' discourses.[1] Rather than the fixity of racial stereotyping, it is the dangerous indeterminacy of 'the Jews' which, I believe, resulted in their construction as a potent threat. This sense of threat was especially expressed in those imaginative and journalistic writings that wished to impose some kind of textual order on the world. As Robert Casillo has shown, in relation to Ezra Pound, the racialized 'Jew' can be thought of as the embodiment of intellectual confusion or the 'negative principle' which opposes the clarity of the image or ideogram. Pound, in a characteristic generalization, was to make explicit this 'negative principle':

You can probably date any Western work of art by reference to the ethical estimate of usury prevalent at the time of that work's composition; the greater the component of tolerance for usury the more blobby and messy the work of art. The kind of thought which distinguishes good from evil, down into the details of commerce, rises into the quality of line in paintings and into the clear definition of the word written.[2]

While Pound is the most articulate and consistent spokesman against this kind of 'semitic confusion', it would be a mistake to mark him out

[1] Harold Fisch, *The Dual Image: The Figure of the Jew in English Literature* (London, 1959) p. 15.
[2] William Cookson (ed.), *Selected Prose of Ezra Pound: 1909–1965* (New York, 1973) p. 76 cited in Robert Casillo, *The Genealogy of Demons: Anti-Semitism, Fascism, and the Myths of Ezra Pound* (Evanston, 1988) p. 35.

as an exceptional figure in this regard. By the inter-war years, as a recent study has shown, writers as various as Graham Greene, Wyndham Lewis and Charles Williams were all to construct 'the Jew' as 'blobby and messy' and to assocate 'semitism' with uncategorizable feminized males or excremental sub-humans. As Lewis's persona, Arghol, was to put it in his *Enemy of the Stars* (1932), 'anything but yourself is dirt. Anybody that is'. For these writers, the racialized 'Jew' was to epitomize what Zygmunt Bauman has called 'aesthetic disgust' or the 'dirt' that has deformed the 'self'.[3] The uncontainable slime of money power, making words indistinct, is clearly foregrounded in this Poundian reading which culminates in T. S. Eliot's *Poems* (1920). Eliot's fear of being Judaized, of unwittingly contributing to an incoherent and confused liberal culture, accounts for the excessiveness of his construction of 'the jew' as an animalistic, diabolic 'other'. The extremity of Eliot's semitic discourse, in other words, can be directly related to his repressed identification with 'the Jew'. But Eliot's particular semitic 'prejudice' is, I want to argue, implicit in all of the writers in this study.

What distinguishes semitic discourse from colonial and racial discourse in general is the extent to which 'the Jew' could directly encroach upon the consciousness of the metropolitan white bourgeoisie. Matthew Arnold's benign self-identification with Moses espying the 'promised land' of 'culture' as well as his 'alien' 'semitico-saxon' racial identity positions him in a particularly intimate relationship with Jews and Judaism. An upwardly mobile Trollope, similarly, gives the rising entrepreneur Anton Trendellsohn his authorial signature ('A. T.') and George Eliot's *Daniel Deronda* (1876) can be said to be predicated on the construction of Jewish nationalism as an 'ideal' for the 'English nation' to follow. The internationalism of the diaspora as well as a 'Jewish' revolutionary prophetic tradition were also represented as exemplary political models by Shaw and Wells. Jewish colonialists or 'orthodox' Jews could, in addition, be constructed as ideal types by Buchan and Kipling or G. K. Chesterton. This fearful recognition of 'the Jew'

[3] Andrea Freud Loewenstein, *Loathsome Jews and Engulfing Women: Metaphors of Projection in the Works of Wyndham Lewis, Charles Williams and Graham Greene* (New York, 1993) and William Chace, 'On Lewis's Politics: The Polemics Polemically Answered' in Jeffrey Myers (ed.), *Wyndham Lewis: A Revaluation* (London, 1980) p. 151 cites *Enemy of the Stars* (1932). See also Zygmunt Bauman, *Modernity and the Holocaust* (Oxford, 1989) p. 46 and chapter 2 for an important discussion of the 'slimy' 'conceptual Jew'.

within the writer resulted in a semitic discourse which attempted to irrevocably banish or contain this confusing 'other'. The closer the 'self' identified, however unconsciously, with the semitic 'other', the more vehement the rejection of this unwelcome double. Hilaire Belloc's supposed 'exotic' foreigness and his traditional supranational religious beliefs have often been seen as the reason for his obsessional focussing on these attributes in European Jewry. Whereas Joyce could playfully identify with Jews as exiled outsiders from received conventions, T. S. Eliot was at pains to distance himself from exactly those 'alien' qualities he shared with many Jews. Ezra Pound, who was often assumed to be 'Jewish', once again makes explicit this horror of becoming semitically indistinct. In a 1915 letter to Joyce, he gives his reasons for refusing to enclose a photograph of himself so that Joyce can recognize him on their first meeting:

I have several copies of a photo of a portrait of me, painted by an amiable Jew who substituted a good deal of his own face for the gentile parts of my own. [Dante] mentions a similar predicament about presenting one's self at a distance. It is my face no I can not be represented in your mind by that semitic image.[4]

Whether a semitic discourse is utilized in an authoritarian or libertarian manner points ultimately to the extent to which a particular individual needs to control his or her uncontrollable semitic 'self-image'. As the twentieth century progressed, however, the belief in the transformative power of *any* one perspective – in the light of the political chaos after the First World War – resulted in a general crisis of representation. Nothing, in other words, could contain 'the Jew' who, especially at this historical conjuncture, signified an 'anarchic' liberalism that was out of control. Such was 'the Jew's' supposed secretive racial agenda; or rampant individualism; or absolute dominance; which positioned them as a force which could no longer be accommodated rationally within European nation-states. Cynthia Ozick has, in this context, described the German 'Final Solution' as an 'aesthetic solution; it was a job of editing, it was the artist's finger removing a smudge, it simply annihilated what was considered not harmonious'. A semitic discourse in liberal England can, in these terms, be implicated in the

---

[4] Forrest Read (ed.), *Pound/Joyce: The Letters of Ezra Loomis Pound to James Joyce, with Pound's Essays on Joyce* (New York, 1967) p. 35 cited in Casillo, *The Genealogy of Demons*, p. 38. Casillo, pp. 298–310 also usefully discusses Pound's repressed identification with his 'Jewish' double, the Prophet Ezra.

Holocaust. While Jews could be constructed as racially inferior – along with other colonized peoples – it is the fascistic imposition of 'order' and 'clarity' on the European continent that gives this study its avowed 'Eurocentric' bias.[5] The writers that we have explored, in short, replicated a semitic discourse that was also utilized in a European context. Nonetheless, it is worth remembering that other British writers, such as D. H. Lawrence, repudiated such Euro-centricism. In *Apocalypse* (1930), Lawrence made explicit his refusal to work within the discursive parameters of *Culture and Anarchy*:

> We accept the Greeks and Romans as the initiators of our intellectual and political civilisation, the Jews as the fathers of our moral-religious civilisation. So these are 'our sort'. All the rest are mere nothing, almost idiots. All that can be attributed to the 'barbarians' beyond the Greek pale: that is, to Minoans, Etruscans, Egyptians, Chaldeans, Persians and Hindus is, in the famous phrase of a famous German professor: *Urdummheit*. Urdummheit, or primal stupidity, is the state of all mankind before precious Homer, and of all races, all, except Greek, Jew, Roman and – ourselves![6]

Lawrence's wholesale rejection of the Judeo-Christian tradition, and his privileging of a pre-biblical 'paganism', clearly discount a prevalent sense of European cultural superiority which underpins the Arnoldian premises of the literature in this work. His spokesman in *Kangaroo* (1923) was thus able to champion the 'older gods, older ideals, different gods: before the Jews invented a mental Jehovah, and a spiritual Christ. They are nearer the magic of the animal world' (229). Unlike Lawrence, what distinguishes the disparate collection of writers in this book is precisely their struggle within the discursive parameters of British liberalism and a European 'culture'. Even James Joyce's *Ulysses* (1922), as has been seen, utilizes an essentially Arnoldian vocabulary to rumbustiously deconstruct the binary oppositions between 'Jew' and 'Greek' or 'Culture' and 'Anarchy'. Molly Bloom's evocation of 'a bigger religion than the jews and Our Lords both put together all over Asia' seems, in this

---

[5] I am indebted to both Bauman, *Modernity and the Holocaust*, and also his *Modernity and Ambivalence* (Oxford, 1991) for the wider European context of this study. Cynthia Ozick, *Art and Ardour* (New York, 1984) p. 165 is usefully cited in this latter work, p. 66.

[6] D. H. Lawrence, *Apocalypse* (London, 1930) p. 87. Further references to Penguin editions of Lawrence's works will be cited in the body of the text. Because Lawrence explicitly rejected the Arnoldian premise of this study, I have not included a detailed consideration of his many racialized Jewish representations. For an unsophisticated account of Lawrence in these terms see John Harrison, *The Reactionaries: A Study of the Anti-Democratic Intelligentsia* (London, 1966).

context, something of an afterthought which, at best, prefigures the unconscious night-time language of *Finnegans Wake* (1939).

It is a particular irony of this study that, in recent years, much of the 'semitic' indeterminacy that we have situated historically has been evoked by cultural theorists in a more generalized post-Holocaust and post-modern context. The impossibility of permanently situating 'the Jew' within any given textual order has been universalized in numerous theoretical works to characterize the absence of any absolute meaning. As with our literary-historical survey, 'the Jew' in the writings of this theory is at the heart of contemporary definitions of European culture and the production of literary texts. Thus Edmond Jabès, characteristically, states that 'First I thought I was a writer. Then I realized I was a Jew. Then I no longer distinguished the writer in me from the Jew because one and the other are only the torment of an ancient world'. In a post-modern context, 'semitic confusion' is not only a virtue but a prototype for the lack of fixity in language as a whole. Instead of attempting to impose a fascistic clarity on 'the Jew', he or she is embraced and rehumanized as a paradigmatic representation of an exuberant post-modernity. The libertarian potential of Joyce's *Ulysses* has, finally, been given full expression. To this extent, as Susan Handelman has argued, the Arnoldian tension between 'Hebrew and Hellene ... renews itself in every epoch, taking another guise, using another language'.[7]

I would, however, like to end with a rather less grandiose claim for the subject of this book. The racialized discourse which constructed 'the Jew' before the Second World War is still, for the most part, blatantly written out of literary-historical studies of nineteenth- and twentieth-century authors. Until those who recall this writing employ a set of reading strategies which can take account of this history of 'semitism' then it will, in effect, still be continuing. It is all very well reconstructing 'the Jew' as the embodiment of post-modern indeter-

---

[7] Susan Handelman, *The Slayers of Moses: The Emergence of Rabbinic Interpretation in Modern Literary Theory* (New York, 1982) p. 3 is an influential work in this regard and cites Edmond Jabès, *Le Soupçon, le desert* (1978) as its epigram. Handelman's study includes a detailed exploration of Harold Bloom, Jacques Derrida and Jacques Lacan in these terms. Her recent *Fragments of Redemption: Jewish and Literary Theory in Benjamin, Scholem and Levinas* (Bloomington, 1991) has extended the discussion to include Walter Benjamin, Emmanuel Levinas and Gershom Scholem. For a more problematic account of a theorized indeterminacy with regard to the Holocaust, which focuses on the work of Jürgen Habermas, Jean-François Lyotard and Hayden White, see Saul Friedlander (ed.), *Probing the Limits of Representation: Nazism and the 'Final Solution'* (Cambridge, Mass., 1992).

minacy and a universal sense of estrangement. But there is also a particular European cultural history to be faced which is, on one level, being effaced by the warm embrace of those that would wish 'the Jew' to be, once again, emblematic. After all, it is precisely this universalizing desire which has, historically, generated a semitic discourse in the first place.

Bibliography

UNPUBLISHED MATERIAL

(A) PRIVATE PAPERS

T. S. Eliot Papers, Houghton Library, Harvard University, Boston, Massachusetts
Rudyard Kipling Papers, University of Sussex, Brighton
Israel Zangwill Papers, Central Zionist Archives, Jerusalem

(B) DOCTORAL DISSERTATIONS

Bayme, Steven 'Jewish Leadership and Anti-Semitism in Britain, 1898–1918' (Columbia University, 1977)

Cesarani, David 'The Zionist Movement in Britain Between the Wars' (Oxford University, 1986)

Chevalier, Esther 'Characterisation of the Jew in the Victorian Novel, 1864–1876' (Emory University, 1962)

Cheyette, Bryan 'An Over-Whelming Question: Jewish Stereotyping in English Literature and Society, 1875–1920' (University of Sheffield, 1986)

Colbenson, P. D. 'British Socialism and Anti-Semitism, 1884–1914' (Georgia State University, 1977)

Feldman, David 'Immigrants and Workers, Englishmen and Jews; Jewish Immigration to the East End of London, 1880–1906' (Cambridge University, 1985)

Gelber, Mark Howard 'Aspects of Literary Antisemitism: Charles Dickens' "Oliver Twist" and Gustav Freytag's "Soll und Haben"' (Yale University, 1980)

Gottleib, Freema 'A Study of the Psychological Development of Leonard Woolf as Reflected in Various Early Writings from 1880–1915' (University of London, 1974)

Guigui, Jacques Ben 'Israel Zangwill: Penseur et Ecrivain' (University of Toulouse, 1975)

Kileen, Janet 'Type and Anti-Type: A Study of the Figure of the Jew in Popular Literature of the First Half of the Nineteenth Century' (University of Kent, 1972)

Klein, Charlotte 'The Jew in English and German Fiction and Drama, 1830–1933' (University of London, 1967)

Kushner, Tony 'British Antisemitism in the Second World War' (University of Sheffield, 1986)

Loewenstein, Andrea Freud 'Loathsome Jews and Engulfing Women: Metaphors of Projection in the Works of Wyndham Lewis, Charles Williams and Graham Greene' (Sussex University, 1992)

Lunn, Kenneth 'The Marconi Scandal and Related Aspects of British Antisemitism, 1911–1914' (University of Sheffield, 1978)

Mayo, Louise 'The Ambivalent Image: The Perception of the Jew in Nineteenth Century America' (New York University, 1977)

Randell, E. F. 'The Jewish Character in the French Novel 1870–1914' (Harvard University, 1940)

Reizbaum, Marilyn 'Joyce's Judaic "Other": Texts and Contexts' (University of Wisconsin, 1985)

Stott, Graham St John 'Under Gentile Eyes: Images of the Jew in the Nineteenth Century Novel of England and America' (Brigham Young University, 1978)

Winehouse, Bernard 'The Literary Career of Israel Zangwill from its Beginnings until 1898' (University of London, 1970)

PUBLISHED MATERIAL

(A) Newspapers and journals

The Eye-Witness
Jewish Chronicle
Morning Post
The New Witness
The Outlook
The Times

(B) Primary Literature (published in London unless stated otherwise)

Allen, Grant *The Scallywag* (1922)

Arnold, Matthew *Culture and Anarchy: An Essay in Political and Social Criticism* (1869)
Essays in Criticism (1865)
Literature and Dogma (1873)
Mixed Essays (1903)
The Poems of Matthew Arnold, 1840–1867 (Oxford, 1909)

Belloc, Hilaire *Emmanuel Burden: A Novel* (1904)
Mr Clutterbuck's Election (1908)
A Change in the Cabinet (1909)
The Place of a Peasantry in Modern Civilization (1910)
Pongo and the Bull (1910)

'The Jewish Question', *The Eye-Witness* (September-October, 1911), 365–589
The Servile State (1912)
The Free Press (1918)
Europe and the Faith (1920)
The Jews (1922)
The Cruise of the 'Nona' (1925)
A History of England, 5 vols. (1925–31)
The Postmaster-General (1932)
An Essay on the Nature of Contemporary England (1937)
Belloc, Hilaire and Hammond, J. L. (eds.) *Essays in Liberalism by Six Oxford Men* (1897)
Belloc, Hilaire and Chesterton, Cecil *The Party System: A Criticism* (1911)
Bennett, Arnold *The Grand Babylon Hotel* (1902)
Besant, Walter *The Rebel Queen* (1894)
Blyth, James *Ichabod* (1910)
Buchan, John *The Half-Hearted* (1900)
The Africa Colony: Studies in the Reconstruction (1903)
A Lodge in the Wilderness (1906)
Prester John (1910)
The Moon Endureth (1912)
The Thirty-Nine Steps (1915)
Greenmantle (1916)
The Powerhouse (1916)
Mr Standfast (1919)
Huntingtower (1922)
The Three Hostages (1924)
The Dancing Floor (1926)
The Courts of Morning (1929)
'Ourselves and the Jews', *Graphic* (5 April, 1930), 12
'The Novel and the Fairy Tale', *English Association Pamphlet* (1931)
A Prince of the Captivity (1933)
Memory-Hold-The-Door (1940)
Butler, Samuel *Erewhon* (1872)
Alps and Sanctuaries (1881)
Caine, Hall *The Scapegoat: A Romance* (1884)
Chesterton, G. K. *Robert Browning* (1903)
Napoleon of Notting Hill (1904)
Heretics (1905)
The Wild Knight (1905 edition)
Charles Dickens (1906)
The Man Who was Thursday (1908)
What's Wrong with the World (1909)
The Ball and the Cross (1910)
Appreciations and Criticisms of the Works of Dickens (1911)

Manalive (1912)
The Victorian Age in Literature (1913)
The Barbarism of Berlin (1914)
The Flying Inn (1914)
The Wisdom of Father Brown (1914)
The Crimes of England (1915)
A Short History of England (1917)
The New Jerusalem (1920)
Eugenics and Other Evils (1922)
The Man Who Knew Too Much (1922)
What I Saw in America (1922)
The Everlasting Man (1925)
The Incredulity of Father Brown (1926)
The Collected Poems of G. K. Chesterton (1927)
Four Faultless Felons (1930)
The Resurrection of Rome (1930)
Autobiography (1936)
The Paradoxes of Mr Pond (1937)
Cleeve, Lucas *The Children of Endurance* (1904)
Conrad, Joseph *Nostromo* (1904)
Tales of Hearsay and Last Essays (1928)
Corelli, Marie *Barabbas: A Dream of the World's Tragedy* (1894)
Temporal Power: A Study in Supremacy (1902)
Free Opinions (1906)
Crosland, T. W. H. *The Absent Minded Mule* (1899)
The Five Notions (1903)
The Fine Old Hebrew Gentleman (1922)
Cumberland, Richard *The Jew* (1794)
Dickens, Charles *Oliver Twist* (1837)
Our Mutual Friend (1864)
Disraeli, Benjamin *Alroy* (1833)
Coningsby (1844)
Tancred (1847)
Lord George Bentinck: A Political Biography (1851)
Lothair (1870)
Endymion (1880)
Donnelly, Ignatius *Caesar's Column* (New York, 1890)
Du Maurier, George *Trilby* (1894)
The Martian (1897)
Edgeworth, Maria *Harrington* (1817)
Eliot, George *Daniel Deronda* (1876)
The Impressions of Theophrastus Such (n.d.)
Eliot, T. S. *The Sacred Wood: Essays on Poetry and Criticism* (1920)
For Lancelot Andrewes: Essays on Style and Order (1928)
After Strange Gods : A Primer of Modern Heresy (1934)

The Rock (1934)
The Idea of a Christian Society (1939)
Notes Towards the Definition of Culture (1948)
Collected Poems 1909–1962 (1963)
To Criticize the Critic and other Writings (1965)
Selected Essays (1966)
'Eeldrop and Appleplex', *The Little Review* (May–September, 1917), 7–19
'American Literature', *Athenaeum* (April, 1919), 236–7
'A Sceptical Patrician', *Athenaeum* (May, 1919), 361–2
'London Letter', *The Dial* 71 (August, 1921), 213–17
'*Ulysses*, Order and Myth', *The Dial* 75 (November, 1923), 480–3
'The Importance of Greek', *The Criterion* 3 (April, 1925), 341–2
'The Bible as Scripture and Literature' (Boston, 1932), unpublished lecture, Houghton Library, bms AM 1691 (26)
'The Approach of Joyce', *The Listener* (14 October 1943), 447
Eliot, T. S. (ed.) *A Choice of Kipling's Verse* (1941)
Ford, Ford Madox *An English Girl* (1907)
The Spirit of the People: An Analysis of the English Mind (1907)
Ancient Lights and Certain New Reflections (1911)
Memories and Impressions (1911)
Mr Fleight (1913)
Ford, Ford Madox and Conrad, Joseph *The Inheritors: An Extravagant Story* (1901)
Forster, E. M. *The Longest Journey* (1907)
Pharos and Pharillon (1923)
Two Cheers for Democracy (1951)
Frankau, Julia *Dr Phillips* (1887)
Graham, Winifred *The Zionists* (1902)
Greene, Graham *Stamboul Train* (1932)
A Gun for Sale (1936)
Brighton Rock (1938)
Grier, Sydney *The Kings of the East* (1900)
The Prince of Captivity (1902)
Haggard, Henry Rider *A Winter Pilgrimage, Being an Account of Travels through Palestine, Italy, and the Island of Cyprus, Accomplished in the Year 1900* (1901)
Harris, Frank *Unpath'd Waters* (1913)
Hope, Anthony *Quisanté* (1900)
Huxley, T. H. *Social Diseases and Worse Remedies* (1891)
Evolution and Ethics (1893)
James, Henry, '*Daniel Deronda*: A Conversation', *The Atlantic Monthly* 38 (December, 1876), 684–94
The Tragic Muse (1890)
The American Scene (1907)
Joyce, James *Dubliners* (1914)

Giacomo Joyce (1914)
A Portrait of the Artist as a Young Man (1916)
Ulysses (1922)
Finnegans Wake (1939)
Stephen Hero (1944)
Kane-Clifford, Lucy *Mr Keith's Crime* (1885)
Kipling, Rudyard *Plain Tales from the Hills* (1888)
Wee Willie Winkie (1890)
Life's Handicap (1891)
The Light that Failed (1891)
The Jungle Book (1894)
The Day's Work (1898)
Kim (1901)
Traffics and Discoveries (1904)
Puck of Pook's Hill (1906)
Actions and Reactions (1909)
Rewards and Fairies (1910)
'The Church that was Antioch' (1929)
Something of Myself (1937)
Lawrence, D. H. *Women in Love* (1921)
The Captain's Doll (1923)
Kangaroo (1923)
Apocalypse (1930)
The Virgin and the Gypsy (1930)
Lewes, George Henry *Actors and the Art of Acting* (1875)
Lewis, Wyndham *The Art of Being Ruled* (1926)
The Apes of God (1930)
Hitler (1931)
Enemy of the Stars (1932)
The Hitler Cult (1938)
The Jews, are They Human? (1939)
Masterman, C. F. G. *The Condition of England* (1909)
Meredith, George *The Tragic Comedians* (1880)
One of Our Conquerors (1891)
Pound, Ezra *The Collected Early Poems of Ezra Pound* (1926)
ABC of Reading (1934)
The Cantos (1934)
Jefferson and/or Mussolini (1935)
Literary Essays of Ezra Pound (1935)
Richardson, Dorothy *Pilgrimage* (1914–38)
Schreiner, Olive *A Letter on the Jew* (Cape Town, 1906)
From Man to Man (1926)
Scott, Sir Walter *Ivanhoe* (1819)
Shaw, George Bernard *Love Among the Artists* (1881)
An Unsocial Socialist (1884)

The Quintessence of Ibsenism (1891)
Man and Superman: A Comedy and Philosophy (1903)
John Bull's Other Island (1904)
Major Barbara (1905)
'Superman and Jew', *Jewish Chronicle* (February, 1909), 20
The Doctor's Dilemma (1911)
Androcles and the Lion (1912)
Heartbreak House (1919)
Back to Methuselah (1921)
The Intelligent Woman's Guide to Socialism and Capitalism (1928)
Too True to be Good (1932)
On the Rocks (1933)
The Millionairess (1935)
Geneva (1939)
Everybody's Political What's What? (1944)
Simons, Oswald John *The World and the Cloister* (1890)
Stoker, Bram *Dracula* (1897)
Thorne, Guy *When it was Dark* (1903)
Trollope, Anthony *The Three Clerks* (1856)
Barchester Towers (1857)
Dr Thorne (1858)
The Bertrams (1859)
Orley Farm (1862)
Rachel Ray (1863)
Can You Forgive Her? (1864)
Nina Balatka (1867)
Phineas Finn (1869)
The Eustace Diamonds (1873)
Phineas Redux (1874)
The Way We Live Now (1875)
The Prime Minister (1876)
Is He a Poppenjay? (1878)
The Duke's Children (1880)
Life of Cicero (1880)
Mr Scarborough's Family (1880)
An Autobiography (1883)
Ward, Mrs Humphrey *Sir George Tressady* (1896)
Wells, H. G. *The Invisible Man* (1897)
Anticipations (1902)
A Modern Utopia (1905)
New Worlds for Old: A Plain Account of Modern Socialism (1908)
Tono-Bungay (1909)
The New Machiavelli (1911)
Marriage (1912)
Liberalism and its Party: What Are We Liberals to Do? (1913)

The Wife of Isaac Harman (1914)
The Research Magnificent (1915)
Joan and Peter (1918)
The Outline of History (1920)
A Short History of the World (1922)
The Shape of Things to Come: The Ultimate Revolution (1933)
Experiment in Autobiography (1934)
The Anatomy of Frustration (1936)
The Fate of Homo Sapiens (1939)
In Search of Hot Water: Travels of a Republican Radical (1939)
The New World Order (1940)
You Can't Be Too Careful (1941)
The Outlook for Homo Sapiens (1942)
Williams, Charles *All Hallows Eve* (1945)
Woolf, Leonard *The Wise Virgins* (1914)
Woolf, Virginia *The Years* (1937)
Zangwill, Israel *Children of the Ghetto* (1892)
  King of the Schnorrers (1894)
Zola, Emile *Nana* (Paris, 1886)

(C) SECONDARY LITERATURE (PUBLISHED IN LONDON UNLESS
STATED OTHERWISE)

Allfrey, Anthony *Edward VII and his Jewish Court* (1991)
Almog, Shmuel (ed.) *Antisemitism through the Ages* (Oxford, 1988)
Appel, Gershon (ed.) *Samuel K. Mirsky Memorial Volume* (Jerusalem, 1970)
Arac, Jonathan *Critical Genealogies: Historical Situations for Post-Modernist Literary Studies* (New York, 1987)
Arendt, Hannah *The Origins of Totalitarianism* (Cleveland, 1958)
Arnold, Thomas *The Inaugural Lecture* (1843)
Attridge, Derek *The Cambridge Companion to James Joyce* (Cambridge, 1990)
Baker, William *George Eliot and Judaism* (Salzburg, 1975)
Barker, Dudley *G. K. Chesterton: A Biography* (1973)
Barker, Francis, Hume, Peter, Iversen, Margaret and Loxley, Diane (eds.)
  The Politics of Theory (Colchester, 1983)
  Europe and its Others, 2 vols. (Colchester, 1985)
Bauman, Zygmunt *Modernity and the Holocaust* (Oxford, 1989)
  Modernity and Ambivalence (Oxford, 1991)
Beer, Gillian *Darwin's Plots: Evolutionary Narrative in Darwin, George Eliot and Nineteenth-Century Fiction* (1985)
Beja, Morris (ed.) *James Joyce: The Centennial Symposium* (Urbana, 1986)
Benjamin, Andrew 'Kitaj and the Question of Jewish Identity', *Art and Design* (Winter, 1988), 61–4
Benstock, Bernard (ed.) *The Seventh of Joyce* (Indiana, 1982)
  James Joyce: The Augmented Ninth (Syracuse, 1988)

Berger, David (ed.) *The Legacy of Jewish Migration: 1881 and its Impact* (New York, 1983)

Bergonzi, Bernard *The Early H. G. Wells* (Manchester, 1961)

Bergonzi, Bernard (ed.) *H. G. Wells: A Collection of Critical Essays* (1976)

Bhabha, Homi 'The Other Question: Stereotype and Colonial Discourse', *Screen* 24 (November–December, 1983), 18–35

'Of Mimicry and Man: The Ambivalence of Colonial Discourse', *October* 28 (1984), 125–33

Bhabha, Homi (ed.) *Nation and Narration* (1990)

Biale, David 'Masochism and Philosemitism: The Strange Case of Leopold von Sacher-Masoch', *Journal of Contemporary History* 17 (1982), 305–23

Bivona, Daniel *Desire and Contradiction: Imperial Visions and Domestic Debates in Victorian Literature* (Manchester, 1990)

Blinderman, Charles 'Thomas Henry Huxley on the Jews', *Jewish Social Studies* 25 (1963), 57–61

Bodelson, C. A. *Aspects of Kipling's Art* (Manchester, 1964)

Bowen, Zack and Carens, James F. *A Companion to Joyce Studies* (Connecticut, 1984)

Boyd, Ian *The Novels of G. K. Chesterton* (1975)

Brantlinger, Patrick *Spirit of Reform: British Literature and Politics, 1832–1867* (Cambridge, Mass., 1977)

Rule of Darkness: British Literature and Imperialism, 1830–1914 (Ithaca, 1988)

Bristow, Edward *Prostitution and Prejudice: The Jewish Fight Against White Slavery* (Oxford, 1982)

Britain, Ian *Fabianism and Culture: A Study in British Socialism and the Arts* (Cambridge, 1982)

Brown, Richard *James Joyce and Sexuality* (Cambridge, 1985)

'Little England: On Triviality in the Naive Comic Fictions of H. G. Wells', *Cahiers, Victoriens and Edouardiens* 30 (October, 1989), 55–65

James Joyce: A Post-Culturalist Perspective (1992)

Buchan, Alistair *John Buchan: A Memoir* (1982)

Buckley, J. H. *The World of Victorian Fiction* (Harvard, 1975)

Budgen, Frank *James Joyce and the Making of 'Ulysses'* (Oxford, 1972 edition)

Camplin, Jamie *The Rise of the Plutocrats* (1978)

Canary, Robert H. *T. S. Eliot: The Poet and His Critics* (Chicago, 1982)

Canovan, Margaret *G. K. Chesterton: Radical Populist* (1977)

Carlebach, Julius *Karl Marx and the Radical Critique of Judaism* (Oxford, 1980)

Carrington, Charles *Rudyard Kipling his Life and Work* (1955)

Casillo, Robert *The Genealogy of Demons: Anti-Semitism, Fascism, and the Myths of Ezra Pound* (Evanston, 1988)

Cesarani, David (ed.) *The Making of Modern Anglo-Jewry* (Oxford, 1990)

Chace, William M. *The Political Identities of Ezra Pound and T. S. Eliot* (Stanford, 1973)

Chappelow, Allan *Shaw: 'The Chucker Out'* (1969)

Cline, C. L. (ed.) *The Collected Letters of George Meredith* (Oxford, 1970)

Coates, John 'Religious Cross-Currents in "The House Surgeon"', *The Kipling Journal* 65 (September, 1978), 2–7

Chesterton and the Edwardian Cultural Crisis (Hull, 1984)

Cohen, Derek and Heller, Deborah (eds.) *Jewish Presences in English Literature* (Montreal, 1990)

Cohen, Joan Mandel *Form and Realism in Six Novels of Anthony Trollope* (The Hague, 1976)

Cohen, Morton (ed.) *Rudyard Kipling to Rider Haggard, The Record of a Friendship* (1965)

Cohen-Steiner, Olivier 'Jews and Jewesses in Victorian Fiction: From Religious Stereotype to Ethnic Hazard', *Patterns of Prejudice* 21 (Summer, 1987), 25–34

Cohn, Norman *Warrant for Genocide: The Myth of the Jewish World-Conspiracy and 'The Protocols of the Elders of Zion'* (1967)

Collini, Stefan *Arnold* (1988)

Colls, Robert and Dodd, Philip (eds.) *Englishness: Politics and Culture 1880–1920* (1986)

Cookson, William (ed.) *Selected Prose of Ezra Pound: 1909–1965* (New York, 1973)

Coren, Michael *Gilbert: The Man Who Was G. K. Chesterton* (1989)

Corrin, Jay P. *G. K. Chesterton and Hilaire Belloc: The Battle Against Modernity* (Ohio, 1981)

Cowen, Anne and Cowen, Roger (eds.) *Victorian Jews Through British Eyes* (Oxford, 1986)

Crawford, Robert *The Savage and the City in the Works of T. S. Eliot* (Oxford, 1987)

Crompton, Louis *Shaw the Dramatist* (Lincoln, 1969)

Daniell, David *The Interpreter's House: A Critical Assessment of John Buchan* (1975)

David, Deirdre *Fictions of Resolution in Three Victorian Novels* (New York, 1981)

Dench, Geoff *Minorities in the Open Society: Prisoners of Ambivalence* (1985)

Derrida, Jacques *Writing and Difference* (1978)

Deutsch, Emanuel 'The Talmud' *Quarterly Review* 123 (October, 1867), 417–64

Dietrich, R. F. *Portrait of the Artist as a Young Superman: A Study of Shaw's Novels* (Gainsville, 1969)

Dobree, Bonamy *Rudyard Kipling: Realist and Fabulist* (1967)

Donaldson, Francis *The Marconi Scandal* (1962)

Doob, Leonard W. *'Ezra Pound Speaking': Radio Speeches of World War Two* (Westport, Conn., 1978)

Draper, Michael *H. G. Wells* (1987)

Duffy, Michael F. and Mittleman, Willard 'Nietzsche's Attitude Toward the Jews', *Journal of the History of Ideas* (April–June, 1988)

Echeruo, M. C. J. *The Conditioned Imagination From Shakespeare to Conrad*: *Studies in the Exo-Cultural Stereotype* (1978)

Edwards, Owen 'Chesterton and Tribalism', *The Chesterton Review* 6 (1979–80), 33–69

Eliot, Valerie (ed.) *The Waste Land: A Facsimile and Transcript of the Original Drafts* (1971)

The Letters of T. S. Eliot: 1898–1922 (1988)

Ellmann, Maud *The Poetics of Impersonality*: *T. S. Eliot and Ezra Pound* (Brighton, 1987)

Ellmann, Richard *Ulysses on the Liffey* (1974)

James Joyce (Oxford, 1983)

Four Dubliners (1987)

Ellmann, Richard (ed.) *James Joyce*: *'Giacomo Joyce'* (1968)

Selected Letters of James Joyce (1975)

Ellmann, Richard and Mason, Ellsworth (eds.) *The Critical Writings of James Joyce* (1959)

Empson, William *Using Biography* (1984)

Endelman, Todd *The Jews of Georgian England*: *Tradition and Change in a Liberal Society* (Philadelphia, 1979)

'Disraeli's Jewishness Reconsidered', *Modern Judaism* 5 (1985), 109–21

Fanon, Frantz *Black Skins, White Masks* (Paris, 1952)

Faverty, Frederic E. *Matthew Arnold*: *The Ethnologist* (Illinois, 1951)

Feldman, David *Englishmen and Jews*: *English Political Culture and Jewish Society, 1840–1914* (New Haven, 1993)

Feldman, David and Jones, Gareth Stedman (eds.) *Metropolis London*: *Histories and Representations Since 1800* (1989)

Fisch, Harold *The Dual Image*: *A Study of the Jew in English Literature* (1959)

Fishman, William J. *East End 1888* (1988)

Foucault, Michel *The History of Sexuality*, 3 vols. (1976)

Friedlander, Saul (ed.) *Probing the Limits of Representation*: *Nazism and the 'Final Solution'* (Cambridge, Mass., 1992)

Garrard, J. A. *The English and Immigration 1880–1910* (Oxford, 1971)

Gates, Henry Louis (ed.) *'Race', Writing and Difference* (Chicago, 1986)

Gelber, Mark Howard 'What is Literary Anti-Semitism?', *Jewish Social Studies* 47 (Winter, 1985), 1–20

Gerber, Richard *Utopian Fantasy* (1955)

Gibbs, A. M. *The Art and Mind of Shaw*: *Essays in Criticism* (London, 1983)

Gifford, Don and Seidman, Robert *Notes for Joyce*: *An Annotation of James Joyce's 'Ulysses'* (New York, 1974)

Gillon, Adam 'The Jews in Joseph Conrad's Fiction', *Chicago Jewish Forum* 22 (Fall, 1963), 34–40

Gilman, Sander *Difference and Pathology*: *Stereotypes of Sexuality, Race and Madness* (Ithaca, 1985)

Jewish Self-Hatred: *Anti-Semitism and the Hidden Language of the Jews* (Baltimore, 1986)

Gilroy, Paul *There Ain't No Black in the Union Jack* (1987)
Gloversmith, Frank (ed.) *The Theory of Reading* (Brighton, 1984)
Gordon, Lyndall *Eliot's Early Years* (Oxford, 1987)
Grainger, J. H. *Patriotisms: Britain 1900–1939* (1986)
Gray, Piers *T. S. Eliot's Intellectual and Poetic Development* 1909–1922 (Brighton, 1982)
Greenblatt, Stephen 'Marlowe, Marx, and Anti-Semitism', *Critical Inquiry* (Winter, 1978), 291–307
Gregor, Ian (ed.) *Reading the Victorian Novel: Detail into Form* (1980)
Gross, John (ed.) *Rudyard Kipling the Man, His Work and His World* (1972)
Grossman, Marshall 'The Violence of the Hyphen in Judeo-Christian', *Social Text* 22 (Spring, 1989), 115–22
Halperin, John *Trollope and Politics: A Study of the Pallisers and Others* (1977)
Hammond, J. R. *H. G. Wells and the Modern Novel* (1988)
Handelman, Susan *The Slayers of Moses: The Emergence of Rabbinic Interpretation in Modern Literary Theory* (New York, 1982)
Harrison, John *The Reactionaries: A Study of the Anti-Democratic Intelligentsia* (1966)
Harty, John (ed.) *James Joyce's 'Finnegans Wake', A Casebook* (New York, 1991)
Henke, Suzette 'James Joyce East and Middle East: Literary Resonances of Judaism, Egyptology, and Indian Myth', *Journal of Modern Literature* 13 (1986), 307–19
James Joyce and the Politics of Desire (1990)
Herring, Phillip *Joyce's Uncertainty Principle* (New Jersey, 1987)
Himmelfarb, Gertrude *Victorian Minds* (1968)
Hirchfield, Claire 'The British Left and the "Jewish Conspiracy": A Case Study of Modern Antisemitism', *Jewish Social Studies* (Spring, 1981), 95–112
Hollis, Christopher *The Mind of Chesterton* (1970)
Holmes, Colin *Anti-Semitism in British Society, 1876–1939* (1979)
Holroyd, Michael *Bernard Shaw: The Search for Love* (1988)
Bernard Shaw: The Pursuit of Power (1989)
Hunter, Lynette *G. K. Chesterton: Explorations in Allegory* (1979)
Huntley, H. R. *The Alien Protagonist of Ford Madox Ford* (Michigan, 1970)
Huttenback, Robert 'The Patrician Jew and the British Ethos in the Nineteenth and Early Twentieth Centuries', *Jewish Social Studies* 40 (Winter, 1978), 49–62
Ingle, Stephen *Socialist Thought in Imaginative Literature* (1979)
JanMohamed, Abdul *Manichean Aesthetics: The Politics of Literature in Colonial Africa* (Amherst, 1983)
Johnson, Iva G. 'Trollope, Carlyle, and Mill on the Negro: An Episode in the History of Ideas', *Journal of Negro History* 52 (July 1967), 185–199
Josipovici, Gabriel *The World and the Book* (1971)
The Lessons of Modernism (1977)

The Mirror of Criticism: Selected Reviews 1977–1982 (Brighton, 1983)

Karl, Frederick *Joseph Conrad: The Three Lives* (1979)

Katz, Jacob *From Prejudice to Destruction: Antisemitism 1700–1933* (Cambridge, Mass., 1980)

Katz, Jacob (ed.) *Towards Modernity: The European Model* (New Brunswick, 1987)

Katz, Wendy *Rider Haggard and the Fiction of Empire: A Critical Study of British Imperial Fiction* (Cambridge, 1987)

Kemp, Sandra *Kipling's Hidden Narratives* (Oxford, 1988)

Kendrick, William *The Novel Machine: The Theory and Fiction of Anthony Trollope* (Baltimore, 1980)

Klein, Charlotte 'The Jew in Modern English Literature', *Patterns of Prejudice* 5 (March–April, 1971), 23–31

Knoepflmacher, U. C. *Religious Humanism and the Victorian Novel* (Princeton, 1965)

Koss, S. (ed.) *The Pro-Boers* (1973)

Kushner, Tony *The Persistence of Prejudice: Antisemitism in British Society During the Second World War* (Manchester, 1989)

Kushner, Tony and Lunn, Kenneth (eds.) *Traditions of Intolerance* (Manchester, 1989)

The Politics of Marginality: Race, the Radical Right and Minorities in Twentieth-Century Britain (1990)

Landau, M. J. *The Jew in Drama* (1926)

Langner, Lawrence *The Magic Curtain* (1951)

Laurence, D. H. (ed.) *Bernard Shaw: Collected Letters 1898–1910* (1972)

Bernard Shaw: Collected Letters 1926–1950 (1988)

Lawrence, Karen *The Odyssey of Style in 'Ulysses'* (Princeton, 1981)

Leavis, F. R. 'George Eliot's Zionist Novel', *Commentary* 30 (1960), 317–25

The Great Tradition (1972)

Levenson, Michael H. *A Genealogy of Modernism: A Study of English Literary Doctrine 1908–1922* (Cambridge, 1984)

Levitt, Morton P. 'A Hero for Our Time: Leopold Bloom and the Myth of Ulysses', *James Joyce Quarterly* 10 (Fall, 1972), 132–46

Levy, Leo B. 'Henry James and the Jews: A Critical Study', *Commentary* 25 (September, 1958), 243–9

Littell, Marcia, Libowitz, Richard and Bodek Rosen, Evelyn (eds.) *The Holocaust Forty Years After* (New York, 1989)

Lodge, David *The Novelist at the Crossroads* (1971)

Loewenstein, Andrea Freud *Loathsome Jews and Engulfing Women: Metaphors of Projection in the Works of Wyndham Lewis, Charles Williams and Graham Greene* (New York, 1993)

Lunn, Kenneth and Thurlow, Richard (eds.) *British Fascism* (1980)

MacCabe, Colin *James Joyce and the Revolution of the Word* (1978)

McCarthy, John P. *Hilaire Belloc: Edwardian Radical* (Indiana, 1978)

McCormack, William J. and Stead, Alistair (eds.) *James Joyce and Modern Literature* (1982)

Maccoby, Hyam 'An Interpretation of "Mr Eliot's Sunday Morning Service"', *Critical Survey* (January, 1968), 159–65

'"The Family Reunion" and Kipling's "The House Surgeon,"', *Notes and Queries* (February, 1968), 48–57

'A Study of the "jew" in "Gerontion"', *Jewish Quarterly* 17 (Number 2, 1969), 19–22 and 39–43

'The Delectable Daughter', *Midstream* 16 (November, 1970), 50–60

'The Anti-Semitism of T. S. Eliot', *Midstream* 19 (May, 1973), 68–79

The Sacred Executioner: Human Sacrifice and the Legacy of Guilt (1982)

MacDougall, A. *Racial Myth in English History* (1982)

Mahaffey, Vicki *Reauthorizing Joyce* (Cambridge, 1988)

Martin, Graham (ed.) *Eliot in Perspective* (1970)

Matthiessen, F. O. *The Achievement of T. S. Eliot: An Essay on the Nature of Poetry* (Oxford, 1935)

Miller, Karl *Doubles* (Oxford, 1987)

Mintz, Alan *George Eliot and the Novel of Vocation* (Cambridge, Mass., 1978)

Mitchell, Gina 'John Buchan's Popular Fiction: A Hierarchy of Race', *Patterns of Prejudice* 7 (Number 6, 1973), 24–30

'In His Image: A Study of the Jews in the Literature of Guy Thorne', *Patterns of Prejudice* 9 (January–February, 1975), 18–24

Modder, M. F. *The Jew in the Literature of England* (Philadelphia, 1939)

Montiero, George 'Christians and Jews in "Mr Eliot's Sunday Morning Service"', *T. S. Eliot Review* 3 (1976), 20–2

Moody, A. D. *Thomas Stearns Eliot: Poet* (Cambridge, 1979)

Morgan, Margery *The Shavian Playground: An Exploration of the Art of George Bernard Shaw* (1972)

Morris, J. A. 'T. S. Eliot and Antisemitism', *Journal of European Studies* 2 (1972), 173–82

Morse, Jonathan *Word by Word: The Language of Memory* (Ithaca, 1990)

Mullen, Richard *Anthony Trollope: A Victorian in his World* (1990)

Myers, Jeffrey (ed.) *Wyndham Lewis: A Revaluation* (1980)

Nadel Ira B., *Joyce and the Jews* (1989)

Naman, Anne Aresty *The Jew in the Victorian Novel: Some Relationships Between Prejudice and Art* (New York, 1980)

Orwell, Sonia and Angus, Ian (eds.) *The Collected Essays, Journalism and Letters of George Orwell*, 4 vols. (1970)

Ozick, Cynthia *Art and Ardour* (New York, 1984)

Parrinder, Patrick *H. G. Wells* (Edinburgh, 1970)

Parry, Benita *Conrad and Imperialism* (1983)

Perl, Jeffrey *The Tradition of Return: The Implicit History of Modern Literature* (Princeton, 1984)

Philipson, David *The Jew in English Fiction* (Cincinatti, 1911)

Pick, Daniel *Faces of Degeneration: A European Disorder, 1848–1918* (Cambridge, 1989)

Pilecki, Gerard Anthony *Shaw's 'Geneva': A Critical Study of the Evolution of the*

Text in Relation to Shaw's Political Thought and Dramatic Practice (The Hague, 1965)

Pinkney, Tony *Women in the Poetry of T. S. Eliot: A Psychoanalytic Approach* (1984)

Posnock, Ross 'Henry James, Veblen, and Adorno: The Crisis of the Modern Self', *Journal of American Studies* 21 (1987), 31–54

Prawer, S. S. *Israel at Vanity Fair: Jews and Judaism in the Writings of W. M. Thackeray* (Leiden, 1992)

Purcell, L. Edward 'Trilby and Trilby-Mania: The Beginning of the Best-Seller System', *Journal of Popular Culture* 11 (Summer, 1977), 62–77

Read, Forrest (ed.) *Pound/Joyce: The Letters of Ezra Loomis Pound to James Joyce, with Pound's Essays on Joyce* (New York, 1967)

Ricks, Christopher *T. S. Eliot and Prejudice* (1988)

Roberts, Neil *George Eliot: Her Belief and Her Art* (1975)

apRoberts, Ruth *Arnold and God* (Berkeley, 1983)

Robertson, Ritchie 'Eliot's Antisemitic Poems', *Jewish Quarterly* 37 (Autumn, 1990), 46–9

Rojak, Chris and Turner, Bryan (eds.) *Forget Baudrillard* (London, 1993)

Rosenberg, Edgar *From Shylock to Svengali: Jewish Stereotypes in English Fiction* (Stanford, 1960)

Ross, Angus *Kipling 86* (Brighton, 1987)

Russell, G. W. E. (ed.) *Matthew Arnold* (1904)
   Letters of Matthew Arnold 1848–1888, 2 vols. (1895)

Rutherford, A. (ed.) *Kipling's Mind and Art* (1964)

Said, Edward *Orientalism* (1978)
   The Question of Palestine (New York, 1979)
   Culture and Imperialism (1993)

Samuel, Raphael (ed.) *Patriotism: The Making and Unmaking of British National Identity*, 3 vols. (1989)

Sartre, Jean Paul *Anti-Semite and Jew* (New York, 1948)

Schlossman, Beryl *Joyce's Catholic Comedy of Language* (Wisconsin, 1985)

Schofield, Martin *T. S. Eliot: The Poems* (Cambridge, 1988)

Schwarz, Daniel *Disraeli's Fiction* (1979)

Searle, G. R. *Eugenics and Politics in Britain 1900–1914* (Leiden, 1976)
   Corruption in British Politics: 1895–1930 (Oxford, 1987)

Senn, Fritz *Joyce's Dislocations: Essays on Reading in Translation* (Baltimore, 1984)

Seymour-Smith, Martin *Rudyard Kipling* (1989)

Shaffer, E. S. *'Kubla Khan' and the Fall of Jerusalem: The Mythological School and Secular Literature, 1770–1880* (1975)

Shaw, Christopher and Chase, Malcolm (eds.) *The Imagined Past: History and Nostalgia* (Manchester, 1989)

Shuttleworth, Sally *George Eliot and Nineteenth-Century Science: The Make-Believe of a Beginning* (Cambridge, 1984)

Sigg, Eric *The American T. S. Eliot* (Cambridge, 1989)

Smith, David *Socialist Propaganda in the Twentieth-Century British Novel* (1978)
  H. G. Wells: Desperately Mortal (New Haven, 1986)
Smith, Goldwin 'The Political Adventures of Lord Beaconsfield', *Fortnightly Review* (April–June, 1878)
Smith, Janet *John Buchan: A Biography* (1965)
Smith, W. S. *Bernard Shaw and the Life Force* (Pennsylvania, 1982)
Speaight, Robert *The Life of Hilaire Belloc* (New York, 1957)
Stanley, A. P. *The Life and Correspondence of Thomas Arnold* (1958)
Steiner, George *Language and Silence* (1967)
  In Bluebeard's Castle: Some Notes on the Re-Definition of Culture (1971)
  Extraterritorial (1976)
Strachey, Lytton *Eminent Victorians* (1918)
Stubbs, Patricia *Women and Fiction: Feminism and the Novel 1880–1920* (Brighton, 1979)
Sultan, Stanley *Eliot, Joyce and Company* (Oxford, 1987)
Super, R. H. *The Chronicler of Barsetshire: A Life of Anthony Trollope* (Ann Arbor, 1988)
Theoharis, Theoharis Constantine *Joyce's 'Ulysses': An Anatomy of the Soul* (Chapel Hill, 1988)
Tomkins, J. M. S. *The Art of Rudyard Kipling* (1959)
Trilling, Lionel *Matthew Arnold* (1949)
  The Liberal Imagination (1951)
  'The Changing Myth of the Jew', *Commentary* (August, 1978)
Turco, Alfred *Shaw's Moral Vision: The Self and Salvation* (Ithaca, 1976)
Turnbaugh, Roy 'Images of Empire: George Alfred Henty and John Buchan', *Journal of Popular Culture* 9 (Winter, 1975), 734–41
Usbourne, Richard *Clubland Heroes* (1953)
Van Wyk Smith, Martin *Drummer Hodge: The Poetry of the Anglo-Boer War (1899–1902)* (Oxford, 1978)
Vincent, John *Disraeli* (Oxford, 1990)
Wall, Stephen *Trollope and Character* (1988)
Ward, Maisie *Gilbert Keith Chesterton* (1944)
Wasserstein, Bernard *Britain and the Jews of Europe 1939–1945* (Oxford, 1979)
Weiner, Martin *English Culture and the Decline of the Industrial Spirit 1850–1980* (Cambridge, 1981)
Weiss, Samuel (ed.) *Bernard Shaw's Letters to Siegfried Trebitsch* (Stanford, 1986)
Weston, Jessie *From Ritual to Romance* (Cambridge, 1920)
White, Hayden *Tropics of Discourse: Essays in Cultural Criticism* (Baltimore, 1978)
Wilk, Melvin *Jewish Presence in T. S. Eliot and Franz Kafka* (Atlanta, Georgia, 1986)
Willey, Basil *Darwin and Butler* (1960)
Williams, Raymond *Culture and Society, 1780–1950* (1958)

The Country and the City (1973)

Wilson, A. N. *Hilaire Belloc* (1984)

Wilson, Angus *The Strange Ride of Rudyard Kipling* (1977)

Wilson, Keith 'The *Protocols of Zion* and the *Morning Post*, 1919–1920', *Patterns of Prejudice* 19 (1985), 5–14

Winter, J. M. 'The Webbs and the Non-White World: A Case of Socialist Racialism', *Journal of Contemporary History* 9 (1974), 181–92.

Wisenthal, J. L. *The Marriage of Contraries: Bernard Shaw's Middle Plays* (Cambridge, Mass., 1974)

Shaw's Sense of History (Oxford, 1988)

Yeazell, Ruth (ed.) *Sex, Science and Society* (Baltimore, 1986)

Index

Adams, Henry, 247–9, 254
Aliens Act, The, 10, 159
antisemitism, literary, 1–3, 235; and
    essentialism, 11; and fixed stereotypes,
    3, 11; reductive definitions of, 8, 58–9,
    69, 138, 162–3, 172, 190; teleological
    definitions of, 2
Arendt, Hannah, 3
Arnold, Matthew, 4–5, 13–23, 53–4, 79, 84,
    92, 93, 139, 140, 269, 271, 273, 274;
    and biblical criticism, 21; and G. K.
    Chesterton, 151, 189–90, 192, 196,
    204; and Benjamin Disraeli, 55, 59, 67;
    and T. S. Eliot, 206, 240, 241, 265;
    and Jewish acculturation, 17, 18, 21–2,
    43–4, 51; and Jewish self-identification,
    22–3, 271; and James Joyce, 206,
    207–9, 210–11, 218, 224–5, 230; and
    the Judaization of his family, 15, 167;
    and D. H. Lawrence, 273; and liberal
    progress, 14, 20; and national
    particularism, 23; and state
    universalism, 23
Culture and Anarchy, 4–5, 10, 13, 14, 18–23,
    43, 55, 100, 148, 206, 207–8, 209,
    224–5, 269; and Christianity, 20–1;
    and cultural transcendence, 5, 13,
    21–2; and Hebraism and Hellenism, 4,
    13, 14–15, 18–20, 151, 189, 206, 211,
    218, 240, 274; and Puritanism, 20; and
    race-thinking, 5, 13, 19–22, 44
Essays in Criticism, 13
'The Function of Criticism at the Present
    Time', 22
Literature and Dogma, 19, 21
'Rachel', 22–3
Arnold, Dr Thomas, 16–17; and Jewish
    emancipation, 16; and racial
    exclusivism, 16–17

Bateson, F. W., 253

Bauman, Zygmunt, 1, 271
Beer, Gillian, 44
Beit, Alfred, 57, 59
Belloc, Hilaire, 149, 150–79, 266; and anti-
    capitalism, 151, 153, 155, 157, 166,
    203, 272; and antisemitism, 151, 156,
    166, 168, 170, 174–5, 176, 177, 179;
    and George Bernard Shaw, 178; and
    the Boer War, 151, 155–6, 157–8, 159,
    163, 166; and Catholicism, 151, 153,
    154, 166, 203, 204; and Cecil
    Chesterton, 167, 174–5, 176, 197; and
    G. K. Chesterton, 154, 182, 183–4,
    187, 191; and Christendom, 150,
    153–4; and William Cobbett, 164; and
    conspiratorial thinking, 165, 167–8,
    173–4, 176, 177, 178; and
    cosmopolitanism, 153, 159, 162, 164,
    166, 173; and Paul Déroulède, 154;
    and Benjamin Disraeli, 161, 171; and
    distributism, 153, 159, 203; and the
    Dreyfus Affair, 150, 154–5, 156, 177;
    and Eduard Drumont, 155; and T. S.
    Eliot, 155; and Englishness, 152–3,
    156, 157, 159, 160–1, 162, 163–4, 166,
    169, 171, 204; and *The Eye-Witness*,
    151, 166, 173, 174, 177; and the
    French Revolution, 150, 154; and J. A.
    Hobson, 156, 157; and Jewish
    plutocracy, 151, 153, 155–6, 158, 169,
    173–4, 178, 204; and Jewish racial
    difference, 151, 154, 167–8, 170–1,
    173–9; and Rudyard Kipling, 177;
    and liberalism, 150, 151, 152, 155, 157,
    159, 166, 174–5, 177, 204; and the
    Marconi Scandal, 151, 172–4, 176–7,
    178; and Karl Marx, 178; and Charles
    Maurras, 155; and Nazism, 178–9;
    and *The New Witness*, 151, 165, 174,
    176; and the Panama Scandal, 155;
    and race-thinking, 151, 162, 166,

293